THE CIA
AND
AMERICAN
DEMOCRACY

D1009146

THE CIA
AND
AMERICAN
DEMOCRACY

THIRD EDITION

Rhodri Jeffreys-Jones

YALE UNIVERSITY PRESS
New Haven & London

For my daughters
Gwenda and Rowen

Printed in the
United States of America
by Vail-Ballou Press,
Binghamton, New York.

Library of Congress Control Number: 2002114384

ISBN 0-300-09948-7 (pbk. : alk. paper)

A catalogue record for this book is available
from the British Library.

10 9 8 7 6 5 4 3 2 1

CONTENTS

PREFACE
TO THE
THIRD EDITION

In the late 1930s Tom Jones, who had been Prime Minister Lloyd George's right-hand man, decided to help those who were fleeing Hitler's tyranny. To this end he worked with the Pilgrim Trust, a private group whose objective hitherto had been the promotion of better understanding between Britain and the United States. In 1938 a Jewish couple, Fritz and Lily Pincus, fled Germany and through Tom Jones were dispatched to Harlech, a village in Wales where, at that time, my mother was organizing the reception facilities for refugees.

Life was hard for the new arrivals. Fritz had been a banker, but in Harlech he tried working as a motor mechanic. All thumbs and no fingers, he was kept on only through the kindness of the garage proprietor. By the war's end he and Lily had moved to London. Fritz worked for the BBC and as a translator. After humble beginnings, Lily found work as a psychologist. A longtime friend of the theologian Paul Tillich, she converted to Christianity. Then she became my godmother, so we were regularly in touch and she proved an inspirational if slightly inquisitorial figure. What was it about my personality, she asked, that made me write about spies?

Lily co-founded the Tavistock Institute for Marital Studies in London, and in later years, she began to write about her psychoanalytical work and became a celebrity: one of her better-known books is *Secrets in the Family*

(1978). Finally, and she told me that this step cost her dearly in terms of emotional stress, she decided to revisit Germany and give a series of radio broadcasts on her life experience since leaving Carlsbad, where she had been born in 1898 (Carlsbad, or Karlovy Vary, was in the German-speaking part of Czechoslovakia that Hitler annexed in 1938). Her objective in giving the autobiographical broadcasts, published as *Verloren-gewonnen: Mein Weg von Berlin nach London* (1980), was to help Germany achieve closure on the Hitler tragedy.

One day, not long after the Syrian-Egyptian Yom Kippur attack on Israel in 1973, Lily expressed to me privately her deep worries about Israel, a nation that she visited regularly and to which she was powerfully attached. The dreadful hostility that Israel endured from its neighbors was, she felt, in good measure owing to Israel's own bad treatment of the Palestinians. The solution lay in moderation and generosity, not in enmity and repression, and it upset her deeply to see fellow-Jews acting in such a ruthless and inhumane manner. She felt that her views were widely shared by Jews in Britain and in the United States, where her brother had settled. Some time later, when she had became well known, I asked her, Are you tempted to rally this strain of Jewish opinion to bring pressure to bear on Israel? The facial lineaments I had grown to love stiffened. I could not *possibly*, she said, I just *couldn't*.

I have narrated this microcosmic illustration of international complexity to show what the CIA is up against. The analysis of foreign affairs is never a simple matter, and no amount of secret probing can reduce to mere logic the complex emotions and feelings of those who influence governments. To expect the director of the CIA to be a Mr. Know It All or a Mr. Fix Everything is to expect too much.

Yet, when dire events like those of September 11, 2001, take place, this is precisely what occurs. The widespread instinct is to point an accusing finger at the CIA, and to demand reform no matter how many dollars it costs, on the assumption that the Agency should be able to wave a magic wand.

This third edition of *The CIA and American Democracy* attempts to make sense of the relationship between the CIA and 9/11. The original edition took the history of the CIA up to the late 1980s. Since then, communism has collapsed in Europe and the Cold War has ended, but new threats have developed. A new prologue therefore addresses the history of the post–Cold War CIA. In it I ask whether the Agency, when it lost its prime mission of watching the Soviet Union, lost its hold on public esteem, leading to poor morale and possibly to mistakes. The prologue focuses, however, on a more recent and pressing concern, the intelligence dimensions of the terrorist attacks of 9/11. I suggest that we expected too much of the CIA, but also that we can expect more than we got from it.

PROLOGUE
September 11
and the
Post–Cold War CIA

T he attack on the World Trade Center
on September 11, 2001, was one of the most distressing events of modern
times. To the perpetrators of the deed, it was a blow struck at the heart of
American capitalism. To the vast majority of others, it was a dastardly attack
on what amounted to a people's palace set in a much-loved city. My own
experience of the World Trade Center is typical. On August 6, 1991, I took
my two little girls up to the top of one of the towers to enjoy the view of the
vast, teeming democracy unfolding far below. A decade later, it was Rowena,
the younger of the two and now a grown woman, who phoned me in a state
of shock to tell me of the attack. Millions of others will likewise remember
for the rest of their lives what they were doing on that day and how they
learned the news.

When an event has been seared into one's mind in such a manner, it is
important to stand back and try to be objective. My purpose in this prologue
is to discuss the intelligence aspects of 9/11, with particular reference to the
subject of this book, the CIA. The strike against the World Trade Center and
the Pentagon had far-reaching consequences for the CIA and the rest of the
intelligence community. It invited fresh thinking on the purpose of secret
intelligence. Perhaps in the heat of emotion it induced new intelligence distortions just as old mistakes were being laid bare. But most conspicuously

the strike prompted a debate about what had gone wrong with American intelligence to make it so blind to the 9/11 plot. Had it been starved of funds or overfed with dollars that made it fat and sleepy? Was the CIA hampered by the requirement that it should cooperate with scheming plodders in the FBI, or should it have operated in closer tandem with the Bureau? Were America's counterspies too politically correct and soft on Arabs, or linguistically negligent, paying too little heed to languages and cultures that spawned hatred of America?

All this relates to the argument in this book, that the CIA's ability to do its job depends, to a great degree, on its standing. If the powers that be are willing to listen to you, you stand a better chance of conveying to them the information that is vital to the nation's security. Various factors affected that standing in the years from the Agency's founding in 1947 to the last phase of the Cold War. But what happened to the Agency's standing after the collapse of the Soviet Union? By the 1990s, did Washington perceive the CIA as essentially a spent force, a Cold War agency that had little purpose? Had the CIA lost its way by the time the terrorists struck in 2001?

The Post–Cold War CIA

A review of the debate on the CIA in the wake of the collapse of the Soviet Union upholds that view to a certain extent, but not conclusively. For if the Agency fell, it also rose again.

In December 1989, General Secretary Mikhail Gorbachev of the Soviet Union and President George Bush met on the island of Malta to declare the Cold War formally at an end, and it soon became evident that American intelligence was entering into a difficult period. The CIA's critics included former intelligence officials like Vincent Cannistraro, journalists like Flora Lewis (*New York Times*) and Mary McGrory (*Washington Post*), and prominent legislators like Senator Daniel P. Moynihan, who recommended the dissolution of the Agency. In part, these critics were motivated by hopes of a "peace dividend," with taxpayers' money being diverted from defense and intelligence to other programs. But they also criticized the Agency's past performance. Richard Pipes, a specialist in Russian history at Harvard University, joined Moynihan in charging that the CIA had failed in its predictive task. Former president Gerald Ford claimed that the CIA had overestimated the Soviet threat in the 1960s. Several critics maintained that the Agency had exaggerated the economic and military strength of the Soviets in the 1970s, adding that it had also failed to predict the fall of Gorbachev in 1991. Others argued that senior Agency officials like Robert Gates had known that the Soviet Union was weakening but had twisted their intelligence output to exaggerate the Communist threat and belittle Gorbachev's reforms, thus helping to fool the American people into accepting President Reagan's expensive strategic plans.

Acting Director of Central Intelligence (DCI) Richard Kerr and former DCIs Richard Helms, James Schlesinger, and Robert Gates came to the Agency's defense. They insisted that the CIA should be left intact and that the nation's intelligence budget should be maintained or even increased. They invented new roles for the Agency, arguing that the evaporation of the Soviet threat made the world more complex and therefore more dangerous. Weapons proliferation was one area that suggested a need for vigilance. There was also a need for an intelligence agency that would address economic, health, environmental, and narcotics problems. With the object of rebutting the critics' charges, former CIA analyst Bruce D. Berkowitz published extracts from CIA documents purporting to show that the Agency had warned of the collapse of the Soviet economy, of the probable fall of Gorbachev, and of the likely disintegration of the Soviet Union.

The CIA's defenders pointed with pride to the Agency's role in Reagan's plan to destroy the "evil empire" of Soviet Communism. Reagan's CIA had sapped the strength of the "Reds" by means of a variety of secret operations. For example, the CIA supplied Stinger ground-to-air missiles to the opponents of the Moscow-backed government in Afghanistan, enabling them to shoot down the regime's Soviet-supplied helicopter gunships and prolong the war at great cost to the Communists (little did they realize that in arming the Taliban they were fueling a future threat to the United States). Similarly, with the help of the Vatican, the Catholic DCI William Casey (1981–87) injected money into Solidarity, the movement that brought down the Communist government in the pope's mother country, Poland. Just as shrewd, the defenders claimed, was Reagan's effort to increase U.S. military spending to a level that would demoralize the Soviets and force them into an emulative expenditure pattern they could ill afford. National security directive NSDD-75 (1983) outlined a plan to bankrupt the Moscow regime. The then-secret document called for "internal pressure on the USSR to weaken the sources of Soviet imperialism."

Vigorous though it was, this defense of the CIA was not strong enough to prevent the controversy from rumbling on. The effectiveness of the CIA's past covert operations was open to question. Had they in the long run shortened the Cold War and brought it to a successful conclusion, or were they one of the principal causes of the Cold War and a provocation that gave the Communists an excuse to cling to power? It is doubtful that objective historians outside the United States will give any prominence to U.S. secret operations and grand deception in their accounts of the changes in the former Soviet Union. John Gooding's respected book *Rulers and Subjects*

(1996) is typical of non-U.S. studies in that it makes no reference to the United States or the CIA in its analysis of the "second Russian revolution." The critics' counterarguments were given new life by a series of further disclosures. Here are some examples, given in order of disclosure rather than occurrence, as it was their disclosure that affected the standing of the CIA. In 1993, evidence obtained by the CIA's archrival, the FBI, led to the arrest of Aldrich H. Ames. Ames had served as head of the Soviet section of CIA counterintelligence. In 1984, he began to sell U.S. secrets to the KGB. The treason led to the deaths of several of America's secret agents. It also enabled Moscow to feed disinformation to the United States: Senate Select Intelligence Committee chair Arlen Specter stated that, because of the KGB penetration, the CIA sent the White House and Pentagon "35 questionable reports." Far from deceiving the Russians, the Americans would appear to have been the victims of a Muscovite deception that caused the Defense Department to waste money on unnecessary projects.

The year 1995 was an embarrassing one for the Agency. R. James Woolsey, DCI since 1993, was forced to resign because he had not disciplined those within the CIA who had failed to root out Ames. In further episodes, the CIA was caught in the act of running economic espionage against two of America's most valued allies, France and Japan. It also emerged that in Guatemala a CIA operative had murdered one American citizen and the husband of another.

The next year was scarcely better. In 1996 it was charged that the CIA's activities in support of the Nicaraguan Contras in the 1980s had been partly financed by the proceeds of crack cocaine sales in inner-city Los Angeles. Although the evidence was inconclusive, the story followed in the wake of an exposé of the Tuskegee experiment, in which 399 African American men suffering from syphilis had been left untreated in order for researchers to study the full course of the disease. Fears of genocide were in the air, and the Congressional Black Caucus demanded an inquiry.

The embarrassments continued in 1997. It emerged that during the Gulf War in 1991, the CIA had kept the U.S. military in the dark about the contents of a storage bunker in Khamisiyah; when bombed by American planes, the bunker released a plume of sarin gas and toxic agents that endangered the health of U.S. soldiers. As if that were not enough, details also emerged of the recent and bloody failure of a CIA-funded coup attempt against Saddam Hussein as well as of CIA assassination plans in 1950s Guatemala, where an Agency handbook had explained how to "purify" a room of a dozen people within twenty seconds.

This tale of woe needs to be placed in perspective. In some cases, the CIA would appear to have been the scapegoat for military and presidential errors. Further, it is axiomatic that a secret agency cannot boast about its successes without betraying its method of operation, so its mistakes tend to hit the headlines to a disproportionate degree. Finally, the history of the CIA suggests an inverse relationship between Cold War intensity on one hand and scrutiny of the Agency's affairs by Congress and the media on the other. It would appear that the press savaged the CIA in the 1990s partly because, in the post–Cold War era, journalists were no longer governed by the imperatives of patriotic loyalty to national-defense institutions. The CIA had become the victim of its own claim to have played a role in the winning of the Cold War.

In spite of these qualifying perspectives, it is plain that the CIA's standing was impaired, and to a measurable degree. Such were the perils of the job that the Agency ran through five directors in the 1991–97 period. In a series of "turf wars," the Department of Defense attempted to dominate the national intelligence effort. Meanwhile, the FBI was challenging the CIA's foreign domain: drawing on a 58 percent budget increase between 1993 and 2001, the Bureau had agents permanently positioned in forty-four countries by the eve of 9/11.

These events occurred against a background of overall intelligence cuts in the early 1990s. Until 1997 the national intelligence budget was kept secret, but it was thought to have reached a peak, in the late 1980s, of between $30 and $36 billion. The official figure released in 1997 was substantially smaller at $26.6 billion. This meant sacrifices: in 1993–94, DCI Woolsey reduced personnel in the CIA by 24 percent. Following these cuts, journalist Tim Weiner noted that morale at the Agency was "lower than Death Valley" (*New York Times*, Jan. 1, 1995).

Upsetting though they were to intelligence officials, these changes did not spell the end of the CIA. For one thing, its budgetary cuts were made from a high base. The new funding levels seemed to be low only when compared with the spending peaks of the late 1980s. Even allowing for inflation, they were not dramatically different from the $20 billion spent in 1981. In light of the potential results of the collapse of the primary enemy, the 1990s cuts were modest.

Even before the Soviet collapse, the American public had shown signs of being open to the idea that the CIA might operate independently of the imperatives of the Cold War. The reception of spy fiction is an indicator of the reading public's readiness to accept diversification of mission. Tom Clancy's Cold War novel *The Hunt for Red October* (1984) sold well, but its highest position on the *New York Times* best-seller list was number three. In contrast, Clancy's *Clear and Present Danger* (1989) hit the number one spot. This tale of the CIA's anti-narcotics operations in Colombia was actually the best-selling novel of any type in the 1980s. By the 1990s, it seemed both evident and acceptable to Clancy fans that the Agency had moved on from its former Cold War concerns. The public's receptiveness to new dangers is underlined in a further best-selling Clancy novel, a work of tragic prescience. In *Debt of Honor* (1994), an enraged pilot crashes his fuel-laden airliner into a joint session of Congress with huge loss of life.

With an eye to increasing its public acceptability, the CIA made a number of changes. DCIs Gates and John M. Deutch (1995–96) advocated more openness and allowed the declassification of carefully selected historical documents. This policy did not satisfy the document-hungry historical profession but was sufficient to provoke DCI George J. Tenet to declare, in his confirmation hearings in 1997, that openness had been carried too far. Nevertheless, Tenet went on to end the secrecy over the Agency's budget. Other reforms, such as cutbacks in the expensive spy satellite program and in covert operations, also commanded respect. Less well received was the attempt, in 1996, to make the CIA director the budgetary and managerial "tsar" of the entire intelligence community.

While the Agency reformed itself and prepared to fight back against its critics, the moderates in the nation's capital steered a course between the abolitionists and the boosters, devising an approach that would ensure public backing for the continuation of the CIA. By 1992, David L. Boren and David McCurdy, chairs of the Senate and House intelligence oversight committees, respectively, had articulated a case for the continuation of a reformed CIA. A sharp increase in congressional oversight in 1992–93 encouraged a sense of shared responsibility for the CIA, thus reducing the possibility of its becoming a sacrificial symbol of the Cold War's end.

In the wake of his accession to the presidency in 1993, Bill Clinton at first seemed to take little interest in the Agency. Like many presidents, he was initially preoccupied by domestic policy. But he had never been anti-CIA; indeed, as long ago as 1969 he had demonstrated his faith in its powers by appealing to the Agency's Richard Stearns for help in avoiding the draft at the time of the Vietnam War. While today it might seem natural to assume that conservative presidents champion the CIA, there is ample evidence to show that liberals had promoted it for decades. Clinton was to be no exception. In 1994, he appointed a presidential commission on intelligence. Under the chairmanship first of Les Aspin and then of Harold Brown, the commission undertook America's biggest-ever single inquiry into secret intelligence. In 1996, the commission recommended that the CIA should continue to function as an independent Agency, that it should reform itself in some respects, and that it should abandon the "intelligence tsar" idea. The report of the Aspin/Brown commission, which had the president's backing, gave the moderates' seal of approval to the CIA.

So the end of the Cold War and the rash of criticism that followed did not fatally injure the CIA. But it must be conceded that, at the time of George

Tenet's confirmation in 1997, there was still some doubt about the Agency's standing. The factors undermining the CIA included lingering doubts about the need for a major post–Cold War intelligence agency and concerns about trustworthiness following the Ames case. But some of the detrimental factors–nagging doubts about the CIA's predictive and analytical performance, continuing concern about its covert operations, and worries about the threat it posed to democracy, especially when the rights of Americans were affected—were less acute than chronic and were rooted in earlier decades. In these concerns, it is possible to see elements of continuity between the pre-1989 and post-1989 history of the CIA, rather than an acute post–Cold War crisis.

Under Tenet, the reputation of the CIA ebbed and flowed, sometimes in ways that prefigured some of the vehement debate that took place after 9/11. There was, for example, the issue of political correctness. Discrimination against intelligence recruits on the basis of class, race, or sexual orientation was challenged on the ground that it deprived American intelligence of talented recruits and of personnel who might be native speakers of useful foreign languages. Changing cultural mores meant that a gay person was no longer vulnerable to blackmail by a foreign intelligence agency, so the politically correct demanded an end to discrimination.

In 1991, the George H. W. Bush administration had initiated a "glass ceiling" study that revealed widespread discontent among women in the CIA over sexual harassment and promotions denial. Four years later, the Agency reacted to a lawsuit by offering retrospective promotions to scores of women, and Nora Slatkin was appointed to the senior post of executive director. President Clinton in August 1995 issued an executive order that forbade discrimination against homosexuals in security clearance procedures, and in the next few months a group of CIA employees established ANGLE, the Agency Network of Gay and Lesbian Employees. The spirit that moved the Clinton administration to be tolerant at home affected foreign policy, too. The president instructed U.S. intelligence officials to help with international peacekeeping efforts. In keeping with this mood, United Nations Secretary General Kofi Annan in 2000 called for an improved U.N. intelligence capability.

Liberalism had its limits, however. In March 1999, the Taiwanese-born scientist Wen Ho Lee was charged with spying for Red China at the atomic weapons research laboratory in Los Alamos. The evidence against him was flimsy. When he was ultimately cleared, civil libertarians complained that Lee's accusers had used "racial profiling" to identify him as a suspect. To these civil libertarians, he seemed to have been arrested for being "Chinese while working in a laboratory," just as traditionally African Americans had been harassed for "driving whilst black" (*Spectator*, June 1, 2002).

Another factor having a bearing on the reputation of the CIA in the Tenet era was Tenet himself. The DCI's parents came from Greece and Albania, respectively (in the 1940s, his mother had narrowly escaped the clutches of Albania's Communist regime). Tenet had the survival instincts and faith in America of a second-generation immigrant. He was able to read the political scene in Washington. He brought to an end the rapid and demoralizing changes in leadership in the CIA by serving to the end of Clinton's second term and then achieving reappointment by President George W. Bush.

To a certain degree, Tenet's reappointment reflected the outlook of the Bush family. Traditionally DCIs had not been political appointees and were not supposed to receive a pink slip upon the advent of a new administration. In 1977, however, the newly elected Democratic president Jimmy Carter had released the senior George Bush, an appointee of the Republican president Gerald Ford, from his post as DCI, in a move widely perceived as political. When the Republican Bush, junior, reappointed the Democratic appointee Tenet, he was, in a significant sense, stating a point of principle. At the same time, Tenet was a consummate politician who had assiduously cultivated the Bushes, for example by throwing a lavish party for Bush senior. Moreover, he had the genuine respect of Bush junior from the beginning. He briefed the president frequently and was even dispatched to undertake a vital diplomatic mission, mediation in the Israel-Palestine conflict. There were those who complained that Tenet was too political. But if presidential access is the criterion, Tenet brought the CIA to one of its highest levels of standing and influence.

With Tenet in charge, rivalry with the ever-expanding FBI continued. But in February 2001 the FBI suffered a setback with the arrest for espionage of Robert Hanssen, a twenty-seven-year veteran of the Bureau and senior counterintelligence official who turned out to have been selling secrets to his Moscow masters since 1985. At the U.S. District Court in Alexandria, Virginia, FBI Special Agent Stefan Pluta served an affidavit in support of Hanssen's arrest warrant setting forth a catalogue of betrayals, all apparently undertaken for money—Hanssen received at least $1.4 million from the Russian intelligence services. The outlook for FBI director Louis Freeh suddenly looked bleak: "Fire Freeh," screamed one headline in the *Washington Post* (Feb. 27, 2001). Perhaps luckily for what remained of his reputation, Freeh did quit the Bureau just in time to avoid excoriation over the cataclysm of 9/11. Thus, Hanssen promised closure on Ames. No longer could it be said that the CIA was uniquely prone to penetration.

With the arrival of Bush junior in the White House, it was immediately plain that secret intelligence would receive a high status and more money. While the CIA may have been the creation of a Democratic president (Harry Truman), it now seemed to be strongly favored by Republicans, notably conservative Republicans and especially the Bushes. Alarm bells began to ring for those who remembered past CIA excesses and who for years had campaigned for restrictions, oversight, and even abolition. But these sounds were soon drowned out by the deafening roar of 9/11.

9/11: Causes, Consequences, Politics, and Significance

The fatalities in the World Trade Center attack exceeded those in the Pearl Harbor attack. Just as Pearl Harbor had propelled the United States into a world war, so, sixty years later, 9/11 would launch the nation into a war against terrorism. Against this grim background, Americans demanded to know what had happened. The question was, How had the nation been caught unawares? To a degree not matched since the mid-1970s, attention focused on the intelligence community and its alleged weaknesses. Immediately after the attack it was assumed that Osama bin Laden and his Al Qaeda terrorist network were responsible for the hijackings and the suicide missions against New York and Washington. The evidence that subsequently unfolded did confirm that Al Qaeda and bin Laden's lieutenants were responsible. But it seemed strange and distressing that intelligence already knew about bin Laden's activities yet seemed incapable of issuing a timely warning to prevent the 9/11 attack and save all those lives.

A widespread view, and one shared by the Bush administration, was that the intelligence community failed to supply a warning of the September attacks because the community was underresourced. In approving in June 2002 the Bush administration's plans for substantial budgetary expansion, the Senate Select Committee on Intelligence maintained that, before September 2001, intelligence "for too long received inadequate attention and insufficient resources."

But this claim invited the question, how much is enough? Even before the advent of Bush junior to the presidency, the U.S. intelligence budget was in its fifth successive year of expansion. The estimated 2000 intelligence budget of $30 billion was larger than all Russian military expenditures combined, and it dwarfed the puny amount Moscow spent on its relatively effective intelligence services. The United States spent five times as much on intelligence as the whole of Europe combined, and no other region of the world could begin to compete with that level of expenditure.

Against this background, some analysts identified qualitative problems with U.S. intelligence performance. In her classic work on the Pearl Harbor attack, the historian Roberta Wohlstetter had suggested that there had been a surfeit rather than a deficit of information. In consequence, U.S. signals intelligence had failed to distinguish between the huge mass of irrelevant "noise" and the much smaller number of significant "signals." The challenge was to collect the right kind of intelligence and to analyze it properly. In similar vein, President Bush's national security adviser, Condoleeza Rice, thought that a crucial FBI memo warning about Al Qaeda plans has been missed because there was "a lot of chatter in the system" (Hersh, p. 40). In the words of a popular phrase, U.S. intelligence "had not connected the dots" (*New York Times*, May 27, 2002).

Some intelligence critics ascribed the predictive incapacity to sheer analytical failure. Others discerned bureaucratic shortcomings. The intelligence community had the right "signals" or "dots," but because of a lack of adequate centralizing procedures, they were not given to the right people, those capable of putting the clues together and interpreting them. While this was perceived to be a general problem, the FBI-CIA rivalry was singled out as a special and tragic issue. As so often in post–World War II history, lack of intelligence coordination became the inanimate villain of the day.

Socially conservative critics saw yet another failing in the system: political correctness. They alleged that this extreme version of liberalism had prevented officials from narrowing their lists of terrorist to focus on young Arab men. Far from being pernicious, "racial profiling" was just plain good sense if you were trying to pin down the Al Qaeda network. Journalist Mark Steyn complained that, under the guidance of misguided national security personnel, airport security and counterintelligence officials would let obvious suspects go free and even harass the innocent to show that they had clean, nondiscriminating hands. In his article "Stop Frisking Crippled Nuns" he wrote of the failure to arrest one would-be suicide-mission pilot: "In August 2001, invited to connect the dots on the [Zacarias] Moussaoui file, Washington bureaucrats saw only scolding editorials about 'flying whilst Arab'" (*Spectator*, June 1, 2002).

Just as damaging, though, was the contrasting charge that U.S. intelligence was too insular to learn about foreign languages and cultures. Notoriously, when the CIA tried to take a leading role in the effort to root out the Al Qaeda network in Afghanistan and to arrest or kill bin Laden, it turned out that the Agency had no capability in the local languages, in spite of having helped train local, Al Qaeda–sustaining Taliban fighters in the 1980s. Nor was the linguistic deficiency limited to languages spoken by relatively small groups of people. Two Arabic-language messages dated September 10, 2001, and warning of an attack the next day—"Tomorrow is zero hour"—were intercepted but not translated in time to be useful (*Washington Post*, June 19, 2002).

To a student of the history of the CIA, the foregoing discussion on causation has a sadly familiar ring. First, the very process of making a scapegoat of the intelligence community and especially of the CIA recalls political opportunism on previous occasions, notably the Bay of Pigs operation of 1961, which led to the resignation of DCI Allen Dulles. The reward of failure is similarly a repetition of history: the political leadership makes a mistake, blames it on the CIA, then calls for more money to remedy the alleged deficiency and to hush up potential critics within the intelligence community with promises of institutional cornucopia. Calls for improved centralization are nothing new—poor centralization at the time of Pearl Harbor was an oft-cited justification for the formation of the CIA. The identification of an enemy within, or "Fifth Column" danger, especially in ethnic or racially defined terms, is as old as the Republic and was a flourishing practice in World War II when the Japanese-American population was interned. As for lack of language proficiency, this, too, was an ancient lament. In the "Factual Epilogue" to their pro-CIA novel *The Ugly American* (1959), William Lederer and Eugene Burdick noted that fewer than three out of ten U.S. officials on duty in Asia spoke the local language, whereas nine out of ten of their Soviet counterparts did (p. 273).

In part because the litany of complaints was familiar, there was at first a certain complacency in the responses to 9/11. Just as the planning behind the Pearl Harbor attack was sometimes depicted as too ingenious to be predicted, so the Al Qaeda terrorists' plot was portrayed as "brilliant." According to the CIA's deputy director for operations, James Pavitt, Al Qaeda's combination of "control," "compartmentation," "discipline," and "fanaticism" made it impenetrable except by means of a defection (Hersh, p. 42).

Such complacency fed on a deafening political silence that lasted for several months after the September depredations. Although the nation was deeply shocked, the president rode high in the opinion polls, and Congress and the press seemed to have dozed off. There was plenty of vituperative patriotism, but little evidence of critical appraisal of what had gone wrong. Was this unusual? After an actual or perceived intelligence disaster, there is normally a spell of bipartisan solidarity, followed after an interval by a partisan political response. This is part of the healthy, adversarial, two-party democratic system. After making a scapegoat of the CIA, an administration typically sets up a preemptive in-house inquiry. Examples given in this book are the Katzenbach probe into the 1967 revelation that the CIA had suborned the National Students' Association and the Rockefeller investigation when it was revealed, early in 1975, that the CIA had run an assassination program. The White House would expect these in-house inquiries to take the heat out of a scandal until people had lost interest, to fend off the possibility of more aggressive congressional investigations, and then to come up with some harmless recommendations meriting just a few paragraphs on the inside pages of the newspapers. Sometimes the tactic worked—the Katzenback inquiry is one example, and the Tower investigation of Irangate

(1987) is another. But sometimes it did not—the Church and Pike congressional hearings on intelligence abuses followed hard on the heels of the
Rockefeller commission.

The post-9/11 silence arose partly out of the fact that America had been
attacked. This is reminiscent of Pearl Harbor; while the Roberts Commission
started investigating the causes of Pearl Harbor within weeks of the attack,
it was not until 1945 that the administration had to face the full force of
congressional investigation. Another reason why critical scrutiny of 9/11
was delayed was that Bush had only recently become president. The
customary honeymoon months had not yet given way to business as usual,
partisan debate. It might be added that, to the overwhelming majority of
Americans, 9/11 was a shock as well as a tactical surprise. In 1941 people
had known that there was a problem with Japan and war had already
broken out in Europe, but in 2001 America was still basking placidly in a
kind of post–Cold War Jacuzzi. Critics of the intelligence community were
equipped to object to its excesses, but not to its predictive shortcomings.

In the wake of 9/11, the standing of the CIA soared to dizzying heights.
People wore CIA T-shirts and applied for jobs in the Agency in the thousands. In a kind of patriotism game, politicians competed with one another
to give most support to the institutions of national security. Confronted with
White House demands for more money to be spent on intelligence, congressional committees for months said, yes, but please accept more money than
you asked for. In a variation on previous preemptive tactics, the White
House placed its trust in the activities of a joint Senate and House investigation of 9/11, trusting that the iconic status of the CIA, Republican strength
in both houses of Congress, and a reluctance on the part of the CIA and FBI
to hand over significant documents would combine to save the president
from any embarrassment in the secret hearings. Not until May 2002 did
serious criticism begin, with demands for an independent commission of
inquiry similar to the Warren investigation of John F. Kennedy's death. This
belated outburst of questioning stemmed from charges that the president had
received warnings of 9/11 and ignored them and that other messages had not
gotten through to him, from indications that the CIA and FBI had withheld
information from each other (there were bitter interagency recriminations
over this), and from the approach of the midterm elections and the
Democrats' need to dent the Republican president's popularity.

In the meantime, the Bush administration had pumped more money into
the intelligence community, a move that was consistent with its pre-9/11
philosophy. Expansionism was back with a vengeance. The CIA's
Counterterrorism Center produced five hundred reports a month, and at
5 P.M. every day DCI Tenet summoned forty officials—a team irreverently
known as the "small group"—to discuss the latest terrorism intelligence
(*Time*, July 8, 2002).

But the president also mooted a major reform of the national security bureaucracy. In June 2002 he proposed a new Cabinet Department of Homeland Security. He said that this would be the greatest reform of its kind since the National Security Act of 1947 that had restructured the armed services and established the CIA. Bush's June 18 press release indicated that the proposed department would "complement" the intelligence-gathering functions of the FBI and CIA and analyze information supplied by those agencies.

The DCI had long tried to act as this kind of leader of the intelligence community, with mixed success over the decades, as the latest rebuff by the Aspin/Brown commission had shown. Now the president proposed to create a new overlord. Perhaps the feuding baronies that made up the intelligence community would rally to the defense of their nation in its hour of need and would support a department whose novelty meant that it had no old enemies. Early reactions certainly indicated an acceptance in principle of the need for cooperation. However, there were also signs of continuing ambition for imperial co-option. In June 27 hearings on the Homeland Security bill before the Senate governmental affairs committee, the new FBI director, Robert S. Mueller, spoke of mutuality of effort, but in language that placed his bureau at the center of things: the FBI's National Joint Terrorism Task Force would, "of course, . . . include the new homeland security department," just as "CIA officers have [already] joined us." Meanwhile the CIA dragged its feet over the involvement of FBI personnel in its Counterterrorism Center. The struggle for control seemed destined to continue.

The terrorist attacks of September 11, 2001, were hugely significant. It is true that the depredation resulted in fewer deaths than other events, such as 1984 chemical plant explosion in Bhopal, India, or aggregated road accidents in the United States itself. But the murderous and hostile intent behind 9/11 was plain and put it into a special category. An attack of this kind on the homeland of a democracy is bound to have major consequences, as the people—the voters—will demand action. America perceived 9/11 as an affront, and that made it one.

To lay the surprise assault at the door of the CIA and the rest of the intelligence community is, however, another matter. The episode was an attack waiting to happen. American policy toward Japan had invited Pearl Harbor, and no amount of moralizing about extremists can undermine the fact that widespread terrorism reflects a deep-seated sense of injustice. American policy toward the Arab and Moslem world cannot be divorced from international terrorism and its practitioners' choice of targets. Intelligence analysts can indicate the flow of the political river, but they cannot change it. It is up to politicians to engineer such changes.

Nor can intelligence agencies, as a general rule, predict where and when the river will burst its banks. Like generals who are good at fighting the last war, they can devise systems to cope with the previous surprise attack. But surprise attack is of its nature and by design nonsystemic. Pearl Harbor, the Yom Kippur War, and 9/11 will never be repeated. The next nasty surprise is unlikely to bear similarities with 9/11 and may have nothing to do with bin Laden and Al Qaeda. It does not take a pessimist to conjure up alternative scenarios now that eight powers can wage nuclear war and others are lining up to develop that capability.

Intelligence agencies can point to such dangers, but expectations should not be high that they can predict the sudden use of weapons of mass destruction or other nasty surprises. Like the police, who can solve only a minority of crimes but still provide a comforting illusion of protection and security, intelligence agencies have an important psychological role to play. To shower the CIA and its ilk with taxpayers' money is to drop pennies into the wishing well—if you are superstitious, it makes you feel better.

With these dampened expectations in mind, it is still necessary to ask what lessons 9/11 holds for the conduct of American secret intelligence. The CIA has always been good at medium- and long-term prediction. That is a skill worth preserving, and here the Agency not only merits but also needs its high standing, if it is to carry its message to a listening White House. It is also possible that one day, the Agency or its siblings will break with tradition and nip a surprise attack in the bud. So there is no need for fatalism in assessing the Agency's weaknesses.

The events of 9/11 do make it clear that the CIA was not cosmopolitan enough, and this is a severe indictment of a foreign intelligence agency. Cooperation in intelligence matters with the United Nations, the European Union, and diverse national governments would bring greater knowledge and wisdom. In dealing with fundamentally different cultures, we are in need of tolerance and understanding. They are needed in the CIA but also more broadly, for as this book argues, the CIA is an integral part of American democracy. And tolerance and understanding are qualities that money cannot buy.

INTRODUCTION

D emocracy depends upon secret intelligence for its survival, yet the relationship between the two has always been controversial, and, at times, mutually harmful. The purpose of this book is to examine those factors which have increased or diminished the effectiveness of the U.S. Central Intelligence Agency (CIA), the main national intelligence organization of the world's leading democracy. Three groups of factors need to be considered. The first is comprised of considerations that affect intelligence work in every country—feudal tyrannies and Communist totalitarian states as much as constitutional democracies. The second group is made up of factors springing specifically from the nature of American democracy. The third group, closely connected with yet in some ways distinct from the second, consists of those elements which have favorably or adversely affected the CIA's standing, for it is the central contention in this book that CIA successes have depended not just on the quality of its analysis but also on its power to persuade.

Uncongenial though the fact may be to ardent democrats, CIA people share certain characteristics that affect non-American intelligence agencies, too. Every prospectively successful intelligence agency, for example, needs to attract good staff. Once it has achieved this goal, it needs to offer sound tuition—as, for example, at the training camp near Williamsburg, Virginia, known as "The Farm." Nor is this enough. An effective agency must, in addition to selecting good people and training them well, induce them to stay on for a substantial period of service in order to benefit from their accumulating experience, without, however, allowing an onset of intellectual, institutional, or behavioral stagnation. Even if the record is good in the foregoing respects, effectiveness will usually depend on the difficulty of the task in hand as well as the competence of the opposition at a given time. Periodic reverses may be expected, and the CIA has by no means been alone in facing the occasional necessity of boosting staff morale—good morale being another ingredient vital to the success of any intelligence agency.

Whether an intelligence organization is located in Washington or Moscow, in the twentieth century or the second, its success depends on its ability to separate analysis from policy advocacy and from action: with the best will in the world, it is difficult to give a fair hearing to reports that undermine policies and actions to which one is committed. One might argue, of course, that, here, democracies have an advantage over the Communists in being less doctrinaire or ideological. Nevertheless, the CIA has not always escaped that international intelligence disease, commitment. Nor has the Agency managed to shake itself entirely free of still another influence that has nothing to do with democracy as such: mirror-imaging, or the potentially misleading belief that other nations are likely to behave in much the same way as one's own. Clearly, then, democracy is not responsible for all of the CIA's problems.

It is nonetheless true that U.S. secret intelligence has in some ways been the prisoner of the very democracy whose citizens' liberties it helps to protect. When the CIA has overstepped certain moral boundaries, domestic politicians have called for greater restraint. At the least suggestion that the CIA is imitating its sworn enemy the KGB, there has been uproar—especially if there seems a danger that Soviet methods will be imported to the United States itself. The result has been an array of statutory limitations on the CIA's freedom of maneuver. The seriousness of democratic restrictions on the CIA needs to be kept in perspective, it is true. For one thing, a democratic society offers an intelligence agency advantages which help compensate for that society's sometimes constricting vigilance. Pluralism and free speech in America's democracy have produced a rich profusion of ideas on every conceivable subject; the CIA has been able to draw on these ideas and, where appropriate, recruit their authors. Of enormous advantage, too, has been that cosmopolitanism which derives from the experience and composition of a nation of immigrants, thus leading to tolerance and understanding, as well as to expertise in the languages and customs of foreign nations. But, of course, the fact that the CIA derives such advantages from American democracy by no means invalidates the case for studying the problems which that democracy nevertheless creates for U.S. secret intelligence.

The CIA has had to operate within the context of America's own form of democracy with its distinctive processes. Notably, the Agency has been enmeshed in presidential politics. For example, its posture on the "missile gap" controversy had a bearing on the 1960 presidential election, and the suppression of its Vietnam estimates influenced the outcome of the 1968 election. As CIA directors are dependent on presidential patronage, they are acutely conscious of the political sensitivity of some of their estimates, and their judgment may be affected accordingly. The presidents themselves are even more politically conscious, a fact which may induce them, in the interest of avoiding political embarrassments, to ask the wrong intelligence questions—resulting in the allocation of inappropriate tasks to the CIA. In spite of the ever-increasing importance of foreign policy, some presidents (and members of Congress, too) have furthermore behaved on the assumption that elections are won or lost primarily on domestic issues. More than one president has impatiently pushed aside foreign-intelligence reports, only then, after an error, to fudge the issue of reform by merely giving the CIA more money. Added to the fact that individual presidents have attended to intelligence problems in a spasmodic and inconsistent manner is the phenomenon of automatic quadrennial discontinuity. The occasional two-term presidency has mitigated the effects of elections on intelligence administration, but, on the other hand, the abrupt endings of the Kennedy and Nixon administrations aggravated the discontinuity in the CIA's tasking.

Some hope for continuous and consistent guidance lay with Congress. Although it is true that many representatives serve for only a short spell, those on influential oversight committees are characteristically veterans of many years' standing. Congress has, indeed, contributed sage advice. In the late 1940s and the second half of the 1970s especially, its members contributed to the CIA's political acceptability and therefore to its effectiveness. On the other hand, there are limits to the beneficial effect of congressional impact. Congress does advise on, consent to, and authorize payment for intelligence provisions, yet, as intelligence is part of the foreign and defense policymaking process, the U.S. Constitution assigns the executive function to the president. Furthermore, in the 1950s and 1960s those responsible for congressional oversight of CIA activities proved languid in the exercise of their invigilatory prerogative and duty, while their critics sometimes allowed political ambition and sensationalism to take the place of seasoned judgment. Congress has on the whole been alert to the CIA's relatively few domestic transgressions, but less consistent in paying heed to the Agency's main, foreign-intelligence function.

Yet there is one aspect of the CIA's foreign-intelligence work that has repeatedly stirred congressional indignation: allegations of excessive secrecy have, in fact, whipped up legislative fury since the early days of the Republic. Here, there is real scope for misunderstanding. In keeping certain information hidden from foreign powers, the director of the CIA must necessarily refrain from instructing (and may even actively deceive) the American people and all but a few of their elected representatives. But as dissimulation is a well-known strategy of the shadier type of politician, and as it might also signify an attempt by a particular president to expand his powers at the expense of Congress, arguments about the need for secrecy often meet with a cynical reception. There have therefore been several crusades to unveil the truth about the CIA's affairs—crusades which have helped to keep the Agency in check, but at the same time made its business public to a remarkable and often embarrassing degree. The effect of the crusades, ironically, has been to make the White House and the Agency even more determined to hush things up: the Eisenhower administration's response to Senator Joseph P. McCarthy's attack on the CIA is a prime example of this. Thus the secrecy issue has occasioned a running battle between president and Congress requiring CIA directors to be adept at dodging the cross fire.

The principles behind American democracy, in addition to its distinctive political processes, have influenced the nature and effectiveness of the CIA's work. American democracy came of age when the revolt by the indigenous white population of the colonies produced a virulent and successful sense of nationhood. Ever since, this experience has been the bedrock of American anti-imperialism, and "nation-building" became one of the CIA's leading activities after its formation in 1947. As a result both of the voters' rejection of domestic socialist parties and of the totalitarian nature of the Soviet socialist state, however, the majority of Americans has come to believe that socialism is almost by definition the negation of democracy, and that no truly indigenous and democratic political movement will opt for left-wing policies. In its foreign covert operations, therefore, the CIA has sometimes had to play, not its trump card—encouragement of local nationalism and pride—but its vulnerable card—opposition to a popular local socialist movement.

A further principle behind American democracy (not just behind congressional criticism of the White House) is the desirability of open government. Faith in this principle is evident all the time, not just in the muckraking crusades of the Progressive era or the 1970s. The extent to which government information is freely available in the United States may not be obvious to American citizens who are used to it and keep on pressing for even more openness, but it is immediately apparent to foreign observers accustomed to the secrecy of their own governments. And as CIA leaders have frequently pointed out, the openness of American society gives Soviet intelligence at least one major advantage over its U.S. counterpart, making counterintelligence a challenging problem for the Agency. On the other side of the coin, it might be added, CIA officials have sometimes made too much of the secrecy of Soviet society, conditioning themselves to ignore those open sources of information which do exist and can be used. So, they have incurred a double penalty on account of the open nature of American democracy.

The fears and expectations behind American democracy influenced the structure and tasking of CIA to a degree that was pervasive on the Agency's performance. When Congress established the Agency in 1947, for example, a growing number of Americans feared that the New Deal had overextended the activities of the federal government; many, also, were determined to prevent the growth of an "American Gestapo." In order to safeguard democracy, Congress gave the CIA jurisdiction over foreign intelligence, leaving to the Federal Bureau of Investigation (FBI) the field of domestic intelligence. From the beginning, therefore, there were squabbles between the CIA and the FBI about demarcation lines for counterintelligence; when the CIA ventured too far into that field in later years, it risked vehement political censure. Another, and much graver consequence of the foreign-domestic split was that CIA analysts came under fire for estimating Soviet capabilities and intentions in isolation from U.S. strength and policy options.

To the dismay of some observers, the majority of Americans expressed, even in the Cold War, a continuing expectation that militarism would be curbed and consumer expectations satisfied. These were complementary goals, for less money spent on relatively expensive, conventional armed forces meant more money spent on consumer goods. In the American democracy, these majoritarian aspirations found expression in policy: a relatively low-cost nuclear defense strategy combined with covert operations at a mere fraction of the cost of conventional military campaigns. American nuclear strategy influenced the U.S. military intelligence appraisal: because of mirror-imaging and self-interest, some senior military analysts erroneously assumed, in the 1950s, that the Soviets were trying to match the American nuclear arsenal (to its credit, though, the CIA itself largely avoided this trap). In pursuit of cheaper options, the administration asked the CIA to run America's covert operations. This led to troubles that made Americans even more reluctant to accept a domestic role for the CIA, for fear that the Agency might import "dirty tricks," applying them to U.S. citizens at home. But the obvious reform—the transference of the CIA's covert operations to a new and separate agency—carried potential danger of an unacceptable kind, the possibility that an agency with no other function than meddling in foreign politics would keep on inventing ever more fantastic and irresponsible schemes simply to stay in business. So the CIA remained in charge of covert programs that threatened constant political trouble at home. Democratic aspirations thus underpinned some of the most intractable problems associated with the Agency.

The effectiveness of the CIA has always depended on the Agency's standing. That standing consists of a number of components. One of these is legitimacy— the degree to which the American people accept the Agency and its work as necessary, and as constitutionally and legislatively authorized. Another component of the CIA's standing at a given time is the credibility of its estimates. The Agency's prestige at home and abroad further affects its standing. Political acceptability is an essential ingredient. Finally, to possess the standing necessary to effective functioning the Agency's leaders must enjoy the respect of their peers among the foreign-policymaking elite in the White House, State Department, Department of Defense, and relevant Senate committees.

There are several reasons why the CIA cannot afford to let its standing slip. One is that ill repute is bad for staff morale, leading to poor performance, inadequate recruitment, and apostasy of a type that compounds the damage. Another is that foreign leaders put small faith in the policies of a nation that has but little respect for its own premier foreign-intelligence agency. Again, unless they enjoy a certain standing, the CIA's leaders can hardly expect the House of Representatives to vouchsafe continuing funds or the Senate to vote unvarying consent to its activities. Prestige is furthermore of great utility with respect to intragovernmental relations: to ensure the respect and cooperation of other branches of the intelligence bureaucracy, of the State Department, and of the military. Above all, the CIA must secure good standing in the White House, the chief consumer of the goods which it produces, for analysis cannot be effective unless it is appreciated, understood, and acted upon.

In certain circumstances, it is true, the CIA's advice might best be ignored, and in such circumstances high Agency standing would impede the proper conduct of foreign policy. If the White House is right and the Agency is wrong, the president must hope to be able to push CIA advice aside without incurring too much political opprobrium or damage. At other times—notably in the cases of Kissinger and Reagan diplomacy—policymakers have ignored CIA estimates, though knowing them to be correct, in pursuit of what they deem to be higher objectives. But it is an underlying theme of this book that CIA intelligence work has been sound most of the time, and that respect for its product is normally a desirable ingredient in the shaping of U.S. foreign policy.

The CIA's leaders have been justified in their protracted campaigns for proper standing, which has been affected by several factors over the years. One factor is the Agency's intelligence performance: it may be true that CIA spokesmen have been occasionally overeager in their claim that they never receive credit for their secret successes, but they are right in stating that the American people cannot forgive their mistakes. Another factor is bureaucratic rivalry and the relative prestige of rival intelligence organizations, notably the military intelligence agencies and the FBI. But a more constant barometer of any agency's standing in Washington is its position in the White House pecking order. The personality and outlook of a particular president, the degree of his respect for and interest in intelligence, and the frequency with which he consults the CIA director have a crucial effect on the Agency's standing (though, conversely, the Agency must already command a great deal of respect in order to win the attention of the president). Nor is mere interest enough: there must exist harmony and loyalty between the CIA chief and his boss in the White House. It is all too easy for a president to make a scapegoat of the CIA when things go wrong in the foreign policy sphere. President Kennedy even argued that this was how American as distinct from British democracy worked: in a serious British crisis, the prime minister would resign; in an American crisis, the president dismissed a civil servant. It is a standard CIA gripe that its director has been the "fall guy" for the president. The gripe is symptomatic of the existence of past misunderstandings that have undermined CIA prestige.

Quite apart from the presidential relationship, the CIA has enjoyed mixed fortunes in democratic politics. For much of the time, the Agency has fared well. Indeed, the little frisson of excitement customarily engendered by the acronym "CIA" is more often indicative of fascination and marvel than of contempt. Yet there have been several setbacks, some of them serious. One cluster of dangers has arisen from personality and circumstance. The ambitions of publicity-thirsty senators have from time to time produced attacks more notable for their ferocity than for their logic. Professionally or ideologically frustrated CIA officers have occasionally resorted to damaging bouts of apostasy. The state of the political climate—whether "Big Government" is in or out of fashion—and the temper of the press—whether it is out for blood or in a "responsible" phase—have clearly affected the CIA's ability to avoid confidence-sapping scandals.

In incurring opprobrium, the Agency has in some ways been the victim of a double excess of democracy. At one end of the political spectrum, libertarians have excoriated the Agency's alleged excesses in propping up foreign right-wing regimes and disregarding civil liberties at home. From a very different perspective, critics like Senators Joe McCarthy and Barry Goldwater have attacked the "liberal" or "left-wing" tendencies that they claim to have discerned in the Agency. The political image of the CIA, whether it derives from the real characteristics of the Agency or from the perception of those characteristics by others, has, in various and sometimes contradictory ways, affected its political fortunes and its ability to perform effectively.

Finally, covert operations have substantially affected the CIA's standing. In the 1950s (and to some extent in the early 1980s, too) such operations enhanced the prestige of the Agency. But, in several ways, they have at other times had the reverse effect, especially when carried to excess. The CIA's foreign covert operations have frequently alienated foreign opinion, although there is certainly a double standard here. In the 1980s America's allies refrained from complaining about CIA covert operations in Afghanistan (where they approved of the objective) but were upset about the use of similar tactics in Nicaragua (where the objective seemed to them less desirable). Many of the attacks on the CIA, furthermore, have been Communist, Communist-inspired, or Communist-manipulated. Other attacks, such as those from Gaullist Frenchmen or from India's Mrs. Gandhi, were non-Communist but opportunistic. Nevertheless, one cannot avoid the conclusion that the CIA's covert operations were a cause of unpopularity in themselves. They diminished the stock of America, as well as the Agency, in foreign eyes, and for this reason senior policymakers in the Department of State and elsewhere took a jaundiced view of the CIA as a whole. Fears that the CIA would import its methods to America, and that operational obsessions were damaging the Agency's analytical performance, strengthened the hand of the critics. At several stages in the CIA's history, the more constructive critics sought practical guidelines that would moderate the Agency's operations without crippling them. The search for these guidelines, as well as the varying fortunes of the operators themselves, is part of the story of the Agency's fluctuating standing and effectiveness.

A historian writing about the CIA is, in some significant ways, at a disadvantage compared with an intelligence expert. The latter may, for example, utilize his intimacy with colleagues and his familiarity with complex weapons systems in a manner which the historian cannot match. The historical approach does, however, offer advantages, these advantages being of a type that is familiar to students of the past in general. By examining the CIA over time, it is possible to appreciate the danger of adopting rigid, unchanging criteria by which to judge the Agency's performance or axiomatic precepts to explain it. Variations in expectations, in political environment, in personality, and in the nature of the tasks prescribed, have all influenced the CIA's effectiveness. For reasons that can only be appreciated in their proper historical setting, the same phenomena have produced different effects at different times. So the student of current intelligence problems might profitably bear in mind the historian's truism: the past does contain some instructive patterns, but history never repeats itself exactly.

The past's instruction begins with the prehistory of the CIA. The Japanese attack on Pearl Harbor, for example, gave a peculiar skew to the Agency's early tasking, for its officials were required to guard against similar surprise attacks in the future. Even after the modernization of the CIA's role, the elimination of surprise has remained an important part of the Agency's job, but now because of a *different* historical phenomenon—the desire of successive presidents to avoid embarrassment in the newly important sphere of world politics. Another legacy was the American democratic habit of criticizing all things secret and all things powerful. Revelations about the Gestapo encouraged this habit, but the habit would not have survived to the present day without being deeply rooted in the American character. Against this background, it is understandable that the CIA's precursors as well as "The Company" itself were concerned to establish their standing in American society; indeed, the need to do so is no recent phenomenon, and not merely the product of short-term factors.

The Agency was, nonetheless, a creation of the postwar years. The first half-decade of peace was one of diverse and sometimes conflicting tendencies: reaction against New Deal-style big government, but creation of the bureaucratic apparatus of the "National Security State"; isolationist yearnings but superpower policies; antimilitary sentiment but growing military commitments. The CIA was on the one hand the product of American distrust. It was to be civilian in character and under the control of the president rather than the armed forces; its domestic role was to be minimal. Even the decision to establish an agency at all had to wait for two years because of the strength of opposition. On the other hand, once it was formed, the Agency was a big-government weapon which could flourish in a democracy with some assurance—indeed, it was the world's first democratically sanctioned secret service. Its leading officials were assembled on the principle of the New Deal's brain trust—they had to be "Top People", both intellectually and socially. Over the years, these Ivy Leaguers were to serve America well (if not infallibly); they excelled at the analysis of diverse problems and proved loyal and impenetrable by any foreign intelligence service. Their fall from grace was to be a product of changing times rather than of declining competence.

In the 1950s, Cold War competition and the mounting urgency of the nuclear threat changed the nature of the tasks facing the CIA and therefore the criteria which contemporaries and historians used to assess its performance and determine its status. Assessment of the Soviet nuclear arsenal and delivery capability was of vital importance, and the Agency's analysts struggled also with problems relating to the economic planning of defense. At the same time, national defense planners gave the CIA an important propaganda role. Furthermore, because America was economizing on its conventional armed forces, the planners gave the Agency a wide mandate to conduct unconventional, covert warfare. The CIA's clandestine propaganda and operations seemed to work well and added luster to the already prestigious agency. It is important to realize, however, that the political climate of the 1950s, as well as the Agency's expertise and good fortune, contributed to the status-boosting judgmental process.

Things went wrong for the CIA in the 1960s. For one thing, whatever one's criterion for judgment may be, its performance declined. The Bay of Pigs fiasco exposed the perils of covert operations and raised the possibility that America, for some years the darling of international opinion, would come to be seen as a cajoling and ineffective bully. The seriousness of the Agency's failure to predict the Soviet nuclear missile buildup in the second half of the decade needs no elaboration. Yet these failures were balanced by successes, and they alone do not explain why the Agency reached its nadir under Presidents Johnson and Nixon. The full explanation has much to do with the political sourness of the years of the Vietnam War. The White House-CIA relationship, which had been excellent under President Eisenhower, deteriorated. Successive presidents directed toward the CIA either an apathy that lowered the Agency's status and effectiveness or an antipathy deriving from personality, from the CIA's social composition, and from class prejudice. And, at the very time when the CIA seemed to count for nothing more than a convenient scapegoat for presidential errors, Congress—the source of the act that had conferred upon the CIA its democratic legitimacy—adopted a more hostile stance consistent with its progressive disillusionment with the performance of the executive branch of government over Vietnam.

The early 1970s were even more upsetting for CIA personnel. The secret agency ironically became the main topic of public debate. There was irony, too, in the fact that covert operations—the source of much pride in the 1950s—were the chief cause of acrimony. But, precisely because the Agency was so susceptible to democratic politics, for the CIA the 1970s were a decade of redemption. The recovery stemmed partly from reforms. Congress set up new guidelines for covert operations. The White House once again began to take the intelligence process seriously.

And, the Agency focused on a task of increasing importance: the verification of Soviet compliance or noncompliance with arms-control agreements.

By the 1980s, the CIA had recovered much of its former standing. Like the more successful of his predecessors, Director William Casey appreciated that in America's democracy a secret service needs publicity. The Agency openly advertised for new recruits; its experts turned up at academic conferences wearing nametags emblazoned "Central Intelligence Agency." In a classic reversal of fortune, the CIA could now expect public plaudits for its dramatically increased and well-advertised program of covert operations. Yet, the political climate had not changed in a uniform manner. Foreign opinion remained largely hostile to the CIA and therefore to America with respect to certain clandestine enterprises—particularly that in Nicaragua. And in the case of President Reagan the Agency had to contend with a new paradox: a keen supporter who was apparently deaf to its advice.

The latter point demonstrates the continuing need for a closer understanding of those factors that have a bearing on the CIA's standing and on its officials' ability to command respect. This question is inseparable from the broader issue of how an intelligence agency may effectively operate in a democracy, and it is a question which the past can help to illuminate.

1

THE
LESSONS
OF
AMERICAN
HISTORY

In the second half of the twentieth century, it has been vital for America to have at its disposal a competent, secret foreign-intelligence agency capable of commanding respect and attention at home. The need for an intelligence organization with high standing stems largely from a modern circumstance: the emergence of the United States as a world power at a time when the Soviet Union, a clandestine society, started to pose a potent threat to world security. The Soviet media simply do not give sufficient information on Russian atomic strength and strategic intentions. There has therefore been a need for clandestine techniques to gauge a purposely concealed threat; and there has been a change in attitudes resulting in loss of status for the State Department and in considerable prestige for a new national-security bureaucracy of which the Central Intelligence Agency is a prominent part.

Yet, the CIA has not always concentrated its main energies on foreign intelligence, and, when it has, it has sometimes failed to impress U.S. policymakers with the significance of its findings. One reason is that White House officials and other Americans have misperceived, or disagreed over, its role. Another reason is that the American spy's search for higher status began prior to the emergence of the Soviet threat and is discernible well before the CIA's formation in 1947. Among the factors worthy of review are not just secret agents' ambitions and taste for publicity, but also presidential desires to circumvent congressional scrutiny, and congressional suspicions of White House conspiracies. These personal and political drives, which still exist side by side with modern security fears and justifications of secret intelligence work, have tended to divert the Agency from its main contemporary functions: the assessment of the Soviet threat, and analysis in connection with arms-reduction negotiations. In the heat of debate, intelligence partisans have sometimes fought for higher standing in ways and for reasons that undermine the real justifications for the agency that they champion.

The justification of a necessary phenomenon by means of erratic reasoning can have distorting and damaging effects on the phenomenon itself. Justifications of the CIA therefore invite scrutiny. One can begin by inquiring what lessons the founders of the CIA drew from American history.[1] By the end of World War II, historical experience had suggested to those concerned with the intelligence problem two sets of principles, each of which produced guidelines—some informal, others official—which governed the performance of the CIA. The first set had to do with efficiency, justifying, for example, a centralized system. The second had to do with restraints on power, or how to keep the intelligence community respectable and status-worthy by saving it from the consequences of its own excesses. The resultant guidelines as a whole proved amply reassuring at the time of the founding of the CIA and underpinned the Agency's "Golden Age" in the 1950s. By the 1970s, however, some of their inadequacies had become painfully evident, and reforms took place. With the wisdom of hindsight, as one might expect, it is possible to discern both the strengths and the weaknesses of the principles behind the original CIA.

One principle that CIA advocates and apologists emphasized was bureaucratic continuity.[2] Their lesson from the past was that the United States had too readily dismantled its spy networks in peacetime, too often been caught unprepared by new crises.[3] Such a viewpoint, however, reflects the grim priorities of the Cold War, when it has indeed been necessary to maintain a permanent vigilance. Before the Cold War, one might argue, bureaucratic rigidity was undesirable. Certainly, in their first century of independence, Americans saw little need for a major, permanent, foreign-intelligence effort. This was largely because they were preoccupied with internal affairs and protected on each side by great oceans. At the same time, successive generations took the pragmatic and perhaps still instructive view that spying should be undertaken at the time and in the manner prescribed by circumstances.

Sporadic though they were, early American espionage efforts did slowly build up an awareness of some of the principles involved.[4] Thus, immediately after the Constitution's ratification, Congress recognized that, in the interest of efficiency, espionage should be an executive prerogative. It voted secret funds to enable the president to make unvouchered payments for intelligence services. President Washington initiated espionage ventures as and when necessary, setting a precedent for his successors.

Presidents never ceased to commission individual clandestine missions, but the hostilities of 1861–65 produced a new need. Spy networks came into being. One of these networks dissolved with the Confederacy, but Lincoln's last cabinet meeting created the present-day Secret Service. The formation of the Office of Naval Intelligence (ONI) in 1882 and the Military Information Division (MID) three years later helped prepare the way for America's emergence as a great power. It was also the beginning of intelligence-agency proliferation and called for some form of coordination. By 1898, the year of the Spanish-American War, technological change had made such coordination more feasible. Secret Service chief John E. Wilkie utilized two recent inventions, the typewriter and carbon paper, to help with the central direction of counterespionage. He was not in a position to centralize foreign, or offensive, espionage, but he did demonstrate the potential of the coordination principle when the Secret Service, with help from the MID and ONI, mounted a defensive watch on a Spanish spy ring run from Montreal. In a blaze of publicity, Wilkie achieved its destruction.

Bureaucratic flux did not mean that the United States was caught unawares in World War I. By then, the Secret Service had ceded pride of place in the counterintelligence field. In 1908 the inauspiciously-named attorney-general Charles Bonaparte had established the Bureau of Investigation. With help from other agencies, the bureau mopped up German secret agents trying to operate in the United States. After the war, the leadership of the FBI, as it was now called, showed a rare gift for publicity and for role flexibility (as evidenced later in the fable of J. Edgar Hoover and his G-men). One American "spymaster" had already come to regard prestige as a goal in itself, rather than as a means to a single end.

President Woodrow Wilson's foreign-intelligence effort in World War I was largely an open operation, conducted through a large-scale, government-financed, instant university known as the Inquiry. Its nonsecret nature reflected Wilson's proclamation of faith in "open diplomacy" and in the relatively accessible nature of the information that U.S. policymakers were seeking. At the same time, the president's advisors did recognize a need for secret intelligence. The State Department took over the coordinating role that the Secret Service had assumed in 1898. The officials of its central intelligence bureau coordinated both counterintelligence and the limited amount of foreign secret intelligence which the United States undertook in World War I. Their office was well-known neither before nor after its later designation, U-1. Its obscurity was, of course, appropriate to its secret function, but, in the context of American democracy, that obscurity also implied low status, and it contributed to U-1's demise in 1927. By this time, however, U-1 had confirmed the principle established by the Secret Service: there was to be civilian control over centrally coordinated intelligence.

In addition to the principles of continuity, executive control, centralization, and civilian leadership, the CIA's founders acknowledged the further principle of legislative sanction. From the beginning, Congress had been alert to possible abuses arising from the president's access to unvouchered funds. Particularly odious was the president's use of secret or executive agents for policy and diplomacy purposes. Long before Henry Kissinger ran into trouble for such activities in the 1970s, James Buchanan was defending secret agents in Cuba against those senators who feared an extension of presidential power and of Southern slavocracy. Later in the nineteenth century, the Hoar amendment allowed that the president could appoint "a mere agent . . . or spy," but "such a person, so appointed, could be in no sense an officer of the United States."[5]

Historical precedent suggested that Congress would also be alert to violations of domestic liberties. Strenuous objections to employers' use of Pinkerton detectives in labor disputes in the 1890s, to the overzealous activities of federal agents in the Red Scare of 1919, to government snoopers trying to enforce Prohibition, to President Hoover's use of the ONI to spy on political opponents, and to employers' renewed deployment of labor spies in the 1930s indicated a profound disquiet about the domestic use of secret agents.[6] Even before the specter of the Gestapo, and, later, the KGB, reinforced such fears, congressmen and their constituents were on guard against an overweaning federal intelligence apparatus. The separation of foreign and domestic spying bureaucracies was an accepted principle by the 1940s.

Another feature of past congressional attitudes toward intelligence matters was that they sometimes stemmed from prejudice or opportunism. Objections to the intelligence services were occasionally spurious. For example, congressmen who opposed the creation of the Bureau of Investigation spoke in the name of liberty, but were influenced by the Secret Service's recent exposure of some of their number who had been engaged in Western land fraud. Diatribes against secret activities welled, at times, from sentiments independent of those activities: Populists' sectional loyalties and hatred of large-scale Eastern capital lay at the root of their objections to Pinkerton detectives to a much greater degree than sympathy with civil liberties. Congressional self-interest and irrationality meant that legislative attempts at intelligence reform could be inadequate or flawed. Legislative shortcomings also produced cynicism and resistance in the intelligence community toward congressional oversight, and encouraged the development of a defensive propaganda that was correspondingly flawed.

The central coordination of foreign intelligence had disappeared with the scrapping of U-1 in 1927, with the result that intelligence gathering was at a low ebb in the 1930s. Army intelligence reached its nadir, judged by both expenditure and personnel, in 1937. The ONI was a little better off, but had nonetheless suffered severe cutbacks. The codebreakers in the Army's Signals Corps were achieving only limited successes on their low budget. One might, of course, argue that none of this mattered. The nation's leaders, especially Roosevelt, needed no intelligence experts to warn them of Hitler's aggressive intentions. It is possible, however, that a better-coordinated intelligence effort might have warned of less obvious threats, notably the ambitions being nurtured—against the dictates of military and industrial reason—in Japan.[7] Furthermore, the Nazi threat was so serious that it demanded complex analysis.

A German spy scare jolted President Franklin D. Roosevelt into an awareness of intelligence needs. In 1938, eighteen members of a Nazi spy ring were arrested. But the jurisdictional lines between the FBI, army intelligence, the New York police, and other interested parties were so confused that the prisoners were poorly guarded, and fourteen of them escaped. Roosevelt demanded better coordination and began to grope his way haltingly forward, first in the counterintelligence field, then more broadly.[8]

The revival of a centralizing mechanism similar to the defunct U-1 should have fallen to Assistant Secretary of State Adolf A. Berle, one of Roosevelt's brain trusters. After his appointment in 1938, Berle did sit in on intelligence coordination meetings but, despite the Nazi threat and American entry into the war, he found the intelligence business dirty and distasteful. He refused to take an initiative.[9] The Department of State thus relinquished control of intelligence, which would be an increasingly important factor in diplomacy. Berle's omission in wartime was to be repeated after 1945, to the chagrin of those who believed that the State Department should be the prime and sole executor of presidential foreign policy.

In search of a man who would take the initiative, Roosevelt turned to Colonel William J. ("Wild Bill") Donovan. Donovan had won his "Wild Bill" nickname for bravery in 1917–18, when he commanded New York's 69th regiment, the "Fighting Irish."[10] His grandfather had been a Fenian immigrant to Buffalo's shantytown. From his quarterback days at Columbia, Donovan was marked out as a fighter on the way to the top. By 1940, he was a Republican, conservative, millionaire recruit to the American business elite. With his enormous capacity for getting things done regardless of the enemies he made in the process, he became a charismatic figure in U.S. intelligence circles.

Roosevelt had known of Donovan since their days at Columbia Law School. In June 1940, he sent him on a mission to assess Britain's chances of surviving the Nazi onslaught. Upon his return, Donovan predicted that Britain would have the will and capability to fight on against the Germans who had already overrun much of continental Europe. His report was important in the diplomatic context, for it helped to correct earlier assessments, notably from Ambassador Joseph P. Kennedy in London, which had been pessimistic about Britain's prospects for survival.

In the context of intelligence history, another aspect of Donovan's report is significant. Navy Secretary Frank Knox had originally charged Donovan with the job of analyzing Britain's handling of Nazi fifth-column activities. Donovan was glad to do so. The British, for their part, were keen to promote the idea that Germany's early victories were the result of dirty tricks, not real military prowess, for that implied that Britain might yet fight off the Nazi assault if only America gave enough assistance. Donovan upheld this idea because he wanted to support the British, and because he wanted Americans to believe the British were worth supporting.[11]

But there was another, equally important reason why Donovan bruited the notion of a Nazi fifth-column menace. This was that it helped him in his campaign to establish a new American intelligence agency. Donovan's syndicated articles on the Gestapo's dirty tricks and psychological warfare paved the way for America's own clandestine ventures in World War II, and foreshadowed the use, in later years, of the KGB bogeyman. He realized that, in the context of an open democracy characterized by vigorous debate on all important issues, he had to publicize his case for a new agency. He resorted to headline-grabbing tactics and dubious arguments in pursuit of what was, indeed, a good cause. Yet, whereas the end did justify the means, the methods he and his successors used had a distorting effect on the end product itself, the American intelligence community.

The British looked forward to cooperating with Donovan, and naturally wanted his enterprise to succeed. Prime Minister Winston Churchill had sent the Canadian industrialist William S. Stephenson to the United States to coordinate British intelligence. Stephenson advised and encouraged Donovan, and helped him to meet the right people in London. In May 1941 Rear Admiral John H. Godfrey, Britain's director of naval intelligence, visited Washington and dined at the White House. He reported rather patronizingly on the inadequacies of American intelligence, but saw some useful strengths to be built on, and recommended Donovan as just the man for the job. On his departure, he left behind his aide Ian Fleming, future author of the James Bond spy novel series, to advise, and liaise with, Bill Donovan.[12]

It was shortly after this that Roosevelt established the office of coordinator of information (COI). Earlier, in April, Donovan had written to Navy Secretary Knox recommending that a new agency be formed for the purpose of coordinating the intelligence effort. He described British secret service arrangements and outlined the features that should appear in an American agency. The president should be in control; there should be no "home duties"; there would be a foreign espionage capability; the proposed foreign-intelligence agency would analyze the information collected by other services, like the FBI and ONI, and coordinate their information-gathering efforts (at the time, the FBI had foreign-intelligence jurisdiction in Latin America). Donovan also told Knox that "subversive operations in foreign countries" would have to be contemplated.[13]

The last point might be said to have been partly established by an opaque phrase in Roosevelt's executive order of July 11, designating Donovan coordinator of information: the COI was "to carry out, when requested by the President, such supplementary activities as may facilitate the securing of information important for national security not now available to the Government."[14] An incorrigible activist, Donovan wanted to launch psychological warfare and paramilitary operations to counter the real or imaginary Nazi fifth-column threat, and to publicize his efforts in order to win recognition and permanence. According to Thomas F. Troy, author of an internal CIA study of Donovan's creative role, from the beginning Donovan thought of analytical intelligence work as a "cover" for secret operations, a bias that continued, according to Troy, in the era of CIA itself and one that constituted a sharp contrast with British practice.[15]

The British influence on Donovan's efforts nevertheless received emphasis in several sympathetic accounts of the CIA's origins. On the one hand, British intelligence was in a remarkable state of decay in the 1930s, being both poorly coordinated and susceptible to dewy-eyed assumptions about German military strength and strategic ambitions.[16] On the other hand, British intelligence officers had improved in the hard school of wartime experience by the time they lent a helping hand to their American counterparts. The Americans knew more about some areas like South America and the Pacific, and the British more about others, notably Germany, so the intelligence services could complement each other quite naturally.[17] Some British individuals were reluctant to give too much help to a nation that was ready to supplant their own country on the world stage and that was ideologically opposed to the British Empire. Nevertheless, the British did hand over some cryptanalytic "golden eggs," did supply ancillary services, and did train a number of Americans who had volunteered to serve as "shadow warriors."[18]

British help and instruction were, to an appreciable extent, important, but actual indebtedness to the British was neither the sole nor the prime reason for extravagant, retrospective acknowledgments of help from across the ocean. Anglophilia helps to explain the emphasis. So does the immodesty of British intelligence veterans like Stephenson, who boasted that they taught the Americans what they needed to know, and even claimed that the CIA's paternity was theirs.[19] More profoundly, the emphasis arose from CIA advocates' search for respectability and standing. The CIA, its critics said, was like the Gestapo or the KGB. No, said the Agency's defenders, it was similar to the more reputable British secret service and, in fact, stemmed from British tuition during the democracy-saving wartime partnership.[20] British provenance tied in with CIA advocacy in another way, too. CIA advocates argued that continuous peacetime intelligence was necessary if America was to be equipped to meet forthcoming crises. They portrayed the intelligence system of the 1930s as having been disgracefully weak, yet, at the same time, praised Donovan's wartime achievements. But if peacetime preparedness was essential to wartime success, why was it that Donovan had done so wonderfully well? The explanation of this "miracle" lay, of course, in the crash instruction course offered by the British.[21] The legend of British help was therefore doubly convenient as propaganda. Unfortunately, its very convenience distracted attention from the American origins of American intelligence, and from more useful and relevant justifications of a central intelligence organization.

In 1941 a major intelligence failure won widespread public support for Donovan's expansionist plans. The surprise attack on Pearl Harbor greatly increased the prospects for an enhanced U.S. intelligence capability both during and after the war triggered by the raid. The carrier-based Japanese airplanes killed 2,403 Americans and destroyed a considerable number of U.S. fighting ships and warplanes. The attack not only plunged America into a second world war, but also shattered forever its sense of geographic seclusion and security. Their new perception of international danger heightened Americans' appreciation of the fact that, on

December 7, 1941, their nation had been caught napping on the intelligence front. Subsequent sifting of the evidence has revealed that there was indeed intelligence failure of two types. The first was a failure of collection. The United States had no spy network in Japan, in spite of the availability of potential intelligence recruits among the West Coast Japanese-American population. The second failure, the COI notwithstanding, was one of coordination and analysis. America had for some time been able to decode some of Japan's secret cables, but the warning signals these cables supplied had not been properly evaluated.[22]

The Pearl Harbor incident had a distorting effect on the CIA's tasking in postwar years: instead of placing a high value on the Agency's analyses of Soviet warmaking prowess and of the prospects for effective arms control, White House officials emphasized the need to predict and deflect surprise attacks. Another effect was, however, to strengthen Donovan's hand. As on similar occasions in the future, intelligence failure led not to retribution and cuts but to reward through bureaucratic enhancement.

On June 13, 1942, President Roosevelt established the Office of Strategic Services (OSS) by military order. Unlike the CIA, the OSS was an agency designed for war. It operated under the authority of the Joint Chiefs of Staff (JCS) and was charged with the collection and analysis of "strategic information" and with the planning and direction of "special services" requested by the JCS.[23] In one way, it is wrong to see in this famous agency a direct ancestor of the CIA, because the OSS had to be more than an agency that might, when peace returned, prevent some future surprise attack. Yet the OSS was a formative precedent of the CIA in several respects. For example, it was denied domestic responsibilities. Indeed, on the day of its establishment, a separate office of war information was created to handle domestic propaganda. The confinement of Donovan's people to foreign propaganda reflected the long-standing police-state fears of Americans who demanded that different methods be used at home and abroad. The separation of domestic and foreign intelligence arrangements was a practice scrupulously followed in future years, with the occasional lapse being severely punished in the media and at the polls.

Another effective OSS precedent was the central agency's noncontrol of code-breaking facilities. International eavesdropping in future years became the responsibility of the National Security Agency, not the CIA. Still another precedent, and one with dire consequences, was its combination in the same units and personnel of two functions, the covert collection of information and covert action. Similar skills were required for the two types of activity, but problems were to arise in future years when covert action came to include, in addition to deniable activities like the offering of bribes to a foreign politician, paramilitary action, an OSS forte under Donovan's inspiration.

Paramilitary actions were too obtrusive for plausible denial. The difficulty was compounded by Donovan's recommendation, at the end of the war, that a peacetime central intelligence service should be accountable to the president, not the

JCS.[24] When this line of authority was in due course established for the CIA, there were complaints that the president could not disown the "dirty tricks" conducted on behalf of the United States. This meant that the CIA invited opprobrium for the one official who personified America more than any other. The CIA's covert activities made the United States unpopular. In turn, concerned Americans pointed an accusing finger at the Agency. The sins of the covert operators were then visited on the clandestine collectors and on the analysts, resulting in the Agency's loss of standing.

Just as important as the organizational legacy was the OSS's gift of experienced veterans to the postwar intelligence world. The OSS had itself inherited some people with useful intelligence experience, but they had come from diverse parts of the intelligence bureaucracy.[25] The CIA, by contrast, inherited a sizable number of veterans from a concentrated source—people who had known each other in the OSS and who constituted a lively postwar old boy network. Four of the CIA's directors (Allen Dulles, Richard Helms, William Colby, and William Casey) were OSS veterans, while a fifth, Walter Bedell Smith, was closely associated with Donovan's wartime outfit. The 1954 Doolittle Report noted that, of "34 key people in the Agency's train of command," 15 had intelligence experience in the OSS or a kindred government service.[26]

It is often remarked that the OSS precedent helps to account for the CIA's penchant for action, as opposed to thought. Some have argued that the preference for action did more than bring the United States into disrepute: it also, effectively, demoted the analysts and belittled their role within the CIA, and, therefore, in U.S. policymaking circles. In qualification of this view, it should be noted that William Langer's research and analysis group in the OSS, almost one thousand strong by the end of the war, contributed heavily to the CIA's personnel.[27] On the other hand, it is true that Donovan sought to achieve a higher standing for the OSS through covert operations. Such activities promised to confer prestige in a wartime situation, as they did at the height of the Cold War in the 1950s; only later did they have the reverse effect.

Operation Torch, launched on November 8, 1942, in Vichy French North Africa, gave Donovan one such opportunity to boost the prestige of the OSS. His organization had built up a network of agents based on the U.S. consuls who remained in various situations in North Africa. This OSS network supplied good military intelligence. Donovan's agents, however, were less successful in the political field. Robert Murphy, Roosevelt's pro-Vichy special envoy in North Africa, backed Donovan's plan to recruit indigenous sabotage and other support for an Allied invasion. In the event, the Allies did invade and, in due course, defeated Rommel's Afrika Corps. But the OSS had overestimated Vichy support, and the progress of the invasion was slower than expected. General Eisenhower, moreover, believed the North African invasion was too risky; from the strictly military point of view, a later, more thoroughly prepared thrust into Europe would have been preferable. Yet, Donovan had chosen his cause well. To satisfy American domestic opinion, Roosevelt had needed an early victory. It was easy enough to gloss over Vichy reluctance and strategic shortcomings and to concentrate instead on victory in the desert and the OSS contribution to it. Donovan's disciples—including Murphy, who went on to a career in the State Department—remembered the way in which the OSS had won its laurels. Operation Torch helped set the precedent for swashbuckling and superficially impressive schemes that were not always based on realistic premises, and which got the CIA into serious trouble after the 1950s.[28]

Myths about the OSS, as well as the reality, influenced attitudes and policies in postwar years. One such belief was that it was unhealthily elitist. Like the CIA later on, the "Oh So Social!" was variously held to be Ivy Leaguish, Wall-Street orientated, reflective of the social composition of the East Coast Establishment, internationalist, interventionist, and conducive to the irresponsible adventurism of recruits with private means. The Groton-Harvard-Yale dude cowboy tendency is, up to a point, verifiable in both the OSS and the CIA. For example, forty-two members of the Yale class of 1943 went into the OSS. Richard Bissell and Tracy Barnes, organizers of CIA covert adventures in the 1950s, were both "Yalies." But not all of the Ivy Leaguers were action men: Harvard's William Langer established the CIA's analytical effort, and Yale's Sherman Kent for many years ran it.[29] Such niceties behind the broad myth were sometimes lost in the heat of debate, or deemed irrelevant to the general point that an unrepresentative minority seemed to be taking momentous decisions behind the shield of secrecy.

Similarly, the OSS and its successor were periodically accused of leftward leanings, on the ground that a few of its members were genuinely of the left, and because Donovan cooperated for pragmatic reasons with the KGB's predecessor, the NKVD.[30] The truth—that the OSS was a broad church—made little difference to rightwing critics of central intelligence later in the 1940s. Opponents of various ideological hues just as blithely fastened on still another notion that sprang, in part, from the effectiveness of Donovan's own propaganda. The OSS director had built up his service as America's answer to the threat of Nazi subversion in foreign countries. But, upon the collapse of Germany, the full horrors of the Holocaust and of the Gestapo's domestic tyranny became apparent. Were the OSS and its proposed successor out to match the Gestapo, or to emulate it? Such a question seemed less absurd in 1945 than it does today. While the OSS was important as a source of inspiration for the CIA and became, in later years, a symbol of respectability, it was something of a liability for central intelligence campaigners in the immediate aftermath of V-J Day.

Americans' experience with foreign-intelligence agencies was still limited in several respects in 1945. There were no precedents for systematic peacetime analysis of the military and economic strength of potential foes or of U.S. capabilities to resist external attack. Americans were not yet fully aware of the role foreign-intelligence agencies might play in arms control negotiations.[31] There was no corpus of intelligence theory to deal, for example, with the relationship of evaluation to decision making. The United States had not yet built a permanent worldwide spy network to mount a preemptive lookout for imminent trouble. It follows that there had been little opportunity to develop an understanding of the limitations of intelligence work: spies cannot warn about every crisis and save every statesman's reputation. Peacetime covert operations had not been undertaken in the first century-and-a-half of the nation's life, so their inherent advantages and disadvantages were not appreciated. Finally, the disbandment of the OSS at war's end testifies to the fact that there existed no ready-made, widely acceptable model for a peacetime central intelligence agency.

Yet, had there lived in 1945 a person gifted with prophetic anticipation of future needs as well as with knowledge of the past, he might have drawn several lessons from U.S. intelligence history and used them to construct useful guidelines for the next generation. That history suggested that America needed an intelligence service, but that it should be capable of adapting to changing circumstances. Central coordination and evaluation were desirable with respect to intelligence data; the success of the State Department's U-1 indicated that policymakers and analysts might profit by working in tandem. Collaboration with the intelligence services of friendly powers seemed likely to produce mutual benefits in the future, as it had done in the past. A string of presidents, including Roosevelt in the case of the COI, had demonstrated the advantages of executive control over secret intelligence. The need for secrecy in intelligence work had always been evident and would doubtless be borne out by future developments.

The past held cautions, too, particularly on the political front. Beware of the Senate, our seer might have warned. The members of that chamber had long been jealous of presidential powers and had repeatedly rebelled over the use of spies, or executive agents, to circumvent senators' desires and undermine the democratic purport of the Constitution. Another clear lesson from the past was: avoid, in both reality and appearance, the introduction of "foreign" skullduggery to the domestic scene; to this end, do not combine foreign and domestic intelligence functions in the same agency.

Above all, the wise person of 1945 might have warned: be secretive, by all means, but in a democracy you must be prepared to emerge from the shadows and proclaim your goals and achievements. The former journalist Wilkie had boosted the Secret Service; J. Edgar Hoover of the FBI was a master of timely publicity, as the case of the G-men shows; Donovan's OSS was first the beneficiary and later the victim of public opinion. In fact, it is quite conceivable that U-1 might have survived, had more Americans heard of it and understood its work. In a democracy heavily influenced by competing interests, and by the media and advertising, publicity was essential to the procurement of proper funding and to the attainment of a standing high enough to ensure cooperation and influence.

So there were several lessons that might have been learned, suggesting at least some of the principles and guidelines necessary for effective postwar intelligence. But there was, of course, no magical seer. As on other occasions, one of history's lessons was that those lessons are sometimes ignored. One of the reasons for this in the case of intelligence history was its discontinuity. In the State Department, it is true, career officers remembered past experiences—but, as we have seen, State lost the initiative in the intelligence field. In Congress, too, long-serving members could apply the lessons of the past—but Congress's role was to oversee, not to initiate or to execute policy. In the White House, discontinuity was an inevitable consequence of the electoral system. In the intelligence community itself, the principles of economy and adaptability had dominated that of continuity, with the result that centralizing arrangements (Secret Service, U-1, OSS) had come and gone. The lack of a continuous intelligence arrangement meant that the accumulation of wisdom proceeded by fits and starts.

A second reason for ignoring past lessons had to do with the propaganda of CIA advocates and apologists. Although publicity was necessary in order to achieve for the CIA a proper measure of support and understanding, the nature of pro-CIA propaganda was sometimes unbalanced in a way that contributed to the distortion of the Agency's mission. Advocates and defenders of the Agency deprecated, and tended to ignore, intelligence arrangements from the end of the Revolutionary War to the creation of the COI, because these arrangements neither matched nor justified the scale and scope of the CIA's operations.[32] CIA partisans redefined the very word *intelligence* to include such activities as covert action, then applied the new definition anachronistically to pre-1941 agencies, which they naturally found wanting and undeserving of serious consideration.[33] By doing this, as well as by invoking the discontinuity-British redemption argument, the CIA propagandists removed from their own field of vision a valuable source of instruction, the past. The Senate's past objections to the use of secret methods to achieve diplomatic goals should have been just one of the lessons for the future. Another was Indian nationalists' objections to arbitrary harassment by U.S. secret agents in World War I—a warning of the likely repercussions of CIA operations in Asia and elsewhere.[34]

Similar myopia affected the opponents of intelligence expansion. For example, belief in the "revisionist" interpretation of U.S. entry into World War II made some critics destructive and obstructive of the principle of intelligence reform. Revisionists attacking the Roosevelt administration held that the president had been either incompetent in connection with Pearl Harbor, or had actually "maneuvered" the Japanese into launching the attack in order to get America into the European war by the "back door."[35] According to this logic, there had been no intelligence failure and there was no need for intelligence augmentation; the OSS, some critics continued, was just another example of overweening New Deal government with, in this case, particularly sinister undertones.[36] People who held these or similar views were disposed neither to study the lessons of intelligence history, nor to seek in that history constructive guidelines for the future.

As the debate on intelligence from 1945 to 1947 was soon to reveal, however, not all historical lessons are ignored or misapplied. An overwhelming majority of

Americans were at least agreed on the kind of intelligence agency they did *not* want: they wanted no mixing of foreign with domestic methods, no American Gestapo. Most Americans wanted a mechanism to guard their own country against surprise attack. This meant that they favored a permanent peacetime intelligence arrangement, and that they had established at least the principle of having criteria by which its efficiency might be judged. It also became clear soon after the war's end that there was a further consensus in favor of intelligence coordination, as well as strong support for civilian, presidential control as opposed to military domination. Additionally, there was support for a measure of congressional supervision. These guidelines were rudimentary, but they were a start. Their main strength lay in their contribution to the founding of an analytically efficient intelligence organization. Their main weakness was that they proved to be an insecure foundation for the establishment of the CIA's longterm standing.

2
THE BIRTH
OF
THE CIA

After 1945 the emergence of the Soviet threat and the inability of war-weakened Britain to do much about it convinced an even greater number of Americans that their nation would need a peacetime central intelligence service. Yet the Truman administration and Congress took some time to recognize that America's wartime ally was now a potential enemy, so progress toward the establishment of a new agency was slow. A minority still resisted the very idea of a central intelligence agency, and there was considerable disagreement over the form it should take. Nor did the matter end when a provision of the 1947 National Security Act did finally establish the CIA and supply it with its legislative charter, for some of the leading supporters of this provision regarded it as no more than an interim arrangement. Still, the original CIA provision was a major step: for the first time, it gave democratic legislative sanction to a foreign-intelligence agency, and it officially approved those intelligence guidelines on which there was common agreement.

Senior figures in the U.S. Navy and Navy Department formed a cohesive group behind the plan for a central intelligence agency, and they supplied a number of blueprints that guided thinking on the shape such an agency should take. At Pearl Harbor, the navy had, of course, suffered the immediate consequences of surprise attack arising from intelligence failure. Subsequently during the war, Undersecretary of the Navy James V. Forrestal advocated closer coordination between the armed forces, in emulation of the British war cabinet system.[1] In June 1945, Forrestal, now secretary of the navy, commissioned the former chairman of the army and navy munitions board, his old Wall Street friend Ferdinand Eberstadt, to study the thorny problem of army-navy coordination. Eberstadt in turn asked Rear Admiral Sidney W. Souers to draft a section on central intelligence.[2] Souers had been deputy chief of naval intelligence in the war. Various naval men, in addition to Forrestal and Eberstadt, now gave him advice and support. In October 1945, for example, Admiral Samuel M. Robinson endorsed an early Souers proposal for coordination through the Joint Chiefs of Staff, and advised an agency "which would obtain its appropriations directly from Congress in a lump sum, and which would not be subject to accounting."[3] Admiral William Leahy, Truman's chief of staff, was another navy man who offered Souers significant advice and support in 1945.[4] Strong naval backing helped Souers to play a key role in the birth of the CIA.

Navy officers were not the only people who, in the immediate aftermath of World War II, searched for constructive guidelines for peacetime intelligence. George S. Pettee had served in the intelligence unit of the Foreign Economic Administration and in the Office of War Information, and he was now teaching at Amherst College. Pettee turned his mind to the theory of foreign intelligence. Like so many Americans, he recalled the failure at Pearl Harbor; he foresaw the need for a "strategic intelligence service . . . for at least a generation to come," and he scorned Congress for its legislative inaction. Pettee went on to argue that a U.S. intelligence service would meet the needs of a world power, correct past ignorance of world politics, and provide a service that academia could not supply. Earlier than most Americans, Pettee openly identified Russia as the main potential enemy. In advance of most people everywhere, Pettee commented on the "failure of British intelligence during the decade before the war," which had arisen from "ideological and intellectual factors," though he praised its integration. An integrated outlook, a combined appreciation of economic and political factors, as well as of the "social-psychological matrix" of problems, should be a feature of U.S. strategy and foreign policy. The obscure Infantry Journal Press published Pettee's *The Future of American Secret Intelligence* in October 1946; only later did his work acquire the status of a pioneering classic. Pettee's endeavors were, nevertheless, symptomatic of the contemporary search for a peacetime intelligence formula.[5]

Wild Bill Donovan's contribution to the contemporary debate was especially influential. Though he had made enemies during the bureaucratic infighting of 1941–45 and had then lost his OSS power base, he was still vigorous in his advocacy, and his views commanded respect because Donovan was so experienced an intelligence officer. It will be recalled that, at an early stage, Donovan had introduced the notion of presidential control over a central intelligence agency. His subsequent correspondence with top people confirms, as one might expect, that he remained a fertile source of ideas on future intelligence arrangements. For example, to one 1945 memorandum outlining the principles which should govern a peacetime intelligence agency, he attached a penciled sheet detailing potential sources of information, all of them in due course exploited by the CIA: independent commercial airlines, shipping lines, communications companies, scientific organizations and institutions, industrial and commercial companies, news agencies, travel agencies, and educational institutions.[6]

Of special interest is the advice Donovan gave on covert operations. According to one theory, Donovan and other opportunists like Robert D. Murphy had promoted certain dubious operations in order to create a role for the OSS in the war, then foisted similarly redundant or counterproductive operations on the CIA in peacetime.[7] It is indeed the case that in his November 1944 report and urgent recommendation to President Roosevelt regarding the establishment and functions of a peacetime central intelligence agency, Donovan mentioned "subversive operations abroad."[8] John Magruder, deputy director for intelligence at the OSS, immediately toned down the implications of his boss's plan—and incidentally introduced a potential guideline—saying that a peacetime agency should only have an instant *capability* for subversive operations, just in case war broke out.[9] In a memorandum to Truman on June 21, 1945, an apparently unrepentant Donovan hinted that the CIA should exercise some control over U.S. voluntary organizations, a classic secret-operations tactic. He claimed that, in behaving offensively toward the Soviets, the American Federation of Labor was playing into the hands of the British who wished to pit America against Russia to enhance their own power.[10] Thus he anticipated what was to be extensive CIA involvement in labor's affairs.

Donovan's anticipation, however, stopped short of public advocacy. In fact, he told an Overseas Press Club dinner in February 1946 that "there is no moral justification for two nations at peace to break the other nations power of resistance or seek to subvert citizens into traitors. In time of peace, therefore, the true scope of intelligence is limited to the setting up of machinery that can gather, evaluate and interpret intelligence concerning other nations."[11] Donovan may well have been disguising his true ambitions in making this statement. Later, he was to deplore the inadequacy of the 1947 CIA provision, urging on the fledgling agency a subversive program which he clearly regarded as a vital if immoral necessity once the Cold War had commenced in earnest. Still, it is notable that Donovan made no attempt to win public support for the principle of covert action in the debate preceding the 1947 provision.

The competing interests and visionaries within the intelligence community produced a number of plans for peacetime centralization. One of these was for a simple extension of Donovan's OSS. The defeat of this plan in 1945 was not so final as it seemed, for the CIA was to inherit several significant ideas and people from its wartime predecessor. A second plan was the expansion of the FBI. The FBI had been active in its opposition to Nazis and Communists in Latin America before and during the war, but the super-FBI plan also went down to defeat. For a brief period, the Truman administration endorsed a third idea, the revival of State Department coordination. This experiment gave way to a final notion with the establishment of the Central Intelligence Group (CIG)—the immediate precursor of the CIA.

Public opinion about these plans, and, especially, public objections and opposition to them, helped determine the shape of the CIA. Public criticism was so strong that it suggests the CIA may have been the politicians' easiest option, an agency imprisoned by democracy, rather than one which was effective in its defense of freedom and shaped by the dictates of operational efficiency. This question clearly worried some campaigners, for they tried to reform the CIA even while it was being created in 1947, and they tried to do so without stirring up too much public discussion. On the other hand, it was the CIA's very susceptibility to democratic debate which gave it its legitimacy and helped it to be effective politically. By the same token, its later evasions of public scrutiny were to bring trouble in their wake. Early criticism of central intelligence proposals were, therefore, by no means unhelpful as the nation's leaders sought intelligence guidelines for the future.

The strength of initial opposition to the CIA may be gauged from the fact that nonsupport began at the top. Two presidents of the United States were there at the creation; neither Franklin D. Roosevelt nor Harry S. Truman declared unequivocal and unwavering support. As a powerful federal agency, the CIA may have seemed a logical extension of New Deal policies which had earlier produced a plethora of central governmental institutions. Certainly Donovan thought, or pretended to think, that Roosevelt backed his conception of a peacetime service. His November 1944 plan envisaging a new central, coordinating "authority" under presidential control which would eliminate "waste," "confusion," and "duplication" was a response to Roosevelt's own request for a proposal.[12] Yet Roosevelt reacted to the plan with caution. He welcomed the idea of "consolidation," but thought it should be restricted to military matters.[13] Just before his death on April 12, 1945, Roosevelt asked Donovan to sound out interdepartmental opinion on the proposed new central intelligence unit. Perhaps because the forceful OSS chief had offended so many departmental officials, Donovan stressed to the new president, Truman, that he had originally submitted "a plan for a Central Intelligence Agency" to Roosevelt "at his request."[14] Clearly, this glossed over the deceased president's reservations about the substance of the proposal and about its political viability.

Precisely because of Roosevelt's well-known temporizing habits, one should be on guard against the proposition that he actually opposed a central agency. What he did leave behind was uncertainty about his intentions. Francis Biddle, attorney general until his dismissal by Truman in May 1945, was one doubter. He reported to the new president on April 20, 1945: "Bill Donovan, of OSS, suggested to President Roosevelt a rather complicated over-all intelligence service in the intelligence field. I think the President was never particularly enthusiastic about it, but asked comments from the various Departments concerned."[15] No doubt FDR had communicated to Biddle his distaste for the CIA proposal; but, after all, the president knew of the attorney general's ambition to consolidate the FBI's intelligence empire, and of his consequent opposition to a new agency outside his own department. Characteristically, FDR had told an official what he wanted to hear, but not definitively, and not in writing. His wait-and-see approach left his views, if he had any, open to interpretation; though friends and foes of central intelligence alike were to maintain that he had favored a kind of CIA, the truth is that his death left the Democratic administration with an ambiguous and potentially divisive intelligence legacy.

Whereas Roosevelt temporized, Truman vacillated. Clark Clifford was one close observer of Truman's intelligence policy. Clifford had some naval experience as well as the advantage of being a St. Louis attorney in touch with the president's "Missouri associates"; his interest was such that he was to keep a critical eye on intelligence matters throughout a long and distinguished career that included a spell as Secretary of Defense in the 1960s.[16] Commenting, in his capacity as special presidential counsel, on a 1946 central intelligence agency plan, Clifford declared it had not been Truman's original intention to establish a new agency.[17] On September 20, 1945, Truman had issued an executive order disbanding the OSS as of October 1, and he demanded a rapid dismantling of the organization Donovan had built up. The president then changed his mind; after some dalliance with a neo-New Deal "alphabet soup" of interim agencies (NIA: National Intelligence Authority; CIG: Central Intelligence Group), he gave his assent to the 1947 law establishing the CIA, as well as to subsequent fortifying legislation. To the fury of the nation's intelligencers, however, this was not his final say on the matter. By the 1950s, he was criticizing the CIA. In 1963 he complained to Senator Wayne Morse that Congress had legislated against his will on the CIA and "upset the applecart."[18] Though he set up the Agency, Truman's endorsement of the institution was hardly less equivocal than that of his predecessor.

The reasons for Truman's original reluctance dictated the terms upon which he dropped his opposition and, therefore, helped shape the CIA. His objections were, in part, personal and reflective of his own personality. It is affirmed in both Truman's testimony and in accounts by others that the vice-president was shaken by Roosevelt's death, and found the burdens of presidential office intimidating in the first few months. Roosevelt had given Truman virtually no briefing on the affairs of state in anticipation of his possible death. Yet the new president was determined to succeed. If he could not transcend the provincialism of his native Missouri, the former presiding judge would make the values of his Independence courthouse the values of the nation. Determined to resist the machinations of the Capitol's power brokers, he was easily slighted by any hint that he lacked presidential capacity, deeply offended by any maneuver designed to channel or frustrate his plans. Donovan miscalculated in invoking Rooseveltian authority for his CIA plan and thus incurred a hostility that was irrational in its intensity. Truman complained in 1954 that he had had a job keeping his bureaucrats in line in 1945. He accused Donovan of being rash and "egotistical," of trying to "set up the FBI as an intelligence service" (never one of Donovan's intentions), and of bullying: "I was afraid of him, to tell the honest truth."[19] Donovan's fate was sealed, and, because his name was so closely linked with it, the proposal for a CIA closely modeled on the OSS suffered a setback.

Truman appears to have been similarly constrained in the case of FBI Director J. Edgar Hoover. Just a week after Roosevelt's death, Biddle told the new president that the "practical approach" to building a peacetime intelligence service would be to expand the facilities the FBI had built up in Latin America since the 1930s.[20] But Truman, in the words of his aide George M. Elsey, "wanted to be certain that *no single* unit or agency of the Federal Government would have so much power that we would find ourselves, perhaps inadvertently, slipping in the direction of, to use a phrase then quite common, a police state."[21] Elsey thought Truman was particularly influenced against J. Edgar Hoover by his close friend Max Lowenthal. A New York lawyer, Lowenthal had served as a staff member on the war expenditure committee Truman had chaired while still in the Senate. He was a strong critic of the FBI, on which he published a book in 1950. Admiral Souers, a senior Truman adviser as well as an intelligence expert, also thought "the President had great faith in Lowenthal," and added he "even had some aversion to" Hoover.[22] Truman ruled out Hoover, in addition to Donovan, as a potential intelligence chief, and, with him, the FBI as a possible nucleus for a central intelligence agency.

Personal feelings, then, as well as the need to establish his presidential authority, led Truman to block the ambitions of Donovan and Hoover, but policy considerations also played an important role. There was, for example, the absence of imminent danger. The Germans surrendered in May 1945 and the Japanese in August. The Red Army was exhausted. In the absence of an immediate military threat, the president could afford the luxury of blocking immediate intelligence proposals.

Another policy consideration that stayed Truman's intelligence hand was the problem of America's image abroad. His inhibition may be illustrated in the case of a particular region, Latin America. Theodore Roosevelt's 1904 Corollary to the 1823 Monroe Doctrine had asserted a U.S. right to intervene, under certain circumstances, in Western Hemispheric countries. Successive interventions proved most unpopular in the countries concerned, and, at the seventh Pan-American conference at Montevideo, Uruguay, in 1933, the United States renounced the right to intervene. When the Nazis began to intervene in South America, the Roosevelt administration countered the threat clandestinely. As Army General Lewis Hershey recalled, more than one agency operated under deep cover: "We had some people in South America that were working with the FBI. They were down there presumably selling automobiles or some damn thing. . . ."[23] Upon the defeat of the Nazis there arose the question of whether Latin American undercover operations, if continued in peacetime, might impugn the good name of the United States.

Director of the Budget Harold D. Smith, a presidential advisor on intelligence affairs, approached Truman in July 1945 about a renewal of the FBI's Latin American funds. He got approval, but noted in his diary that Truman "had some question, from the standpoint of good neighbor relations, about our having the FBI in Latin America."[24] Truman never gave up this reservation about foreign covert activities. In his 1964 criticism of the CIA, he focused his attack on its "cloak and dagger" operations and their effect on foreign opinion of the United States.[25] In 1945 his reservations formed one more reason for holding back from a major new intelligence enterprise.

Truman's concern about the possible development of an American police state was the single most important factor in causing him to block early central intelligence agency proposals. This concern ensured, too, that he would endorse only such proposals that divided, and therefore weakened, the intelligence community's police powers. The contemporary image that haunted him was that of Nazi Germany's Gestapo. In December 1945 Harold Smith told him the FBI had cost $49 million that year, compared with less than $9 million in 1939. Only loyalty to his newly appointed attorney general Tom Clark kept the president from cutting the FBI's budget drastically. To Smith, he repeatedly expressed concern about "building up a gestapo."[26] In an off-the-record press conference not long after the establishment of the interim Central Intelligence Group (January 22, 1946), Truman was pressed to explain why the attenuated CIG did not include the FBI. He replied that "we have to guard against a Gestapo. . . . You must always be careful to keep [national defense] under the control of officers who are elected by the people, then you won't have any trouble in the future."[27] The president—and, possibly, Congress—would supervise central intelligence unimpeded by any bureaucratic czar or unelected cabinet official. A powerful intelligence agency was simply not on the president's agenda in January 1946.

Truman's "gestapo" reservations would not have survived if they had sprung from personal idealism alone. If he was conscious of the importance of Latin American opinion, he was even more alert to the possible reactions of his own countrymen. He realized that the gestapo issue might fuel a popular crusade. In his *Memoirs*, he recalled an April 26, 1945, conversation with Harold Smith during which he presented the police-state aversion in terms of public opinion, not personal conviction: "I told Smith one thing was certain—this country wanted no Gestapo under any guise or for any reason."[28]

The popularization of the gestapo charge had been, and was for some time to remain, largely the work of the *Chicago Tribune* journalist, Walter Trohan. Trohan had been with the *Tribune*'s Washington bureau since 1934. The paper put him in charge of the bureau in 1947, a position he occupied until 1969. He exemplified the isolationist, conservative viewpoint of his paper's readers and proprietor, Colonel Robert R. McCormick. As late as 1970 he still believed that not only the United States but Britain as well should have stayed out of World War II. Russia and Germany, the totalitarian dictatorships, should have been allowed to slug it out alone and weaken one another, leaving Western democracy supreme. Instead, the West's policy had helped build up Russia.[29] Worse still, the New Dealers planned to introduce totalitarian phenomena at home. When Trohan received accurate, leaked information about Donovan's secret plan for a postwar central intelligence agency, he believed he had confirmation of this sinister plan.

Trohan broke the story in the *Tribune* and other McCormick papers on the morning of Friday, February 9, 1945. Headlines proclaimed "New Deal Plans Super Spy System" and "New Deal Plans to Spy on World and Home Folks; Super Gestapo Agency is Under Consideration." Elaborating in the text, Trohan noted that the new organization would be OSS-based. Stella Frankfurter would "pick key personnel at the suggestion of her brother for Donovan." Stella's brother Felix, Harvard law professor, Supreme Court justice and Roosevelt advisor, had been one of the sponsors of the New Deal's breed of Ivy Leaguish Bright Young Men—and he was anathema to the *Tribune*'s anti-elitist readers. Trohan complained that the authority of FBI Director J. Edgar Hoover—a permanent fixture in the iconography of the American Right—would be undercut. Not surprisingly, there has been a tendency to assume that Hoover was the source of the leak, though a more likely suspect is the towering New Deal bureaucrat Harry Hopkins, who thought the OSS was immoral and saw Donovan as a potential political menace.[30] It is true that Hoover, who had feuded with the OSS during the war, had cause to be pleased with Trohan's agitation, just as he had cause to be dismayed when Truman later applied the "Great Gestapo Fear" to the FBI.

Donovan was furious. The disclosure was "in the nature of a treasonable utterance" and should be investigated by "a judicial or quasi-judicial body armed with the power to subpoena and to compel testimony under oath."[31] But no such inquiry was launched, and routine investigations came up with nothing more revealing than categorical denials from the various departments that had handled the secret memoranda. The attempt to discredit Donovan's enemies failed. Donovan proved justified in his foreboding that the leak, probably a deliberate attempt to sabotage his CIA proposal, would arouse opposition in Congress. In any case, the times were not propitious for the perpetuation of big government institutions. Clare E. Hoffman, a Republican congressman from Michigan and opponent of that wartime big government manifestation, the Office of Price Administration, dubbed the Donovan proposal "another New Deal move right along the Hitler line." Democrats and Republicans in both houses of Congress denounced the central intelligence agency idea in anti-Gestapo terms.[32]

Unappeased by the death of Roosevelt, the disbandment of the OSS, or the return of Donovan to private business, McCormick journalists continued their opposition to central intelligence. Trohan disliked Truman, who reciprocated by calling him an "S.O.B."[33] In May 1945, with the new president in office, he again lashed out at the OSS as having been "scarcely more than an arm of the British Intelligence Service."[34] Two years later, in June 1947, when the CIA proposal was before Congress, Trohan's *Washington Times-Herald* colleague John O'Donnell reported that "veteran intelligence experts" foresaw a "super-duper gestapo-OSS cloak-and-dagger organization." He attacked the move toward monopoly, expansion, and centralization. Three days later Trohan wrote under the headline "U.S. Sets Up 'Gestapo'," but used an additional comparison: "Agents of the CIG have begun operations on the pattern of the Soviet secret police, the MVD, or Nazi

gestapo agents, both of whom usurped diplomatic and intelligence functions."
Trohan rolled the two totalitarianisms into what one pair of historians has labeled
the "Red fascism" image; the message was, however, clear enough. The CIA was
opposed as a menace to the rights of Americans at home and their true interests
abroad.[35]

With horrible images of World War II fresh in people's minds, the gestapo
metaphor stood out against the background of traditional U.S. antiauthoritarian
rhetoric. It encouraged president and Congress to preclude the possibility of an
intelligence monopoly. Domestic police powers were prohibited to the CIA; the
FBI had to give up its Latin American empire and concentrate on domestic work,
to the exclusion of foreign intelligence. Thus were allayed, at least for the time
being, fears of an American police state. In the long term, the separation of CIA
and FBI functions brought peace of mind but, with it, alarming stories of rivalry
and lack of cooperation between the external and internal guardians of security, as
well as fears of weakness in counterintelligence and vulnerability to deception
operations mounted by unfriendly powers. If the danger lay more in the appearance than in the reality, it was a danger nonetheless in that it sapped confidence in the intelligence community. As for the short term, the overwhelming
rejection of the plan-that-never-was, or "super-Gestapo" proposal, left an intelligence void that needed to be filled.

Since majority opinion dictated that an intelligence service would be an exclusively foreign-intelligence service, the Department of State was the logical place for
it. After all, intelligence had been successfully coordinated there in World War I
and the 1920s. When Truman disbanded the OSS, he had relocated William
Langer's research and intelligence outfit in the Department of State, which, therefore, had already been made to take one step in the desired direction. The measures
he was now about to take reflected the president's view that his precursor, Roosevelt, had deliberately but mistakenly ignored the State Department, which, Truman was convinced, should enjoy policymaking primacy.

On September 20, 1945, Truman directed Secretary of State James F. Byrnes to
"take the lead in developing a comprehensive and coordinated foreign intelligence
program for all Federal agencies."[36] Byrnes had requested a prominent role for
State in intelligence. Soon, however, he began to display impatience at being the
"undertaker" for wartime agencies (he got the Foreign Economic Administration
and Surplus Property Administration, as well).[37] He was heavily committed to
foreign travel and diplomacy, and he left what must have seemed a bothersome
administrative detail to his subordinate, Dean Acheson.

Acheson, in turn, persuaded Byrnes to entrust intelligence planning to Colonel
Alfred McCormack. McCormack was a successful lawyer who had joined the War
Department in 1942, and had been given the job, in 1945, of molding State's
research and intelligence services out of the OSS veterans it had inherited. In
response to his superiors' instruction to develop a coordinated system, McCormack immediately came up with a peacetime plan, which he proceeded to advo-

cate vigorously.[38] McCormack did not think there should be an independent central intelligence agency. Instead, he called only for the creation of a national intelligence authority under the direction of the secretary of state,[39] which would have a secretariat and provision for liaison with other intelligence groups. The plan is reminiscent of U-1. Unlike the 1920s system, however, it lacked the prestige of descent from a successful wartime setup.

The McCormack plan ran into such ferocious opposition that the president abandoned not just that particular proposal but the whole idea of State Department domination in the intelligence field. According to Acheson, some of the most damaging opposition came from within the State Department. He himself supported the notion of State's intelligence dominance, for "intelligence is information, a key to decision."[40] Nor was the undersecretary lacking in weight, for in Byrnes's absences, he was acting secretary much of the time. The problem lay with conservative chiefs of the regional divisions of State who resented the advent of a powerful group of newcomers who might interfere with what they regarded as their own, perfectly adequate, intelligence arrangements. Testifying before a Senate subcommittee in 1954, Spruille Braden openly confirmed his earlier opposition. Braden had been chief of the Latin American division of the State Department: "We . . . resisted this invasion of all these swarms of people . . . mostly collectivists and 'do-gooders' and what-nots."[41]

Braden's 1954 language reflected the McCarthyite influence then prevailing. However, it was not unrepresentative of an incipient anti-Red campaign that had helped to scupper the McCormack proposal in 1946. The charges originated in the State Department, one of whose officials claimed that the ideology of the Department's 850 OSS recruits sponsored "a socialized America in a world commonwealth of Communist and Socialist states."[42]

The Democratic chairman of the House Committee on Foreign Affairs made a similar remark about McCormack and his former intelligence group in the War Department (fifteen of whom had joined the State Department unit): they had "strong Soviet leanings."[43] The House Military Affairs Committee charged that McCormack's group contained "pro-Communists." No proof was adduced in support of these contentions at the time, though it may be significant that McCormack's group included Herbert Marcuse, the Marxist philosopher who later became an apostle of the New Left. The House Appropriations Committee cut $4 million from McCormack's budget. In his fighting letter of resignation, McCormack stated that the remains of his unit were to be spread between the geographic divisions, and that this "dismembered" intelligence system would be unworkable.[44]

Apart from internal State Department opposition and anti-Red scaremongering, a number of other considerations militated against the acceptance of the McCormack proposal. Unfortunately for McCormack and his supporters, the moment was unpropitious. Congress and the whole nation were in the hunt for budget cuts in the wake of the massive appropriations of World War II. Not until the intensification of the Cold War did Congress loosen the foreign-policy and defense purse strings and realize that a cent spent on intelligence might save a dollar elsewhere. Leadership was another factor. Acheson later wrote of "indecision in high places," a thinly veiled reference to his disappointment with Truman.[45] It is true that Truman vacillated. He had little trust for any establishment, and was inconsistent in the support he gave the State Department. The trust Truman placed in Acheson, "a prize bloom from the garden that had long produced the American elite" (Groton, Yale, Harvard Law School under Felix Frankfurter), was exceptional.[46]

In addition to all the other problems, there was the military nail in the State intelligence coffin. Rear Admiral Souers told the State Department:

> Recent experience has shown all too readily that as long as the Army and Navy may be called upon in the last analysis to support the nation's foreign policy, the Services should have a voice reaching the President as unmistakable as that of the State Department.[47]

It was hard to give up the glories and appropriations of victorious world war. Souers realized that some compensatory bureaucratic morsels could be wrung from Congress by waving the bloody flag. This close advisor of the president argued against State Department control and in favor of an increased military role in America's intelligence system. The services wished to keep their own intelligence arms intact. If there had to be a central system, they demanded a major say in it.

Several factors combined, then, to ensure that State Department control of central intelligence would not come about. Truman took up McCormack's proposal for a national intelligence authority, but his directive of January 22, 1946, gave it oversight of the Central Intelligence Group, which had been more under the influence of the military than of the State Department. The failure of the State Department to dominate intelligence, first evident on the eve of World War II, had been confirmed.

After the collapse of the McCormack-Acheson plan, the nation nudged toward a full-service CIA through a process of accretion and refinement. Among a plethora of propositions, a proposal circulated by Souers in the fall of 1945 began to make headway.[48] This was an identifiable step in the direction of the final institution. It embraced principles later enshrined in law: establishment of a CIA, which had not been envisaged in State's plan; control by the president through an NIA dominated by the military; and a catchall "broad interpretation" phrase—the proposed CIA was to "perform such other functions and duties related to intelligence as NIA may from time to time direct."[49]

The proposal had powerful backing from the Joint Chiefs of Staff, who had been considering such a move for several months, referring to it as the "JCS Plan." Truman's intelligence policy also began to make headway on account of the political skills of Admiral Souers. Like Truman and like the CIA's first director, Admiral Roscoe C. Hillenkoetter, Souers was a product of Missouri. The president is said to have liked New Deal ideas, but not some of the Ivy League New Dealers who went along with them. Commendably, Souers was a graduate not of Harvard, but of Miami University in Oxford, Ohio, not a manipulator of inherited wealth, but a self-made linen service magnate and refinance expert. He had reorganized the once-defunct Missouri State Life Insurance Company into a new, national concern. His talent for restoring the fortunes of lost causes was to be an asset. So was Souers's World War II career as a reservist with a high rank in naval intelligence. On the other hand, Souers' reservist status distanced him from the professional military hierarchy. According to the *St. Louis Post-Dispatch*, this outsider status impaired his empire-building capacity; from the perspective of a president who had advanced no further than a captaincy in spite of a valorous World War I record, it may have been an advantage.[50]

Souers emerged at President Truman's right hand. According to a leading Spanish newspaper, he was the "gray eminence" in the way that Harry Hopkins had been for Roosevelt.[51] Rubbing away at the hybrid genie of Wilsonian and Rooseveltian politics, the *Washington Post* said Souers was to Truman "a sort of Harry Hopkins and Colonel House combined."[52] Truman would not have demurred. Recommending Souers's integrity in 1954, he declared: "You can depend on this guy. He was one of my greatest assets."[53]

On January 24, 1946, just two days after establishing the interim CIG, Truman celebrated its birth with a little ceremony. He conferred upon Souers, its first director, a black hat, a black coat, and a wooden dagger, playfully referring to him as "director of centralized snooping" and as "Chief of the Gestapo," remarks which confirm that by this time, if not earlier, the president's main gestapo fear sprang from possible political reaction to a central intelligence agency, not from personal convictions.[54] Under the new arrangement, the army and navy preserved their own intelligence services intact. They also received dominant representation on the National Intelligence Authority, which supervised the CIG. The NIA was made up of the secretaries of state, war, and navy, with a presidential representative. Souers ran a small, coordinating staff of eighty. Since Truman felt that even State Department officials thought him ignorant and conspired to keep him that way, Souers tried to supply him, through the CIG, with succinct summaries of world events and trends.[55]

Under Souers, the CIG retained its modest dimensions. One reason was that the Soviet Union had not yet assumed the appearance of an exceptionally dangerous threat to national security. In October 1945, Admiral Robinson had identified America's potential enemies as Germany, France, Britain, Brazil, and Japan, as well as the Soviet Union.[56] At about the same time, Donovan assured Truman that Soviet educators were teaching the virtues of peaceful coexistence with the United States.[57] As Souers later remarked in defending Truman's apparent lack of urgency on the intelligence front, everyone had difficulty, at first, in making the transition from treating Russia as an ally to treating her as a real, potential enemy.[58]

Soon after the cozy ceremony to install Souers as America's first director of central intelligence, Russo-American relations deteriorated. On February 9, 1946, Stalin stated in a public speech that Communism and capitalism were incompatible, and that the world economy would have to be transformed on Communist principles. In the wake of this announcement, it became clear that the Soviet-backed Warsaw government was not going to allow free elections in Poland. The United States and the Soviets were also bickering over arrangements to prevent the proliferation of nuclear weapons and, ominously, they failed to reach agreement. On March 5, Winston Churchill made his famous Iron Curtain speech in Fulton, Missouri. Though he was out of office, his remarks summed up the Cold War attitudes now emerging both in the West and in the East. Against this background, intelligence expansion was assured.

On June 10, 1946, Lieutenant General Hoyt S. Vandenberg took over as CIG's director, serving until May 1947. Vandenberg's appointment did not signify that Souers had fallen from grace. Souers had been reluctant to take on the CIG directorship in the first place.[59] In 1947, he became the first executive secretary of the National Security Council (NSC), which supervised the work of the CIA, staying on in that capacity until 1950. He preferred to remain the gray eminence of U.S. intelligence, working at the president's side rather than directing the daily business of the CIG or the CIA. Vandenberg, in contrast, relished the task of building up a central intelligence organization. He expanded the CIG staff from Souers's meager eighty to just over eighteen hundred. He allocated to his staff the labor-intensive task of collection, as well as their existing evaluation duties. One-third of Vandenberg's CIG employees worked abroad. The new director ensured that some of the OSS's more gifted veterans would stay on in the intelligence community to become the luminaries of the future. One of these was James Angleton, who became the CIA's counterintelligence chief. Another was future CIA director Richard Helms.[60]

Supporters of central intelligence now mounted a campaign to give their proposal legislative status. Though the ONI and the MID were not congressional creations, the Secret Service and the FBI operated within a legal framework, and the central-intelligence campaigners of 1946–47 correctly anticipated that it would be advantageous to establish the democratic authenticity and respectability of their agency. The appointment of Vandenberg seemed propitious, for he was the nephew of the powerful senator Arthur H. Vandenberg, the Republican architect of postwar bipartisan foreign policy. The buildup of the CIG was already being protected on the congressional flank. The Vandenberg avuncular connection also augured well for the congressional legitimization of a central intelligence service, hitherto authorized by executive orders only.

Opposition, however, entered a new phase. In the White House, George M. Elsey fixed his attention on the expansionists. In April 1942 the ONI had assigned Elsey to the White House Map Room, the nerve center of presidential intelligence in World War II. He stayed on under Truman to serve the president as a naval aide and special assistant until 1951. In spite of his naval background and the fact that the CIG was the outgrowth of a Navy plan, Elsey mounted a sniping campaign against the CIG and its proposed successor, the CIA.

Clark Clifford's tactical approach was slightly different. He decided to boost the capabilities of the CIG as a preemptive measure. In July 1946, the special counsel leaked a story to Arthur Krock of the *New York Times*.[61] Krock dutifully reported that Truman was the best-briefed president ever; since Vandenberg's takeover, he had received a "correlated" daily "intelligence" summary. Donovan's mistake had been to advocate an editing role for the OSS. If only FDR had been as well informed as Truman, Krock continued, fewer concessions would have been made to the Soviet Union; if only the CIG system were to continue, America might at last emulate the British. Not surprisingly in view of his own background, Elsey objected to the publicity campaign in praise of the CIG. Its "morning summary is not an 'evaluated' job at all"; the Map Room and Department of State had served Roosevelt with briefings in no way inferior to those of CIG.[62]

In spite of such differences, the two officials evinced a similar reserve about the proposed CIA bill, and a skepticism that went beyond the bounds of normal legislative scrutiny. Just before the Krock leak, Clifford commented on the "proposed bill for the establishment of a Central Intelligence Agency" being circulated by Vandenberg. He criticized the loose use of the word *intelligence*. It seemed to include domestic activities, and it implied that the CIA would "attempt to control" the "FBI and other intelligence agencies." In January 1947 Clifford told Vandenberg that Truman would not be calling for a CIA in his State of the Union message. Both the president and his chief of staff, Admiral William D. Leahy, "felt that it was undesirable and unnecessary to bring this matter to the attention of the Congress at the present."[63]

Vandenberg kept on pushing, and the White House kept on resisting. Elsey complained to Clifford in March that the "CIG is up to its old tricks again," trying to push through a CIA bill that would give it separate statutory authority and strengthen its powers.[64] Truman, who had enough troubles in Congress without offending Vandenberg's senatorial uncle, remained reticent about his precise requirements, if he had any. In a private letter to Senator Wayne Morse in 1963, he apparently disclosed that he had had some reservations: "Congress decided to pass a law forcing me to use, in the agency, some people who were not familiar with what was wanted and who were very anxious to help those who were opposed to what I was trying to do."[65] The indictment may simply reveal that by 1963 the aging ex-president's mind was wandering, yet his unease about the 1947 law, or the 1949 law, or both, does seem probable. After the passage of the 1947 act, indeed, Elsey continued to oppose the expansionists, who had now introduced a separate, augmentary CIA bill. On one occasion he noted Clifford's comment that a proposal had been "ignominiously dropped after our scathing criticism of it."[66] To put it mildly, the CIA proposal did not enjoy unqualified support in the White House.

The creation of the CIG had been a defeat for the State Department. In the first two months of 1947, legislative consultations over the CIA provision offered an opportunity to rally opposition, within the department, to what was regarded as an attempt to militarize foreign policy. Clark Clifford and Dean Acheson instructed Charles Fahy, the department's legal adviser, to collect opinion on the fourth draft of the proposed national security law. Fahy had been general counsel to the National Labor Relations Board in the 1930s, advisor to the United Nations general assembly, and chairman of Truman's commission on racial equality in the armed forces in the later 1940s. Formerly director of the legal division of the U.S. military government in defeated Germany, he had firsthand knowledge of war crimes and gestapo methods, and he had also run afoul of another totalitarianism, as his division had held "a large number of reports of investigations of war crimes involving Soviet nationals," but the Soviet authorities had refused to cooperate in their prosecution.[67]

Fahy consulted William A. Eddy, a respected OSS veteran who was in the process of reviving McCormack's former State Department intelligence team. Eddy stated that a CIA might possibly be useful in time of war, but not in peace, when there was no justification for the idea that "political and intelligence activities" would be "completely dominated by the Armed Forces" through the CIA.[68] Spruille Braden said he shared the "alarm" already expressed by Dean Acheson. The proposal for a CIA supervised by a National Security Council (NSC) infringed "our constitutional responsibilities for the conduct of foreign affairs under the President." The NSC was "a body in which the State Department would be outnumbered five to one [seven to one, it transpired] and could develop into a branch foreign office."[69]

Fahy communicated the consensus view to the president in the name of the secretary of state, warning that the department's "collection and evaluation" powers should not be subordinated, "especially during times of peace" and stating that the proposed NSC-CIA powers "seem almost unlimited." In further comments on the eighth draft, Eddy repeated what he portrayed as strenuous departmental objections to the military's proposed domination of the intelligence evaluation process.[70] The objections were doomed as an attempt to galvanize the State Department to block the CIA proposal. A military man, General George C. Marshall, succeeded Byrnes as secretary of state in January 1947. Two factors predisposed Marshall to accept the principle of centralized intelligence on military lines. He was a long-standing advocate of military unification, and he had helped reorganize G-2 (Army intelligence) during the war. Marshall underwrote Eddy's reconstruction of State Department intelligence, but did not support his subordinates' objections to alleged military preeminence in the proposed CIA.

Further objections to military domination and leadership came, however, from the press. The *Washington Post*, which in March 1947 was "wholly in sympathy" with the CIA proposal, nevertheless issued the following warning: "Dominance by the military could easily ruin the agency's effectiveness and leave the country once again with the same warped, one-sided interpretation of intelligence that led to

Pearl Harbor." The *Post* feared that a military director of the CIA would necessarily reflect the bias of the service he came from and would have to return to: he
would counsel more tanks if he came from G-2, more planes if from A-2, more
ships if a naval man. Right into the 1950s the *Post* continued to portray CIA
directors' military provenances as a source of weakness.[71]

The hearings and floor debate that preceded congressional endorsement of the
CIA furnished yet another opportunity for counsel and criticism. Allen W. Dulles,
already a veteran of American intelligence in both World Wars, and destined to be
the CIA's longest-serving director, 1953–61, could not testify in person before the
Senate Armed Services Committee and the House Committee on Expenditures, but
he sent a memorandum on the CIA proposal to the respective chairmen, Chan
Gurney and Clare Hoffman.[72] In the interest of "economy and efficiency," Dulles
thought the CIA should absorb the evaluative functions of the Department of
State, with which good relations should nonetheless be maintained.[73] Of more
significance in April 1947 was Dulles's emphasis on the need to civilianize central
intelligence. Whereas many CIA critics deplored the CIG's military leanings from a
civil libertarian viewpoint, Dulles advanced a more functional argument:

> The prime objectives today are not solely strategic or military, important as these
> may be. They are scientific—in the field of atomic energy, guided missiles, super-
> sonic aircraft, and the like. They are political and social. We must deal with the
> problem of conflicting ideologies as democracy faces communism, not only in the
> relations between Soviet Russia and the countries of the west, but in the internal
> political conflicts within the countries of Europe, Asia, and South America. For
> example, it may well be more important to know the trend of Russian communism
> and the views of individual members of the Polit Bureau than it would be to have
> information as to the locations of particular Russian divisions.[74]

Dulles's plea for demilitarization and his implementation of that principle in
future years were to be controversial. One set of detractors saw him as a blindly
anti-Communist believer in the fifth-column menace; another, using the Bay of
Pigs debacle as a prime example, lambasted the allegedly amateurish conduct of
the CIA's paramilitary operations. Military critics and their sympathizers believed
that military operations and the intelligence behind them should be left to professional soldiers, or eschewed. In 1947, however, these criticisms had not been
anticipated. The support given to civilianization by Allen Dulles stood him in good
stead, if accidentally, in libertarian circles and contributed to the liberal image of
the CIA and its director in the 1950s.

Speakers in the floor debate on the CIA took to heart the libertarian dimension
of the antimilitary argument. Indeed, the debate rested deeply in the shadow of
New Deal and wartime centralization of power, and of the odious totalitarian
practices of Hitler's Germany. Congress modified Vandenberg's bill with the
intention of countering dictatorial tendencies and of furthering traditional demo-

cratic practices. Congressman Clarence J. Brown, a member of the Republican hierarchy who had been weaned on anti-New Deal rhetoric, led the attack on what he thought would be a further extension of unchecked federal power.[75] Cross-examining Navy Secretary and CIA advocate James Forrestal in the course of House hearings, he said no president should have "a gestapo of his own." If the FBI and the Secret Service operated "under certain restraints by law," so should the CIA.[76]

The military did not go undefended in the debate. Maryland's Democratic senator, Millard E. Tydings, wondered whether it "was a wholesome thing" that the CIA "reports directly to the President" without any direct control by the military services.[77] Styles Bridges, a Republican senator from New Hampshire who claimed the voters had rejected New Deal principles in the 1946 midterm elections, insisted that the separate services keep their own intelligence facilities.[78] On the floor of the House, Fred E. Busbey, G-2 veteran and Illinois Republican, saw no reason why the CIA should be given the same kind of overlordship as the OSS, which had, he erroneously stated, tampered with Army intelligence reports from Yugoslavia because "the men at the head of OSS did not agree with the principles of Mihailovich but were favoring the principles of Tito, the Communist dictator of Yugoslavia today."[79]

The outcome of the military-influence debate was a compromise. Clarence Brown demanded an amendment with the wording "the director shall be ap-pointed from civilian life by the President, by and with the advice and consent of the Senate."[80] The House agreed to the amendment, and the ultimate statute did provide for senatorial approval of both the director and the deputy director. The law stipulated, however, that the director or his deputy could be a military man, provided at least one of the positions was occupied by a civilian. Military men could also take comfort from their generous representation on the National Security Council which guided the CIA, on which the State Department was heavily outvoted; but the president, in principle, at least, remained in control.[81]

The dispute over the military-civilian mix in the CIA was one of the more striking ingredients in the 1947 intelligence debate. The proponents of military-dominated and civilian-dominated intelligence neutralized each other in such a way that a novel arrangement had to be devised. The CIA was similarly the indirect product of the propaganda issued on behalf of individual intelligence agencies already in existence: the FBI, ONI, MID, and State Department distrusted each other so much that their spokesmen preferred to yield central direction to a new agency, rather than lose out to an old rival. The debate over the CIA makes it plain that the Agency sprang from these factors, as well as from a desire for cost efficiency, from memories of Pearl Harbor, and from an emerging consensus on at least some of the guidelines that should govern a U.S. foreign-intelligence agency.

In explaining the birth and early character of the CIA, it is helpful to note one curious omission from the debate leading up to the law of July 26, 1947. Respond-ing to the imminent collapse of British aid to anti-Communist forces in the Greek civil war, Truman made his famous March 1947 plea to Congress to step into the breach with a $300 million appropriation. Yet in spite of the anti-Communist tenor of the Truman Doctrine, and in spite of the presence of anti-Communists in Congress, nobody mentioned the Soviet Union or its clandestine services in the congressional debate on the CIA provision of the National Security Act. Congressmen were introspectively concerned with gestapo-like tendencies at home, rather than with the external Soviet challenge to which Truman was already responding. So the initial CIA did not have as one of its explicit guidelines the organization and sponsorship of programs to frustrate Soviet ambitions.

Section 102 of the 1947 National Security Act, which contained the CIA provision, set forth a number of explicit, democratically approved guidelines for U.S. foreign intelligence. About half of the relatively brief section dealt with the military-civilian balance. The section went on to stipulate that the CIA should coordinate the intelligence effort, should correlate and evaluate intelligence but without diminishing the right of other government agencies to do the same thing, should have access to the product of those other agencies including FBI information, should eschew police and internal security functions, should report to the president through the National Security Council (which replaced the National Intelligence Authority), and should "perform such other functions and duties related to intelligence affecting the national security as the National Security Council may from time to time direct."

The act reflected the consensus on U.S. intelligence that had begun to emerge prior to 1945, and which took coherent form during the debate of 1945–47. In retrospect, the 1947 legislative guidelines can be seen to have contained both strengths and weaknesses. Over the years, the mix of military and civilian elements proved to have been judicious; the Agency could and did, at times, act as a brake on plans for military expansion based on self-serving military estimates of Soviet strength and intentions. The restriction of the CIA to foreign work was wise, not so much from the operational viewpoint, but because it made the CIA more acceptable to the American voter and preserved the appearance as well as the reality of freedom in the world's model democracy. On the other hand, the concession of autonomy to other foreign-intelligence organizations created a management problem and led to proliferation, duplication, and confusion, especially as successive CIA directors failed to exert sufficient control to be able to coordinate properly the U.S. intelligence effort. Additionally, the open-ended commitment to "other functions" indicated that the job of setting the CIA's agenda was still unfinished in July 1947. Central-intelligence boosters had begun to plan more expansive guidelines well before the National Security bill became law, and events soon played into their hands.

3

THE MISTS OF BOGOTA
Expansion and Obfuscation

Expansion and obfuscation characterized the infant CIA's history between 1947 and 1950. In the course of deliberations on the central-intelligence section of the 1947 National Security Act, the CIG's legislative liaison officer Walter L. Pforzheimer withdrew a clause authorizing "covert and unvouchered funds" because it would "open up a can of worms," but he noted "we could come up with the house-keeping provisions later on."[1] In 1949 a further act of Congress achieved that purpose. Additionally, the National Security Council issued a stream of secret, enabling directives. The Agency's budget, personnel, facilities, and functions therefore expanded sharply.

Few people knew the precise extent and nature of the expansion. The deliberations of the National Security Council were more than a closely guarded secret: Congress did not extensively debate the 1949 act, and its members were not keen to delve into the doings of the mushrooming national security bureaucracy, for they voted against a modest proposal for an intelligence watchdog committee. Only among the cognoscenti did an increasingly sophisticated, if deliberately secretive, discussion occur. Officials and experts concluded that the avoidance of Pearl Harbor-type surprise attacks was not enough; they developed a theoretical framework for intelligence; they introduced the notion of "national intelligence estimates"; they debated the place of intelligence in overall U.S. strategy.

With the constraints of public opinion a mere secondary consideration for the time being, the question of which guidelines were proper for a democracy's intelligence agency became less urgent. Even the innately cautious Truman and

Souers sanctioned operations of a type that they might have condemned before the spring of 1947. In due course, greater freedom of scope led to excess and disgrace, yet it also encouraged innovation. The CIA's intelligence work steadily improved, because even though secrecy may have invited criticism in an open society it also enhanced the CIA's imperviousness to foreign penetration and deception and, therefore, strengthened the quality and integrity of its analyses.

The causes of the CIA's secretive expansion are also of some interest. The Cold War lay at its root: while the Soviets argued that the CIA instigated the Cold War (and there may be a particle of truth in this), the expansion of CIA activities was more a symptom than the cause of the deterioration in Russo-American relations. The resurgence of Soviet military might posed an intelligence challenge to a nation that wished to deploy its resources intelligently, as did Soviet support to foreign Communist parties and insurgent groups. Soviet espionage thus created a need for counterintelligence and both invited and justified American offensive espionage in return. The Agency's growth, then, was a specific response to the Kremlin's plans for expansion, some of them figments of Western imagination, others real enough.

Important though the Cold War was, however, there were other causes of the CIA's expansion, among them a need to control the clandestine operations of certain private anti-Communist groups. In other cases, private groups appealed to the CIA for support. To accommodate these needs, the Agency incorporated the organizations concerned or used money to control them indirectly. The significance of this cause of expansion is that the Agency appears to have been affected by the buccaneering spirit of some of those whom it swallowed up in the name of greater responsibility. Just as ironic was a further cause of augmentation, failure: Pearl Harbor had spurred intelligence growth during and after the war. Similarly, allegations of failure in Bogota, Colombia, in 1948, led not to a punitive contraction of the intelligence community, but to renewed expansion.

It is, of course, obvious why CIA officials and their supporters aimed at secrecy: they had to conceal their goals, methods, and sources from the intelligence services of the Soviet Union and other potential enemies. Although administration officials appreciated this, they also had other motives, such as the concealment of incompetence or shielding the true nature of American intelligence operations from public scrutiny. Truman did not trust Congress on the intelligence question. He may well have been correct in his suspicion that there would be rebellion over issues like covert operations and CIA infiltration of private organizations. He saw no reason why he should reveal secrets that would gratuitously stir up even a minority opposition.

The early development of the CIA owed much to the successes of one man and the imputed failures of another. Even before the passage of the 1947 National Security Act, Allen W. Dulles effectively argued the case for further legislation that would legitimize activities while allowing for flexibility and secrecy. In closed testimony to the House Expenditure Committee, he urged the recruitment of

"American businessmen and American professors and Americans of all types and descriptions who travel around the world," and he also urged Congress, "not in too much detail, however," to "define the nature and functions of the Central Intelligence Agency."[2] To some extent, he was preaching to an already receptive audience. Senator Millard Tydings had earlier complained of "a void in the bill" where the CIA's functions were concerned and had welcomed CIG director Vandenberg's assurance that "the enabling act is prepared."[3] Yet Dulles was still surprised by the warmth of his reception. On his return to New York he told David Bruce (former OSS secret intelligence chief and future ambassador to Britain) that he "couldn't have had a better reception or a more intelligent line of questions . . . Frankly, it was most encouraging."[4]

The future CIA director made a favorable impression partly because of the prevailing mood in Congress and partly because of a widening appreciation of the need for secret intelligence. But most of all, he succeeded because he was by nature a publicist. As a child, Dulles had had to have a corrective operation on his club foot. Unlike the protagonist of Somerset Maugham's *Of Human Bondage* and unlike the British novelist himself, who with Dulles had been a secret agent in Switzerland in World War I, Dulles shook off the effects of the impediment to become a socially robust adult and a man of considerable charm. Perhaps reacting against his family's early attempts to conceal his infirmity, he developed a gift for persuasion and publicity. Even as a six-year-old, he had written and published a treatise on the Boer War, demonstrating an anti-imperialist sympathy that was all the more remarkable for being in defiance of his family's beliefs. As OSS station chief in Switzerland in World War II he put a plaque on his door indicating who he was. With inspired timing he published in 1947 a work called *Germany's Underground*, drawing upon the knowledge he had built up while conspiring with Hitler's internal enemies. He did not need to spell out the allegorical message: if democratic elements could oppose one imperialist dictatorship, they could, with similar clandestine outside help, oppose another. Teeming with interesting stories, the book was an early indication of how Dulles would hold audiences spellbound in the future, both in arguing for a stronger CIA and during his long spell as its director.[5]

Like Dulles's successes, the alleged shortcomings and failures of Roscoe H. Hillenkoetter contributed to the CIA's secretive expansion. "Hilly" succeeded Vandenberg as director of central intelligence in May 1947, presiding over the last months of the CIG and remaining at the CIA's helm until October 1950. As the U.S. naval attaché in France, Hillenkoetter had briefed Donovan on German "fifth-column" tactics during the emissary's 1940 visit to Europe to assess Britain's ability to survive. He thus knew something of intelligence, but differed from Donovan himself—whom Truman still rejected as too abrasive—in being more cautious about undertaking covert missions.[6]

Hillenkoetter's caution was one of the factors that led to his denigration by contemporaries in the 1940s and by historians later. At the same time, his alleged demerits and the presumed failings of the CIA under his leadership complemented, in a strange way, the Dulles campaign, for they confirmed the need for more and more resources to be poured into intelligence. His unfortunate reputation was therefore a self-correcting feature. His character and record may also be more directly redeemed in spite of the judgments pronounced upon them, many of which have been arbitrary. To one historian, Hilly remained "a sea captain in mind and heart"; to another, he was "an amiable and innocuous naval career man."[7] According to his contemporary and subsequent detractors, he lacked the rank to command respect and cooperation from senior Washington officials and the military chiefs (his promotion to rear admiral came only just before his CIA appointment). He was chiefly concerned, the indictment continues, with the naval career to which he readily returned in 1950; he lacked the dynamism to forge a proper intelligence organization.[8] The question at issue is whether these judgments exaggerate the distinction between the first director and his successors, underestimate the difficulties facing a pioneer, and treat too lightly some of the CIA's early achievements.

Those who accused Hilly of being undercommitted to his job were in some cases influenced by their belief that the director of central intelligence should be a civilian.[9] Contemporaries too casually assumed, also, that Hilly's tenure would be a short one like that of his predecessors (Souers: six months; Vandenberg: nine months). In fact, Hilly stuck to his job for three years, five months, and seven days. Of the thirteen men who served as director of central intelligence during the post's first forty years, only four served for a longer period.

Hilly was accused of recruiting dross. Those whom he hired were, according to a senior contemporary covert-action specialist, "a bunch of old washerwomen exchanging gossip while they rinse through the dirty linen."[10] Needing to hire a lot of people quickly, the director used the *lateral transfer* device of recruiting from other departments, including the military, some of whose intelligence specialists would otherwise have left government service because of demobilization. To the critics, this was the "dead wood" of the future. One might respond that Hilly had to get his men from somewhere—that future directors were not faced with the same pioneering task. Furthermore, the critics sometimes had an axe to grind, believing for example that more OSS veterans should have been hired.[11] But when OSS veterans did return to the intelligence service, they, too, were variously attacked for being rash adventurers, elitist, and ill-educated. Criticism of Hilly's recruitment performance must have been well founded up to a point, but its main significance is that it further concentrated people's minds on the need for intelligence reform.

The most serious criticism that Hilly had to endure centered on the CIA's intelligence performance. Under his direction or misdirection, the Agency is supposed to have rendered substandard evaluative reports to the president. Vandenberg had established an office of research estimates to prepare these reports, and to the end of Hilly's tenure ORE continued to prepare monthly reviews of the world situation. One problem, here, was that the CIA had no authority to oblige other branches of the intelligence community to cooperate in producing a coordinated, or "national" estimating process. The Agency also lacked the capability to conduct independent investigations to check the accuracy and objectivity of reports it received from other agencies, which may well have contributed to a lack of incisiveness. According to the ORE's critics, its reports were shortsighted instead of helpfully predictive, factual rather than analytical, a source of paperwork for the president rather than a shortcut to the essential truth.[12] Public allegations of intelligence failure in specific crises further undermined Hilly's reputation. Such allegations may be taken seriously up to a point: the CIA's performance in the 1940s is unspectacular when one considers that the Soviet Union's subversion and deception techniques were then in their relative infancy. Yet, three mitigating factors must be borne in mind: long-term predictions never did become a CIA forte and were probably beyond the capability of any intelligence agency; "paper mountains" were to be an increasing problem in future years and were by no means a distinctive feature of Hilly's overlordship; unenlightened White House attitudes were often a product of presidents' impatience with complex and politically unrewarding foreign-policy issues, not just a consequence of CIA incompetence.

Here again, the principal importance of this criticism after 1947 is that it contributed to a myth that generated action: allegations of intelligence incompetence were sufficiently forceful to spur growth as well as the development of greater secrecy than the dictates of national security required. Indeed, the fact that these allegations inspired growth rather than the CIA's termination suggests that some of the critics may have been concealing an underlying faith in the Agency's efficacy.

From the Agency's inception, critical attention focused on the competence or otherwise of its appraisal of the threat that the Soviet Union posed directly and through surrogates. George F. Kennan, the expert on Russia who was chief of the State Department's policy planning staff, had dramatized that threat in his pseudonymous article on "The Sources of Soviet Conduct" in the July 1947 issue of *Foreign Affairs*. Among the minority of analysts who disagreed, arguing that the United States exaggerated the Soviet threat, there were those who tended to blame the CIA. The Agency's own Soviet expert Harry Rositzke remarked on the inadequacy of early espionage against the Soviet Union. Not until 1949, Rositzke wrote, did the CIA start dropping its own secret agents into Russia. "It was our almost total ignorance of what was going on in the 'denied area' behind the Iron Curtain," he maintained, "that helped create the false image of a super-powerful Soviet Union."[13] Yet Rositzke and others who could perceive the shortcomings of the early CIA could also discern grounds for hope, and they went on to enjoy long careers with the Agency.

The known record suggests that, from the very first month of its existence, Hillenkoetter's CIA did contribute to America's understanding of her most powerful potential foe. In August 1947, Hilly, still writing on CIG stationery, circulated a special evaluation based on a document that had been stolen from a Russian intelligence official in "one of the Soviet Satellite Countries" and microfilmed before being returned to his safe.[14] The document envisaged a split in the Politburo between Molotov and Vishinsky on the one side, and Mikoyan and Voznessensky on the other. Minister of Foreign Affairs Vyacheslav Mikhaylovich Molotov was a proponent of Cold War intransigence. Backed by the security agency MVD, he believed that U.S. capitalism would collapse and that, in anticipation of that gratifying event, the Soviet Union should continue her unyielding policy, whatever the cost to herself.[15]

Minister of Foreign Trade Anastas Ivanovich Mikoyan saw things differently. He stressed the damage already done to the Soviet economy by World War II. He warned against self-inflicted wounds and the fortress mentality, arguing that Russia's European satellites, having been an advantage initially, were now a burden.[16] Hillenkoetter's special analyst complained that he had no means of verifying the accuracy of the report—a clear reference to the CIA's desire to build up its independent collection capability. He thought, however, that the document was not a plant and that it was plausible.[17] Hilly's endorsement of the document's interpretation suggests the early CIA did not take the simplistic view that the Kremlin's attitudes were monolithic or that its intentions could be taken for granted.

The Agency's analysts were also capable of putting the Soviet threat into perspective. In September 1947, the CIA circulated the first of its monthly reviews of the "world situation as it relates to the security of the United States." The historian Walter Laqueur has remarked that this laid out guidelines that long remained in force and that it was a "fairly realistic estimate." The review stated that only the Soviet Union, among foreign powers, was in a position to threaten the security of the United States, but the Soviets were "presently incapable of military aggression outside of Europe and Asia," even if they were "deliberately conducting political, economic, and psychological warfare against the United States."[18] Although there was a hint, here, that the Soviet Union would resort to clandestine methods on a global scale, it would be too harsh to conclude the CIA did nothing to counter the image of a "superpowerful" foe.

Hilly's CIA has been conversely accused of complacency, of predictive failure relating to the Soviet threat to U.S. national security. The most famous case is its failure to pinpoint the date of the anticipated Soviet detonation of an atomic bomb.[19] An earlier CIG estimate had put the likely date of the first A-bomb test at 1950. In December 1947 the CIA predicted the Russians would be unable to test the device until 1951. In fact, they did so successfully in September 1949.[20] This was a predictive failure, yet the CIA was wide of the mark by sixteen months, an appreciable but surely not disgraceful margin of error. Even though the Agency at times downplayed the direct Soviet military threat, it was neither complacent nor disastrously incompetent in its assessment of it.

The Agency was furthermore alert to and thoughtful about problems elsewhere, recognizing that the Kremlin was not the source of every challenge to U.S. security and interests. In April 1948 one of its reports correctly predicted "increasing political instability and nationalism" in the Philippines.[21] In June, the CIA reported on the activities of wealthy American businessmen who were illegally or extralegally shipping arms to Europe, the Middle East, and Central and South America to the possible detriment of U.S. interests and lives. In December, the Agency circulated dispatches regarding the activities of Nicaragua's Anastasio Somoza, who had temporarily given up the presidency of his country only to orchestrate an invasion of neighboring Costa Rica.[22] In the same month, an Agency memorandum recommended support for the center-left Labor Party (MAPAI) in Israel's first election: "Power in the hands of the extreme right would result in intensified nationalistic demands for territorial and economic expansion. Power in the hands of the extreme left would lead to closer ties with the USSR. Either development would prejudice the strategic interests of the U.S. in the Near East."[23] In assessing the intelligence performance of the early CIA, it would be wrong to concentrate exclusively on alleged predictive oversights and to ignore the Agency's alert and, sometimes, intelligent watch on developments in a wide variety of foreign nations.

The point is vividly illustrated in a further, December 1948 memorandum. Issued by Hillenkoetter, the memorandum confirmed the imminence of Chiang Kai-shek's downfall—Chiang did in fact resign from China's presidency in January 1949. More strikingly, the CIA memorandum referred to the likelihood that the victorious Mao Tse-tung would "turn his forces against the Moscow-dominated Chinese Communists."[24] In retrospect, that prediction may not seem surprising. In a footnote to his 1937 best-seller *Red Star Over China*, American journalist Edgar Snow had noted Mao's intention, once victorious, to regain control of Russian-dominated Outer Mongolia.[25] The formal friendship pact between the Soviets and Chiang in 1945 is a further indication of potential friction between the Communisms of Stalin and of Mao. Yet, the CIA's December 1948 prediction is striking in three respects. First, it was premature: in the winter of 1949–50 Mao had to visit the Soviet Union, cap in hand, to request economic aid. Second, however, it did anticipate the long-term trend in Sino-Soviet relations. Third, it flew in the face of the emergent conspiracy theory that would portray Mao's government as "a tool of Russian imperialism in China" and present worldwide Communism as an indivisible menace.[26] Thus the early CIA's analysts cannot be held accountable for later policies—such as clandestine raids against mainland China—which forced the Communists together rather than splitting them apart.

Whatever the actual record, the campaign to improve the CIA's clandestine capabilities sprang in part from its perceived espionage shortcomings. At the same time, the campaign reflected a desire to enter the secret propaganda field, a desire which fitted in with overall U.S. strategy. In the summer of 1947, Congress approved the European recovery program. Known as the Marshall Plan, it provided for billions of U.S. dollars to be pumped into the Western European economies. Some supported the plan for generous humanitarian reasons, others because they thought that by making Europe self-reliant America would be able to retreat into its former isolationism. Still others perceived in an enriched Europe a potential market for U.S. exports. None of these various reasons affected the CIA directly. What did affect the Agency was the one point on which most of the plan's supporters agreed: by making Western European countries more prosperous and attractive than their Soviet bloc neighbors, the plan would undermine the appeal of Communist parties in forthcoming elections.

Some of the CIA's more powerful boosters believed the Agency should have a vital supplementary role in stopping the spread of Communism. In August 1947, Wild Bill Donovan had a conversation with newly appointed defense secretary James Forrestal on the steps of Columbia University's library. Though immersed, by now, in private practice on Wall Street, the former OSS chief had kept abreast of foreign events and pressed his views on "the effectiveness of clandestine assistance to the French in their resistance to communism." Donovan outlined to Forrestal the nature of the Communist threat in France, basing his remarks on his own observations during a recent visit. The French Communists, he said, were buying up copies of literature that might embarrass them, purchasing printing presses, "and carrying on all these activities which characterize a psychological warfare operation." Though a lone secretary in the Paris embassy was doing his best, the United States had no effective official counter to this activity.[27]

Money was the prescription Donovan urged. Better news service should also be provided in France, and Russian tactics explained to the American people in a series of articles. The American Federation of Labor was already assisting the anti-Communist component of the French labor movement. According to Donovan, the knowledge that this assistance came from an American source boosted the morale of the anti-Communist French workers. On the other hand, such assistance was neither enough nor appropriate in its provenance. There was an imminent possibility that American and French private money would be pumped into the anti-Communist campaign. "But," Donovan wrote Forrestal, "I am sure you would think it unwise to let this pass beyond your control."[28]

Donovan was lobbying the right man. Forrestal pushed hard for the adoption of the former OSS chief's plan. He discussed it with Admiral Leahy, Truman's chief of staff and intelligence adviser. Leahy was receptive to the French question and knowledgeable about it; as America's ambassador to Vichy France he had witnessed the clandestine techniques of the Vichy government and taken a hand in the OSS's Torch operation in North Africa.[29] Forrestal commended Donovan and his plan to other officials, too. Donovan placed great faith in the defense secretary, telling him that "there is no one who can take the lead in this but you."[30] In common with a number of conservative-minded critics, he regarded his fellow Wall Street alumnus as one of the few patriots in the Truman administration.[31]

Forrestal shared this view of himself, working so hard in pursuit of Cold War objectives that by early 1948 he was showing the signs of strain that led to his ultimate breakdown and suicide in the following year. It was a dedicated man indeed who in October 1947 preached at Donovan the very sermon that Donovan had just scripted for him: the French operation would "require plenty of brains, persistent follow-up, and above all, money."[32]

The CIA did step in with secret propaganda funds, and—possibly for this reason among others—the French Communists failed at the polls. It should be noted that rumors eventually spread about other types of CIA activity. The Agency allegedly had links with the Corsican gangster syndicates in Marseilles. It reportedly armed these gangsters, who had previously worked against local Communists for the French fascists and, during the war, for the Nazis. Several strikers were murdered in Marseilles before the collapse of the Communist-led general strike on December 9, 1947.[33] If the CIA was indeed involved, it was a foretaste of things to come—but in 1947 the main emphasis was on covert propaganda, not covert action of a more drastic type.

In October 1947, just as Donovan and Forrestal were conferring, an event occurred that added urgency to American deliberations. At a conference in Warsaw, Communist leaders from the Soviet Union, France, Italy, Bulgaria, Czechoslovakia, Hungary, Poland, Romania, and Yugoslavia met to establish Cominform, a collective propaganda agency. Although it was to prove a failure in the long run and was dissolved in 1956, in the fall of 1947 it seemed a challenge worthy of response. The State Department already had an office of international information. The budget of this agency for open propaganda soon increased from $24 million (1948) to $120 million (1951).[34] In the meantime, U.S. officials decided to resort, in addition, to psychological warfare.

The term *psychological warfare* had taken hold in military circles in World War II, when General Eisenhower had established and used a psychological warfare board.[35] It referred to covert operations that boosted the morale of friends or undermined the morale of enemies. In the context of European politics in the late 1940s it meant, for example, the issuance of unattributed publications, false attribution, forgery, and the secret subsidization of publications. As these activities were intended to help achieve diplomatic objectives, Forrestal wanted the State Department to be in charge. Secretary of State Marshall refused. He feared that American diplomacy would lose credibility if a covert operation came unstuck and could be traced to his department. But, in December 1947, the situation was resolved. National Security Council directive number 4/A put the CIA in charge of covert "psychological" operations, with the State Department supplying policy guidance.[36]

While these decisions were being taken, the CIA was already in action in Italy. George Kennan later explained that the Communist problem in Italy had been one of the main reasons for giving the CIA its covert-operational capability in 1947–48:

We were alarmed at the inroads of the Russian influence in Western Europe beyond the point where the Russian troops had reached. And we were alarmed particularly over the situation in France and Italy. We felt that the Communists were using the very extensive funds that they then had in hand to gain control of key elements of life in France and Italy, particularly the publishing companies, the press, the labor unions, student organizations, women's organizations, and all sort of organizations of that sort, to gain control of them and use them as front organizations.[37]

The CIA's Italian venture was a democracy-propping operation, for the Italians were looking forward to elections in the spring of 1948. In fact, about one-third of the CIA's interventions in the future were to take place in "pro-Western" democracies; President Ford eventually claimed that the CIA's prime covert-operational duty was to shore up well-established democracies.[38]

The selection of Italy for special attention, however, was by no means a matter of democratic principle alone. The country was strategically important. The National Security Council noted that the peninsula flanked the Balkans and dominated the Mediterranean. It was a potential base for eastward air strikes, and it could be used to guarantee—or, in the wrong hands, impair—oil supplies from the Near East. In February 1948, the National Security Council declared it to be essential to the U.S. national security that Italy be preserved from external attack and from subversion by "Soviet dominated communist movements within Italy."[39] When Italy became a member of the North Atlantic Treaty Organization, the need to protect NATO secrets made it essential to keep Communists out of the Italian cabinet. Thus the CIA remained committed to its Italian operations for strategic as well as ideological reasons.

The Italian intervention is of further interest for the way in which it was conducted. In their study *Gli americani in Italia* (1976), the journalists Roberto Faenza and Marco Fini pointed out that there were strong World War II precedents for U.S. covert operations in Italy. These included Counter Intelligence Corps activities, which continued until 1947, and the famous recruitment of the Mafia via Italian-American links to ease the path of invading U.S. armed forces. They also included dealings between Donovan and the antifascist philosopher and historian, Benedetto Croce.[40]

Though the Mafia link was to recur at a later stage in the CIA's history, it was the political link that proved important in the 1940s. The Liberal Party had won a respectable fourth place in the preindependence election of 1946, and Croce remained at its head until December 1947. After that, its fortunes plunged, but by this time the CIA had widened its political base, largely at Forrestal's instigation. In January 1948, Forrestal urged Hillenkoetter to intensify covert action. The CIA director was reluctant because of his nervousness about the repercussions of possible exposure, and because he and the Agency's legal counsel doubted that the National Security Act gave the CIA the authority to launch operations without the advice and consent of the Senate. But with Truman's tacit support, Forrestal and Marshall overruled him.[41]

On December 22, 1947, Hilly had already set up a special procedures group to direct such covert operations as might be authorized. He placed James Jesus Angleton in charge in Italy. Angleton's personality was in some ways better suited to counterintelligence, the job that ultimately made him legendary. Tall, thin, and forbidding, he has variously been described as a cold fish, a snob, an Anglophile, an introvert, and as man of paranoid suspicions. Yet he knew Italy, his father having been an Italian-based businessman. Indeed, as editor of the Yale literary magazine *Furioso*, Angleton had published poems by one of Italy's most fervent American admirers, Ezra Pound. During the war, Pound broadcast profascist propaganda from Rome. It is doubtful that Angleton shared Pound's antisemitism, but he did share his conservatism. Angleton may not have been an inspirational character but he was knowledgeable, an instinctive anti-Communist, and a dedicated worker of the type who would sleep in his office rather than waste time commuting. By early 1948, he was using ample funds to subsidize the center-right in Italian politics, and to manipulate opinion through forgeries and other devices. He received help both from non-Communist Italians and from Americans like the ex-Communist Jay Lovestone, disburser of the AFL's foreign assistance in Italy and elsewhere.[42]

Because the Communists did not win in Italy in 1948, the CIA operation in that country was chalked up as a success. There may, of course, have been other reasons for the election result. Perhaps a majority of Italians were anti-Communist to begin with. Additionally, overt U.S. propaganda made it clear whom the Americans wanted to lose, and this may have had a greater psychological effect than covert financing, especially as open propaganda was linked with the dangling carrot of Marshall Plan aid. Secret donations could not boost morale in quite the same way as overt support, since their provenance was, by definition, unknown to all but a few initiates. Nonetheless, CIA officers began to believe they could work wonders through secret financial manipulation. William Colby recalled that he had arrived in Italy in 1953 with "an unparalleled opportunity to demonstrate that secret aid could help our friends and frustrate our foes without the use of force or violence." Miles Copeland raised the expectation to the level of a simple generalization: "In an election in such-and-such a country the KGB backs a candidate, the CIA backs a candidate, and the CIA candidate wins."[43]

The prospect of success in Italy did little to allay the fears of those who believed the Soviet-dominated Communists were on the move in the early months of 1948. In March, air force intelligence (A-2) predicted an immediate Red Army attack on Scandinavia. The CIA scotched the falsely-based rumor, but the war scare was still unnerving.[44] Events in Czechoslovakia were equally unsettling. In February and March the Russian-backed Communists in that country executed a coup that ended democracy in one more nation. Allen's brother John Foster Dulles, foreign-policy advisor to Republican presidential aspirant Thomas E. Dewey, now proposed a "counter-cominform" that would combat European Communism on both sides of the Iron Curtain, utilizing "underground movements" in the East. On April 9, the *Washington Post* revealed the existence of the plan.[45]

On that same day, events took a serious turn in America's own hemisphere. The Colombian capital Bogota was hosting the Ninth International Conference of American states. The leading item on the conference agenda was the drafting of a charter for the proposed Organization of American States (OAS). At the same time, the U.S. and Latin American delegations entertained additional ambitions of a contrasting nature. Many of the Latin American delegates hoped the eponymous head of the U.S. mission would announce a Marshall Plan for the Western Hemisphere. But Marshall aimed instead to strengthen the U.S. policy of "containment"—stopping the spread of Soviet-backed Communism. It was a shock to both parties when, on April 9, a street assassin felled Liberal Party opposition leader Jorge Eliécar Gaitán. His death triggered widespread rioting and destruction, with twelve hundred deaths in Bogota and extensive damage to the Capitalio, the seat of the conference. In addition to unnerving the Pan American delegates, the upheaval sparked a serious controversy in the United States.

Contemporary explanations of the rioting varied. A senior Scripps-Howard journalist thought that the "amazing precision of timing" indicated a first-time intrusion into Latin America of European-style Communist techniques.[46] Marshall blamed Communists and the Soviet Union directly.[47] According to veteran Latin American reporter Duncan Aikman, the problem was that Colombia had been "bedeviled more than any other land in South America by fanatical rightist politics," a circumstance that enabled the Communists to make the "hay burn" after the fire had started.[48]

Back in the United States, people immediately demanded to know why the CIA had not warned the American delegation of the impending riot, in time for precautions to be taken. After all, declared Clarence J. Brown, who had been troubled by the creation of the CIA and was now chairman of the House committee set up to investigate the Bogota incident, the Agency had been "created for the exact purpose of keeping top American officials advised as to activities in foreign countries which might in any way affect or endanger the welfare of this nation."[49] Dewey spoke on the radio of "a shameful example of unbelievable incompetence . . . We apparently had no idea what was going on in a country just 2 hours flying time from the Panama Canal."[50]

The truth is that there was no CIA intelligence failure at Bogota. Hilly pointed out in testimony to the Brown committee that he had warned on January 2 and again on March 23 about plans to harass the U.S. delegates. The *Washington Post* noted that he had even gone public, "in order to establish his point." In an effort to find a substitute scapegoat, Hillenkoetter claimed that O. J. Libert, the State Department's advance delegate in Bogota, had blocked his warnings in the belief that the local police could maintain order and not wishing to cause unnecessary alarm to U.S. delegates. The State Department, Hilly told Brown, had a veto power over CIA operatives who might wish to make facts known to other government officials locally, or to higher officials in Washington via the director of central intelligence.[51] Perhaps Hilly was unaware that Ambassador Willard C. Beaulac had, quite independently of the CIA, warned Marshall on March 22 that "Communists and left wing Liberals" might try to disrupt the conference.[52]

Bogota was demoralizing for Hilly and his colleagues not because they had failed, but because they could be portrayed as having failed. Given the nature of the democratic process and the proximity of a presidential election, Dewey naturally exploited the event. For the same reason, Marshall could not be expected to admit he had been duly warned but had taken no precautions. Hilly knew his agency was young and vulnerable, and that powerful rivals, like FBI director J. Edgar Hoover, lay in the wings. The FBI had after all lost its Latin American empire upon the CIA's creation: the *Washington News* ominously juxtaposed remarks about the recall of five hundred FBI agents in 1947 with others about the CIA's shortcomings in 1948.[53] Through no fault of their own, Hilly and his colleagues were in trouble.

Perhaps because he was politically vulnerable, Hilly agreed to a proposal for a permanent congressional watchdog committee. The Atomic Energy Act of 1946 had established a precedent whereby Congress could discreetly supervise a top-secret government agency: to monitor the Atomic Energy Commission, it had established the Joint Committee on Atomic Energy, composed of nine members from the Senate and nine from the House, with not more than five from the same political party in each instance. In the aftermath of Bogota Edward J. Devitt of Minnesota, a former intelligence officer who had won a purple heart in World War II, made a thirty-minute speech in the House proposing a similar eighteen-member joint committee for the CIA. White House zeal for obfuscation and a lack of congressional enthusiasm ensured the defeat of Devitt's proposal in spite of Hilly's support. Thus the CIA was deprived of a committee that might well have been a source of useful, responsible criticism, on the one hand, and a shield against opportunist or irresponsible charges, on the other.[54]

Bogota may not have produced closer congressional supervision, but it did have other consequences. Wilmoore Kendall, who served in the intelligence unit of the State Department and in the CIA in 1946 and 1947, respectively, noted one effect of Bogota on the Agency and on expectations surrounding it. In an essay which came to be regarded as a classic in U.S. intelligence theory, he warned of a "compulsive preoccupation with *prediction*, with the elimination of 'surprises' from foreign affairs." According to Kendall, "the shadow of Pearl Harbor is projected into the mists of Bogota, and intelligence looks shamefaced over its failure to tell Secretary Marshall the day and hour at which a revolution will break out in Colombia."[55] The CIA's nervousness is not surprising in the light of events that unfolded in the aftermath of Bogota. The Communists' blockade of West Berlin—imposed on the opening day of the Republican Party convention—provoked inevitable charges about nonprediction.[56] Then, in August 1948, there broke the sensational allegation that Alger Hiss, formerly a Roosevelt aide, had been a Soviet agent. This theory, fanned by protracted trials, by Hiss's conviction, and by subsequent revelations about Soviet espionage, strongly suggested that America should be more vigilant to and suspicious of Communist machinations. Thus Kendall's plea for a more thoughtful approach to intelligence did not in the short run dissuade the Agency from concentrating on predictions of a type designed to protect politicians from embarrassment. Because of this preoccupation, Hilly's colleagues soon acquired the reputation of "crying wolf."

The Bogota riots also had a marked effect on the CIA's covert operations. For one thing, the charter of the OAS—agreed on in April as the riots raged—undermined the principle of nonintervention endorsed by President Roosevelt in 1933. To be sure, some clauses in the charter forbade foreign intervention in the affairs of any American nation. But the conference as a whole had yielded to U.S. pressures for greater security, rather than to demands for a Marshall plan. Articles 24 and 25 of the charter affirmed the right of American nations to intervene in the affairs of a particular American nation which was under threat. Translated into plainer language, this loophole meant that the United States could intervene to stop a Latin American nation from going Communist. The charter's ambiguity, however, suggested it would still not be prudent to intervene openly: clandestine methods would be more diplomatic.[57]

The logic of Bogota seemed to be that the CIA's covert capabilities should be strengthened. Since there had been no predictive failure, as the cognoscenti must have known, this made more sense than reforming the intelligence structure. There would be no major problem politically, as the Dulles brothers had already persuaded Dewey of the need for an improved covert action capability. Stephen J. Spingarn, assistant general counsel in the Treasury Department and special assistant to President Truman, now exploited the Bogota incident to press for an extension of the CIA's psychological warfare tactics beyond propaganda, and over a wider geographic area. He enjoyed the backing of a numerous and powerful group, the organized veterans of the army's counterintelligence corps. The Italian election result of April 18, a defeat for the world's second-largest Communist Party, came at an opportune moment for covert operations expansionists like Spingarn. In May 1948, Kennan reaffirmed his support, recommending that there should be better provision for political warfare. In June, the National Security Council issued directive 10/2[58]

NSC 10/2 canceled and superseded NSC 4/A. "Taking cognizance of the vicious covert activities of the USSR" and its satellites, it established a new covert operational branch within the CIA "in the interests of world peace and U.S. national security." This branch would undertake more than the chiefly media-related activities authorized under NSC 4/A. Its "covert operations" would have to be of a type for which "the U.S. Government can plausibly disclaim any responsibility," and could not involve "armed conflict by recognized military forces," but they included "propaganda; economic warfare; preventive direct action, including sabotage, anti-sabotage, demolition, and evacuation measures: subversion against hostile states, including assistance to underground resistance movements, guerillas and refugee liberation groups, and support of indigenous anti-communist elements in threatened countries of the free world." It was in the aftermath of Bogota, therefore, that the United States committed itself to establish, though not necessarily to deploy, a full range of covert-operational capabilities. Representatives of the secretaries of state and defense—the 10/2 Panel—were to supervise such operations, with the National Security Council exercising a mediatory role in cases of disagreement. The CIA would be the agency responsible for covert operations because it already conducted "espionage and counter-espionage operations abroad." The title of the new branch, the Office of Policy Coordination, is sometimes regarded as a euphemism, and it certainly concealed the true nature of some of the CIA's activities, but it should be noted that it reflected the NSC's desire that covert operations should be "planned and conducted in a manner consistent with U.S. foreign and military policies and with overt activities."[59]

Frank G. Wisner became assistant director for policy coordination on September 1, 1948. The Soviet spy and British traitor Kim Philby described him as "a youngish man for so responsible a job, balding and running self-importantly to fat."[60] Born to a wealthy Southern family, Wisner had graduated in law from the University of Virginia. In the war, he served as OSS station chief in Romania, and he met future CIA directors Allen Dulles and Richard Helms. The assistant director moved in a charmed circle of lawyers, OSS veterans, and wealthy people. In the opinion of maverick CIA operative E. Howard Hunt, Hilly was only "Wisner's nominal superior" and lacked his "political power base," which included both Forrestal and Marshall.[61] Wisner succeeded in bolstering the Office of Policy Coordination's position in Washington's byzantine bureaucracy. He presided over its early budgetary expansions, and from 1952 to 1958 served with the enhanced rank (number three in the CIA hierarchy) of deputy director for plans, orchestrating the "Golden Age" of covert operations before his nervous breakdown, and his ultimate suicide in 1965.

The new arrangement did not calm the fears of those who considered American intelligence to be inadequate. Very few Americans knew about the National Security Council's secret directive, so very few were reassured by it. Those who did know about it included some who thought it could be improved, others who thought it did not address the right problem. So the debate about secret intelligence continued.

In the course of 1948 and 1949, Allen Dulles's influence on the intelligence debate increased. In January 1948, Admiral Souers in his capacity as National Security Council executive secretary had demanded and received a summary of the Wall Street lawyer's April 1947 testimony.[62] Sensing a need to respond to criticism, Truman thereupon agreed to a three-man investigation of the CIA and other intelligence agencies. He placed Dulles in charge of it—possibly a preemptive move, in view of Republican presidential candidate Dewey's association with

Allen's brother, future secretary of state John Foster Dulles. Matthias Correa was a sleeping member of the team, though his wartime navy department service with intelligence expansionist Forrestal signified, from Dulles's point of view, that his inactivity would be benign. The third, more active, member, was William H. Jackson, the hard-drinking author of a wartime report on British intelligence, and a devotee of counterintelligence. On May 10, 1948, Souers was able to reassure Spingarn that Jackson "is familiar with the British intelligence set-up," and that he had been given a copy of Spingarn's April 1948 memorandum on counterintelligence.[63]

The Dulles-Jackson-Correa committee reported to the National Security Council on January 1, 1949. The authors of the report shrewdly pointed to America's intelligence advantages in having a cosmopolitan population and in being technologically advanced. Reflecting Allen Dulles's conviction that "free men could be more efficient than the unfree," they were optimistic about the future.[64] But they were critical of the CIA as then constituted. They emphasized the deficiencies of the intelligence briefs of the Office of Reports and Estimates, "which by no stretch of the imagination could be considered national estimates." To achieve "national" or supra-sectional estimates, the committee recommended stronger coordination by the CIA of the efforts of the intelligence community as a whole. It thus identified a management problem that was to stay with the CIA for many years. Second, the committee recommended that there should be a fusion of the Office of Special Operations, which ran the CIA's spying activities, with the Office of Policy Coordination: "These operating functions are so inter-related and inter-dependent that they should have common direction at some point below the Director of Central Intelligence."[65] Though NSC 10/2 had recognized the similarity of spies' and operators' tradecraft, it had separated them bureaucratically, an arrangement that Dulles regarded as nonsensical.

Well before the committee reported, Dulles was leaking his points of view to the press. As early as 1947, New York Times journalist Hanson W. Baldwin, in a book called The Price of Power, had called for improved collection facilities for the CIA and for greater central authority in the matters of evaluation and coordination; he had quoted with approval Dulles's pro-civilianization argument that the CIA should be above military as well as political faction. In July 1948, he wrote an influential five-part series of articles on "Intelligence." In these contributions to the Times, he admitted the CIA was showing some competence in assessing Soviet military intentions, but pointed to CIA-State Department feuding over Bogota, alleged that the FBI had burned its Latin American files rather than surrender them to the CIA, and endorsed Allen Dulles's plea for stronger coordination. In the same series, Baldwin backed the John Foster Dulles proposal for "secret operations," though he added that these ought to be supervised by a congressional committee like the one which watched over the United States Atomic Energy Commission.[66]

Baldwin also supported and advised the task force on national security organization. This operated under the chairmanship of Ferdinand Eberstadt within the

Hoover commission, a body which Congress had established in 1947 with the duty of finding ways to improve efficiency in the executive branch of government. Eberstadt consulted, in addition to Baldwin, a variety of congressmen, government officials, and other informed individuals, including Souers, Leahy, Vandenberg, Forrestal, and future CIA directors Walter Bedell Smith and John McCone. He believed that the CIA was the "logical arbiter of differences between the services."[67] His committee's January 1949 report to Congress recommended that a top-level evaluation board be established within the CIA, that improvements should be effected in the CIA's relations with other departments and agencies, and that coordination be improved. Additionally: "The battle for the minds of men may decide the struggle for the world. The Committee found present facilities and mechanisms for the waging of psychological warfare inadequate."[68]

By this stage a consensus was beginning to emerge on the need for intelligence coordination. Army, navy, and air force intelligence appeared to be exaggerating Soviet strengths in particular areas in order to procure appropriations for more tanks, ships, and plans, respectively, and a civilian-dominated, authoritative CIA appeared to be the answer to this problem. This was indeed the theme of Sherman Kent's classic work *Strategic Intelligence for American World Policy*, completed in October 1948 and published in the following year. By then a history professor at Yale, OSS veteran Kent insisted that, for checking purposes, the CIA should have access to the raw materials on which the military intelligence services based their conclusions. Like Dulles and Baldwin, Kent also advocated a civilian director for the CIA, but he further warned against the creation of a major independent espionage capability for the CIA, a move which might provoke dangerous rivalry with its intelligence siblings. As it was, he anticipated a "five-year storm" of hostility from the CIA's rivals. Kent's views commanded respect in the National Security Council, whose endorsement of CIA hegemony remained circumspect.[69]

The CIA's failure to win a powerfully dominant position in the intelligence community did not stem from any failure on the Truman administration's part to appreciate the urgency of the international situation. The problem was that the consensus on intelligence reform was neither clear cut nor easy to gauge in the absence of a thorough public debate. As Kent foresaw, the military intelligence chiefs perceived the intelligence challenge in predominantly military terms and fought to retain the independence of their own agencies. They were prepared to tolerate a civilian intelligence agency, but not to surrender to it.

In any case, a closer examination shows that U.S. foreign-intelligence theorists were not unanimous in their conceptualization of the CIA's task. Wilmoore Kendall in his 1949 essay criticized the principles being advanced by OSS veterans. Luxuriating in their wartime experiences, these veterans looked to "a Golden Age situated, like Spain's, in the past." They were of poor quality, and the nation's human intelligence resources would "remain hopelessly inadequate throughout the predictable future." Kent's book was in his view a failure, for it exemplified the current overreliance on historical method—on the "analysis" of "raw material" leading to predictions—instead of tackling the *theory* of intelligence. According to Kendall, Kent's intelligence function stopped "at the three mile limit" in that he did not advocate a *combined* assessment of foreign circumstances and U.S. policy options: he took no "cognizance of United States policies alternative to the one actually in effect, such problems being 'domestic' matters."[70] Against the background of such forceful and intelligent criticism it was all the more difficult to advance the CIA's claims to supremacy within the intelligence community. Kendall's contribution, though, did serve the useful function of increasing the sophistication of U.S. thought on intelligence matters: by the late 1950s, it had taken its place alongside the books by Pettee and Kent as part of the collective wisdom on U.S. intelligence theory. Such forceful intellectual debate about the intelligence function was limited to a small circle. Still, it could not have occurred in such an informative manner in less open democracies, let alone in a closed society. The U.S. democratic tradition, though an encumbrance to secret organizations in some ways, did contribute to the speed with which America was able to adapt to its role as an intelligence superpower.

Nevertheless, the foregoing debate took place largely on the theoretical plane and was confined to the professionals. Public debate on that important piece of enabling legislation, the Central Intelligence Act of 1949, was limited both in terms of its extent and its content. The bill and the proposals that preceded it did run into some opposition, but of a type that was predictable to the point of staleness. The irrepressible Trohan suspected a conspiracy by the "Eastern internationalist bloc" and denounced William H. Jackson as "a known admirer of the British intelligence system."[71] Senator William Langer continued the domestic fixation, perceiving a New Deal-style plot against American liberties. So did Congressman Vito Marcantonio of New York, a former aide to Fiorello La Guardia and a radical advocate of the rights of labor. Marcantonio believed Congress was legislating in a mood of "hysteria" and that the CIA would be used "to spy on labor and carry out antilabor activities." But Congressman James Wolcott Wadsworth of New York protested there was "nothing secret" about the need for espionage, while Senator Burnet Rhett Maybank of South Carolina stressed that the bill was "a typical example of the working of our legislative process as provided by the Constitution."[72] After closed hearings and brief debates in the course of which Congress accepted an amendment strengthening the prohibition on the CIA's domestic activities, both houses passed the bill "without knowing," according to Langer, "what all of its provisions meant."[73]

The 1949 law set the seal of congressional approval on the CIA, a seal that remained unbroken until December 1971, when Congress cut off the Agency's funding for operations in Laos and Cambodia. The act's language was obscure in the sense that it did not specify the Agency's functions. Instead, it set forth what legislative liaison officer Pforzheimer had earlier described as "house-keeping provisions." The law allowed the CIA a seal of office, authorized training for CIA officers (for example in labor and scientific organizations), and specified their employment conditions (hospital expenses, storage of furniture while on foreign service, and the like). It did not establish the CIA's supremacy over other agencies. It did permit the CIA to borrow personnel from other agencies, to ignore the immigration laws in recruiting up to one hundred defectors per annum, and to use funds in a discreet and flexible way calculated to enhance its espionage duties. Notably, the 1949 act gave detailed and specific authority for the use of secret funds. The 1947 provision had given the director the duty of protecting secrets about "sources and methods"; now, the 1949 Act gave him the power to create secrets to protect. The new law authorized the director to receive, exchange, and spend money without giving an account to Congress in accordance with the laws governing other agencies. For "confidential, extraordinary, or emergency" operations, the accounting would be "solely" on the director's certificate, which would be "deemed a sufficient voucher for the amount therein certified."

Given the fillip of the 1949 act, the CIA's covert operations expanded. The personnel and funds at the disposal of the office of policy coordination rose from 302 and $4,700,000 in 1949 to 2,812 (plus 3,142 overseas on contract) and $82,000,000 in 1952.[74] Much of the additional effort went into an expanded propaganda program. In 1949, secret CIA funds set up the ostensibly private Radio Free Europe, which beamed propaganda toward the Eastern bloc exclusive of the Soviet Union; under a similar arrangement Radio Liberty broadcast to the Russians from 1950.[75] On April 20, 1950, President Truman called for a "campaign of truth" against Communist propaganda: the CIA-financed radios were to complement the State Department's openly funded Voice of America radio station in a massive program projecting the image of the United States. Meanwhile, the CIA continued to finance organizations whose leaders might be expected to express non-Communist or anti-Communist views. American Federation of Labor conduits remained in use. One of those involved in another program, FDR's cousin Frederick Delano Houghteling, noted that CIA financing of the anti-Communist activities of American students abroad was under way by 1950. At the time, most Americans were unaware of or incurious about such activities, while foreigners were still grateful for U.S. wartime aid and the Marshall Plan, and not yet cynical about the new great power as it made its global debut.[76]

The financial procedures authorized by the 1949 act made it easier for the CIA to develop covert programs of a nonpropaganda type. The Agency's acquisition of air transport facilities, for example, increased its capability for covert action, including action of a paramilitary type. The impetus for this move came, in part, from the desire—expressed by Donovan and shared by others—to control potentially embarrassing private activities. In June 1948, there had appeared a CIA report on "Clandestine Air Transport Operations by U.S. Citizens and U.S. Owned Aircraft in Areas Outside the U.S." The authors of the report complained that "certain wealthy private American interests" were smuggling military supplies and aircraft to sensitive areas in Central and South America and Europe. These might well fall into Soviet or other left-wing hands. In fact, Service Airways of Burbank, California, were already playing into Russia's hands by supplying arms to Jews in Palestine. The chain of transactions included not only a fake corporation in Panama, an apocryphal Rome headquarters, and a prominent Jewish financier, but also Italian socialists "following the party line laid down by the USSR." The authors of the CIA report believed that such activities, if allowed to continue freely, would harm U.S. interests and prestige.[77]

The initiative for governmental takeover of maverick airlines came from a private corporation. Civil Air Transport (CAT) had been formed just after the collapse of Japan, and at first prospered in strife-torn China. Its financial backers, Major General Claire L. Chennault and former Roosevelt adviser Thomas G. Corcoran, began to panic at the prospect of Mao's victory. They appealed for government funds, to be so administered that CAT could be "militarized" at short notice. They proposed to assist Nationalist forces, to stop and indeed reverse the "domino" process in Southeast Asia, and to halt Soviet expansion in its tracks, as well as to bail out their by-now ailing corporation.

Hillenkoetter, Wisner, and other CIA officials supported the plan. CAT operated for the CIA from October 10, 1949, and formed the first component of the Agency's worldwide aerial empire. The arrangement was formalized under liberal Delaware laws in 1950, when the cover holding company, Airdale Corporation, was formed. Air America and Southern Air Transport were later incorporated as CIA cover proprietaries in a similar manner to operate in other parts of the globe. The CAT-Airdale transition was by no means a smooth one. The State Department at first opposed the plan, but was brought round by the promise that the CIA would not compete with private airlines, as well as by the argument that CAT needed to be kept out of the hands of "uncontrolled purchasers." The Chinese Nationalists wanted control; CAT's original operators loved to go it alone; only in 1955 did the CIA feel fully satisfied with the degree of authority it had managed to assert over its proprietary. Such difficulties notwithstanding, the CIA did acquire one of the prerequisites of effective paramilitary operations, airpower.[78]

Soon after the enactment of the 1949 law, the CIA became involved in its first attempt to topple a foreign government. Its target was the Communist regime in Albania, headed by the World War II partisan leader, Enver Hoxha. Hoxha leaned on Moscow for support against the neighboring Yugoslavs, who had split with Stalin in 1948, but the British Secret Intelligence Service (M.I.6) planned to topple his regime, weakening further the Stalinist grip in the Balkans. Truman had already stepped in against the neighboring Greek Communists at the behest of the impoverished British. Now, the CIA supplied unvouchered funds as British secret agents infiltrated Albania, operating from the then-British island of Malta. Kim Philby recalled Wisner's remark: "Whenever we want to subvert any place, we find that the British own an island within easy reach."[79] In the event, Hoxha's efficient counterintelligence service mopped up the Anglo-American secret agents, whose security procedures were far too lax. The Russians knew about the operation anyway, for the SIS-CIA liaison officer in Washington was none other than their own spy, Philby.[80] Poor security on the British side would in future years further undermine an intelligence partnership which the Americans, with superior resources and rapidly improving organization, needed less and less.

The Albanian affair invites a reconsideration of the claims by both Truman and Souers that the CIA became obsessed with covert operations only after their departure from office. Contrary to what they implied, the Albanian operation does seem to have set an earlier precedent, even if the CIA acted through British surrogates. It should be noted that Souers objected not to operations as such, but to "so much emphasis" on operations.[81] There is also a distinct possibility that Souers distinguished between desirable and undesirable operations. He described himself as "just left of center" politically, and even the Communist Philby conceded that the CIA's penchant for supporting right-wing dictators did not develop until *after* the Albanian affair.[82] Truman and Souers were reluctant to use covert action, and democratic in their aims. But they were not in principle opposed to the foreign-policy instrument which Wisner, helped by the 1949 act, forged. In fact, under their aegis covert action was to be enshrined as part of overall U.S. strategy as set forth in NSC 68, which the CIA's Ludwell Lee Montague helped draft.[83] Issued on April 14, 1950, the famous directive called for a nuclear and conventional military buildup, but additionally for covert operations to subvert Communist regimes.[84]

It may be concluded that, between 1947 and 1950, congressional legislation and National Security Council directives broadened considerably the scope of the CIA's operations. The sometimes reluctant and often maligned Hillenkoetter had presided over this process, and over at least some triumphs in the fields of both intelligence and secret propaganda. Yet, much had been lost in the mists of Bogota and in the debate that followed the riots. Gone was any immediate prospect of a long-term, stable relationship with Congress. Gone, too, was any degree of certainty about the desirable scope and nature of the CIA's covert operations. In the realm of intelligence, there was even more uncertainty. Gone, apparently, was the narrow assumption that the CIA had simply to avoid a repetition of the Pearl Harbor-type predictive failure. Even as they began to grapple with the new notion of national intelligence estimates, however, the CIA's analysts were under continuing pressure to avoid errors of the predictive type. The presumption of such an error, indeed, was to lead to Hillenkoetter's final disgrace in the summer of 1950.

4

SURVIVING
McCARTHY
A Weakness
for
Immunity

At dawn on June 25, 1950, over one hundred thousand soldiers from Communist North Korea crossed the thirty-eighth parallel, invading the republic to the South. With United Nations backing, President Truman committed the United States to the defense of South Korea. In the fighting which ensued, an estimated three to four million people died before the two sides agreed to a mutually unsatisfactory stalemate. Thousands of American soldiers fell in battle. Many thousands more were wounded, including the only son of Allen Dulles: Allen Macy Dulles, Jr., never recovered fully from the effects of the bullet which passed through his brain.

Korea opened a new phase in the CIA's history. Because the Communists had caught their Southern neighbors unawares, the CIA took the blame for yet another "intelligence failure." The Truman administration made a scapegoat of Hillenkoetter, then built up the Agency still further under his replacement, Walter Bedell Smith. The new director both improved the CIA's estimating machinery and developed its covert operational potential. His work was appropriate and well received on account of a further consequence of the Korean war. The war's unpopularity in its later stages reminded the nation's leaders of their compatriots' deep-seated hostility to conventional militarism, and it nudged them in the direction of reliance on nuclear deterrence on the one hand, covert action on the other. Smith's reform of strategic estimates as well as clandestine missions could not have been better timed.

Still another of this war's consequences had a major if indirect impact on the

CIA. It fueled the idea that there was something rotten in the federal government, unleashing the anti-Communist crusade led by Senator Joseph R. McCarthy of Wisconsin. Having already investigated and demoralized several branches of the government, McCarthy tried to scrutinize the most secret bureaucracy of all. But Allen Dulles, a patriot by repute and by sacrifice as well as by inclination, had the prestige to withstand the onslaught. By now in charge of the CIA, he inflicted on McCarthy his first—and decisive—defeat. Dulles's triumph had several consequences for the CIA. Especially in light of the disarray of other branches of government, it boosted the Agency's standing and shed a roseate glow on its personalities and actions. It contributed to the illusion of CIA liberalism—and, later, to the myth that its officials displayed a liberal bias in their Soviet estimates. Finally, it encouraged Dulles in his successful pursuit of immunity from all types of thoroughgoing congressional oversight. In the long term, this quest for immunity ran into the obstacle of American democracy, resulting in a clash that ended the prestige which Dulles had so brilliantly built up. This clash was all the more serious because excessive secrecy had, ironically, blinded people to the virtues as well as to the faults of the CIA.

The North Korean onslaught had indeed caught American forces unawares, but not because of a paucity of warnings by the CIA. As early as February 28, 1949, the Agency had warned that such an attack was "highly probable" in the wake of projected U.S. troop withdrawals.[1] Yet, Defense Secretary Louis A. Johnson declared that the intelligence reports he had received too often cried "wolf," so it was difficult to know what to believe; there had been no specific warning to the armed forces of the Communist offensive in Korea. Commenting at the end of July on rumors that Hilly was to be replaced, an editorial in the *Washington Post*, too, noted the "CIA's tendency to cry 'wolf' in its reports."[2] Allegations about past predictive failures had evidently panicked the CIA into issuing an indiscriminate profusion of warnings in an attempt to insure against potential criticism. Indeed, when the Agency gave Truman its immediate reaction to the North Korean surprise attack, it suggested it was "undoubtedly undertaken at Soviet direction" and was "a diversionary action to cover an attack on Formosa."[3] The evocation of the Kremlin bogeyman in this way shows that the CIA was underestimating autonomous tendencies in Korea at the same time that it was still covering itself against guessed-at contingencies by crying "wolf".

One of Korea's intelligence lessons was that the CIA should be built up and allowed greater scope to conduct its own research into local conditions. The commanding officer of U.S. forces in the Far East, General Douglas MacArthur, had refused to allow the Agency to operate in his theater. According to one of the CIA's lines of defense, the Agency's estimates consequently suffered from a damaging lack of local information, a fault also said to have affected the OSS, similarly kept out by MacArthur.[4] The logic of this defense was that the CIA should be given wider responsibilities together with more assets. MacArthur's defiance of presidential authority and his dismissal by Truman in April 1951 lent credibility to the view that the CIA had been obstructed by an irrationally intransigent foe and should now be bolstered. The reward for intelligence failure, as in the cases of Pearl Harbor and Bogota, was to be intelligence expansion.

A more immediate consequence of the Korean debacle was that the CIA had to serve as a scapegoat, for there was a distinct possibility that the American public would blame politicians for U.S. unpreparedness in the face of attack. From the administration's viewpoint, there was an ominous ring to Hilly's congressional testimony and press leaks. A worried Democratic Senator told Truman on June 27, 1950: "The testimony which is being offered to the Appropriations Committee indicates that although for more than a year Central Intelligence has been reporting evidence of aggressive preparations in North Korea, no steps have been taken. . . . "[5] One could indeed argue that Truman and his advisers, preoccupied with other problems like Formosa (Taiwan) and too impatient to read CIA reports carefully, were "deaf" to important signals. Even after the outbreak of the war with its implicit intelligence lesson, American officials continued to ignore CIA warnings. Notably, U.S. troops pressed on into North Korea in spite of an accurate CIA prediction that this action would provoke Chinese retaliation on an overwhelming scale.[6] Truman could see that if he did not find a way of indicating his disappointment with the CIA, the nation might blame the president instead. He therefore dismissed Hillenkoetter.

In a report issued on December 11, 1950, Lieutenant General Walter Bedell Smith intimated that the Soviet Union was "directing . . . local Communist aggression in the Far East."[7] Truman had picked out the "Beetle" to replace "Hilly" about a month after the North Korean assault, and the new man took over on October 7, 1950. As his remark indicates, Smith was no more sensitive to indigenous Korean tendencies than his predecessor. Yet from the domestic political standpoint, this mattered less than the fact that he had unchallengeable credentials: he had been Eisenhower's wartime chief of staff. Just as important were his anti-Soviet leanings, for Senator McCarthy was already making charges about pro-Communists in the government. Smith had recently been ambassador to the Soviet Union and had exemplary right-wing, hard-line opinions, many of them recorded in his timely 1950 memoir. By 1949, he declared, "wartime cooperation with the capitalistic world was being portrayed by Soviet propaganda as an unholy alliance." He proclaimed that Moscow had been behind not just the Communist takeover in Czechoslovakia, but also labor strikes in France and Italy aimed at destroying the effectiveness of the Marshall Plan.[8]

At first, Smith did seem a satisfactory solution to the CIA's potential problem with Congress. In the absence of a joint congressional committee of the type which Devitt had unsuccessfully proposed in 1948, the chief responsibility for dealing with the Agency had fallen to the Senate Armed Services Committee and to a subcommittee within it that met, from time to time, to consider intelligence matters. On August 24, 1950, the Armed Services Committee held a confirmation hearing for General Smith. Its chairman, Maryland's Millard E. Tydings, told

Smith his knowledge of Russia and his military service made him an ideal selection as director. Senator Leverett Saltonstall inquired solicitously after the general's health. Senator Estes Kefauver sounded the only note of criticism in demanding that the CIA extend its subversive activities to divide opponents in Asia: "I hate to see the yellow people united in their opposition to us." Senator William F. Knowland declared that the CIA had given exemplary early warnings on the Korean invasion, but had been ignored. General Smith amused his audience with a war story, a practice later repeated by Dulles in testifying to admiring congressional committees. Other Senators having expressed their respect for the "Beetle," the hearing, a formality from the outset, drew to a close on a note of approbation and hilarity, as Tydings stated he had no intention of subjecting the formidable nominee to the "third degree."[9]

Smith was himself optimistic about the reception he could expect, telling an Army friend in September 1950 that there was "some comfort . . . in the fact that I am taking over at a time when the nation is keenly aware of the need for an effective intelligence organization and I can confidently expect wholehearted support from every quarter."[10] What could not be foreseen in 1950 was that Smith would be incapable of resisting McCarthyist hysteria. The penalties of resistance were intimidatingly evident by the fall of 1950 when Tydings, who had robustly attacked McCarthy over his accusations, went down to defeat in the midterm elections. Two years later, Smith swam with the McCarthyist tide when he told a congressional committee that "there are Communists in my own organization," though he had been unable to detect them.[11]

In spite of that remark, Smith is usually portrayed as having been one of the CIA's most respected directors. He had the good fortune of avoiding—whether through sound judgment or good luck—any major predictive failures in the course of his tenure, October 1950 to February 1953. He also impressed people on account of his dyspeptic disposition, thought to be the combined consequence of an exhausting army career and constant stomach complaints. In January 1951, he brought in Allen Dulles as deputy director for plans, promoting him to deputy director of the CIA in August, but such signs of favor would from time to time give way to peremptory remarks like "Dulles? Dulles, Goddamit, get in here!"[12]

Dulles thought Smith lacked the imagination and character to deliver anything other than mimetic intelligence, being just a good administrator adept at carrying out orders.[13] Be that as it may, Smith did command admiration for the way in which he asserted his authority with a minimum of fuss. According to a March 1951 *New York Herald Tribune* story the five-star general was obtaining what he wanted from other agencies because, unlike Hillenkoetter, he could pull rank to get his way; thus, for example, he gained access to new areas like local signals intelligence without ruffling too many feathers, and he managed to reduce interagency feuding.[14] Under Hillenkoetter the Intelligence Advisory Committee, a body dating from the CIG and composed of the heads of other agencies, had taken on supervisory instead of advisory functions. Smith simply told them he was in charge. With similar authority, he would telephone Pentagon colleagues with requests like: "I want you to get over here and decide whether Russia is going to invade Poland."[15]

Smith liked to present President Truman with just one, uncontradicted intelligence assessment, his own. To that end, he made a serious attempt to unify the estimating process. By 1950 the Office of Research and Evaluation had succumbed to the effects of departmental parochialism; finding it impossible to obtain other intelligence bureaus' golden nuggets, it produced purely internal CIA estimates that did not utilize the resources of the U.S. intelligence community as a whole. To help him shake up the intelligence management structure, Smith brought in as deputy director of the CIA William H. Jackson, one of the authors of the Dulles-Jackson-Correa report of 1949. Jackson lasted for only a short period (October 7, 1950 to August 3, 1951) before yielding the deputy directorship to Allen Dulles, but he served long enough to persuade Smith to replace the Office of Research and Evaluation with the Office of National Estimates (ONE).

To organize the ONE, Smith appointed William Langer. The new recruit was a Harvard professor who had written with great distinction on European and U.S. diplomatic history. In 1947, the Rockefeller Foundation had given him a grant through the Council on Foreign Relations to write an account of American entry into World War II. The announcement of this grant provoked a furious attack from isolationist and revisionist critics of the Roosevelt administration, such as Trohan, Beard, and Tansill. According to them he epitomized the "Establishment," belonged to an "interventionist, Anglophile clique," and was "A Hired Liar."[16] Undeterred, Langer, on the basis of privileged access to still-classified documents, published in 1952 his seminal though subjectively anti-isolationist, pro-preparedness account of America's entry onto the world stage.[17] By this time he had not only set up the ONE but also singled out a successor who would consolidate his scholarly approach: Sherman Kent, another Ivy League historian, a Yale professor who could draw on the expertise he had accumulated while researching his 1949 book on intelligence theory. Kent continued in charge of the ONE until 1967.

In addition to his academic qualities, Langer had the temperament necessary to deal with a man like Smith. He believed in recruiting only top-quality people; when Smith offered him a staff of two hundred for the ONE, Langer is reputed to have said "I can do it with twenty-five."[18] The ONE's staff never did exceed the thirty to seventy-five range over the years: Langer handpicked the original bunch. These professionals were complemented, within the ONE, by a board—senior people with practical experience who could temper with pragmatism the intellectually derived findings of the analysts. By November 1950, the board consisted of an economist, four historians, one retired general, and one lawyer. To further modify what was still an academically biased process, Jackson hit on the idea of the "Princeton Consultants," people like George F. Kennan and atomic scientist Vannevar Bush. Four times a year this group would meet—at Jackson's home near

Princeton or at Princeton University's Gun Club—to mull over and improve the ONE's latest problem-orientated national intelligence estimates. Both as deputy director and as director of the CIA, Allen Dulles regularly flew up to Princeton to listen to the consultants.[19]

Smith's tough and elaborate shake-up of the estimating process impressed a number of his contemporaries and has been portrayed in retrospect as a notable achievement, partly because the people selected for advancement in this period served for many years and then gave a glowing account of the reforms which had benefited them.[20] For a while, because of Smith's personality and his successor's qualities, the system did work without any severe political dislocation. Furthermore, Smith achieved other reforms. He developed the CIA's collection, scientific, and information-distribution facilities, grouping these various functions into a new directorate for intelligence in January 1952. On the other hand, the ONE was not the final solution to the problem of intelligence coordination. Other agencies continued, over the years, to withhold their cooperation or criticize the CIA's analyses. Proliferation complicated the problem of intelligence management. For example, while the formation of the National Security Agency on November 4, 1952, may have been a timely boost for advanced-technology signals intelligence, the NSA reported to the Department of Defense, presenting another management challenge just as Smith and Langer appeared to be making headway in reducing interagency difficulties.[21]

Smith cherished an ambition to be more than just a bureaucratic reformer. He looked for a field of activity that would allow him to establish the CIA in the public esteem, and he was sufficiently realistic to perceive that this would not be in the field of intelligence. "Only two personalities," he told the senators at his confirmation hearing, might satisfy the "popular conception" of what a director of central intelligence should be: "One is God, and the other is Stalin, and I do not know that even God can do it because I do not know whether he is close enough in touch with Uncle Joe to know what he is talking about."[22] The CIA directorship, he confided to a business acquaintance,

is one of those jobs where one can never be right as the American people expect the incumbent to be able to predict with accuracy just what Stalin is likely to do three months from today at 5.30 a.m. and, of course, that is beyond the realm of human infallibility. Furthermore, whenever there is a failure, everybody begins to shriek "intelligence" and with a political November coming up, the immediate prospect is even more gloomy.[23]

Appreciative of the limitations of intelligence and the political pitfalls associated with it, Smith ironically turned to *covert* activities as a way of securing some *demonstrable* success which could, if necessary, be used to protect himself and the CIA politically. As he was a fervent Cold Warrior, and covert operators targetted the Soviets, this course of action was in any case congenial to him. He began to develop contacts even before taking office. For example, he arranged to see the philosopher Sidney Hook to discuss "matters of mutual interest"; Hook was soon to start planning international conferences for the CIA-funded Congress for Cultural Freedom, and to choose editors for its London magazine *Encounter*.[24] Another former socialist contacted by Smith was the labor leader David Dubinsky. Dubinsky proved to be a link with American Jewry as well as with the AFL, a piece in that intricate mosaic of New Deal-style liberalism that was rapidly frosting over as part of the Cold War process. While Wisner provided some of the introductions, Smith set the tone, congratulating, for example, the Jewish Labor Committee's Conference to Stop Communist Aggression for its "direct refutation of the Communist lie that our workers are willing to accept anything less than unregimented liberty."[25] Thus, although much of his planning and recruiting was necessarily clandestine, Smith was able to conduct a public relations campaign quite openly. In December 1950, he told a group of cabinet members and congressional leaders—in a statement duly recorded in the press—that it might be necessary to foment "counterrevolutions in the small countries the Soviet has enslaved."[26] Smith realized that a judicious airing of its actual and potential goals could enhance the Agency's prestige.

In spite of his public relations successes, Smith did not in practice succeed in relaxing the guidelines for the CIA's covert operations. The Albanian subversion attempt continued during his directorship, but still through British surrogates. Surrogacy operated elsewhere, too. Just before Smith took over at the CIA, Colonel Edward Lansdale arrived in the Philippines. There, he worked on behalf of the Agency to help defeat the "Huk" left-wing insurgency movement: however, he offered advice and resources rather than direct participation, the native Filipinos in this case being the CIA's willing—and effective—surrogates.[27]

In several cases, the CIA did not so much offer its services as respond to requests for help. Thomas A. Braden, who administered CIA grants to anti-Communist fronts between 1950 and 1954, commented on the prior anti-Communism of some of his organized-labor recipients: "when they ran out of money they appealed to CIA."[28] The CIA did not have a monopoly even on passive responses: on April 4, 1951, Truman established a separate psychological strategy board, which was soon being plagued for money by anti-Communist student organizations (the CIA stepped in, however, to organize the funding).[29] When the CIA concocted more active plans of its own for foreign interventions, such as a scheme to overthrow the Guatemalan government, the Truman administration dragged its feet.[30] Under Smith's leadership, therefore, the CIA continued to build up its clandestine networks, but, by comparison with later years, they were never fully unleashed.

In the field of covert operations, as in the intelligence field, Smith's main contribution was a bureaucratic reorganization. The Dulles-Jackson-Correa report had recommended a fusion of the spying and covert action bureaucracies. Dulles had argued that it was silly to keep apart people who had the same tradecraft, for the separation would lead to a duplication of skills and to one group of spooks tripping over the other. By 1952, feuding between the Office of Special Operations (in charge of spying) and the Office of Policy Coordination (in charge of operations)—over personnel, salaries, and status—had become chronic. In August 1952, Smith created a directorate of plans, giving Dulles the job of translating policy into plans and giving him the rank of deputy director of the CIA. Under Dulles, Wisner was assistant director with the duty of implementing plans for both spying and operations. This reform was important in two respects: it put CIA officials directly in charge of the Agency's operations (previously they had carried out secret operations at the behest of State and Defense), and, as Dulles was now number two in the CIA hierarchy, it enhanced the status of the covert operators within the Agency.[31]

To characterize the emergent CIA of the early 1950s, it is appropriate to look beyond policy, organization, and individual directors' personalities to ask what kind of employees, in general, did the Agency recruit? What was their quality, their social and educational background, their ideology? These questions, and the various responses to them, were controversial at the time. They have also provoked profound disagreement since; assumptions about the CIA's makeup and outlook have affected both the Agency's standing and the shaping of U.S. foreign policy.

The CIA's first director, Hillenkoetter, had had to contend with complaints about the poor quality of his recruits. In 1954, in the immediate wake of major recruiting efforts in the early 1950s, President Eisenhower asked Air Force Lieutenant-General James H. Doolittle to examine the cost efficiency of the CIA's covert activities.[32] In his report, Doolittle mentioned contemporary gripes about there being too much "dead wood" in the Agency, where the mediocre tended to linger on "through inertia or because of a desire for financial security." He observed that the CIA's recruitment program on college and university campuses met with mixed success:

> Many applicants find the necessary clearance procedures unpalatable and annoying. Some are repelled by misunderstanding of the purpose of polygraphic examination and the techniques employed. Some (particularly in scientific fields whose future professional reputation may depend upon publication of papers, etc.) are unwilling to accept the implications of a lifetime of anonymity, or of life under a pseudonym.[33]

While the CIA was studded with talented individuals and may well have been collectively better staffed than rival intelligence agencies, the overall quality of its personnel remained open to question.[34] Contemporaries realized that this was the case: the debate about the quality of the CIA's personnel showed no signs of abating.

Even more damaging, potentially, was the charge that the CIA's leadership came from a narrow, privileged social stratum, suggesting to some that it was not only selected on grounds other than merit, but also undemocratic and unrepresentative of the American people at large. Stewart Alsop, a journalist who knew and admired some of the CIA's top officials in the 1950s, noted that their enemies labeled them "the Ivy Leaguers, the Socialites, the Establishmentarians," though he himself coined the alternative epithet, "the Bold Easterners." Alsop professed nostalgia for the prep school decade, "when the CIA was positively riddled with Old Grotonians." According to Alsop's list of examples, Groton had produced Richard Bissell, Tracy Barnes, John Bross, William Bundy, Kermit Roosevelt, Archibald Roosevelt, and W. Osborn Webb.[35]

Full information on the socio-educational background of the CIA leadership is not available because the Agency has concealed the identities of some of its people—partly to protect national security, partly to shield the individuals concerned from attack, and doubtless to some degree in order to cultivate a clandestine mystique. Still, such evidence as exists tends to confirm that the CIA leadership was elitist by educational background. That leadership appears to have included more Ivy League graduates than the civil service leadership as a whole, and more Harvard-Yale-Princeton alumni than two other groups for which figures are available: 1,032 "key federal executive appointees" 1933–65, and 234 "key American foreign-policy decision-makers" 1944–60. Fully 25 percent of the CIA's top people appear to have obtained at least one degree from Harvard.[36]

To be sure, the CIA's image as the secret last bastion of mugwump privilege must be modified in some ways. Top U.S. diplomats dealing with Russia from 1933 to 1947 had a much higher Harvard-Yale-Princeton quotient than the CIA in the succeeding period.[37] A Harvard degree and WASP pedigree were no guarantee of promotion to the CIA elite: according to one 1951 recruit, "It would have been better if I had gone to Princeton and been a member of OSS. I was not a Catholic, nor an East European ethnic, I just did not fit into the ruling cliques in the Clandestine Services."[38] Advancement and policy determination may also have owed as much to OSS background and big business contacts as to Ivy League education. In any case, it is held that the CIA, like other branches of government, looked to more egalitarian campuses from the 1950s on.[39] Such an effort at more democratic recruitment could also be taken to signify that the Agency considered itself to be as elitist as Alsop claimed, to a degree that needed correction. It is significant, too, that a number of presidents and Senate critics have regarded the Agency as elitist and conspiratorial. Their complaints were partly opportunistic and partly colored by their own social backgrounds: most of them were "outsiders." But their perceptions and portrayals were influential nonetheless.[40]

Yet another assertion about the CIA was that it was biased on a "liberal" or even "left-wing" direction. David Atlee Philipps, in retirement after holding senior positions in the Agency, commented that "the majority of the people" he met in the 1950s "fit the pattern of Ivy League, OSS, and liberal." William Colby, a future CIA director who took charge of political operations in Italy in the fall of 1953, later wrote of the Agency's "opening to the left" in that period. Tom Braden, Frank Wisner, Lyman Kirkpatrick, Tracy Barnes, and Richard Bissell were among the senior or rising CIA officials reputed to have liberal sympathies. Another was Cord Meyer, according to Colby an official of "firmly liberal coloration," who specialized in working with private groups like students' organizations and wished to recruit the adherents of "democratic socialism" in Europe.[41]

Portrayals of the CIA as "liberal" or "soft" on Communism were to damage the Agency on more than one occasion but were at least partly based on an illusion— as the case of Cord Meyer illustrates. Meyer joined the CIA in 1951 at the behest of Allen Dulles. In the 1940s, he had crusaded on behalf of a United Nations-based world federalism, serving until the fall of 1949 as president of the United World Federalists. In this period a friend had poked fun at Meyer, describing him as a naive "Ivy League liberal." Soviet propagandists saw things from an entirely different standpoint. They attacked the "world government" idea as an American imperialist plot, and Moscow Radio denounced Meyer personally as "the fig leaf of American imperialism." Disillusioned through direct personal experience, as well as by the grim turn in world events, Meyer went to work for the CIA.[42] No doubt he, like others in the CIA, saw in Europe's social democrats a force that was both implacably opposed to Communism and likely to undermine support for Communist parties in free elections. Pragmatism, as much as ideological sympathy, dictated that they, along with other anti-Communist groups, should be supported.

American liberalism has various meanings, but it can be said that disillusionment and pragmatism were among the factors that impelled some of the CIA's *reputed* "liberals" to join the ranks of the "neoliberals" (later known as "neoconservatives"), a group described by one authority as "liberal advocates of 'hard anti-Communism'."[43] It should also be noted that Smith, Angleton, and other leading CIA officials never were anything but right-wing. After Truman's departure from the White House, furthermore, the CIA helped several right-wing dictatorships. Although Agency officials have hinted from time to time that they have tried to engineer the downfall of some right-wing dictatorships of the more invidious type, they have never claimed success, nor has success been attributed to them. Yet, the Agency has claimed success in toppling leftward-leaning governments, including democratically elected ones. Of the three charges against the collective CIA leadership—that it was relatively mediocre, elitist, and liberal/leftist—the last is the least credible.

Upon the election of Dwight D. Eisenhower in 1952 Smith, bored with the CIA and getting more irascible by the minute, accepted an alternative job—that of undersecretary of state. Dulles took over at the CIA, in spite of Smith's objections that he was overenamored with covert operations, and in the teeth of the rival candidacy of seventy-year-old Bill Donovan.[44] Referring to Dulles, historian Stephen B. Ambrose has remarked that the "most famous Director of Central Intelligence was a liberal."[45] Perhaps this reputation derives, in part, from Dulles's opposition to the German Nazis in the 1930s, his support for the British stand against Hitler, and the fact that he was the CIA's first civilian director, having been preceded by a military man of outspoken conservative views. But Dulles was not a New Deal Democrat; he supported Dewey and was appointed by Eisenhower. His ideology is uncertain. He would cooperate with Nazis or anyone else, if he believed that to be in the American interest. He aspired to be, above all, a pragmatic patriot.

Dulles was a member of the East coast elite as defined and despised by its political opponents. Educated at Princeton, he was associated with the Wall Street law firm of Sullivan and Cromwell, and in the 1930s he had performed some notable legal services for its major corporate clients, such as the United Fruit Company.[46] His grandfather John W. Foster had been secretary of state in 1892–93 (and had started the practice of using U.S. military attachés for intelligence purposes). His uncle-by-marriage Robert Lansing had been secretary of state from 1915 to 1920, the period when Allen Dulles first entered the service of his country as a foreign secret agent. His brother John Foster Dulles became secretary of state on January 31, 1953, helping to ensure that Allen would take up the CIA post twenty-six days later.

This almost incestuous job-fixing by an elite was not new in the U.S. intelligence community. In World War I, Lansing's number two at State, Frank Polk, had laid the groundwork for the central intelligence organization U-1. His assistant, Gordon Auchincloss, had like Polk attended Groton and Yale. Auchincloss was also married to the daughter of Colonel E. M. House, President Wilson's close adviser. Both the World War I clique and the Dulles brothers succeeded as a team; they were loyal to their country and to each other in a trade long marked by treachery; they effectively guarded secrets in the interests of national security.[47] Allen Dulles's selection, it should be added, was due as much to his unquestionable expertise as to his family connections and socio-educational background: he had served as a secret agent in both world wars, then advised on the structuring of the early CIA. Yet in spite of these attributes, Allen Dulles epitomized a high-handed tendency that some people considered to be both distasteful and dangerous in a republican democracy. On the eve of his takeover as director, two *Washington Post* editorials scored the "freelance irresponsibles" in CIA who were subsidizing neo-Nazis and conspiring with United Fruit in Guatemala; another of the Agency's major trials was about to begin.[48]

Congress was the source of the trouble. Though Congress had placed the CIA on trust in the 1940s and had rejected the option of an oversight committee, there was nothing to prevent it from changing its mind. In any case, in America's parliamentary democracy, Congress from time to time passed laws that affected the Agency, and congressional opinion therefore had to be heeded. One example is the internal security law or McCarran Act, passed over Truman's veto in 1951. The act placed several restrictions on civil liberties, drove the Communist party underground, and prevented the admission to U.S. territory and citizenship of radical aliens. Truman's 1950 veto message made it clear that he had consulted the CIA, whose officials had earlier objected that they might lose their supply of informative defectors.[49] In addition to the need to secure congressional cooperation in occasional matters of this kind, it was necessary to ensure the annual appropriation of funds. The CIA's money came, via disguised accounts, from the department of defense's budget. In 1952, it began to receive additional resources from a contingency reserve fund, set up to take care of unexpected large-scale expenditures. To ensure the smooth flow of its unvouchered funds, the CIA had to avoid offending Congress generally, and more specifically the Senate Armed Services Committee and the House Appropriations Committee Defense Subcommittee, whose chairman's certification of the CIA's budget constituted congressional approval.[50]

The attack, when it came, focused not on the CIA's allegedly irresponsible covert operations abroad but on the unrepresentative nature of its hierarchy. Like other prominent critics of the CIA in the future, Senator Joseph R. McCarthy hailed from the western interior and had presidential ambitions. A tribune of the have-nots and outsiders, he had already taken to great lengths his campaign to smear as pro-Communist a wide range of privileged Americans including Secretary of State George Marshall and his successor Dean Acheson, "the Great Red Dean." He denounced Acheson's "crimson crowd" who had betrayed American boys dying in Korea: "the Communists within our borders have been more responsible for the success of Communism abroad than Soviet Russia."[51] With the tacit approval of the Republican party leadership, he continued to smear the Washington elite in the presidential election of 1952, contributing to the Democrats' defeat. He did not desist in 1953, in spite of the fact that Eisenhower was now in the White House, so that his allegations were potentially damaging to his own party. Little did he imagine that his bluff would be called by a CIA director from the very class whose softness McCarthy so despised.

McCarthy had for some time intended to launch what would have been the first major congressional investigation of the CIA. According to his associates he had already accumulated "tons" of documents, with the unofficial cooperation of Agency officials including Bedell Smith himself, in preparation for the one inquiry that "interested him more than any other."[52] The timing seemed right in 1953, for McCarthy wished to divert attention from a political indiscretion by one of his researchers, Dr. J. B. Matthews, who had claimed that the Protestant clergy of America contained in their midst five thousand Soviet agents. But President Eisenhower appears to have been more shrewd, foreseeing that the demagogic senator might well impale himself by attacking a superpatriotic institution. To safeguard his own position, the president nonetheless ordered his own investigation into the CIA, the Doolittle inquiry.[53]

The official whom McCarthy singled out as his first potential victim was an ideal focus for the senator's obsessions and fears. William P. Bundy had joined the CIA in 1950 to work in the ONE and on liaison with the National Security Council. Acheson's son-in-law and a Dulles recruit, he had attended Groton and Yale. In his demeanor, according to one journalist, he was a "snob."[54] J. Edgar Hoover told McCarthy that Bundy had donated four hundred dollars to the Alger Hiss defense.

Thus did one scion of the establishment subsidize another who had been accused of espionage on behalf of the Soviet Union and, additionally, of masterminding the 1945 McCormack plan to set up within the State Department a leftist "super duper [intelligence] department."[55] When McCarthy's attack on the CIA met with resistance, the *Chicago Tribune* vented its spleen on Bundy's backers. They consisted of "New Deal Democrats" who had "an appalling record of bringing Communists into the public service and protecting them there." The said Democrats were backed up by interventionist newspaper proprietors, and by "New Deal Republicans." The latter, according to the *Tribune*, included both Dulles brothers.[56]

McCarthy was forced to back down in Bundy's case. He failed to obtain compliance to a subpoena requiring the CIA official to testify before his Committee on Government Operations Subcommittee on Investigations. Whereas Bundy stayed with the CIA until 1961 and went on to become an assistant secretary in both the Defense and State departments, Matthews had to resign. This was the beginning of the end for McCarthy. In the context of CIA history, it is pertinent to inquire what, or who, obliged the senator to desist. In the Senate, those whom the *Chicago Tribune* derided as "New Deal Democrats," notably Almer Stillwell and Mike Monroney, labored in the CIA's defense out of disgust with McCarthy, and in the hope of achieving for the Truman administration a kind of vindication by implication. At the same time, more than one journalist noted President Eisenhower's desire to cut McCarthy down to size, now that the demagogue had served his fleeting purpose: the defeat of the Democrats in 1952.[57] Eisenhower sent his vice-president, Richard M. Nixon, to see McCarthy and work out a compromise that was in fact a defeat for the Wisconsin senator: McCarthy's committee was conceded the right to subpoena CIA officials in exchange for a promise that it would not in fact do so.[58]

The Bundy backdown entered the annals of CIA history as a victory for Allen Dulles. Dulles certainly took a stand. The CIA's congressional liaison officer, Walter Pforzheimer, notified McCarthy by telephone that Dulles would not cooperate with his committee. Dulles threatened to fire any CIA employee cooperating with McCarthy. The recently installed director told Eisenhower he would resign unless the president pressured McCarthy to call off his investigation. Dulles identified the CIA in the public mind as the only government agency to have stood up to Joe McCarthy, an achievement which did wonders for morale in "The Company."[59]

Although the CIA fought off Senator McCarthy, it did not remain entirely free of McCarthyism. Instead of taking pride in their vindication, some of those falsely accused took fright and adopted the outlook of the very people who had impeached them. Cord Meyer is an example. On August 31, 1953, with Allen Dulles conveniently abroad, Meyer was suspended from duty on the ground that he was a security risk. A few days later, the young Yale graduate was handed a summary of the series of flimsy smear charges leveled at him in an FBI report: for example, he had signed a statement issued by the National Council Against Conscription, an organization subsequently smeared as a Communist front. To the delight of Allen Dulles, who supported him through his travail, Meyer cleared himself and was reinstated.[60] Yet the smear episode did not recall Cord Meyer to the more tolerant beliefs he had entertained prior to his 1940s skirmish with Soviet propagandists. Instead, it confirmed him in his bitter hostility toward the Soviet Union. In his 1980 memoir he complained that some liberals had gone soft on Communism because McCarthy had made anti-Communism so invidious: "By falsely accusing so many of being Communists who were not, [McCarthy] gave real Communists the protective coloration of injured innocence. . . . McCarthy's legacy lives on in the continuing conviction of many people that any attempt to uncover evidence of Communist spying or political manipulation must be part of an attempt to rekindle the hysteria of the McCarthy era."[61] It is plain that in his own case McCarthyism had the reverse effect: never again did he wish to seem "soft" on Communism or blind to what Dulles in 1954 termed "commie cold war techniques."[62]

Allen Dulles's anti-McCarthy stand failed to convince at least one analyst. George F. Kennan, preeminent among America's Russian experts and a leading architect of Truman's foreign policy, had been one of the Princeton consultants working on a contract basis for Bedell Smith's CIA. His task had been to review the estimates that fell within the range of his considerable knowledge, and Smith, understandably, had been "extremely anxious" to continue with Kennan and to employ him on a more regular basis.[63] Allen Dulles felt the same way. But Kennan's response was influenced by the treatment of his friend John Paton Davies, Jr. Davies was a State Department official who had incurred the wrath of the China lobby in the 1940s by telling the truth, namely that Chiang's position was weak and getting weaker. When it emerged that he had, in November 1949, tried to use the CIA to put out feelers to China's ascendant intellectuals, the McCarthyites hounded him. Though Acheson had to yield to McCarthy in some cases, Davies survived the Democratic administration only to be dismissed by John Foster Dulles on November 5, 1954. Disgusted, Kennan refused to work for the CIA in the new Republican administration.[64]

Yet, according to one school of thought, the Dulles victory against McCarthy at least ensured a change in the character of job applicants. In the 1960s Robert F. Kennedy told his radical-student biographer, Jack Newfield, that

> many of the liberals who were forced out of other departments found a sanctuary, an enclave, in the CIA. So some of the best people in Washington, and around the country, began to collect there. One result of that was the CIA developed a very healthy view of Communism, especially compared to State and some other departments. They were very sympathetic, for example, to nationalist, and even Socialist governments and movements.[65]

Even though Kennedy was knowledgeable about the CIA, his pronouncement needs to be treated with caution. He had worked as counsel for McCarthy, so his inversion of values invites speculation. Having subsequently worked closely with the CIA while he was attorney general in his brother's administration, he probably wished to enhance his prospects on the presidential campaign trail by presenting the CIA and therefore himself in a way that would be less uncongenial to Newfield and the radical/liberal constituency he represented. Certainly, he did not back up his point with a convincing list of "liberals" who joined the CIA in the wake of McCarthy's rebuff.

On the other hand, even if subjectivity and ambition colored Kennedy's judgment, it was not without a grain of truth. The CIA and its front organizations did offer to a lucky few a refuge from McCarthyism. William Welsh, the first president of the National Students' Association, said that his fellow-officers turned to the CIA for help not just because they wanted money, but also because they were under McCarthyite attack and the CIA link offered them a kind of insurance.[66] McCarthy's attack on the overtly run Voice of America may well have encouraged the development of the CIA's clandestine radios beyond the point which might otherwise have seemed reasonable. Tom Braden explained the political advantages of secrecy as they appeared to his CIA colleagues in the Cold War-McCarthy days: "The idea that Congress would have approved many of our projects was about as likely as the John Birch Society's approving Medicare."[67] Roger Hilsman, who as a member of the Kennedy administration tried to cut the CIA down to size, also explained some of the secret subsidies by saying that McCarthyism had driven such financial arrangements under cover: "The State Department should have supplied the money, but Congress wouldn't give it to them."[68] None of this amounts to proof that "liberals," however defined, flocked to the CIA from 1953 on. But McCarthyism does appear to have encouraged the secret subsidization of organizations that might otherwise have been supported openly—and with much less danger of subsequent controversy.

McCarthyism and the CIA's will and ability to resist it therefore bred not so much liberalism as a myth of liberalism within the Agency, a myth that had dangerous consequences. For one thing, it invited debunking in future years. Then again, some CIA officers developed such high expectations concerning the Agency's likely support for democracy, self-determination, and social reform that they were bitterly disillusioned later on; a few of these turned to apostasy, contributing to a serious weakening of the Agency. Most damaging of all, the myth that the CIA was "liberal" in the sense of being "dovish" encouraged people outside the Agency to query its estimates—on the Vietnam War, for example, and on Soviet military strength. Those who queried the CIA's estimates in such ways did so partly on the basis of sound evidence, but mostly through prejudice and ignorance. The final legacy of McCarthyism, though, was that it discredited the notion of congressional oversight and therefore contributed to much ignorance—about matters which were justifiably secret, to be sure, and also about the CIA's misdemeanors—but, above all, it contributed to ignorance about the true nature, significance, and quality of the Agency's intelligence work. Dulles, confident following his success against McCarthy, believed that he should and could resist every attempt at thoroughgoing congressional oversight. That he had every prospect of succeeding became evident during a congressional campaign which began on July 20, 1953, when Senator Mike Mansfield introduced a resolution demanding a joint committee on central intelligence.

Mansfield was a Democratic freshman senator from Montana, a state with a relatively small number of voters and no great wealth. Within Montana, he had been a spokesman for the have-nots, the unionized miners as opposed to the corporations and cattlemen. Lacking wealthy backers and a populous power base, he used the publicity-conferring intelligence issue to make a name for himself. In that respect, he was similar to McCarthy. Mansfield, however, was interested in oversight reform for its own sake and furthermore regarded his move—made in the immediate aftermath of the Bundy affair—as a counter to McCarthy's irresponsible efforts. Affording minor coverage, the United Press reported Mansfield's proposal as "an outgrowth of Sen. Joseph R. McCarthy's threat to have his Permanent Senate Investigating Subcommittee investigate the CIA."[69] But President Eisenhower lumped the proposals together, telling a friend in Congress that "he was damned if he was going to let McCarthy have any other area wherein he might get a foothold" and that Mansfield's measure "would be passed over his dead body."[70]

Frustrated in 1953, Mansfield reintroduced his resolution in March 1954. Senate Armed Services Committee chairman Leverett Saltonstall opposed him, arguing that two subcommittees in each house, one each from the respective Armed Service and Appropriations committees, already devoted part of their attention to the CIA. Hanson Baldwin, the journalist who had been an early supporter of and consultant on the CIA, now came to Mansfield's aid. He claimed that the Agency's intelligence efficiency and cost efficiency should be scrutinized, and that a proper oversight committee would safeguard the CIA "against irresponsible attack." Mansfield presented a similar argument, saying the scrutiny he proposed was essential "to the security of the Intelligence Agency itself."[71] Dulles disagreed. In an angry letter to journalist Walter Lippmann, who had argued that "secrecy is not a criterion for immunity," he claimed that previous congressional investigations had already destroyed CIA operations.[72] Mansfield's 1954 attempt at oversight foundered in the Senate Rules Committee. Baldwin now tried to stir things up by publishing his claim—often repeated thereafter—that the CIA was spending one billion dollars annually. Dulles replied with furious denials, though he did not feel constrained to offer specific figures.[73] Dulles won the day: privately, Baldwin had to acknowledge that McCarthyism was discrediting the Mansfield proposal.[74]

In November 1954, Dulles demonstrated his confidence about appropriations in making a successful request for a new headquarters building which would be sufficiently central to make the director "immediately available to the President and the National Security Council."[75] He may have felt further encouraged when, in December, the Senate voted to censure McCarthy. This certainly removed one menace. Of course, it removed also a major constraint on "responsible" congressional reformers. The following year, 1955, was to be the peak one for congressional oversight proposals, with the figures for the decade being: 1950–52 (0); 1953 (5); 1955 (28); 1956 (2); 1957 (17); 1958 (7); 1959 (18); and 1960 (4).[76]

Mansfield was once again behind the main proposal, which had thirty-five cosponsors in the Senate in January 1955. McCarthy's disgrace was not the only encouraging factor. The Hoover Commission, which was once again investigating the intelligence community, had lent its weight to the Mansfield campaign by recommending a joint congressional oversight committee. Mansfield and his emulators in the Senate could also hope to profit from a thaw—temporary, it transpired—in the Cold War. A Soviet-American summit meeting was under discussion; the "spirit of Geneva" culminated in a July 1955 meeting in the Swiss city between Eisenhower and the Soviet leadership.[77] The relaxation in tension and therefore of the patriotic imperative may well have encouraged criticism of the national-security establishment.

Dulles's defeat of the 1955 proposals was a tribute to his tact as well as to his firmness. In November, for example, he made a statement whose deferential tone set a precedent for future directors faced with similar challenges: "As regards the idea of a Congressional Committee for CIA, I have always taken the position that this was primarily for Congress to decide."[78] On February 6, 1956, Eisenhower assisted Dulles by setting up the President's Board of Consultants on Intelligence Activities. Its chairman was James R. Killian, president of MIT, who was already in charge of a Surprise Attack Panel set up by Eisenhower in 1954. Among the board's members were Admiral Souers (an insurance against partisan attack) and Henry M. Wriston, president of Brown University and an authority on executive-congressional friction over the use of secret agents.[79] The appointment of the invigilatory board helped defuse the campaign for congressional oversight, but Dulles still suffered setbacks in Congress. On February 23, 1956, the Senate Rules Committee voted eight-to-one in favor of the latest Mansfield proposal. But a coalition of senators, including Stuart Symington—former Air Force Secretary and future CIA scourge—supported Dulles. Then, in the course of the debate, the sponsors of the bill found themselves embarrassed by the support of McCarthyists. Mansfield lost this battle by twenty-seven votes to fifty-nine.[80]

Meanwhile, Dulles supporters in Congress were busily outflanking the reformers. The CIA-supportive Armed Services and Appropriations committees in both the House and the Senate established specific intelligence-oversight committees in the 1956–57 session. These met irregularly and had meager staffing. To Dulles they were commendably discreet, but to an authoritative critic they were "oversight windowdressing," successful attempts to divert attention from more serious reform.[81] McCarthy's death in 1957 from a final excess, alcohol, removed an impediment to oversight rather than a potential scourge. In the same year, however, Mansfield became assistant majority leader and Democratic whip in the Senate, so he no longer needed to make his mark by making trouble. His 1958 oversight proposal never reached a vote, and it was his last attempt at reform. At the cornerstone-laying ceremony for the new CIA headquarters in Langley, Virginia, in November 1959, both the CIA and its director were at the height of their powers, apparently triumphant in the field of appropriations and unchallengeable through the democratic process.

It should not be assumed too readily that the defeat of Devitt-Mansfield-style oversight proposals was an unqualified tragedy for the proper conduct of U.S. intelligence activities. It is true that Dulles and his friends were obsessive about secrecy and disposed to cover up evidence of incompetence or wrongdoing by the CIA on the pretext of protecting national security. Yet the CIA did need to guard certain secrets, and it is possible that extended oversight, especially by critical and partisan senators, would have produced leaks. That, certainly, was what happened in the 1970s. Furthermore, it is unclear why Mansfield and his colleagues wished to scrutinize only certain CIA activities, or indeed which activities those were. As one former CIA director pointed out in 1981, some senators who were later to round on the CIA's covert operations had themselves sanctioned them in the Cold War years.[82] After all, one of the Mansfield group's arguments had been that oversight would help establish the CIA's respectability. They offered no new or additional guidelines for the CIA's covert operations or intelligence or counterintelligence. They were advocating democracy to no purpose.

Even so, on balance the CIA's immunity from critical-yet-responsible congressional oversight was unfortunate. The single joint committee Mansfield proposed would have been preferable to a McCarthy investigation, and it might well have forestalled the leak-prone committee proliferation of the 1970s. Such congressional oversight might also have enhanced the element of continuity in U.S. clandestine policy. Opinions vary on the desirability of continuity, some fearing bureaucratic atrophy and others seeing it as an essential element in intelligence success.[83] Yet senators—usually serving longer terms than presidents or CIA directors—might have contributed an awareness of the lessons of history without necessarily condoning organizational calcification. In time, rigorous oversight might additionally have eliminated some abuses of the type that were not only regrettable in themselves but also potentially harmful to the CIA, even if it is true that Mansfield had no immediate guidelines in mind. Finally, the absence of a credible probing mechanism encouraged suspicion and meant that members of Congress and their constituents were in danger of being blinded not just to shortcomings and mistakes, but also to the intelligence achievements of the CIA, and particularly to the Agency's objectivity.

5

THE GOLDEN AGE OF OPERATIONS

On February 28, 1975, veteran CBS journalist Daniel Schorr filed another story: "President Ford has reportedly warned associates that if current investigations go too far they could uncover several assassinations of foreign officials in which the CIA was involved. The President reportedly indicated that this would embarrass the government and damage relations with at least one foreign country." CIA director William Colby had recently briefed Gerald Ford on assassinations, and, Schorr said, the president had been "reportedly shocked." The commentator concluded on a note that combined sepulchral humor with ominous prescience: "Colby is on the record as saying, 'I think that family skeletons are best left where they are, in the closet.' He apparently had some literal skeletons in mind."[1]

President Ford failed to stop the major investigations under way in the press and Congress, with the result that Americans and foreigners alike feasted on stories about CIA covert operations. One of these concerned, for example, the activities of the Agency's "Health Alteration Committee": it emerged that, in 1952, the CIA had made an arrangement with the army's biological laboratory at Ford Detrick, Maryland, for the storage of biological agents and lethal toxins. By 1970, when President Nixon ordered the destruction of the materials, the laboratory had stored botulus, shellfish, and snake poisons, as well as ingredients for generating anthrax, valley fever, brucellosis, salmonella, and smallpox. The 1975 investigations thus produced some of the most dramatic and suggestive revelations about the CIA's covert operations, yet they were just part of a long series of exposés to which the Agency has been subjected in America's open society.[2]

Covert operations and stories about them caused serious embarrassment to the United States over the years, as well as damage to the CIA's effectiveness in some important ways. The Agency had been allocated a role in the battle for men's minds; yet, as the historian Henry Commager put it, CIA activities resulted in the "alienation of much of world opinion." Many experienced commentators agreed with his verdict.[3] The diplomatic repercussions of covert operations alarmed those responsible for competing with the Soviet Union for the affection, trust, and loyalty of other nations. Roger Hilsman, who in the Kennedy administration was director of the State Department's Bureau of Intelligence and Research and assistant secretary of state for Far Eastern Affairs, believed "covert action" had been "overused as an instrument of policy, and the reputation of the U.S. suffered more and more. Too heavy reliance on the techniques of secret intelligence, in sum, so corroded one of our major political assets, the belief in American intentions and integrity, as to nullify much of the gain."[4]

The CIA's covert operations undermined confidence in the Agency within the United States, and therefore impaired its effectiveness. In alienating foreign opinion and trust when they were supposed to be achieving the opposite, the Agency's officials looked foolish and incompetent. The CIA's leadership also seemed to be preoccupied with operations at the expense of intelligence. The quality of the Agency's intelligence performance came to be doubted for this reason, among others. Still another deleterious consequence of foreign covert operations was that they came to be regarded as having a symbiotic relationship with the CIA's domestic infractions: people feared the Agency might import foreign methods to the United States. Finally, an influential minority of Americans—by no means all of them impractical idealists—voiced moral objections to some of the things the Agency was doing. The criticism that arose because of these various doubts impaired the CIA's morale and cohesion. More seriously, it so damaged its prestige that the Agency's standing as an important contributor to foreign-policy deliberations slipped. The voice of neutral intelligence became a muted one. This was a high price to pay for the inclusion of a covert-operational capability in America's premier foreign-intelligence organization.

Yet, the foregoing problems became acute only in response to the changing perceptions and attitudes of the 1960s and 1970s. In the 1950s, or to be more precise between the inauguration of President Eisenhower on January 20, 1953, and the Bay of Pigs fiasco on April 17, 1961, the CIA's covert operators enjoyed their golden age. It was a period of continuing expansion and of operational good fortune, as well as a time when most Americans and a great number of their friends abroad looked favorably on adventures whose details may have been secret but whose general nature and purpose were widely appreciated. Indeed, there is some ground for saying that the CIA's operations in the 1950s had the reverse effect of its operations in later decades: they contributed to the standing and prestige of the

Agency. In later years, the CIA's covert action activities may have seemed over-developed, ill-conceived, the product of hysteria, and out of control, as indeed they occasionally were. To Senator Walter F. Mondale, the Agency's senior critic in the 1970s and 1980s, the Agency had "a record which is completely beyond under-standing."⁵ But there was widespread approval of the Agency's activities in the 1950s, and this approval helps explain its embarkation on some of the coun-terproductive projects which later critics found so difficult to explain.

The CIA's recourse to dangerous schemes seemed perfectly sensible in the 1950s. Their long-term effects had not been predicted and were to some extent unforeseeable. At the time, they seemed suffused with a justifying rationality. The reasoning of the 1940s continued in force. For example, while National Security Council directive 5412/1 (March 12, 1955) differed from the earlier NSC 10/2 in using more ponderous and less academic language, it still defined "covert opera-tions" in the same way as "all activities . . . so planned and executed that any U.S. Government responsibility for them is not evident to unauthorized persons and that if uncovered the U.S. Government can plausibly disclaim any responsibility for them." This directive also listed the covert operations the CIA was expected to undertake as:

> Propaganda, political action; economic warfare; escape and evasion and evacua-tion measures; subversion against hostile states or groups including assistance to underground movements, guerillas and refugee liberation groups; support of indige-nous and anti-communist elements in threatened countries of the free world; decep-tion plans and operations; and all activities compatible with this directive necessary to accomplish the foregoing.⁶

Members of the Eisenhower administration therefore accepted the earlier concep-tualization. At the same time, they tried to develop the reasoning behind covert operations. Psychological warfare, or "psywar," attained the status of a scientific doctrine. Similarly, a doctrine was invented for counter-insurgency. These covert doctrines were consistent with the "New Look" in defense thinking as explained by Secretary of State John Foster Dulles in January 1954, and in speeches by other senior officials. Eisenhower rejected the massive military expenditures required in NSC 68, expenditures which he believed would ruin the U.S. economy. Using his authority as a successful general, he limited the size of conventional forces. In-stead, he built up nuclear air strike capability—and the covert operational arm of the CIA. It seemed rational to adopt clandestine methods, which by comparison with conventional war were relatively humane as well as inexpensive. These methods seemed the natural complement to "massive retaliation."

With the benefit of hindsight, it is possible to see that at least two ingredients were absent from the generally hard-headed reasoning behind the 1950s opera-tions. One was the provision of that military professionalism necessary to the operational success of some of the CIA's larger enterprises. The other was a set of guidelines to ensure that existing wisdom was applied, and to impose restraints on operators who might succeed in the short-term, narrow sense, but whose work would undermine the U.S. interest, security, and morality in the longer term. In retrospect, for example, it is clear that the expedient of assassination was unacceptable to the American people for reasons both moral and political. Such unacceptable practices were adopted in the 1950s from ignorance of the likely future reaction in the wake of disclosures. Had there been closer congressional supervision, certain mistakes might have been avoided, and the CIA might have had a clearer idea of the restraints necessary to its long-term good name and success. However, the difficulty was that even in an open society like the United States, there could not be candid, public, and prior discussion of the methods of a secret foreign-intelligence agency like the CIA: in such matters, time would be the stern instructor.

The excessive nature of some of the golden age's covert operations stemmed in large part from overenthusiasm and overconfidence. One source of overenthusiasm appears to have been the continuing "voluntarist" element in or associated with the CIA. The Agency had interested itself in groups like the airlines and student and labor organizations at least partly in order to restrain their activities, but this was not always easy. Though it would have been administratively sensible to anticipate the 1976 merger between Radio Free Europe and Radio Liberty, for example, Smith and Dulles kept them separate because they were easier to control that way. In spite of the fact that the radios were wholly subsidized by the CIA, Dulles and Wisner were "apprehensive" about their "strength and independence," since they seemed to their admirers to be taking the battle to the enemy in a way in which the pusillanimous Voice of America did not. In the McCarthyite years, who would dare strike at Radio Free Europe, which had set itself up as the local radio for "Warsaw and Lodz, Prague and Brno, Budapest and Bucharest, Sofia and Plovdiv," with a view to being "a surrogate free press for the captive peoples"?[7] A few of the Agency's fronts and occasionally its components, too, retained or became suffused with the buccaneering spirit of the very element it had set out to control. Compartmentalization within the Agency—designed to limit the damage if enemy intelligence penetrated one section—made it difficult to assess, or fully control, the activities of every enthusiast within the Agency. The adventurous element, sometimes labeled the "Cowboys," played a discernible role in the history of the CIA.

More damaging to the long-term prospects of the CIA's undercover operations was the unrestrained application of concepts which, though valid in themselves, were only practical in the right circumstances. The doctrine of psychological warfare was one of these concepts. In the later stages of the Truman administration, there had been growing uncertainty about psychological warfare. Bureaucratic experimentation was a symptom of this, one result of which was Truman's secret directive establishing the Psychological Strategy Board, a National Security Council subcommittee consisting of Undersecretary of State James Webb, Deputy

Secretary of Defense Robert Lovett, and the CIA's "Beetle" Smith. According to its historian, Edward P. Lilly, the board's purpose was to plan the use of the information media in coordination with the actual or threatened use of military, diplomatic, or economic force, to influence the attitudes and actions of "enemy, neutral, and allied people."[8] But the board did not last long, and not only because of the bureaucratic jealousy it inevitably inspired: in February 1952, former Hoover Commission member George E. Taylor told the board's director "there is no such thing as psychological warfare in intelligence or research as distinct from intelligence and research necessary for the formulation of national policy particularly in its political aspects."[9] The board had ceased to be active by the end of 1952, and on September 2, 1953, held its last meeting.[10] Thus the Truman administration wavered at least in its bureaucratic resolve. The Eisenhower administration, in contrast, pressed on boldly with psychological warfare.

In their enthusiasm, Eisenhower's officials sometimes forgot one of the fundamental principles of covert operations, a principle explained in identical phrases in NSC 10/2 and 5412/1, "support of *indigenous* and anti-communist elements in threatened countries of the free world."[11] Henry Kissinger spelled out the indigeneity requirement for the benefit of the Psychological Strategy Board in July 1952. Kissinger was at the time a teaching fellow at Harvard and had already impressed the board with a report about Japan.[12] He now described Germany as "the keystone of American efforts in Europe." The Germans were virulently anti-American and might even turn to Russia for aid in asserting their independence, which would be a manifestation of "reverse Titoism." American anti-Communist propaganda was crude, "all too reminiscent of the propaganda of Goebbels." The Voice of America and U.S.-sponsored publications like *Die Neue Zeitung* were no substitute for indigenous advocacy. A more careful assessment of the "psychological climate" suggested a less legalistic and more "unofficial" approach: "study groups, cultural congresses, exchange professorships and intern programs, wherever possible under non-governmental auspices." There should be an appeal to youth "through a number of young Americans strategically placed in key universities."[13] So, according to Kissinger, the United States should build on indigenous forces in the countries where there was cause for concern, using clandestine methods for fear of provoking a nationalist reaction against American assistance. His analysis may be faulted on the ground that clandestine assistance, when exposed, confers instant unpopularity on donor and recipient alike. But the cultivation of foreign nationalisms which he recommended might well have succeeded to a greater extent, had it been pursued with the circumspection and subtlety which he urged.

President Eisenhower himself was the nation's prime enthusiast for psywar tactics. As we have seen, covert operations were a part of his New Look strategy and consistent with his desire to avoid bloody and expensive conventional warfare. But he did not support psywar merely by default: he was on the contrary a convinced supporter of the idea on practical, political, and moral grounds. On the practical level, he was convinced of psywar's efficacy in the past. He had backed psychological tactics in World War II. Then, as Army Chief of Staff in 1947, he called for the preparation of a list of potential Italian covert action agents to be drawn up and handed to the CIA.[14] On the political level, he recognized psywar's utility in the face of McCarthyite criticism: his administration's apparent impotence in the face of Communist advances could be explained away on the ground that unspecifiable clandestine operations were afoot. The CIA, Eisenhower told McCarthy's supporter Senator William Knowland, was achieving great things which he could not reveal; in fact, he "knew so many things [he was] almost afraid to speak to [his] wife."[15] A final factor confirming the president's faith in "dirty tricks" was his conviction that the other side was using them, making adherence to old-fashioned morality impossible:

> Truth, honor, justice, consideration for others, liberty for all—the problem is how to preserve them, nurture them and keep the peace—if this last is possible—when we are opposed by people who scorn . . . these values. I believe we can do it, but *we must not confuse these values with mere procedures, even though these last may have at one time held almost the status of moral concepts.*[16]

The election of a president with such views was one boost to the psychological warfare component of covert operations. Another was Eisenhower's selection of an administrative assistant for psychological warfare activities. This was Charles Douglas ("C. D.") Jackson, a 51-year old who had excellent qualifications for his job. Before entering Princeton, he had been educated in Switzerland, and he spoke French and Italian fluently. He was further equipped for cultural propaganda by virtue of his musical interests, lifelong association with *Time, Life,* and *Fortune* magazines, World War II propaganda activities, and service as Radio Free Europe president, 1951–52. His marriage into the Astor family and extreme hostility to Communism made him acceptable in conservative circles, though he was reputed to have "liberal" credentials. Jackson felt that America's image abroad was of crucial importance to U.S. foreign policy, and that every act and statement by the U.S. government had a psychological impact in this regard. For example, tariff alterations would affect world opinion—as could an inspirational pronouncement like Eisenhower's "Atoms for Peace" address to the U.N. General Assembly, a speech which "C. D." helped draft. With the same goal in mind, Jackson persuaded Eisenhower to set up an inquiry into psychological warfare. Eisenhower made him responsible for it in January 1953; by May, Ike was listing Jackson as one of his administration's best prospects, a man of possible presidential caliber.[17]

It is true that not every omen favored the CIA's psychological operations in the early Eisenhower years. The Asian writer L. Natarajan had already devoted two whole chapters in his *American Shadow Over India* (1952) to the denigration of U.S. intelligence activities: "Intelligence and propaganda are the left and right hands of American diplomacy."[18] The extreme left-wing tone of his book—it attacked the British Labour party and merited a Moscow edition in 1953—at least partly undermined its appeal. Much more effective and widely read, however, was British novelist Graham Greene's *The Quiet American* (1955), written from the perspective of a worldwise English journalist who encountered Pyle, the CIA's man in French Indochina. Greene had met the prototype four years earlier during a visit to Saigon: he "had never before come so close to the great American dream which was to bedevil affairs in the East."[19] His fictional journalist liked Pyle, in spite of the fact that he stole his mistress and cleaved with Ivy-Leaguish confidence to half-baked ideas. Still, the book was a devastating attack on the CIA, whose sense of morality Greene depicted as being incomprehensible to Vietnamese Catholics.[20]

Yet in spite of these early warning signals, the CIA's covert anti-anti-Americanism campaign seemed to be going well. The Agency managed to protect for the time being its own cover and its front organizations' appearance of indigeneity. The Paris-based Congress for Cultural Freedom, for example, received its funds from the CIA, and in 1953 it began to sponsor a whole family of publications—but the fiction remained that *Encounter* was British, *Preuves* French, *Tempo Presente* Italian, *Forum* Austrian, *Hiwar* Lebanese, *Cuadenos* Latin American, and *Chinese Quarterly* Chinese.[21] In any case, it is not entirely clear that knowledge of the source of subsidy would have provoked any great scandal in the 1950s. Even in the more critical 1960s, when there was a fuss in the United States about the Congress for Cultural Freedom's finances, the English journalist Malcolm Muggeridge alleged the disclosures caused "scarcely a ripple" in Europe.[22] In the 1950s, the United States was supremely powerful militarily and economically, and it inspired awe for that reason. It was also still relatively new to the world stage and had yet to incur the chronic unpopularity that sooner or later attaches to every great power. Because of America's prestige, U.S. policymakers did not operate in a hostile environment. It seemed natural to suppose that the CIA's clandestine methods—as well as open policies like Marshall Aid, educational exchanges, and information programs—had helped create this favorable atmosphere. The idea seemed all the more plausible because the Agency was reputedly "liberal" and therefore well equipped to deal with twentieth-century European anti-Americanism which, in contrast to nineteenth-century anti-Americanism, seemed predominantly left-wing in character.[23] All in all, the omens for psywar's success were sufficiently propitious to encourage confidence in its overall efficacy.

Early successes in other covert-operational spheres compounded this confidence. Of particular significance here was the "counterinsurgency doctrine" that U.S. officials developed. The doctrine, a set of tactical principles, was a method of combatting left-wing insurgency and of stopping the spread of Communism by the surreptitious means which the Kremlin as well as the White House increasingly favored as the high costs of nuclear or conventional war became ever more glaringly apparent. Theodore Shackley, a senior covert-operations specialist who spent twenty-eight years with the CIA, described counterinsurgency as "the third option," the alternative to diplomacy (often ineffective) and war (too dangerous).[24]

The counterinsurgency doctrine developed and gained official acceptance in the United States because of events in the Philippines. In April 1948, the CIA had prepared a "special evaluation" on the islands following President Manuel Roxas's fatal heart attack. Roxas had been acceptable to the United States because of his opposition to the Hukbalahap. The "Huks" were nationalist guerilla fighters. At the turn of the century, they had terrified occupying U.S. soldiers with their ferocity: prior to an attack, they would screw up their testicles until, bestialized by the resultant pain, they would fling themselves in ritualistic fury upon their American oppressors. In World War II, the Huks once again formed guerilla groups, this time to harry Japanese occupying forces. By 1948, according to the CIA report, they were "left-wing" and threatened the shaky administration of Elpidio Quirino, the new president who, though lukewarm toward the United States, was considered a lesser evil worth supporting.[25] The CIA's assessment of Huk strength proved to be accurate: by 1950, the Huks were in virtual control of the main island of Luzon, and American policymakers feared a threat to their strategic installations there, at the very time when they needed them for Korean operations.

In September 1950, Lieutenant Colonel (later Major General) Edward G. Lansdale returned to the Philippines. He had previously served there in World War II, for the OSS and for military intelligence. Before that he had been with a San Francisco advertising agency, and Lansdale never lost the taste for publicity and indeed the gift of persuasion. In evolving his counterinsurgency philosophy he exhibited naive idealism on the one hand, shrewd foresight and insight on the other. Fond of referring to Franklin, Paine, and Lincoln, he said he took his "American beliefs" into "those Asian struggles." He took a dewy-eyed view of Filipino-American relations, seeing no cause for resentment in the U.S. suppression of the "so-called Philippine Insurrection" (1899–1902) and subsequent domination of the islands. But he was otherwise perceptive, realizing earlier than most that the conventional Korean war was an anomaly, that left-wing insurgency was the problem of the future, and that the answer would have to lie in popular government in the areas affected.[26]

On his 1950–53 tour of duty Lansdale—ostensibly an air force officer but in reality funded and directed by the CIA—befriended and supported the popular leader most likely to succeed.[27] By 1953 Ramon Magsaysay had defeated Quirino at the polls, and by 1954 he had driven the Huks into the Sierra Madre, a range of mountains away from the densely settled areas of Luzon. Analyzing this achievement, CIA counterinsurgency expert Douglas S. Blaufarb drew attention to a number of points. Among them were the indigenous nature of the anti-Huk campaign, the preservation of morale-boosting democratic processes in the Philippines during the operation, the advisory rather than participatory role of the

Lansdale team, the dependence on light infantry units rather than on heavy engagements, and psychological warfare (rumor campaigns, exploitation of local supersititions, et cetera). William Bundy (the CIA official who survived McCarthy's wrath) described Blaufarb as a "mainstream 1930s-vintage liberal."[28] This, perhaps, accounts for Blaufarb's emphasis on another aspect of the anti-Huk campaign, reform. For example, the U.S. Army's contribution to the "psychological" war was the construction of four thousand prefabricated schoolhouses in the Philippines.[29] Such reforms were no doubt popular locally and went hand in hand with the emphasis that Lansdale and Blaufarb—like Kissinger—placed on indigenous feeling and on the cultivation of local nationalism. The Lansdale-Blaufarb-Kissinger outlook was characteristic of, and therefore credible in, the citizens and envoys of a highly literate and democratic country which had fought its own war of independence.

But could the opinion-manipulators from the CIA manufacture nationalism in the American image at will, in countries around the world where the prospects might be less than promising? Such a rash supposition would probably never have been made, even in the sanguine 1950s, but for two influential episodes, both of them political coups in Third World countries.

In August 1953, riots and fighting between soldiers on the streets of Tehran ended the Iranian government headed by Prime Minister Mohammed Mosaddeq. The imperial government of the shah—Mohammed Reza Shah Pahlavi—took the place of Dr. Mosaddeq's administration. It is possible to interpret this event as having been in the interests of the United States in a number of ways. Dr. Mosaddeq had been one of the first nationalist leaders to threaten the wholesale nationalization of "colonialist" oil installations. The coup not only prevented this, but also gave Gulf, Standard of New Jersey, Texaco, and Socony-Mobil a 40 percent share of Iranian oil rights.[30] This benefited the individual American corporations, but also, depending on the historian's particular perspective, served any one or combination of the following national goals: it protected the flow of oil to the American economy in general; furthered an oil-for-coal fuel substitution that undermined the power of Communist-led West European miners' unions; broke the British oil monopoly in Iran; destroyed the potential menace of an oil-enhanced power bloc based on the Moslem faith and extending from the Atlantic to the Pacific Ocean; diminished the Moslem threat to the fledgling state of Israel; and ended the danger of Soviet encroachment on the oil-rich gulf and the Indian Ocean.[31]

According to CIA mythology, a team of just five Agency officers, equipped with a one-million-dollar slush fund in five-hundred-rial ($7.50) notes, organized the coup from a Tehran basement.[32] Kermit ("Kim") Roosevelt oversaw the operation, which included the hiring of weightlifters as muscle-men and the organization of paid street mobs. Kim was a grandson of President Theodore Roosevelt, as well as FDR's cousin and an OSS veteran. His team's designation as "Cowboys" would have tickled his grandfather, the keen dude rancher who shot to prominence in the 1898 Cuban war by leading the "Rough Riders" in their famous charge up San Juan hill.

The CIA's Iranian escapade throws light on the attitudes of Presidents Truman and Eisenhower, respectively, toward peacetime covert operations involving the use of force. In 1951, the Truman administration had told the British government it would not tolerate the use of overt military force except in an extreme circumstance such as Soviet military intervention.[33] According to Kim Roosevelt, the Democrats ruled out covertly-exercised force also. Roosevelt had to wait for the new Republican administration before taking action in Iran, for President Truman would never have approved of the plan, and Bedell Smith distanced himself from it. Immediately after Eisenhower's inauguration, however, Smith's deputy Dulles set the wheels in motion.[34]

Kim Roosevelt took for himself and for the CIA full credit for the coup, epitomizing the "promotional" style that came to be associated with the Agency's covert operators. A trained historian, Roosevelt had already supervised production of the OSS's war report. In 1979, insensitive to the current U.S.-Iranian crisis, he was to publish his book on the 1953 coup, contributing at the nadir of the CIA's fortunes to the image of the 1950s as an intelligence "golden age."[35] Not that he waited that long to bruit the story of the Agency's prowess: on his way home from Tehran, he stopped off in London to tell his story to the ailing British prime minister, Winston Churchill.

Churchill professed deep admiration; nevertheless, the CIA's impact should not be too hastily assessed. Iranian politics at the time were inherently unstable and riven by passionate enmities of diverse types, so it cannot be taken for granted that Mosaddeq would have survived but for the CIA's intervention. Moreover, the CIA was not the only foreign institution with a vested interest in Mosaddeq's overthrow. The Anglo-Iranian Oil Company (later British Petroleum) is suspected of complicity in some quarters.[36] The CIA's Middle East veteran Wilbur C. Eveland has also noted the British secret intelligence service's claim "that Roosevelt really did little more than show up in Iran with CIA funds to encourage agents the British had organized and then released to American control." Be that as it may, the coup became, in Eveland's words, "the most publicly flaunted CIA 'secret' accomplishment."[37] The CIA's Cowboys were able to chalk up "Iran, 1953" as a victory comparable with "Italy, 1948" and "Philippines, 1950–54."

The case of "Guatemala, 1954" was similarly presented as a victory for the Cowboys. To the accompaniment of remarkably little bloodshed, the CIA engineered the downfall of the democratically elected leftward-leaning president Jacobo Arbenz Guzman, and his replacement by Colonel Carlos Castillo Armas, soon a notorious dictator. "Voice of Liberation" broadcasts purporting to emanate from rebel transmitters within Guatemala actually came from powerful external CIA stations; they accused Arbenz of ineptness and alleged that the prime minister had Communist sympathies. According to CIA Latin American specialist David

Atlee Phillips, the State Department's protest in May 1954 that a Czech arms shipment was on its way to Puerto Barrios was just a psychological warfare ploy.[38] In June 1954, the CIA employed what Phillips called the "final big lie," the dissemination of an apocryphal story about a strong overland invading force of rebels. By this time, "rebel" pilots—some of them on loan from the CIA's secret airline Civil Air Transport—were flying real missions against Guatemala. President Eisenhower personally authorized a vital additional airstrike, in spite of the danger of blowing the CIA's cover. Arbenz resigned on June 27, and sought refuge in the Mexican embassy.[39]

Various reasons might be advanced for the CIA's removal of a democratically elected Latin American leader. The involvement in the operation of E. Howard Hunt, one of the Agency's "mavericks," might suggest a certain amount of unauthorized initiative. President Eisenhower and Secretary of State John Foster Dulles, however, approved of "Guatemala, 1954" just as they had of "Iran, 1953." Instead, the operation might be represented as an instance of "blind" anti-Communism. The historian Richard Immerman suggests Arbenz was dubbed a Communist because he failed the metaphorical "duck test," defined by Admiral Souers as follows: "If he quacks like a duck and waddles like a duck, you just assume he's a duck."[40]

But the duck test alone does not explain U.S. reaction to Arbenz. U.S. intervention in 1954 came largely because a specific American interest was threatened: the United Fruit Company, dubbed "El Pulpo" (the Octopus) in Latin American rhetoric. United Fruit was well entrenched in the Guatemalan economy and feared the effects on its profits of the social experimentation going on in that country. Beginning in 1950, it retained some gifted lobbyists and publicists whose brief was to convince the U.S. government and people that Guatemala was edging toward Communism. Tom Corcoran, the former New Dealer who had helped persuade the CIA to take over Civil Air Transport, recruited "liberal" support; others played the Right. After the successful coup, Corcoran secured the appointment of his friend "Beetle" Smith to United Fruit's board of directors; nor was it disadvantageous to the firm that it still retained the services of the Dulles brothers' law partnership.[41]

The Guatemalan operation might be portrayed as having had more constructive causes, or at least consequences. It helped to protect U.S. hegemony over the approaches to the strategically important Panama Canal. On a wider plane, it postponed the day when there might be a challenge to U.S. hemispheric control. According to Phillips, Eisenhower believed the CIA had "averted a Soviet beachhead in our hemisphere."[42] Such speculation must be kept in perspective, for, above all, the operation is significant for what it was not. Far from being a subtle encouragement to indigenous forces, it was a crude and none-to-clandestine blow against local nationalism and democracy. The future revolutionary Che Guevara narrowly escaped with his life in the final hours of the Arbenz regime: he, like Cuba's Fidel Castro and like many others throughout Latin America, took careful note of U.S. priorities in 1954. Yet at the time the overthrow of Arbenz merely reinforced the illusion, within U.S. government circles, that the CIA could work wonders.

Eisenhower and his advisers were nevertheless aware that their luck could change, and that damage might stem from any serious exposures about the CIA's covert activities. They therefore took steps designed to minimize the extent of such damage, should the occasion arise. In considering what measures to take, however, they failed to entertain the notion of restraint in the operations themselves. Instead, they opted for, and placed excessive faith in, bureaucratic tinkering. In the process, they endorsed a self-contradictory and fallacious corollary to *plausible deniability*, that of *circuit breaking*.

In March 1953, Eisenhower started his quest for improved bureaucratic procedures by creating the post of Special Assistant to the President for National Security Affairs. The first such assistant, Robert Cutler, organized an administrative shake-up. An early outcome of this was the Operations Coordinating Board (OCB), designed to succeed the Psychological Strategy Board as the guidance body on covert operations. The OCB proved useful as a means of backing requests for money for unforeseen expenses, though it still left important decisions to a limited group identical to the former NSC 10/2 panel.[43] Then, in March 1955, NSC 5412/1 established the 5412 Committee or Special Group, with the stated task of authorizing covert operations. Membership of the committe varied on an ad hoc basis depending on the nature of the task in hand, but its core was little different from previous committees: the secretaries of defense and state or their representatives, the director of the CIA, and the president's representative as chairman. One senior Agency official described the covert operational procedure as follows: the special group chairman would take to the president a plan already approved by Allen Dulles and by State, then hand the decisions down.[44]

The new procedure had an impact on policymaking and on perceptions of the CIA in at least one sense: it projected into the intelligence world some powerful new personalities. Gordon Gray, the special group's first chairman, was already a weighty figure. A broadcasting executive, he had served Truman as secretary of the army, as first director of the Psychological Strategy Board, and as Atomic Energy Commission chairman (he launched the hydrogen bomb program and presided over the controversial hearing which led to the withdrawal of security clearance from Robert J. Oppenheimer, the father of the U.S. atom bomb). Gray went on to become special assistant to the president for national security affairs between 1958 and 1961, creating for that post its modern and controversial importance in foreign affairs. Another figure involved in the new procedure was Nelson D. Rockefeller, chairman of the operations coordinating board at the time when the special group was set up. Robert Murphy, who as Eisenhower's undersecretary of state generally had the duty of giving his department's approval or disapproval to proposed covert operations, headed another 1970s inquiry into the CIA. Such circumstances suggest that the special group may have made up in human terms what it lacked in novelty: the identity of its founders was important at least in the sense that it helped convince some latter-day critics that there existed a conspiracy of silence regarding the CIA.

Behind the special group reform lay some expectations of crisper initiative, better control, and stricter authorization procedure. Had the group laid down a good set of operational criteria and guidelines, it would indeed have performed a valuable function—but this would have required a consistent effort. In practice, the group's revolving membership met irregularly, to assess the "feasibility" of specific projects rather than to discuss the desirability of types of project. Further-more, in the words of an official historian, the group failed to establish "clearly de-fined criteria" even as to which projects should or should not come before it.[45] The CIA itself complained in the 1960s that the criteria were "somewhat cloudy."[46]

Eisenhower's fundamental expectation of the special group was that it should strengthen "plausible deniability." According to Gray, the group's main purpose was "to protect the President" by ensuring that the CIA did not act in such a way as to embarrass the nation or its chief executive.[47] But a distinction might here be made between the two: while there was a need to protect the nation against foreign opprobrium which might follow future debacles and exposures, there was also a need to protect the president against congressional attack in the light of the Mansfield campaign. According to testimony by former CIA director Richard Helms given in the 1970s, the special group "was the mechanism . . . set up . . . to use as a circuit-breaker so that [covert operations] did not explode in the Presi-dent's face and so that he was not held responsible for them."[48]

The fallacy here was that the special group could at the same time be a secret committee and a publicly displayed "circuit breaker" in times of trouble. Over the years, the group was to be disinterred and reburied in a series of farcical attempts to deceive public opinion: for example, it was renamed the 303 Committee and the 40 Committee under Presidents Johnson and Nixon, respectively, after its exis-tence had been "exposed." Experience was to show that the special group's existence protected neither president nor nation, and certainly not the CIA. The Bay of Pigs debacle and Watergate showed that the president could not evade the consequences of his actions through such a device. As to the reputation of the United States, foreign opinion made no distinction between the president and an executive committee because the distinction was irrelevant to the citizens of nations affected by what the CIA did. As it turned out, a more satisfying method of vindicating president and nation was to blame the CIA when things went wrong. As one Agency veteran put it, "it is part of the CIA director's job to be the fall guy for the President."[49]

In the short term, though, both Eisenhower and the CIA got away with it, or at least escaped lightly the consequences of operations which were becoming in-creasingly risky. This escape was not because the special group counseled restraint or invoked itself as a circuit breaker. Rather, other factors preserved the golden age's sheen: the exceptional cohesiveness at the apex of the Eisenhower administration (so Allen Dulles was not yet made a "fall guy"), the continuation of the Cold War outlook and of popular U.S. loyalty to its artefacts including the CIA, certain rash actions by the Soviet Union, and some effective domestic public relations work by Allen Dulles and his friends.

Eisenhower and the CIA also had a lucky escape, or at least partial escape, in the case of the Hungarian uprising. In the 1952 presidential campaign, and thereafter through pronouncements by John Foster Dulles, the Republican leadership had promised to "liberate" Eastern Europe. Foster Dulles saw "disintegration from within" as the safe alternative to a "head-on collision" with "the empire of Soviet Communism."[50] Such rhetoric caused one analyst to redefine psychological warfare as "a robust faith in the efficacy of public posture."[51] It was also a useful way of diverting the East European ethnic support from Senator McCarthy's camp without unduly alarming the rest of the American electorate.

The promise was, however, delivered to the peoples of Hungary, Poland, and Czechoslovakia, as well as to their enfranchised cousins in the United States. From its Munich base, Radio Free Europe broadcast Khruschev's de-Stalinization speech in 1956. In this secret speech—the CIA had obtained a copy by clandestine means—the new leader seemed to promise a more liberal approach. Freedom enthusiasts at Radio Free Europe's Hungarian desk further encouraged anti-Soviet nationalism by hinting at American aid, should there be an uprising. It is questionable whether their broadcasts were a significant factor in encouraging the revolt; on the contrary, East European dissidents (subsequently smeared as tools of the CIA and U.S. imperialism) strongly resented any suggestion that they had been externally manipulated. Whatever the truth of the matter, Hungarian students and workers made a determined and indigenous effort in Budapest, where they killed 7,000 Russians and lost 30,000 dead themselves before Khruschev's force of 200,000 troops backed up by 2,500 tanks and other armored vehicles broke their resistance.

Psychological tacticians generally, and the CIA in particular, were now blamed for having sparked a revolt they could not support. An investigation by Konrad Adenauer's West German government cleared Radio Free Europe of the charge of reckless behavior, but within the CIA the disaster caused agony. Wisner suffered his first breakdown; Radio Free Europe personnel drifted away, discouraged. According to C. D. Jackson, America's psychological warfare efforts as a whole declined after Hungary. Jackson had resigned from his White House post after only fourteen months. Eisenhower's failure to replace him after his departure in April 1954 meant that he was the last as well as the first administrative assistant for psychological activities. John Foster Dulles blocked the president's subsequent attempts (in 1957 and 1958, respectively) to bring in the ambitious psywar expert as assistant for national security affairs or as secretary of state.[52]

After the failure of the Hungary uprising, Jackson fumed at Allen Dulles and Cord Meyer for not expanding psywar. He stressed the need for such expansion: the Soviets were, for example, "with almost diabolical skill," beginning to hand out college scholarships to young Africans. Meyer told Jackson he was listening to exaggerated stories and assured him that he was continuing his efforts to safeguard the world's youth against Communism. Unappeased, Jackson resigned from the board of the Free Europe Committee in December 1958, telling John Foster Dulles in the following year that if he did not support Radio Free Europe, he might as well let it go out of business.[53]

In Jackson's view, the Eisenhower administration had faltered in its commitment to psychological operations. It is perfectly true that the Hungarian tragedy demonstrated the inefficacy of secret propaganda against brute force and caused some people to change their expectations about what the CIA might accomplish in Eastern Europe. Yet the affair must be put in perspective. The ill-advised Anglo-French-Israeli attack on Egypt happened at roughly the same time, inviting anti-Western opprobrium of a volume that dwarfed criticism of the CIA's role in Hungary. As for Hungary itself, there can be no doubt that it was primarily a psychological disaster not for the United States and the CIA, but for the Soviet Union. All over the world, dedicated socialists began to leave the Communist party. Never again could the Russians credibly claim that they, not the Americans, were the true respecters of self-determination. The Soviet tanks may have answered CIA propaganda in Hungary, but they also performed for it a great political service, especially in the Third World.

The CIA suffered further covert operational setbacks but still escaped any crippling disgrace. One such setback was the failure of its attempt to topple the government of Indonesia, led by the supposedly leftward-leaning president Achmed Sukarno. In May 1958, Indonesian government forces shot down a Civil Air Transport B-26 aircraft while it was on a bombing and strafing mission in support of the hoped-for rebellion. The CIA's involvement became apparent and the plot collapsed. Another setback was the inability of Edward Lansdale, in a series of sabotage and psychological-rumor operations from 1954 on, to topple the Communist government of North Vietnam. The guru of counterinsurgency, it appeared, was fallible. However, it should be noted that this operation, like the Indonesian one, aimed to overthrow an existing government, not to thwart insurgency in a friendly state, the true purpose of the counterinsurgency doctrine. In South Vietnam, where the government was anti-Communist, Lansdale's theories still appeared to be viable: as affirmed in their acclaimed novel *The Ugly American* (1959) by William J. Lederer and Eugene Burdick.[54]

Support continued for the increasingly accident-prone covert operational program partly for old reasons (very few people wanted conventional warfare or nuclear hostilities) and partly for new ones. Among the latter was Khruschev's formation of the Committee for State Security (KGB) on March 13, 1954. At first, the KGB's main role seemed to be to assist Khruschev eliminate the secret-police-state tyrannies of the Stalinist era, Stalin having died in 1953. Toward the end of the 1950s, however, the KGB intensified its external efforts. Just like their counterparts in the U.S. organization formed seven years before their own, the KGB's officials assumed an increasingly prominent role in foreign affairs, especially after the appointment of their new chief Alexander Shelepin in 1959. In the same year, the KGB set up a disinformation department under Ivan I. Agayants, an event of considerable significance for the history of CIA estimates. But from the covert operators' point of view, Department 13 was just as important. This was a successor to the *mokrie dela*, established in 1936 with the object of murdering Trotsky (assassinated in Mexico in 1940), Trotskyists, and other foreign residents unacceptable to the Soviet leadership. Clearly, Khruschev was not going to take de-Stalinization too far.[55]

The intensification of Soviet clandestine efforts inspired imitation by the CIA, enabled the Agency's protagonists to justify some of their more ruthless efforts, and invited retaliation. Supporters and critics alike discerned a tendency for the CIA to imitate the KGB. An Agency veteran, for example, praised Cord Meyer's International Organizations Division because its "method of operation was to copy the Communists' technique."[56] A state department veteran was more critical but made the same point in accusing the CIA of "slavish imitation" of the KGB from the 1950s on.[57] So long as such CIA actions could be presented as a *response*, they could be adequately defended. Thus CIA officials and their supporters in Congress presented KGB activities as one of the main justifications for U.S. "dirty tricks." It became standard practice to include in congressional reports on U.S. intelligence methods appendixes with such titles as "Soviet Intelligence Collection and Operations against the United States."[58] Finally, KGB methods appear to have provoked retaliation, no doubt partly from a spirit of revenge, and partly as a deterrent against future KGB excesses. For example, senior Agency officials including Richard Bissell (Deputy Director for Plans, 1958–62) described the CIA's efforts to neutralize Fidel Castro as a response to the KGB's Department 13.[59]

The rise of Castro was itself a quite separate and independent cause of the continuation and even intensification of the CIA's covert operational program. Castro and his followers marched in triumph into Havana on New Year's Day 1959, putting an end to the right-wing dictatorship of Fulgencio Batista. His acceptance of support from Communist elements within Cuba, his early cancellation of promised elections, and his evident revolutionary appeal throughout Latin America alarmed American policymakers. On January 19, Gordon Gray complained that the special group was not being kept fully informed by Allen Dulles, and he declared that the group would in future take the initiative in moves to appeal to youth and student movements in Latin America, counteracting the appeal of the young and dynamic Castro. Ten days later, Eisenhower convened a small meeting, telling Gray and Dulles that future records of special group deliberations should be kept ultrasecure, that planned operations should not be notified to the Joint Chiefs of Staff or National Security Council, but that he, personally, should be "kept adequately informed."[60] The president had taken a preparatory step toward introducing an official, top-secret U.S. policy of assassination.

Castro was the CIA's first and prime target: on December 11, 1959, J. C. King, the head of its Western hemisphere division, recommended the "elimination" of the Cuban leader.[61] Within a few months, Eisenhower sought to widen the program. Batista had taken refuge in the Dominican Republic, then under the tyrannous rule of another right-wing dictator, Rafael Leonidas Trujillo. The Dominican leader was campaigning against Castroism but, because of his notorious association with terrorism, corruption, and murder, Eisenhower's officials regarded him as a liability. On May 13, 1960, President Eisenhower met with Assistant Secretary of State for Latin American Affairs R. Richard Rubottom and four other officials. According to the "top secret" transcript of the conversation:

> Mr. Rubottom said that Trujillo is involved in all sorts of efforts all over the hemisphere to create disorder. The President commented that Castro is also, and he would like to see them both sawed off.[62]

While assassination as an official policy appears to have been sanctioned at the apex of U.S. government, there can be no doubt that it had its firm adherents within the CIA, as well. For example, in July 1960, the CIA's acting station chief in the Dominican Republic recommended Trujillo's "assassination" as the best method of dispensing with his influence. In another case, that of Patrice Lumumba of the Congo (now Zaïre), it is unclear whether the decision to assassinate came from Eisenhower or from the Agency. In August 1960, the chief of station in Leopoldville cabled that the Congo might well be on the brink of becoming "another Cuba." Eisenhower told Gray the CIA's plans for political action were too weak: the situation demanded "very straightforward action." In the light of the Cuban and Dominican precedents, the president probably needed to say nothing more explicit than this. At any rate, Bissell promptly ordered the devising of an assassination plot. The CIA delivered "rubber gloves, a mask, and a syringe" to the Congo. A "lethal biological material" was to be injected into Lumumba's food or toothpaste.[63]

Castro and Trujillo survived Eisenhower's presidency, while local rivals put an end to Lumumba before the CIA could act. Yet it is clear that both the president and the CIA had accepted the principle of assassination. The administration thus remained committed to covert actions of the most drastic type in spite of ominous difficulties in Indonesia, North Vietnam, and Hungary. Indeed, covert operations were addictive. One State Department historian suggested that, once the CIA had destroyed the natural balance of politics in a country like Italy, its artificially stabilizing presence was permanently required thereafter.[64] Roger Hilsman, a high intelligence official in the Kennedy administration, thought the CIA had been "hooked" in another way, too: how could it stop subsidizing political parties in Japan, Italy, and France, when there was a danger that aggrieved former recipients of support might vengefully expose their previous CIA link?[65] Willard Matthias of the CIA's Office of National Estimates drew attention to yet another problem, the chronic importuning of the CIA by foreigners taking advantage of the Cold War:

Individuals or groups calling themselves Castroists or Communists might stage revolutionary attempts or initiate guerilla movements, not on the orders of Moscow, [Peking], or Havana, but in the hope of gaining their support. Similarly, individuals or groups may organize or execute plots to gain U.S. support.[66]

Within the CIA, there was, as one operator put it, a "publish or perish" impetus: "You had to develop operations or you would fade away."[67] Nor was it in the self-interest of individual presidents to exercise restraint. Once the hidden hand of the United States had been perceived in one event, it would be assumed to exist in every conceivable case, whether or not a particular president was observing a self-denying ordinance: if such a president did restore good faith, his successors, not he, would be the likely beneficiaries. For a variety of reasons, then, the CIA's covert operations proved addictive.

A final reason for the survival of covert operations is that the advocates of such ventures were gifted publicists. As a rule, the action men gave the appearance of being extroverts who were unimpeded by introspection, self-doubt, or excessive modesty.[68] Their cloak-and-dagger work encouraged vigorous storytelling and advocacy—it contrasted with analytical work that frequently remained top secret long after the event and was invariably dull to all but the experts. The covert operators' gift for publicity was particularly felicitous, of course, in a democracy, a type of society in which so much depends on persuasion. The CIA's publicists, however, stood out from their counterparts in other democratic societies like Britain, where fiction was sometimes the best guide—and an unreliable one at that—to the arcane world of secret intelligence. In America spy fiction remained poor in quality, but the public were able to form an opinion on the basis of a deluge of what passed for fact.[69]

Allen Dulles followed Donovan's example in becoming a master of publicity. An able raconteur with a fund of stories, he was able to disarm both Congress and the public. He skillfully turned foreign criticism into an asset at home, keeping extensive files on overseas press comment on himself largely with this end in view.[70] For example, the Soviet propagandist Ilya Ehrenburg denounced him as even more dangerous than his brother the secretary of state, writing in *Isvestia* that should the CIA director ever enter heaven, he would "be found mining the clouds, shooting up the stars and slaughtering the angels."[71] Dulles delighted in prefacing some of his speeches with such quotations—Soviet denunciation being particularly useful in the light of McCarthy's attack on the CIA as a "liberal" or "leftist" institution. These speeches made Dulles a well-known figure in contrast to the chief of the British secret intelligence service, whose name was a secret. He openly addressed various organizations, for example, the Overseas Press Club, the Women's Forum on National Security, and the Conference of National Organizations.[72] Nor did he desist upon his retirement, producing in 1963 a respected work called *The Craft of Intelligence* and, characteristically, going to great lengths to publicize it.[73]

Important though Dulles was, CIA publicity was not the work of one man alone.

Several personalities associated with the Agency's covert operations strove to enhance the CIA's image at home. Kim Roosevelt never shirked the limelight, while C. D. Jackson and Gordon Gray were publicists by profession as well as by inclination. E. Howard Hunt is alleged to have helped write *The Craft of Intelligence* and, in the 1960s, even wrote a series of novels to enhance the all-action CIA myth.[74] To some extent, then, the golden age was really a Gilded Age—bearing a further resemblance to Twain's epoch in that it led to an orgy of muckraking, and, in the 1970s, to reform. Nonetheless, publicity was a factor that gave a protective sheen to covert operations in the 1950s and delayed the tarnishing process thereafter.

Intelligence veterans are sometimes puzzled or embittered by the fact that operations of the type which contributed to the prestige of the mid-1950s CIA later came to be regarded as a liability to the Agency and to America.[75] In the 1950s, there were some sound reasons for covert operations as opposed to other types of action, and U.S. strategists devoted a good deal of thought to them. Indeed, the rational basis of the operations has made it **seem** even more absurd that they should have fallen from grace. Yet that very appearance of rationality was a source of weakness, for it encouraged overconfidence, **an** overconfidence that was further nurtured by the mid-1950s operational successes. Overconfident as they were, America's covert operational strategists failed to entertain the notion of restraint; they failed to develop criteria to determine which operations should be seriously examined, let alone an enforceable set of general guidelines. Their failure contributed to some post-golden age CIA operational and political debacles. Ironically, the mid-1950s operational successes thus ensured, even if they postponed, an hour of reckoning. Only in the charmed 1950s did they contribute unequivocally to the image of an Agency that was effective both in action and, by implication, on the intelligence front.

6

INTELLIGENCE
IN THE
GOLDEN AGE
The Fight
for
Credibility

In the 1970s, a loosely knit group of critics known as *neoconservatives* accused the CIA of having underestimated the Soviet threat to the security of the United States. The critics advanced various hypotheses to explain the alleged error. Some believed the Agency's estimators to be biased in a liberal, pro-Soviet direction. Others thought its leaders had been so preoccupied with covert operations that they allowed the estimators to become lax and incompetent. According to a further argument, the CIA was poorly staffed, either because it failed to pick the best Soviet experts, or because America's universities had failed to produce Soviet experts of sufficient caliber.

All this, one might think, suggested a need for recrimination about the 1950s, the decade in which McCarthy accused the CIA of being pink, in which covert operations flourished to an unprecedented degree, and in which James Doolittle complained about the dullness of the Agency's recruits. The neoconservatives chose instead to castigate CIA performance in the 1960s. One reason for this is that the Agency's intelligence performance in that decade did leave something to be desired, even if its shortcomings were later exaggerated. Other reasons included the general obnoxiousness, to conservatives, of the 1960s (protests against the Vietnam War; permissiveness; expanding federal regulation of industry), as well as stories about Soviet deception, and the CIA's alleged subordination of historians with a sound grasp of Russian thinking to the new technologies of the computer age.

The 1950s, by contrast, presented a reassuring spectacle. The officials of the earlier decade seemed admirably alert to Soviet military buildups and remorselessly suspicious of Kremlin intentions before the age of deception began in earnest with the creation of the KGB's disinformation department in 1959. And if some neoconservatives criticized the CIA for its apparent obsession with covert operations, they were outweighed by those who wholeheartedly admired those operations because of their anti-Communist tenor.

In one sense, the neoconservatives were correct. The CIA's intelligence record in the 1950s was not a bad one. Weaknesses in its performance, such as its presumed failure to penetrate in a comprehensive manner Russia's political and defense establishments, did not dangerously curtail its overall effectiveness. The Agency was fulfilling its original purpose as a neutral intelligence organization, an achievement confirmed by McCarthy's attack and by his defeat. What the neoconservatives as well as other analysts failed to perceive or acknowledge was the degree to which the Agency's success depended not just on its objectivity, but also on its *reputation* for objectivity. In the American democracy, the executive sometimes has to ignore even an infallible source of intelligence, if that source lacks credibility and standing in the eyes of State and Defense department officials, of Congress, and of the people. As the historiography itself suggests, the CIA's achievement in the 1950s was to do with persuasion, as well as with analytical skill.

The CIA's neutral reputation during the greater part of the Eisenhower presidency meant that the White House could afford to listen to what the Agency said. But that reputation rested, in turn, on a political foundation. While there was harmony and unity of purpose within the administration, the Agency retained its credibility. When that harmony began to crack even during Eisenhower's presidency, fissures developed within the intelligence community and weakened its authority. These fissures widened in later years; with the CIA's reputation plunging for other reasons, too, they ultimately led to the neoconservative attack which all but destroyed American faith in the CIA's Soviet estimates. Bearing in mind the fact that neoconservative criticism was as much a political symptom as an objective critique, it is evident that even the tranquil 1950s harbored the beginnings of a future intelligence storm.

Indeed, Allen Dulles himself identified one source of future controversy when he argued that the intelligence agency of a free society was at an inherent disadvantage. His March 1954 interview with *U.S. News and World Report* was entitled "We Tell Russia Too Much." The CIA director explained the Soviet Union's intelligence advantage:

> In the first place, they have far greater facilities for operating in the United States than we have behind the Iron Curtain. Also we Americans publish a great deal in our scientific and technical journals and in congressional hearings. And, of course, in our free system of government, what we do in the field of legislation for national defense is open to the public. I would give a good deal if I could know as much about the Soviet Union as the Soviet Union can learn about us by merely reading the press.

Sometimes I think we go too far in what our Government gives out officially and in what is published in the scientific and technical field. We tell Russia too much. Under our system it is hard to control it.[1]

Dulles was right. Future attempts to curtail the outward flow of high-technology information were not a resounding success: the necessary restrictions on free expression were too high a price for America's democracy to pay.

One of Dulles's motives in drawing attention to a genuine weakness in a democracy's intelligence system may have been to distract attention from the specific shortcomings of the CIA and of himself as its director (after all, in 1949 he had spoken of democracy's inherent *advantages* in the intelligence field). Several leading authorities on the CIA have accused Dulles of being a poor manager of the intelligence community. Like all his predecessors and successors, he had to wear two hats, one as director of the CIA, the other as director of central intelligence with the task of coordinating the whole of the U.S. intelligence effort and producing single, authoritative estimates. According to his detractors, Dulles failed to devise a management system for providing coordinated estimates and too often adopted a mere compromise position when confronted with two or more estimates at variance with one another produced by diverse branches of the intelligence community. Because of his fuzzy-mindedness or because of his preoccupation with operations, Dulles sat on the fence instead of developing criteria for deciding one way or another.[2]

Dulles appears in a worse light still when one considers President Eisenhower's suppression of the 1954 Doolittle Report. Doolittle complained of poor management at the CIA and also alleged, in a meeting with Eisenhower in October, that the CIA was poorly staffed, that Allen's fraternal link with the State Department was unhealthy, and that the CIA director was too "emotional" in his approach to intelligence problems. But Eisenhower, having commissioned the Doolittle inquiry chiefly in order to outflank McCarthy, was not disposed to listen. He told Doolittle bluntly that he rejected his findings.[3] Even though this is a good example of the intra-administration cohesiveness that protected Dulles and the CIA in the 1950s, the incident does not inspire confidence in Dulles's CIA.

Yet the criticism of Allen Dulles overlooks several factors: the benefits flowing from John Foster's support, the so-often incomplete and ambiguous nature of the evidence which confronted Allen Dulles when he was under pressure to make up his mind, the necessity of taking a politically defensible line in order to ensure that the CIA was taken seriously, and the possibility that a strong interest in covert operations did not preclude dedication to intelligence aspects of the Agency's work. According to Board of Estimates member DeForest Van Slyck, Allen Dulles "worried over each strategic estimate."[4] As for the bad management charge, it is notable, first, that no director before or since Dulles has been credited with success in this regard, and, second, that good management in itself cannot solve intelligence problems; indeed, preoccupation with managerial solutions can stultify imagination.

A review of the CIA's intelligence assets and performance in the 1950s suggests that though Agency officials were notoriously boastful about some achievements and sometimes hinted unconvincingly about "unsung successes" where none existed, there was an overall competence about their work.[5] Indeed, some of the "unsung successes" were real enough. For operational reasons, even the politically-minded Dulles had to keep quiet about certain achievements. For example, he did not challenge the view that the CIA had failed to penetrate the Soviet Union, instead pointing out that penetration was difficult because of the closed nature of Russia's dictatorial society.[6] The Russians have contributed to the impression that there was no penetration: according to the Soviet historian Yakovlev, the vigilance of the ordinary people of the socialist countries led to the "100 per cent liquidation" of CIA agents.[7] Yet, according to one CIA veteran writing in 1974, "literally thousands" of CIA agents had penetrated Communist countries, including the Soviet Union, "over the years."[8] That is no doubt true, if one includes the camera-laden tourists recruited by the CIA via travel agencies and other institutions to photograph strategic installations while overflying the Soviet Union. But the "thousands" may also include a minority of infiltrated agents unacknowledged by the Soviets because of ignorance, face-saving requirements and the dictates of counterintelligence, and unadmitted by the Americans for obvious reasons; certainly, the CIA recruited some agents locally.

One factor that encouraged American discretion—and obscured a potent intelligence asset of the early 1950s CIA—was the use by U.S. intelligence services of Nazis known to have committed war crimes and crimes against humanity. The logic behind the deployment of German intelligence officials with a shady past but with access to Soviet information seemed clear to their American employers: why bother about Jews already dead, when the top priority was to protect U.S. and allied lives from future Soviet attack? Given the revulsion which the Holocaust had engendered, however, there was good reason to disclaim U.S. contacts with certain insalubrious individuals. One such individual was Klaus Barbie, the "butcher of Lyon." Though he was already suspected of having committed atrocities in France, this former Gestapo official was taken on and protected by the U.S. Army's Counter Intelligence Corps because of his knowledge of Communist techniques and his access to an anti-Communist ring of agents. In 1951, though knowledge of Barbie's atrocities was by now confirmed, U.S. officials connived in his escape to South America via the underground "rat line" already established for such purposes. Once in Bolivia, Barbie continued his nefarious activities, which included drug trafficking and government terrorism, until the Reagan administration insisted on his extradition in 1983.

The issue was still so sensitive that a special U.S. government inquiry was set up on March 14, 1983, to examine the CIA connection with Barbie both before and after his arrival in Bolivia.[9] The report is notable not just for its negative conclusion, but for its assumption that the CIA-Nazi link was potentially injurious. When these links were first forged, the case for circumspection was even more pressing and gave further encouragement, if any were needed, to those who wished to wrap U.S. anti-Communist espionage in a blanket of absolute secrecy.

A proven example of a German asset to the CIA is to be found in General Reinhard Gehlen. Because of the unwelcome hostile propaganda that would have been generated on account of his previous services to Hitler, and because of his widely presumed postwar adherence to Nazi beliefs, as well as for the usual operational reasons, the CIA kept quiet about Gehlen.[10] Yet, one can say that, unlike Barbie, Gehlen was able to provide the U.S. intelligence community with underground links to East European informational sources, a significant building block in the CIA's courtship of defectors.

In World War II, Gehlen had headed the Germans' military intelligence service in Eastern Europe. His reports on Soviet military strength and war aims were sufficiently accurate to be, from October 1942 on, profoundly depressing from the German point of view. An enraged führer demanded his dismissal in 1945, and Gehlen made a timely escape from the doomed Reich. After an interlude, Gehlen set up an organization in collaboration with the U.S. army's G-2, or intelligence section, still with the Russian-watching brief. Seeing a further opportunity with the formation of the CIA, he broke with G-2 and in 1949 entered into a written contract with the new intelligence organization that broadened the scope of his operations to include political, economic, and technological espionage. Building on the agent network he had established in Hitler's days, he constructed a new intelligence empire. At first, the CIA claimed exclusive jurisdiction over his services and spy network, forbidding him to have any official contact with Bonn. But, in 1956 the West German government took over his operation, doubtless still liaising with the CIA. Gehlen remained until 1968 head of the Bundesnachrichtendienst, the West German secret service.[11]

A partial version of Gehlen's exploits has entered literary circulation in spite of the CIA's reticence, because the German intelligence chief was such a self-promoter. He even wrote a memoir claiming, like the British, to have taught the CIA people all they needed to know.[12] Gehlen owed his survival in intelligence circles in the decade of the Nuremberg trials to his utility as a Russian expert. The Western powers, the United States included, had neglected Eastern European espionage in World War II, because Russia was an ally. This meant that Gehlen's network was a precious asset. To preserve his own position and, perhaps, to enhance Germany's postwar strategic status, Gehlen sold himself as that most vital type of Cold War asset, an anti-Communist Russian expert. As a result, his reports tended to exaggerate the expansionist intentions of the Soviet Union, a bias which impressed the army, but the CIA only to a lesser extent.

The CIA treated Gehlen with caution and ensured that he was kept as a very junior partner, yet his utility and initiatives were respected. One of these initiatives came to light because it failed. In 1955, the CIA acted on an idea of Gehlen's worked out in conference with Allen Dulles. The Agency built a thousand-yard tunnel from the American sector of West Berlin into East Berlin, in such a way as to enable Russian telephone conversations to be tapped in this vital strategic area. George Blake, a British secret service employee who turned out to have been a double agent, betrayed the plan to the Russians. In April 1956, they invited journalists to inspect the tunnel and its electronic equipment in a ritualistic display of anti-U.S. espionage propaganda that involved no loss of face and no lost counterpenetration opportunities. The tunnel thus became a known example of Gehlen-CIA cooperation. The U.S. decision to implement the tunnel plan presumably reflected the confidence created by previous, unrevealed projects. Its exposure also meant Gehlen was placed at arm's length; it was in 1956 that he started to work officially for Bonn. By this time, he was losing his usefulness for the CIA. His East German network, the cornerstone of his general anti-Russian operations, succumbed to penetration by the opposition. Gehlen also overreached himself by interfering in West German politics.[13]

Until the mid-1950s setbacks, Gehlen's organization gleaned information about the Soviet Union and Eastern Europe by interrogating German prisoners of war as they returned from the East and by recruiting agents in East Germany. His spy network was thus German-based and stopped at the Russian border. The Soviet espionage gap was filled to a modest extent, at least, by a "defector in place." Lieutenant Colonel Pyotr Semyonovich Popov worked in Vienna for the GRU, the highest echelon in Soviet military intelligence. From 1952 to his presumed execution in 1959, he worked also for the CIA.[14] According to accounts given by CIA veterans, Popov gave the Agency information about Soviet missile systems. William Hood, for thirty years an employee of the OSS and CIA, rather grandiosely claimed that Popov "trundled bales of top-secret information out of the secret centers of Soviet power. In the process he shattered the Soviet military intelligence service . . . and saved the United States half a billion dollars in military research."[15] Though it may be true that the CIA failed to recruit any important agents on its own in the Soviet Union, there was, then, consolation in the fact that it had alternative "humint" sources at its disposal.

Other strengths helped compensate for possible weaknesses in the U.S. espionage system. One of these was the CIA's Economic Research Area group, set up in 1950 to study the Soviet economy. By 1953, the group was in a position to suggest that there might be a distinction between the weaponry the Russians knew how to produce and the weaponry they could afford to produce.[16] Another strength was high-technology surveillance. From the late 1940s, airborne electronic eavesdropping equipment deployed along the Soviet Union's borders picked up internal transmissions, helping for example to locate a missile testing site at Kaputsin Yar. By 1955, a radar station in Samsun in Turkey was monitoring the testing program in Kaputsin Yar; the United States established similar facilities in

Iran and Pakistan.[17] A third strength of the 1950s CIA was James Angleton's successful operation of counterintelligence. To some, Angleton's obsession with compartmentalization and his suspicion of the Soviet Union's every move smacked of paranoia, but chronic skepticism is no fault in a counterintelligence chief. Angleton helped to ensure that—as far as is known—the CIA was not penetrated. His constant alertness to possible Soviet deception ploys made the CIA's estimates of Communist resources and intentions more reliable. One illustration of CIA alertness is a 1951 estimate that interpreted the "temporary" relaxation in Soviet posture as a "different method of political and psychological warfare, to lull the West into a false sense of security and undermine growing NATO strength."[18]

To assess the CIA's efficacy in its primary intelligence role, eyeing the Russians, it is useful in the first instance to survey the period up to 1956, a year when several new developments were to change the picture. In this period as in others, strategists both East and West were to some degree the prisoners of their own political environments. They reacted to internal circumstances as well as to the actions of the other side. So the story of the arms race and of U.S.-USSR intelligence rivalry is in one sense about an asymmetrical relationship. Thus the Soviets did not respond immediately to America's strong nuclear challenge. Proud memories of the Red Army's World War II victories dictated the continuation of a massive conventional force which could threaten NATO and allow a "hostage Europe" policy. Stalin's death in 1953 did not change matters overnight. Russian leaders remained prisoners both of the past and of a strong conventional military lobby. Khruschev achieved a slight redistribution of resources, but the Soviet nuclear strategy remained one of "minimum," as distinct from America's "massive," deterrence.[19]

The CIA responded, in the period before 1956, by overestimating the Russian nuclear threat. This hawkish attitude derived in part from hostility and ignorance, in part from mirror-imaging. In the 1940s, American experience seemed to suggest that missiles would be less efficient than bombers, so U.S. estimators erroneously assumed the Soviet Union would, like the United States, concentrate on bomber production.[20] In fact the Russians not only clung on to conventional strategy but also, insofar as they did modernize, bypassed intercontinental bombers in favor of a rapid missile-testing program. Yet in the early 1950s the United States proceeded on the assumption that the Russians—like the Americans—were mass-producing long-range bombers. Air Force intelligence (A-2) had a vested interest in making that claim.

The claim, however, could not have been welcome to Eisenhower, who wished to curtail arms manufacturing in the interests of world peace, a balanced budget, and a healthy economy. But he would not risk halting the arms race unilaterally, and he could not risk an agreement with the Russians without some means of first ascertaining their strength and then of verifying that they were sticking to their side of the bargain. At a summit conference in Geneva in July 1955, the president made his imaginative "Open Skies" proposal, whereby America and Russia could overfly each other's territory checking on military installations and factories. But the

Russians could already find out about many U.S. installations because of America's open society, and they refused to make what they regarded as a unilateral concession. Lacking evidence to the contrary, Dulles endorsed the A-2 estimates, which thus dominated the NIE 11–4s (the Office of National Estimates' National Intelligence Estimate dealing with the Soviet strategic threat). Only subsequently did it become plain that A-2 and the compliant CIA had seriously overestimated Soviet long-range bomber production; in 1955, then, the CIA's incipient intelligence strengths had not yet borne full fruit.[21]

For the CIA, 1956 was a year of triumphs, of promise, but also of potential discord. The Agency enjoyed a public triumph when, in February, its officials obtained a copy of Khruschev's secret de-Stalinization speech. In April, the Communist authorities in East Berlin made a great display of their exposure of the CIA's tunnel, but the *Washington Post* hailed it as an example of "Yankee ingenuity," and a CIA analysis of world opinion showed the tunnel had enhanced "U.S. prestige."[22] Such triumphs pale into insignificance, however, compared with the Agency's achievement in this year of an independent estimating capability. The importance of this achievement should not be exaggerated, for the CIA was often called upon to confirm that the Soviet Union was *not* doing something, and it is always hard to prove a negative. But at least the Agency was now becoming capable of corroborating or casting doubt upon the findings of other components of the intelligence community. By the spring of 1956, the analysts of the economic research area group were already suggesting that the Soviets could not be manufacturing long-range bombers on anything like the scale and speed postulated by the air force.[23] In mid-June 1956, the first U-2 flight started a process that was to confirm the doubters in their opinions.

Earlier, in 1954, Allen Dulles had asked his special assistant Richard M. Bissell, Jr., to take up the concept of a high-flying airplane with the capability of taking photographs of Russian items of possible strategic significance. Bissell's drive and genius were to contribute decisively to the rapid fruition of the U-2 project. Even as a child, Bissell had demonstrated a mastery of detail: his researches as a juvenile railroad buff were uncannily appropriate to his later work, for Soviet railroad lines were one of the indicators as to the location of offensive missile sites. After Groton and Yale, Bissell studied at the London School of Economics in its socialist heyday. He taught economics at Yale and MIT before entering government service, his duties including a spell as acting administrator of the Marshall Plan prior to his engagement by the CIA in 1954. Bissell rose to become deputy director for plans (1959–62). As well as being physically dominant at 6'4" and having a forceful if urbane and courteous personality, Bissell was from the beginning a commanding intellectual figure within the Agency.[24]

Bissell's project was run and financed by the CIA, with jealous but effective assistance from the air force. Special cameras were developed for use in the resultant aircraft, the U-2, which could fly at 80,000 feet, beyond the range of Soviet surface-to-air missiles though not, as it turned out, radar. The plane could in one flight take up to 4,000 high-definition photographs of an area 2,174 miles long and 30 miles wide. Expert analysts could use them to identify groundlevel objects with a diameter as small as 12 inches.[25] By May 1956, a unit of four planes and six pilots was stationed in Turkey and ready to go. The flight authorized by Eisenhower the next month—its flight path included Moscow and Leningrad—was the first of about two hundred. The planes photographed factories and military sites in the Soviet Union. With the new evidence in hand, the CIA had by 1960 reduced its estimate of Soviet bomber production to 19 percent of the figure mooted by A-2 in 1956.[26]

Just as the CIA was developing its capability to impose objectivity on the national estimating process, the Agency began to run into new political trouble. This was never to reach critical proportions in the Eisenhower presidency, but it was an ominous indicator of what lay ahead and therefore invites comment. James R. Killian was one critic. Killian in his various advisory capacities had encouraged the development of new photographic techniques and had the scientist's sharp eye for fact as distinct from speculation; Eisenhower was to show his regard for Killian's expertise by appointing him special assistant for science and technology in 1957. In his memoir, Killian revealed that he had been a powerful doubter: he recalled that the president stuck by his intelligence chief, thus failing to recognize or at least remedy the "administrative inadequacies of Allen Dulles" in arriving at an adequate Soviet estimate.[27]

Some real and alleged nonstrategic intelligence failures added to Dulles's discomfiture. The CIA had failed to predict an uprising in East Berlin in 1953; then, on November 23, 1956, the Agency was once again taken by surprise by the Hungarian uprising. The Hungarian revolt thus cast the CIA in a bad light for intelligence as well as for operational reasons. Just after Hungary, Eisenhower appointed General Lucien Truscott to survey the CIA's activities; by the time Truscott reported in the following year (accusing the CIA of devoting too much attention to covert operations), the ever-prudent president was beginning to worry about the escalating costs of the billion-dollar-per-annum agency, one of whose purposes, after all, was supposedly the implementation of a dollar-saving strategy.[28]

Their alleged nonprediction of the Anglo-French-Israeli attack on Egypt on October 31, 1956, was a further setback for Allen Dulles and his CIA colleagues. Egypt's president Gamal Abdul Nasser had nationalized the Anglo-French Suez canal on July 26. From the American point of view, this act in itself did not mean Nasser had fallen into the Communist camp; instead, he appeared to be playing off East and West, with every prospect that the West might ultimately be in a position to offer him the better deal. The Anglo-French-Israeli attack was therefore precipitate. At the very least, the United States needed advance warning in order to prepare her diplomatic posture. Her allies did not supply this warning.

The widely presumed failure of U.S. intelligence to supply the warning instead meant that America had also missed an opportunity to dissuade her allies from undertaking a risky adventure—an adventure that seems even more foolish in retrospect because it discredited Western democracies just as they were poised to extract maximum propaganda benefit from the Soviets' brutal contemporaneous exercise of force in Hungary. There has been considerable speculation about this presumed intelligence failure. For example, some accuse James Angleton, who had close links with Israeli intelligence, of suppressing indications of the attack because he sympathized with its objectives, while others report that he was furious at being kept in the dark by his Israeli friends. But there is some doubt as to whether the CIA was, in fact, caught unawares. The Agency's deputy director for intelligence Robert Amory (who had the advantage of a distant cousin sitting in the British cabinet) predicted the attack to within twenty-four hours, and a U-2 plane photographed the air strike against Cairo's military airport as it actually happened. Amory's liaison man in London, Chester Cooper, complained that Washington simply did not listen. It does seem likely that a warning from a single official, even one so senior as Amory, on this occasion proved insufficient to alert a president in the final throes of his re-election campaign.[29]

With the election just a few days away, it was imperative that Eisenhower should not take the blame himself. The president announced that he had first read of the Suez attack in the newspapers. Thus CIA officials once again had to face charges of incompetence. In January 1957, for example, Cooper was summoned to Washington to explain why he had not sent a warning about the British intention to attack.[30] Dulles therefore had to defend his agency. Though he had personally been skeptical of Amory's prediction of imminent attack, he denied that Eisenhower had been left unwarned, leaking the story that the president would have known about the imminence of an attack if only he had read his intelligence reports. It should be emphasized that this Eisenhower-Dulles breach was brought on by particularly stressful circumstances and was uncharacteristic of the generally harmonious executive-CIA relations in the 1950s. Yet it illustrates the endemically problematic nature of the White House-intelligence relationship, and it may have encouraged others to take issue with the CIA and its intelligence estimates in the later 1950s.[31]

In the fall of 1957, the CIA's estimates became not just a source of internal disagreement, but an issue in public debate leading to the notorious "Missile Gap" controversy and to serious if often unfounded doubts about the CIA's efficacy. Subsequently declassified documents show that the CIA's own analysts had suspected in advance that Russia intended to "leap-frog" the bomber stage and advance directly to the testing of intercontinental ballistic missiles.[32] For three years, also, the Agency had been warning that the Russians planned a satellite launch. But, since knowledge of the precise state of one's intelligence about a potential enemy's capabilities and intentions would have been of use to that enemy's counterintelligence experts, the CIA had kept the Russians—and necessarily the American people—in the dark. This made the launch of the Soviets'

Sputnik satellite on October 4, 1957, doubly distressing to that majority of Americans who had come to regard U.S. technological superiority, not to mention open government, as the norm, and who were now ready to listen to critics of the administration and particularly of the CIA who claimed that the Russians had been allowed to steal a march.

The Gaither Report leak made things worse. Eisenhower had appointed a civilian group under the Ford Foundation's H. Rowan Gaither to examine U.S. strategy, and its report of November 7, 1957, stressed the Russians' shift to missiles. The Gaither Report cited the CIA's latest estimate that 100 Russian intercontinental missiles carrying megaton nuclear warheads would be in place by early 1960. This estimate, when leaked, was bad enough. Worse still were rumors of the air force calculation in the same November 1957 National Intelligence Estimate: 500 Soviet missiles in place by the middle of 1960, and 1,100 a year later. The air force estimates took no stock of the CIA's economic calculation that the Soviet defense industry was incapable of producing more than 50 missiles per annum (the *total* number of SS-6 intercontinental missiles deployed by 1961 in fact turned out to be only 50). Against this background, Dulles was obliged to testify defensively to a Congress that contained intelligence critics like former air force secretary Stuart Symington.[33]

Allegations about CIA underestimates and their consequences gathered momentum at the end of the 1950s. Foreigners as well as Americans began to believe them. In February 1959 the pro-Labour party British Sunday newspaper, *Reynolds News*, attacked the CIA. The paper rehearsed the story of the CIA's covert operations and rejoiced at the illness which was to force John Foster Dulles's retirement in April: "Without Big Brother to protect him, it looks as if Little Brother's days in Washington are numbered also." To its familiar left-wing line, the paper added the "revelation" that the CIA had "deliberately faked intelligence reports of Soviet missile progress to suit the Administration's 'balanced budget' policy."[34] In order to maintain the CIA's and America's strategic credibility at home and abroad against the background of such attitudes, Allen Dulles had to tread warily.

The CIA director's masterly grasp of publicity therefore continued to be a precious asset. He was, for example, careful to counter any suggestion that the Soviet leadership might be duping the CIA. Thus he reacted to a story that arose from Khruschev's visit to America in September 1959. This was the celebrated occasion when the Soviet premier met everyone from Eisenhower to Marilyn Monroe, referred to his liking for America's "amiable and kind-hearted people," and hinted at a termination of the Cold War.[35]

The story was about the encounter between Dulles and Khruschev at a White House dinner on September 15. The atmosphere was evidently relaxed. CBS reporter Paul Niven recalled in an 8 A.M. broadcast the next morning that "the Soviet Premier was in his best bantering form."[36] Introduced to Dulles on the receiving line, Khruschev was interpreted as saying "Oh yes, I know of you. I read your reports." After dinner, the men separated from the ladies and stood around in small groups drinking coffee and smoking cigars. Vice-President Nixon led Dulles across to have another word with Khruschev, who was with Lyndon B. Johnson and other senior congressmen. According to John Horner of the *Washington Star*, Dulles now said to Khruschev, "I suppose you read some of our intelligence reports."[37] The next day, Dulles's assistant suggested the CIA simply confirm the Horner version, which several newspapers had taken up. But the CIA chief issued a clarifying memorandum. In this, he playfully acknowledged Khruschev's badinage about sharing agents and paying them "only once" to save money, but he also offered the correction that it was Khruschev, not he, who supposed the Russians were acquiring CIA documents.[38]

In an effort to defend his own and the CIA's credibility, Dulles publicly stressed those of his beliefs that identified him as being alert to the Soviet menace. His frequent emphasis on the threat posed by growing Soviet economic might is an example of the way in which he combined conviction with political instinct. This was by no means a straightforward matter, however, for his insistent warnings of growing Soviet strength offended those who were too prejudiced to concede the Communists could do anything right. *Fortune* magazine, for example, took the weakness of the Soviet economy to be an axiom of its C. D. Jackson-style psychological warfare campaign. It had poured scorn on Soviet economic performance since 1953; it vilified the Congress for Cultural Freedom in February 1957 for daring to sponsor a conference highlighting Soviet economic advances; in May 1958 it turned its editorial wrath on Dulles. Dulles was also constrained by the fact that Soviet strength, if proved, would be yet another challenge to Eisenhower's attempt to restrict defense expenditure and would seem to discredit some of the underlying assumptions of the CIA's own economic research area group. He had to balance such considerations against the benefits of realism, and of taking a credibility-enhancing posture as an apostle of the Soviet economic menace.[39]

Dulles's typewritten notes for a March 1959 speech in Atlantic City, New Jersey, show, moreover, that he was aware of a weakness in his publicly stated economic argument. Although in the text he observed that the "average growth rate" in the Soviet Union's gross national product had been "twice that of the USA over last decade and more than three times over the last five years," he added by hand the parenthetic qualification "lower base."[40] Later in the year, after Khruschev's visit had raised hopes of detente, Dulles nevertheless underlined his hawkish public stance. In lengthy congressional testimony on the Soviet economy he claimed:

> The major thrust of Soviet economic development and its high technological skills and resources are directed toward specialized industrial, military and national power goals. A major thrust of our economy is directed into the production of the consumer type goals and services which add little to the sinews of our national strength.[41]

This analysis implied that Americans needed to spend more, not less, on weapons and that they needed to accept some sacrifices in the process. As in the case of his critique of an open society that told the Russians too much, he was underlining the inherent vulnerability of a democracy in the face of totalitarian threat. While he was genuinely worried on both counts, by showing himself alert to the Soviet challenge he was also, in each case, taking care of the CIA's credibility and standing.

Similar political caution may well have been at the root of Dulles's overestimate of Soviet missile strength in 1960, a presidential election year. That year's national intelligence estimate put the number of Soviet intercontinental ballistic missiles at 400 by mid-1963. The army and navy estimates were lower at 200, the State Department and Joint Chief of Staff estimates were higher, and the air force's ᴄstimates the highest at 700 (the actual Soviet figure was 150 by 1963). The CIA figure of 400—which led to the deployment of precisely that number of *American* missiles by 1963—has been characterized as "an attempt for institutional compromise rather than a logical extension of concrete analysis."[42] The compromise, and others before it, led critics to suppose that Dulles was a poor manager of the intelligence community. Such a supposition is, however, untenable. For one thing, it overlooks the CIA director's political shrewdness. If he had forced through a lower figure, it is conceivable that many would have disbelieved it, and that few would have trusted the CIA thereafter. Thus, he would have surrendered the intelligence field to the military, contrary to his own principles and with a real danger of even greater exaggerations of Soviet strength in the future.

There is, moreover, a further reason why Dulles had to be cautious about his Soviet missiles estimate in 1960. Together with the CIA and America as a whole, he was the victim of an intelligence gap, a gap that helped perpetuate the myth of the missile gap. The gap in intelligence consisted of U.S. ignorance about the current state of Soviet missile deployment. The CIA knew about Soviet missile testing centers at Kaputsin Yar and Tyuratam, but had not yet located an operational launching site. Once one of these had been identified, photograph analysts would know what to look for in scrutinizing film of other areas of the Soviet Union under suspicion. Until this breakthrough, there was no way of discounting the contentions of air force analysts to whom, the critics complained, "every flyspeck on a film was a missile."[43] In the absence of a decisive intelligence breakthrough, Allen Dulles understandably stuck to his compromise position in spite of the palpably self-serving nature of air force claims.

By the spring of 1960, combined assessment of communications intelligence and agents' reports indicated there might be an intercontinental ballistic missile base under construction at Plesetsk. Eisenhower authorized a U-2 overflight to confirm or discount the possibility. But the Russians could track the U-2 by radar, and they had also improved the range and accuracy of their ground-to-air missiles. At this of all times, the plane appears to have developed an engine fault causing loss of altitude (the details are still unclear); at it was passing over Sverdlovsk on May 1 on the way to its target, the Russians shot it down.

The "U-2 Affair" was a setback in more ways than one for the CIA and the United States. James Killian argued that the plane's loss was in itself evidence of intelligence failure; he claimed "the CIA long before should have brought to bear hard-nosed scientific and military judgement on the possibilities of the plane's being shot down and of the growing Soviet capability to attack the plane." The Agency and the air force had misled Eisenhower, who was unaware that the Russians had repeatedly tried to shoot down earlier U-2 flights, and who believed that, in the event of an accident, both plane and pilot would be destroyed. He would have been still more reluctant to authorize the Powers mission—especially on the Communists' festive May Day—if he had been properly briefed on the intensity of Russian feeling about the overflights. But, even at a time when America was pressing for detente, the CIA's analysts proved insensitive to Russian opinion.[44]

Dulles offered his resignation and Eisenhower, in a typical display of loyalty, refused it. At first the president, suffering as he was from technical misapprehensions, issued denials. But Francis Gary Powers, the U-2 pilot, had managed to bail out, and the Russians captured not only him but also fragments of the aircraft. They withheld this information from the U.S. government until Eisenhower had issued his denials and then produced both pilot and wreckage, demonstrating to a startled American people that their president would lie to them. Eisenhower refused to apologize and Secretary of State Christian Herter invoked the circuit-breaking mechanism: "Specific missions . . . have not been subject to Presidential authorization."[45] This was unconvincing as well as untrue. The insulted but jubilant Russians had a show trial and put on a U-2 exhibition in Gorky Park, thus treating the episode as a propaganda victory.

More seriously, the U-2 affair set the seal of doom on the already precarious Russo-American summit meetings on which Eisenhower had been pinning his hopes for a safer world. U.S.-Soviet relations were already deteriorating because of renewed friction over the status of Berlin, because the Chinese were attacking Khruschev's "soft" policy toward America, and because the Soviet leader was by now determined to build a nuclear defense—in response to the U.S. air force's mounting arsenal of bombers and missiles and as a solution to Russia's problem of overexpenditure on conventional armies. The U-2 affair thus aggravated an already serious political situation.[46]

Additionally, the shoot-down perpetuated the intelligence gap. The CIA's Soviet analysts now had to turn to new sources of information. After the Russians' Sputnik launch in 1957 (which, incidentally, led to routine Soviet aerial inspection of U.S. military sites), Eisenhower had secured the creation of the National Aeronautics and Space Administration. Richard Bissell recognized the intelligence possibilities, and the Administration made large sums available for the development of reconnaissance satellites through the budgets of the Department of Defense, National Security Administration, and Air Force. On August 19, 1960, Discoverer 14 became the first U.S. spy satellite to achieve operational efficiency. It was designed to eject a film capsule that was then recovered in midair. In due course, remarkably detailed photographs were taken even from the range of ninety to one hundred miles at which the satellites operated.[47]

The August 19 flight passed over Plesetsk. The recovered photographs revealed railway tracks absent from World War II German intelligence maps. This was suggestive, for it was known that Russian missiles were so large and cumbersome that they needed to be transported by rail. By June 1961, photo technology and analysis had so improved that the Discoverer program for the first time yielded accurate knowledge about the appearance of a Soviet offensive missile site. Many previously suspected sites could now be discounted. From April 1961, Oleg Penkovsky further assisted the CIA's analysts. A colonel in Soviet military intelligence (GRU), Penkovsky served as a "defector in place." Prior to his arrest in the fall of 1962 and execution by firing squad, he supplied the Western powers with thousands of pages of secret strategic documents, some of which contained information that could be usefully collated with satellite evidence. The combined picture destroyed the "missile gap" theory.[48]

This, however, did not happen until well after the 1960 presidential election. The initial Discoverer photographs, though suggestive, were of relatively poor quality. The intelligence gap persisted throughout 1960. Had the CIA's analysts utilized open sources—Russian official documents revealing the Communists' ideology, strategy, and intentions—Dulles might have been more reassuring about the Soviet threat, for no attack was planned. But, conditioned by the belief that only the United States had documents open to inspection, the analysts neglected this source.[49] Dulles, unwilling to risk his country's security or the integrity of the CIA's analysts, refused to defer to the judgment of those skeptics within his agency who suspected the conclusions and motives of air force analysts.

His stance was of considerable significance for the election campaign. Two of the aspirants for the Democratic nomination, Senators Stuart Symington and John F. Kennedy, had been laboring the missile-gap issue since 1958. Kennedy, who won the nomination, had to live down his father's World War II reputation as an appeaser; he tried to present himself as the young, virile successor to a faltering Eisenhower, by this time suffering from a faint heart, he implied, as well as from heart disease. He made a major issue of foreign policy. The 1960 Democratic platform pledged a military buildup to close the alleged missile gap. On the eve of the presidential election, Khruschev foolishly made a table-thumping speech at the United Nations, bragging that Russia's factories were turning out missiles "like sausages." This mistimed piece of psychological posturing kept the missile gap to the fore as an issue in the election that Kennedy so narrowly won.[50]

In later years, the CIA was accused of having worked on behalf of John F. Kennedy in the 1960 election campaign. This belief was a symptom, as well as a cause (if a minor one) of the dislocation in America's intelligence efforts in the 1960s and 1970s. According to Lyndon B. Johnson, a rival for the Democratic nomination before becoming Kennedy's running mate, the CIA worked behind the scenes at the Democratic convention on Kennedy's behalf.[51] As Johnson did not elaborate, his allegation may be ignored. More seriously, Richard Nixon, the Republican candidate in the 1960 election, believed the CIA—instructed to brief the Democractic candidate—deliberately withheld from Kennedy the knowledge that there was, in reality, no missile gap, the omission being a tactic calculated to secure Nixon's defeat. It is true that in the course of an August 3, 1960, briefing Kennedy asked Dulles "How do we stand in the missile race?" and that the CIA director replied evasively that the Defense Department "was the competent authority on this question." In light of the reply, writes Eisenhower's biographer Stephen Ambrose, "Kennedy felt free to continue to speak of a 'missile gap'."[52] One might read into this circumstance a disposition on Dulles's part to favor Kennedy and help him defeat Nixon.

But it seems more likely that Dulles was governed by other factors. According to a recent Allen Dulles biographer, the CIA director had been affected by the recent death (on May 24, 1959) of his brother, the secretary of state; having been an emotionally "liberal" foil to John Foster, he now veered, still emotionally, to a more conservative, hawkish stance to compensate for the fraternal loss.[53] Other factors are also more likely to have influenced Allen Dulles's judgment than antipathy toward Nixon. Among these were political prudence, the CIA's concentration on Soviet to the exclusion of U.S. strength, and the intelligence gap. The existence of the intelligence gap, in particular, exonerates Dulles from charges of supine compliance with palpably erroneous assessments, charges of the type that may be leveled at some of his successors.

In view of the CIA-White House rifts later on, it is worth inquiring why Johnson and Nixon expressed such suspicion of the CIA. One reason is that both were chip-on-the-shoulder outsiders with a grouse against the Eastern establishment of which CIA was a part, and to which the affluent, Harvard-educated Kennedy seemed to them to be attached. The fact that Kennedy was a Catholic and in some ways at odds with the establishment did not dispel their suspicions. Nixon, it is true, did at times seem capable of distinguishing between elitist cohesion and elitist conspiracy: reassuring McCarthy in 1953 about William Bundy's contribution to the Alger Hiss defense fund, he said: "Joe, you have to understand how those people up in Cambridge think. Bundy graduated from the Harvard Law School, and Hiss was one of its most famous graduates"—and there was nothing more to it than that.[54] Yet, he was in general suspicious of officials from a specially privileged background. It should be added that both he and Johnson were embittered by their 1960 defeats, a factor which further colored their judgment. It is also significant that they both singled out the CIA as a cause of their 1960 reverse *after* the Agency's disgrace at the Bay of Pigs, in an era when the CIA was becoming everyone's favorite scapegoat.

What further jaundiced Nixon's view of the CIA in 1960 was the fact that the Agency did nothing to stop Kennedy's exploitation of the Cuban issue. Nixon gave his version of events in an early memoir, *Six Crises*. He told of his shock when, on October 20, 1960, his opponent advocated "U.S. intervention in Cuba." Kennedy had attacked the Republican administration for its reluctance to help Cuban exiles invade their motherland and put an end to Castroism: "Thus far," said Kennedy, "these fighters for freedom have had virtually no support from our government." Nixon was angry because the administration did have secret plans for a paramilitary invasion, plans which the vice president endorsed and which, he claimed, had been revealed to Kennedy in the course of a CIA briefing at Hyannis Port, Massachusetts, on July 23, 1960.[55]

The Kennedy camp's defense, that the CIA did not tell JFK about the planned invasion, has been described by one biographer as "disingenuous."[56] Certainly, Kennedy appears to have been remarkably uninquisitive about the Republican administration's plans, when one considers his usual thirst for details about "dirty tricks." The story is told of Ian Fleming's dinner with the Kennedys on March 13, 1960. Responding to what he assumed was a humorous question, the novelist (according to his biographer) "developed a spoof proposal for giving Castro the James Bond treatment." For example, he suggested that the removal of Castro's beard would diminish his appeal to the whisker-conscious Cubans. The interest here lies less in the influence Fleming may have had on the CIA's depilatory plans, than in the young senator's amused curiosity about unorthodox methods. The CIA's John Bross was another guest at the dinner party, and within half an hour of the evening's end Dulles was on the telephone obtaining an account of Kennedy's outlook.[57] Eisenhower approved a Bissell "paramilitary force outside of Cuba" plan on March 17. In light of Dulles's knowledge about Kennedy's curiosity, it would seem odd that Kennedy did not learn of that plan at the July 23 briefing.

Two factors should be taken into account, though. One was Eisenhower's reluctance to divulge secrets to the "young whippersnapper" and his foreign-policy advisors. Another is the incremental nature of the planning for the invasion. Not until August 18, well after the Hyannis Port briefing, did the retiring president allocate the substantial sum of $13 million to the Castro-toppling program.[58] Though Dulles might have gone further to neutralize the issue and Kennedy might have tempered his ambition with curiosity, neither was involved in active deception. This was by no means clear to Nixon, who on the stump attacked Kennedy's invasion proposal in order to conceal the administration's own plans. It is not surprising that in this case Nixon saw himself as the patriot, Kennedy as the rogue, and the CIA as the willing accomplice. The 1960 election campaign therefore contained more than one source of future White House-CIA discord.

In retrospect, the CIA's golden age invites a sober assessment. The era's covert operations were excessive and stored up trouble for the future. Eisenhower's determined efforts to limit military expenditure and reach an arms agreement with the Russians foundered for a variety of reasons, one of which was the inability of the CIA to specify authoritatively and continuously the Soviet Union's precise offensive atomic strength. This shortcoming induced Dulles to exaggerate Soviet strength in order to outflank his critics, especially in a Congress never fully taken into the CIA's confidence.

At the same time, Dulles should be credited with having overseen some notable achievements. He helped Americans understand the importance of intelligence in arms-reduction negotiations, smoothing the way toward public acceptance of expensive aerial and space research. Because of his colleagues' skills and his own caution and political astuteness, Dulles preserved the CIA's credibility. He did so in the face of mounting odds, for toward the end of Eisenhower's presidency that credibility came under threat for reasons that sometimes had little to do with the Agency's professional standards. In his farewell address, Eisenhower warned of a "military-industrial complex" that had a vested interest in the arms race. Military challenges to the CIA's neutral, civilian estimates were a mounting problem; indeed, the military was on the point of achieving a new, unified voice: the Defense Intelligence Agency. Just as serious was the threatened politicization of intelligence. Alleged intelligence failures at Bogota, Korea, and Suez had already formed a backdrop to earlier presidential elections; none of them was more significant than the missile gap and Cuban issues in 1960. Not the least of Dulles's achievements, in the light of these potential dangers, was that until April 1961 he kept America on his side.

7

PRESIDENTIAL SHAKE-UP
Kennedy and the Bay of Pigs

The prejudices and ambitions of 1970s politicians partly account for the retrospective view that the CIA was an ailing institution in the 1960s. At the same time, that view has a basis in fact. The Agency failed to exert an optimal intelligence influence because it became accident-prone, because some of its reasoning was faulty, and because, with waning political confidence in the integrity and status of its product, that product came to be ignored or treated lightly. The failure of some of its covert operations and the exposure of others made matters worse because they showed that the CIA was operationally vulnerable and because, in a changing political climate, they made the Agency seem a diplomatic liability instead of an asset. Once U.S. and world opinion had received intimations of the CIA's mortality, the Agency's senior officers began to lose the power of persuasion and, toward the end of the Johnson administration, the self-confidence to exercise independent judgment.

These troubles were rooted in the earlier history of the Agency. Ever since the 1940s its leaders had contended with libertarian criticism, bureaucratic rivalry, right-wing attacks, and charges of incompetence. Overconfident investment in covert operations that led to serious trouble in later years was also a legacy of the period before 1960. Hitherto, however, the Agency had not only escaped lightly but basked in the esteem of an overwhelming majority of Americans. Beginning with the Kennedy administration, the rot set in. The decline came not only because of the legacy of the Truman-Eisenhower years but also because of the Agency's mistakes in the 1960s and because of deteriorating White House-CIA relations in the Kennedy-Johnson-Nixon era. It was not new for critics to portray the CIA as a menace to the democratic process; now, however, democratic politics seemed a real threat to the standing and effectiveness of the Agency.

Even though the Agency made scientific and technological advances in the Kennedy years, it also organized the disastrous Bay of Pigs invasion and then performed in a less than inspiring manner in relation to the Cuban missile crisis. Furthermore, quite independently of these events and apparently justifiably in the light of them, President John F. Kennedy set in motion an intelligence shake-up, a shake-up that rattled the CIA's morale and invited all and sundry to reconsider its standing in the national-security and foreign-policy bureaucracies.

It was not immediately apparent that the Kennedy succession would alter the CIA's status. To every outward appearance, the White House-CIA relationship continued unimpaired from Inauguration Day on January 20, to the Bay of Pigs fiasco on April 17, 1961. To the annoyance of a small coterie of liberal friends who were beginning to regard Allen Dulles and the CIA as liabilities, the president-elect had already announced that the director, together with J. Edgar Hoover at the FBI, would be staying on. Arthur Schlesinger, Jr., the historian who served on Kennedy's White House staff, interpreted this as part of the "strategy of reassurance" adopted by a narrowly elected president in order to show the nation that he represented all citizens, not just the young, the radical, and the dispossessed. Another factor, as intelligence analyst William Corson shows, is that CIA officials, armed with a psychological profile of the successful candidate, played on his intellectual pride which inhibited his desire to ask simple but necessary questions that might have produced embarrassing answers harmful to his working relationship with their colleagues. Thus the early Kennedy-CIA relationship was ostensibly a cozy one.[1]

There is, however, evidence which suggests that, because of the new president's determination to run things differently, White House-CIA disharmony set in even before the Bay of Pigs. Kennedy's special assistant for national security affairs, McGeorge Bundy, explained to a congressional committee in the mid-1960s that the National Security Council, the CIA's controlling committee, played a less significant role under the new president. The State Department and Kennedy's personal staff, including Bundy himself, played a relatively greater role. These new arrangements, which Bundy later described, understandably caused some early friction. Dulles tried to smooth things over. On February 5, 1961, for example, he wrote to Bundy to correct the "misunderstanding" that the NSC and CIA had been running U.S. policy in the Congo.[2]

Some senior state department officials scented an opportunity, even before the Bay of Pigs, to put the Agency in its place. Undersecretary of State Chester Bowles believed the CIA had been given too many responsibilities and recommended a reorganization. Secretary of State Dean Rusk turned to Roger Hilsman, Kennedy's selection to head State's Bureau of Intelligence and Research (INR). Hilsman, a Texan educated at West Point and Yale, had led an OSS commando unit in Burma

(1944–45) and had also worked for the CIA itself. He described Rusk's February 1961 brief as "an assignment to look at the role of CIA and the relations between CIA and the Department of State in line with President Kennedy's call for the State Department to lead." There was no secret about Hilsman's opinion that intelligence should be integrated with policy decisions and run by policymakers; he had developed the theme in his book *Strategic Intelligence and National Decisions* (1956). Affecting the present tense of the tough guy, he later recalled how, in the early weeks of the Kennedy administration, "there isn't any place to go but down for CIA, you see."[3]

The anti-CIA attitude was also to be found among other Kennedy diplomats. John Kenneth Galbraith, the Harvard economist chosen by Kennedy as ambassador to India, wrote in his diary well before the Bay of Pigs incident: "My briefing this morning was by the CIA and on various spooky activities, some of which I do not like. I shall stop them."[4] Such desires to curb the CIA were not universal, and in some memoirs they may well have been an invention of hindsight, but they did exist in some diplomatic quarters before, and independently of, the Cuban fiasco.

Kennedy's own approach to the CIA was governed, in part, by his desire to break with tradition once he had performed the ritual of reassuring Americans they would not have their society changed overnight. Like Franklin D. Roosevelt, he wanted to forge, within the central government, an instrument of reform. Unlike FDR, he envisaged the immediate application of renewed presidential vigor to foreign, as well as domestic affairs. Like any new president, he had to impose his personal authority, as distinct from the authority of his office, on the officials and bureaucracy around him. It is possible that Kennedy, in some ways an untried and unproven young man, felt this need psychologically to a greater extent than some other presidents. In order to assert his power, it was necessary for him to shake things up and throw his weight around. The way in which he did so mattered less than the fact of his doing it.

According to the defenders of Kennedy's CIA policy, the Agency was from the beginning a logical and justifiable target. Schlesinger described the combined effects of the Dulles partnership and the "lucky success in Guatemala": the CIA's budget grew to exceed State's by 50 percent, it had better personnel in many areas; its local station chiefs were sometimes more powerful than the U.S. ambassador; its intelligence operations were out of State Department control, and its covert operations threatened to become so. Hilsman painted a similar picture. Perhaps unaware of the fact that State Department intelligence control had no basis in law or the Constitution and had existed only in World War I and its aftermath, he attacked the supine behavior of his predecessor: "With Hugh Cuming in INR the CIA got so it was running the foreign policy of the United States."[5]

Hilsman set about the process of, as he saw it, reforming the part of the intelligence community over which he had influence. He cut those of the INR's activities which relied on CIA funds (biographical and country-by-country compilations) "to be free of them so I could fight them." He obtained better access to

information about the CIA's covert operational planning "and was able to influence and cut down CIA after that power fight." All this was consistent with
Kennedy's desire to exert greater personal influence over foreign-policy formation,
and to do so through the instrumentality of the State Department, which was to be
refurbished as a presidentially controlled coordinating agency and brain trust.[6]

It was consistent, also, with the demotion of the NSC noted by McGeorge
Bundy, a prime beneficiary of the change. Eisenhower had used the NSC for the
purpose for which, among others, it had been intended, the overall policy direction
of the CIA. He had occasionally resorted to ad hoc methods, for example by
appointing the outsider John McCone of the Atomic Energy Commission to the
NSC. But he had exercised control over the CIA—firm control, according to future
CIA director McCone—in a formal manner at NSC meetings. The 1960 election
result changed all that. Chester Cooper, now on the White House staff, recorded
that the Kennedy administration thought the NSC was "ossified." So Kennedy cut
through existing procedures, substituted a "dynamic and bright staff" of his own
choosing, and, in so doing, Cooper contended, "broke the link between the policy
maker [the president in the NSC] and the intelligence analyst [the CIA]."[7]

Kennedy reduced the general influence of the NSC by the simple expedient of
ignoring it. He also removed one of its specific functions, the coordination of
covert operations. Under Eisenhower this was, in theory at least, the job of the
NSC's Operations Coordinating Board. Kennedy heeded the complaints of those
who regarded the OCB as a "paper mill" and abolished it in February, 1961.
According to one veteran of both the OCB and its predecessor the Psychological
Strategy Board, he failed to appreciate that the committee's members had trans-
acted much of their business informally, over Wednesday luncheons and on the
telephone, and that OCB members had usefully discussed means for the implementation of policy decisions.[8] The abolition of the OCB was significant for other
reasons, too: it demonstrated the president's willingness to challenge accepted
procedures and authority, and it removed a potential scapegoat should a covert
operation go wrong. As the Bay of Pigs episode was soon to show, the CIA itself
would have to be that scapegoat.

Deputy director for plans Bissell's plot to topple Castro was well advanced by
the time Kennedy entered the White House. The Guatemalan government had
allowed the CIA to train a Cuban exile force on its territory. The plan was to
invade Cuba with a small contingent and establish a beachhead in anticipation of a
popular rising in support of the counterrevolution. Surprise and therefore secrecy
were essential ingredients in the scheme, and U.S. involvement was, of course, to
be plausibly deniable. Already committed to the exiles' cause because of his
campaign rhetoric, Kennedy approved this plan and authorized the mission.

At 7:45 P.M. on the evening of April 16, 1961, the seven-ship invading armada
dropped anchor in the Bay of Pigs, an area selected for its seclusion and for the
swampy approaches that would preclude counterattack from Castro's forces. At
11 P.M. Pepe San Román, the invasion commander, went on deck for a breath of

air. He was astonished to be greeted by a shoreline of twinkling lights. In the past three years, unknown to the invasion's planners, the Bay of Pigs had become Playa Girón—a Cuban equivalent of Coney Island—with solid roads crossing the swamps to the delectable beaches. Román's discovery was but the prelude to a rude awakening. Many planning errors had been made, and mistakes continued as the invasion went badly wrong. The fourteen-hundred invaders suffered heavy bombardment. Within seventy-two hours they were utterly defeated. The cover story collapsed, and CIA involvement was blazoned across the world to the acute embarrassment of the United States.[9]

The various contemporary explanations of the operational failure at the Bay of Pigs not only throw doubt on the competence of those involved, but they also illuminate the divisive effects of the episode. Bissell, for example, blamed Kennedy for not authorizing a U.S. airstrike in support of the invasion; perhaps he inwardly contrasted Kennedy's inaction with Eisenhower's bold and decisive support of the 1954 Guatemalan operation.[10] In turn, Kennedy's own inquiry, the Taylor commission, while pointing to poor coordination as one factor, criticized the CIA, especially on the point of overcentralization.[11]

Such was the CIA's stranglehold on the project that vital information did not get through to the president. Thus, although the success of the enterprise depended upon a spontaneous rising of the Cuban people in support of the invaders, Kennedy did not see Office of Naval Intelligence reports casting doubt on this possibility. He obtained a distorted view of the project because it was monopolized by Bissell and his covert action chief Tracy Barnes at the deputy directorate for plans. Kennedy was enamored of the brilliant Bissell and placed too much faith in his judgment. Able though he was, Bissell was a poor counselor on Cuba. Hilsman noted that both Bissell and Dulles, upset by the failure of earlier preemptive moves to get rid of the repressive Batista, had become "emotionally involved" in the Castro issue, to the detriment of their operational judgment.[12]

The degree to which Bissell and Barnes shut out intelligence advisers to the Joint Chiefs of Staff and the State Department, not to mention their own colleague, CIA Deputy Director for Intelligence Robert Amory, was no doubt exaggerated in retrospect as everyone ran for cover and claimed they had had no say in the disastrous decision.[13] Nevertheless, the need for secrecy in planning a surprise attack does seem to have accentuated the evils of compartmentalization, so that Kennedy became a victim of the plan's enthusiasts. Bissell and Barnes, in turn, formed intelligence estimates of the likely success of a plan of which they were the chief advocates, hardly an ideal arrangement.

Recrimination over responsibility for the Bay of Pigs took place between the White House and CIA, within the CIA, and, just as significantly, between the CIA and the military. General George H. Decker, chief of staff of the U.S. army, 1960–62, naturally tried to distance the Joint Chiefs of Staff from the disaster and, in doing so, indicated that the CIA had been monopolistic as well as incompetent. This interpretation of events can only have encouraged the advocates of a more powerful military input to U.S. intelligence estimates: in August 1961, these advocates won the day with the establishment of the Defense Intelligence Agency, one of the CIA's potent rivals in future years. According to Decker, the Joint Chiefs of Staff had been "on the sidelines as observers and advisers." The operation had failed because their stipulations and guidelines had been ignored. Decker shared the naval intelligence view that the Cuban people would not have risen in support of the invasion, and he asked why it was left to military professionals to ask the political questions their civilian bosses had left unanswered.[14]

Decker also criticized the operation for its lack of one ingredient essential to its success, surprise. He was right, for the Latin American world had expected the CIA to act. To the CIA, the replacement of Arbenz by a right-wing dictator in 1954 seemed a shining precedent; to Latin American revolutionaries, however, the Guatemalan episode was a warning, and a signal that prepared them against a surprise attack on Cuba. For example, on March 12, 1960, a full year before the Bay of Pigs invasion, a Guatemalan exile publicly predicted there would soon be a covert attack on Cuba, possibly from a base in Honduras. As time went by, American intentions became increasingly obvious. Questioning Secretary of State Christian A. Herter in an executive session of the Senate Foreign Relations Committee on January 6, 1961, Senator Wayne Morse drew attention to rumors about a CIA invasion. There was open speculation in both Latin America and in California about the CIA's training base in Guatemala. In the event, Castro was so well informed about the invasion plans that, four days before the exiles' assault, he rounded up thousands of suspected opponents to guard against the insurrection the Americans hoped for. The policy of secrecy had kept American officials in the dark, but not, apparently, the Cuban leadership.[15] The CIA made serious intelligence errors in failing to assess correctly the outlook and military preparedness of the Cuban people.

The Bay of Pigs fiasco resulted in a severe loss of caste for the CIA. Abroad, opinion of the Agency sank to a low point—not because people suddenly awoke to the perfidiousness of its actions, but because the awe-inspiring institution had at last shown itself to be vulnerable. One can more effectively speak ill of the mighty once they have fallen, and Castro lost no time exploiting the apparent weakness of the CIA. In a television address immediately following the Bay of Pigs invasion, he traced the covert nature of U.S. interventions to the now much-tarnished Rooseveltian undertaking, in 1933, not to intervene openly in the internal affairs of sovereign American states. The fate of Arbenz had been a warning to Cuba. The Bay of Pigs episode was a grim reminder of what might happen to any American sovereign state. Should the United States make another such attempt, the whole of Latin America would arise.[16] Castro, according to his critics within the CIA, had been an enemy of the United States ever since his participation as a young man in the Bogota riots of 1948.[17] Now, the Bay of Pigs disaster had given him a new and dangerous lease of life.

The Bay of Pigs made the CIA a favorite scapegoat of foreign politicians of all hues, not just those on the Left. The proven involvement of the Agency in one foolish conspiracy stimulated endless allegations of further plots. Some of these allegations were serious, as for example in France, an important NATO ally whose friendship America could ill afford to lose. Just after the CIA's abortive attempt to remove Castro, French newspapers and politicians accused the Agency of trying to overthrow the government headed by Charles de Gaulle. According to their allegations, the Agency conspired with Maurice Challe and others to depose and assassinate de Gaulle in order to frustrate the French president's attempt to give Algeria its independence. The CIA's motive, according to press reports, was to preempt a Communist takeover in France, which was envisaged should Algeria with its extreme right-wing French settlers be lost.[18]

The truth was rather different. Far from fomenting right-wing colonialist plots, the CIA had taken an option on Algerian independence. Between 1958 and 1962, when Algeria gained independence, the Agency organized secretly vouchered educational grants for students who had already been expelled from French universities for Algerian nationalist activities.[19] Nor did the CIA encourage President Kennedy to back another horse, once the Algerian loyalist rebellion had started on April 22, 1961: on April 24, Dulles specifically warned the chief executive that the insurgent leaders would not get the necessary support in metropolitan France.[20]

These factors, however, could not be made known at the time. In the immediate aftermath of the Bay of Pigs, there was a natural reluctance to believe the disclaimers that came from Dulles on May 1, and from President Kennedy at a Paris press conference on June 2, 1961. Kennedy had almost called off his goodwill visit to France because of Foreign Minister Maurice Couve de Murville's innuendo about CIA involvement in Algeria.[21] In the event, he opened the press meeting with style: "I am the man who accompanied Jacqueline Kennedy to Paris," but he still glumly noted, as he fended off a question about CIA complicity, "the good will of this visit may be rapidly diminishing."[22]

There have been various suggestions about the provenance of the Kennedy-CIA-de Gaulle conspiracy theory. The version favored by the CIA was that the rumors, though they appeared in conservative newspapers, were the result of a successful KGB disinformation ploy.[23] Another possibility is, however, that it was a French disinformation ploy, one that may, paradoxically, have had its basis in French annoyance at America's sympathies with the Algerian anticolonialists. The CIA had helped a leading literary opponent of French colonialism, Franz Fanon, to an extent that apparently annoyed de Gaulle.[24] Kennedy himself had supported the Algerian anti-imperialist cause in a 1957 speech that provoked the suspicion, among domestic critics, that he was lukewarm toward NATO. Yet, eminent French officials spread the story that the CIA supported the attempted loyalist coup. *U.S. News and World Report* perhaps guessed as well as any source why such anti-American rumors were apparently credited in responsible French circles:

[There was] a search for scapegoats, particularly for non-French scapegoats.

It was against this background that officials of the French government, including Cabinet Ministers and other high officials, privately encouraged the idea that U.S. generals were to blame for supporting the conspirators.[25]

Whatever the explanation, anti-CIA-type anti-Americanism had become an article of faith, or at least of expediency, in certain conservative French circles.

The Bay of Pigs debacle had further unfortunate consequences in Africa south of the Sahara, where Kennedy hoped to nurture local nationalisms as a bulwark against Soviet-orchestrated Communist expansion. To the dismay of some of its supporters like C. D. Jackson and to the surprise of some Communist commentators, the CIA had made a late start in sub-Sahara Africa, ignoring the vast region for much of the 1950s.[26] Now, the Cuban catastrophe made local politicians acutely suspicious of the Agency's intensifying activities.

One of the CIA's tactics in Africa's new and politically mercurial nation states was to court various opposition factions, a prudent precaution or a dangerous provocation according to one's point of view.[27] In 1961, Agency officers made overtures to Kwame Nkrumah's opponents, concentrated in exile in Togo, just in case the charismatic socialist slipped back down the greasy pole of Ghanaian politics. Not surprisingly in the aftermath of the Bay of Pigs, knowledge of this made the Ghanaian president and his supporters nervous. The semi-official *Ghanaian Times* claimed that American blacks were engaged in African subversive operations. Nkrumah warned U.S. ambassador William P. Mahoney about the CIA: "We've got to keep an eye on these people."[28]

The Bay of Pigs episode tainted many of America's overseas ventures, even the Peace Corps. Launched on March 1, 1961, the Peace Corps helped young American volunteers to serve overseas, offering assistance to underdeveloped regions and countries. As well as being a means of extending practical help, and of channeling the idealism of American youth, it was an inspired public relations exercise. Radio Moscow immediately charged that the Peace Corps was a collection agency for Allen Dulles. Then, taking advantage of the Bay of Pigs scandal, the Soviet news agency Tass announced that the head of the Peace Corps, Kennedy's brother-in-law R. Sargent Shriver, was a "CIA Agent." Kennedy subsequently acknowledged the CIA was a public relations liability when he instructed the Agency not to use the Peace Corps for any undercover activities whatsoever. The stigma remained, however. When Shriver flew to Accra in 1963 "to inform Nkrumah that President Kennedy had given his direct personal assurance that no one in the Peace Corps was in any way connected with the CIA," the *Ghanaian Times* responded with blank incredulity.[29]

Although it is probable that only a minority of left-wing Africans genuinely feared the CIA, the nationalist imperative dictated that others should denounce the

Agency, too, to avoid being dubbed, in the telling words of one historian of the Congo, "CIA puppets."[30] International hostility of either type meant that it was no longer so feasible for CIA officers to present themselves as the natural allies of indigenous local forces, as demanded in psywar and counterinsurgency doctrine.

The Bay of Pigs made the Agency a diplomatically embarrassing institution to such a degree that State Department officials campaigning to diminish CIA influence on the making of U.S. strategic and foreign policy found new support. The Cuban disaster jolted U.S. opinion makers into reappraising the CIA's role, because, whereas previous abortions like the attempts to remove Sukarno had been unspectacular and far from the continental shoreline, the Cuban defeat could not be ignored. It inspired, for example, a small cluster of books that, for the first time, offered critical yet responsible analysis of the CIA—they were written from neither a Communist nor a self-serving standpoint. These books included Andrew Tully's general critique *Central Intelligence Agency: the Inside Story* (1962), Paul W. Blackstone's attack on covert operations as short-term palliatives in *The Strategy of Subversion: Manipulating the Politics of Other Nations* (1964), and the influential best seller *The Invisible Government* (1964), in which journalists David Wise and Thomas B. Ross criticized in detail the Bay of Pigs operation and the CIA's other clandestine activities.[31]

These works indicate that a long-term trend of skepticism about the CIA's worth had set in. More immediately, Congress launched an investigation into the abortive mission. Senator Wayne Morse, chairman of the Foreign Relations Committee's Subcommittee on American Republics Affairs, publicly attacked the administration on April 27, 1961, for its cavalier disregard of the Senate's right to be consulted over foreign policy. Within three weeks, the Committee on Foreign Relations had questioned the following leading officials on Cuba: Secretary of State Dean Rusk, Allen Dulles and Richard Bissell of the CIA, Adolf Berle and Chester Bowles of the Department of State, and General Lyman K. Lemnitzer, chairman of the Joint Chiefs of Staff.[32]

Yet, the Committee let the CIA off so lightly that Bissell kept his good humor. Morse was in the event only "a little surprised" at some of the support logistics, while former air force secretary Symington pointed out that the CIA was not the U.S. government and then launched a diversionary attack on poor U.S. airlift capacity. Mansfield commended Bissell for his "candor," and apologized to the deputy director because the lights had gone out during the hearing. Bissell quipped: "I trust our influence is not so baleful that it would affect even the lighting system."[33]

The Senate had held back for several reasons. It was in a poor position to criticize the actions of an agency it had consistently refused to oversee. There was no rising Young Turk in a position to supply leadership. The Cuban problem was not a major domestic issue affecting U.S. citizens. Finally, the Cold War was raging anew, and not only in Cuba. Just after Kennedy's inauguration, Patrice Lumumba had been assassinated in the Congo (by local rivals who preempted the CIA's own plot).[34] This plunged the mineral-rich nation into civil war, with Kennedy strongly committed to the right-wing factions. Meanwhile, the U.S. once again confronted the Eastern Bloc over Berlin, Kennedy taking a strident stand and the East Germans for their part erecting the infamous Berlin Wall. Against the background of these events, no senator wished to seem disloyal to the chief executive, so the CIA's hour of legislative reckoning was once again postponed.

But CIA officials did not escape the wrath of the president. The Bay of Pigs was the beginning of the end of an era of White House-CIA harmony. Given the pecking-order nature of Washington's governmental bureaucracy, this rift was to lower the Agency's stock in the foreign-policy-making community.

At first, the enraged Kennedy stayed his hand for reasons of political expediency. He ignored the circuit-breaking mechanism whereby he could have attempted to blame a National Security Council committee for the failure—a wise decision not just because this particular subterfuge was barely credible at the best of times, but also because the operation was so large scale that nobody would have believed the president knew nothing about it. The operation was "plausibly deniable" neither for the United States nor for the president. Just four days after the abortive landing, in fact as soon as the scale of the disaster was known, the president told the press the responsibility for the Bay of Pigs was his; on Monday, April 24, he added that the decision was his "sole responsibility." This response was much admired; General Decker, for example, later described it as "a very noble thing." What seemed consistent with the president's public statements was his refusal to fire Dulles and Bissell.[35]

Political shrewdness underlay Kennedy's policy. The wound had to be stitched up quickly to forestall the actions of foes who might wish to take advantage of the weakened state of the Democratic administration. Schlesinger recalled the president saying that so long as he kept on Dulles, a Republican appointee, "the Republicans would be disinclined to attack the administration over the Cuban failure." Another politically beneficial aspect of Kennedy's response was its speed. Surely, in taking the blame on himself before launching an inquiry, the president was giving his officials the benefit of the doubt? He was supporting—or perhaps covering up for—his men in a manner which, admirable on one level, left room for speculation on another. Kennedy gently prodded the speculation: "Victory has a hundred fathers," he declared to newspapermen, "and defeat is an orphan." By the very process of adopting the orphan so conspicuously, Kennedy fueled speculation about the real paternity of the Bay of Pigs fiasco.[36]

Then, one day in May, the president told Dulles, Bissell, and deputy director Charles P. Cabell they would be replaced "after a decent interval." Accounts of the occasion and of the exact wording vary, but they agree on the substance of what Kennedy told Bissell: "If this were the British government, I would resign, and you, being a senior civil servant, would remain. But it isn't. In our government, you and Allen have to go, and I have to remain."[37] Thus Dulles and his colleagues met the same fate as Hillenkoetter before them, though on this occasion they had to take responsibility for an operational as opposed to an intelligence failure. It was a humiliating experience: Dulles's own press files show that journalists simply assumed, by August, that he would have to go; Bissell's successor as deputy director for plans noted the dismissals were unambiguously "the sad outcome of the Bay of Pigs."[38] The dismissals were an enduringly bitter pill for Dulles and Bissell to swallow, and in later years both indicated their resentment at the presidential verdict.[39] Dulles had no facesaving military or other public career to which he could return. His fate was a stern warning to future intelligence officers who might be tempted to risk their careers by speaking out forcefully or taking an adventurous initiative.

At first, it appeared that the Kennedy administration might go further in its chastisement of the CIA. In particular, Undersecretary of State Chester Bowles pressed for more severe action. Bowles, who had been one of the inspirations behind the Kennedy presidential campaign, was an archetypal Yankee anti-imperialist who wanted to safeguard America's position as the standard-bearer of decolonization in Africa. Not everyone in the State Department shared his views, but there was widespread resentment in the department and in the diplomatic service at the way in which CIA chiefs-of-station in various countries were allegedly preempting or embarrassing local U.S. ambassadors. Indeed on April 15, 1961, Secretary Rusk had had to write to Prime Minister Lee Kuan Yew of Singapore, apologizing for a clumsy attempt by CIA officials to bribe the premier with the princely sum of $3.3 million, to ensure his nondisclosure of an earlier, equally clumsy CIA effort to suborn the Singapore secret service. To hush the matter up, Rusk promised that the officials responsible would be punished. But the affair incensed Hilsman and Bowles and when the Bay of Pigs immediately followed the Singapore humiliation the undersecretary seized his opportunity: "I recommended to Rusk that the CIA should be abolished and its functions absorbed by officers more directly responsible to the [State] Department."[40] Kennedy did make a concession to his campaign mentor: on May 20, 1961, he sent to U.S. ambassadors a circular letter prepared by Bowles, stressing the seniority and coordinating responsibilities of American ambassadors abroad.[41]

But Kennedy's disappointment over the Bay of Pigs—a single if major episode—in no way undermined his firm faith in the principle of covert operations, and in the CIA's mission to carry them out. There are numerous indications of his enthusiasm, which he made no particular effort to hide. In 1959, he had called for a new type of response: "Our nuclear retaliatory power is not enough . . . It cannot protect uncommitted nations against a Communist takeover using local or guerrilla forces."[42] He not only dined with Ian Fleming, but flaunted his taste for James Bond fiction as a "publicity gag."[43] He was also greatly taken by Edward Lansdale, whom he met early in his presidency and with whom he discussed the situation in Vietnam.[44] As Lansdale's friend Lederer put it, counterinsurgency experts wanted to Vietnamize the anti-Communist struggle in Vietnam, and so ensure that the few Americans who went out there were "good Americans": "As there aren't enough geniuses to go around, we have to school, educate, enema, and beat the middle class intellectuals" to make them knowledgeable and tough.[45] Kennedy put Lansdale in charge of a special task force in Vietnam and, from 1961 on, Lansdale pressed his "de-Americanization" argument both privately and publicly.[46] In the long run he lost his attempt to apply the Philippine formula in Vietnam. Yet, elsewhere in Southeast Asia the CIA option did prevail over the military solution, and even in Vietnam serious conventional military escalation did not begin until the Johnson administration. President Kennedy's adoption of Lansdale and his techniques was therefore an important indication that the covert approach of the Eisenhower years would be continued.

Far from being warned against covert operations by the ignominy on Cuba's beaches, Kennedy defiantly accused the Communists of a "monolithic and ruthless conspiracy that relies primarily on covert means for expanding its sphere of influence," and promised to redouble his efforts.[47] His appointment of a board of inquiry on the Bay of Pigs was a means to that end, rather than an effort at open-minded assessment of the role of covert operations in U.S. foreign policy. The members of the board were Attorney General Robert Kennedy, Admiral Arleigh Burke, and Allen Dulles. The chairman was retired army chief of staff Maxwell D. Taylor. In his book *The Uncertain Trumpet* (1960), Taylor had criticized the Eisenhower administration's overreliance on nuclear deterrence. This seemed promising to the advocates of larger conventional forces, but Taylor's "flexible response" doctrine also offered hope to counterinsurgency advocates: in one passage the general referred to the limited wars then in progress in Malaya, Vietnam, Laos, and the Middle East: "While our massive retaliatory strategy may have prevented the Great War—a World War III—it has not maintained the Little Peace."[48]

Several witnesses before the Taylor inquiry argued that covert action should be improved, not stopped. Edward Lansdale said the Bay of Pigs operation had been properly a CIA activity, but the political aspects had been neglected. Former director Bedell Smith thought covert operations might be taken away from the CIA, but they ought to continue: "It's time we take the bucket of slops and put another cover over it." When the Taylor Committee reported formally (but secretly) to the president on June 13, 1961, it concluded that "paramilitary operations such as Zapata [the Bay of Pigs invasion] are a form of Cold War action in which the country must be prepared to engage."[49] In spite of Smith's suggestion, the inquiry accepted Dulles's argument (a reiteration of the 1949 Dulles-Correa-Jackson recommendation) that a single roof should shelter the spies and the operators—there was to be no Balkanization of the plans directorate. In future, however, covert operations were to be on a smaller scale and less detectable. Kennedy accepted these recommendations, keeping an eye on the CIA's budget, limiting the scale of its operations, but continuing them with, if anything, renewed vigor.[50]

In the fall of 1961 it became clear to all that Kennedy would continue to favor the covert Cold Warriors, even if there was more than one cause of the renowned Thanksgiving Day Massacre, the firing of CIA critic Chester Bowles. Dean Rusk had failed to galvanize the "beast of Foggy Bottom" which remained, its White House critics thought, slow, indecisive, cumbersome, and inefficient—and therefore incapable of meeting what Hilsman had described as "Kennedy's call for the State Department to lead." The Massacre did not so much achieve efficiency as offer up a sacrificial lamb for its nonachievement. Undersecretary Bowles, the lamb in question, was hardly responsible for alleged inefficiencies, but suffered from the disadvantage of belief to an embarrassing degree in the ideals professed by President Kennedy. In the words of one State Department diehard, "the trouble with Chet Bowles and Soapy [G. Mennen] Williams [Assistant Secretary of State for African Affairs] was that when they saw a band of black baboons beating tom-toms they saw George Washingtons."[51] Bowles had to go because he believed in genuine nationalism, instead of synthetic nationalism engineered by secret means.

In reaffirming his support for covert operations, Kennedy sought to ensure that in the future he would be better advised, and so he established bureaucratic machinery strongly reminiscent of that which Eisenhower had used. Thus, he revived the president's Board of Consultants on Foreign Intelligence Activities, whose pro forma collective resignation in anticipation of his inauguration he had originally accepted as part of his initial shake-up. He now re-installed the board's former chairman Killian, and, as members, other old Eisenhower hands including Langer, Murphy, and Gray.[52]

Also under review in the immediate aftermath of the Bay of Pigs were the bureaucratic provisions for authorization, planning, and circuit-breaking in relation to covert operations. In spite of his disgrace the eponymous deputy director of plans chaired a "Bissell committee" to review procedures.[53] Out of this review emerged three key committees. The special group continued to operate, consisting in the fall of 1961 of Maxwell Taylor, McGeorge Bundy, deputy undersecretary of state U. Alexis Johnson, deputy secretary of defense Roswell Gilpatric, Joint Chiefs of Staff chairman Lyman L. Lemnitzer and, of course, the director of central intelligence. This group would meet at two every Thursday afternoon. Then, it would resolve itself into the Special Group (Counterinsurgency), being joined by the attorney general, Robert Kennedy. The Special Group (Counterinsurgency) would devote its attention to clandestine means of blocking Communist insurgency in Laos, South Vietnam, and Thailand. Later still, the same group would transform itself into the Special Group (Augmented). By this time, Fowler Hamilton of the Agency for International Development and the broadcaster Edward R. Murrow (famous for his stand against McCarthyism and now director of the U.S. Information Agency) would be in attendance. President Kennedy told Taylor to be careful to conceal the activities of this last group. Its object was to get rid of Castro.[54]

Whereas the removal of Castro had been an important objective before and during the Bay of Pigs operation, immediately afterwards it became an obsession of the Kennedy brothers and some CIA officials. The Kennedys' response stemmed in part from a desire to get even. There was also a more rational and consistent element in their thinking. National Security Council staff member Michael Forrestal (the son of Truman's defense secretary) observed that both the Kennedy brothers and particularly the younger—soon dubbed "Mr. Counterinsurgency"—had been influenced by a Khruschev speech delivered in December 1960. In this speech, the Soviet premier noted that atomic warfare was impossible, and that Korea had discredited conventional warfare; so, internal, revolutionary, warfare was the way forward for the Communists. Counterinsurgency and in the Cuban case clandestine counterrevolutionary activity therefore seemed the proper course for Americans, whose horror of nuclear war and distaste for draft-based wars (evident in Korea, soon to be confirmed in Vietnam) complemented the attitudes of the Russians.[55]

The debate about how to eliminate Castro and the means eventually used in the attempt illustrate some of the dangers inherent in covert operations. One plan was to support leading Cuban dissidents. But these dissidents could be highly individualistic, unamenable to U.S. discipline, and—contrary to the express wish of the president—indiscreet. So, in the words of one White House official, the CIA at first favored "a CIA underground formed on criteria of operational convenience rather than a Cuban underground formed on criteria of building political strength sufficient to overthrow Castro."[56]

Lansdale, who returned from a Saigon trip in November 1961 and was immediately conscripted to run an anti-Castro program (Operation Mongoose), in principle preferred indigenous groups. But he could see that the ground was barren. Castro, he told President Kennedy, "had aroused considerable affection for himself personally with the Cuban population."[57] The United States would therefore need to coax Cubans to change their minds about Castro, putting them in the right frame of mind to start a counterrevolution on their own initiative. But Lansdale's scheme failed miserably. Lansdale found it difficult to control the CIA's Miami station, whose overfinanced and overzealous staff launched pointless sabotage operations that only increased Castro's popularity. As Lansdale confessed with rueful hindsight: "We have a tendency as a people to want to see things done right—and, if they aren't, we step in and try to do things ourselves. That is fatal to a revolution."[58]

In addition to running its Mongoose operation, the CIA continued to try to implement its plans—first hatched under Eisenhower—to assassinate Castro. When some details leaked out in later years they caused a sensation, for they contained compelling elements: money, sex, revenge, and conspiracy to murder. Some of the more salacious revelations told of the involvement in the scheme of Robert Maheu (an ex-FBI man employed by oil tycoon Howard Hughes), of Maheu's recruitment of hoodlums Sam Giancana and John Rosselli, and of President Kennedy's politically indiscreet relationship with Judith Campbell, a woman passed on to him from Frank Sinatra via Giancana.[59] Apart from their use of mobster gunmen, CIA officers dreamed up schemes to slip Castro the hallucinatory drug LSD via a cigar, to give him a pen with a poison tip, to cripple him with exploding clamshells while he dived in the Caribbean, and to sprinkle his shoes with a depilatory to make his beard fall out and with it, according to the psywar experts, his Latin machismo.[60]

John F. Kennedy's own assassination in 1963 fueled later speculation that Castro knew the CIA was trying to kill him and got to the U.S. president first. Thus there has been extensive debate about whether President Kennedy knew the CIA was trying to kill Castro. The evidence is still inconclusive.[61] That does not, of course, rule out the Cubans' revenge or preemption motive, for they may have thought John Kennedy was behind the CIA murder conspiracies, even if he was not. Interesting though all this may be for its human interest or as a "ripping yarn," however, speculation about revenge assassination plots has been significant for the CIA not in itself, but for its effects. For when details of the assassination conspiracies emerged in the mid-1970s, they linked the Agency in the public eye with unsavory practices, with the death of a president, and with the political destabilization of the mid-1970s. The Agency's standing suffered accordingly.

And although the CIA did not feel the full force of public ire until the 1970s, under the Kennedy administration its officials continued with a full panoply of operations that rubbed salt in the Bay of Pigs wound and diminished the stature of the Agency even in the 1960s. The Agency's operations in the Congo made it a byword for iniquity. In Indonesia it pursued a more moderate policy toward President Sukarno in the wake of its 1950s plotting, but in the Western Hemisphere its diverse actions continued to fuel anti-Americanism; indeed they encouraged the spread of Castroism and the near deification of Castro's revolutionary emissary, Che Guevara. In Ecuador, for example, the Agency contributed to the overthrow of President Jose Velasco Ibarra's regime, installing instead Carlos Julio Arosemena. Then, when Arosemena displeased the CIA, the Agency used its grip on the local labor movement, among other factors, to destabilize his government which fell, in its turn, in July 1963. Robert Kennedy was keen on the use of the labor component, which in domestic politics was part of the still-surviving 1930s coalition that made up the Democrats' power base. In 1963, the CIA, through its labor contacts, engineered a general strike in British Guiana that contributed to the fall of democratically elected Cheddi Jagan.[62]

By this time, the CIA was also running a "secret" war in Laos. The operation had begun on a small scale in 1962, as an attempt to prevent a takeover by the Pathet Lao and their North Vietnamese Communist allies. Prevented by the 1954 Geneva accords and by the prospectively high costs from intervening openly, the Kennedy administration resorted to the clandestine option. The CIA recruited groups of local hill tribesmen known collectively as the Meo to fight against the insurgents. Though fewer than ten CIA officers were involved at the outset, the aim soon became to exploit the Meo as a strategic asset rather than to help them in their push for self-determination. With the full knowledge of leading U.S. senators as well as officials, the Meo were encouraged to fight a large-scale war of oblivion. A quarter of a million of them overlooked the strategic Plain of Jars in 1962; thirteen years later, a mere ten thousand survivors escaped into exile.[63]

Such actions offended those U.S. diplomats who were worried about international opinion. These diplomats also saw cause for concern in the continuation of covert subsidies. Under Kennedy, for example, the CIA still largely financed the international activities of the National Students' Association. Ralph Dungan, who as first president of the NSA had been present at the creation of the CIA link, in fact became one of President Kennedy's White House aides. Robert Kennedy later made it clear that the program had not been an instance of CIA adventurism. It had been run from the White House, with close supervision by McGeorge Bundy. In 1961, this type of propaganda subsidy was also extended to the "International Affairs Fund" of the American Newspaper Guild. These types of activity were bitterly objected to by Chester Bowles, who thought propaganda subsidies should have been openly given. Bowles subscribed to the view that responsibility for these subsidies had been foisted on the CIA "under pressure from the White House, State Department and Bureau of the Budget, as well as from its own empire builders."[64] But although the initiative came from elsewhere, it was the CIA which had to bear the opprobrium when the schemes were exposed.

John F. Kennedy continued with the extensive covert operational program of the Eisenhower years even after its partial exposure at the Bay of Pigs made it doubly provocative. On the other hand, in Dulles's successor John McCone he chose a man who opposed assassinations, revitalized the intelligence process, and made an effort to restore the CIA director's standing in the intelligence and foreign-policymaking community. McCone was a Catholic with well-known anti-Communist opinions that won plaudits from the conservative press. The *U.S. News and World Report*, for example, depicted him sympathetically as "a man with a slide-rule mind who never forgets he is dealing with human beings." The future intelligence director had been born in San Francisco, studied engineering for a brief spell in California, did not attend an Ivy League college, and became a millionaire shipbuilder. He had undergone an impressive apprenticeship for the CIA job. After serving as assistant to defense secretary Forrestal in 1948, he was air force undersecretary, 1950–51. Then he worked on Henry M. Wriston's federal committee on foreign service reform. Eisenhower appointed him chairman of the Atomic Energy Commission, and in that capacity he learned about Russian nuclear capabilities. His spell at the AEC also demonstrated that he was no mean politician. He had worked harmoniously with the AEC's congressional oversight committee. No rigid ideologue, he had dealt fairly with the public corporation, the Tennessee Valley Authority. In spite of his right-wing views, he had also coped well with the Oppenheimer problem. In fact, he had done a repair job on post-Oppenheimer AEC morale and could thus be seen as the ideal man to repair the post-Bay of Pigs CIA.[65]

McCone's takeover on November 29, 1961, brought hope for an intelligence upturn. For one thing, the White House seemed determined to make up for past deficiencies: the appointment of Chester Cooper as a White House-CIA liaison officer promised to restore morale by facilitating the optimal consumer-producer relationship long advocated by intelligence theorists. As Cooper put it, his job was to alert the CIA in advance to the kind of estimates, say on the Sino-Indian conflict or Cypriot terrorism, which the White House staff anticipated they might need.[66]

Once McCone had settled in to his new job in the CIA's new $46-million headquarters, his personality disarmed several potential critics. A few were no doubt reassured by the new director's efforts to stop political murder plans.[67] In more general terms, Hilsman recalled that "everybody thought McCone was going to be a bad guy. And basically he turned out to be a good guy." McCone knew that Killian, chairman of the Foreign Intelligence Advisory Board, had opposed his appointment as director "on the basis that I was more of an outspoken anti-communist than should be in that position and I was incapable of making a fair evaluation and that my estimates would be slanted." In the event, the two men sunk their differences and developed a "very intimate" relationship. Ray Cline, appointed deputy director for intelligence in 1962, was effusive about what he regarded as a halcyon intelligence interlude: McCone "is the only DCI [director of central intelligence] who ever took his role of providing substantive intelligence analysis and estimates to the President as his first priority job, and the only one who considered his duties as coordinating supervisor of the whole intelligence community to be a more important responsibility than the CIA's own clandestine and covert programs."[68]

McCone impressed his colleagues as a director who was determined to ensure the high quality of the CIA's estimates. A long-serving member of the Office of National Estimates described him as "going over each line" of a particular estimate "as if it were a corporate mortgage."[69] Another colleague recalled the new director telephoning Sherman Kent of ONE very early in the morning with blunt requests like: "On page 20, you say this. . . . Can you prove it?"[70] McCone impressed people through his determination to shake up the estimating process in the intelligence community, and he managed to impose at least some measure of authority on the community as a whole. Defense Secretary Robert S. McNamara allied with him in this respect, for although McNamara's Defense Intelligence Agency was to be a challenge to the CIA's authority in the longer term, McNamara needed all the help he could muster to fight off the air force's attempt to control aerial reconnaissance and Soviet military estimates, and he therefore backed Mc-Cone. The president also made known his unqualified support. On January 16, 1962, Kennedy issued a directive instructing McCone to exert more authority over the entire intelligence community.[71]

McCone was determined to improve the quality, coherence, and standing of the CIA's military estimates by strengthening the scientific research component within the CIA. This was to be a long battle, but external and internal factors played into his hands. Externally, the air force's position was weakening: the creation of the National Aeronautics and Space Administration in 1958 had deprived it of overall direction of aerial and space research; the palpably self-serving nature of its estimates on missiles had undermined its credibility; and McNamara was a formidable foe. Internally, the retirement of Bissell in February 1962 removed the man who had supported Dulles in his opposition to scientific reform (whereas apathy had governed Dulles's response, Bissell had opposed change because he wished to remain in control). By August 1963, McCone had completed his reform campaign and the CIA now had a new deputy directorate.[72]

The addition of the Directorate for Science and Technology to the existing ones for intelligence, plans, and administration meant that a number of allied functions were now collected under one roof. The new deputy directorate incorporated the former Office of Scientific Intelligence (established in 1949), Electronics Intelligence (the interception of foreign radiomagnetic radiations like radar), and various personnel including a data processing staff. One objective was an interchange of experts with the nongovernmental scientific community, and salary levels were to be commensurate with this revolving door principle. Appropriately, the first deputy director for science and technology, Albert Wheelon, had himself joined the CIA in the late 1950s from a private technical research firm.[73]

McCone's scientific reform was the culmination and epitome of a trend in the CIA away from human intelligence. His innovation met with stiff resistance at the time and has remained controversial since. To his contemporary and later critics McCone was variously second-rate, the fourth choice for the job, prejudiced against the Ivy League, and ambitious to exert an improper influence on policy. The indictment continues and is savage. With Kennedy's help, he is supposed to have started the process whereby the "prudent professionals" replaced the "bold easterners." Imaginative historians and secret agents alert to Soviet intentions and deceptions therefore gave way to dull, slide-rule scientists who measured only the obvious. The quality of recruitment, furthermore, far from improving with McCone's higher salaries, fell away as the Bay of Pigs and later the Vietnam War discouraged the better applicants from applying to an increasingly tarnished agency. The process had thus started which led to a dangerous underestimate of Soviet capabilities. There is some irony in this collective indictment: the CIA is supposed to have become "soft" on the Russians just when its "liberal" reputation was on the wane.[74]

Much of the criticism of McCone and of the changes he initiated has been subjective in origin and unbalanced. There is also much that can be said in defense of the reforms he introduced, and of the performance of the Agency under his direction. For example, the CIA's increasing technological sophistication meant it could verify Soviet observance or nonobservance of the atmospheric nuclear test ban treaty—ratified in the Senate in 1963 after McCone had satisfied first his own doubts and then others' on the feasibility of verification.[75] However, there were real shortcomings for the critics to note. They had already pointed to the Agency's failure to give adequate forewarning of the construction of the Berlin Wall in 1961, or of the rift between Syria and Egypt in the same year. Restrospectively, they were to complain about the CIA's nonprediction, during McCone's tenure, of the political decline of Khruschev leading to his fall from power in 1964.[76]

The Cuban missile crisis is the most important of the events illuminating the deficiencies of the CIA in McCone's day, and it helps explain why the Agency did not bounce back to enjoy its former standing. In the summer of 1962, Soviet engineers forged ahead with secret construction work preparatory to the installation of nuclear-tipped missiles in Cuba. These missiles had a range of 2,200 miles and would have been within a few minutes' flying time of major eastern seaboard cities in the United States. McCone, more imaginative than his critics were prepared to concede, warned in August that the Russians might well be planning such a move in Cuba. New York's Republican senator Kenneth Keating also warned, in September, that Cuban exiles were telling stories of missile-site construction. However, McCone was relying on instinct and Keating on rumor laced with midterm election political opportunism. In the aftermath of the Castro revolution and the Bay of Pigs fiasco, the CIA had no reliable spy network in Cuba. With McCone on honeymoon on the French Riviera with his second wife, the Agency produced what one authority has called its "notorious 'September estimate'," dismissing the missile hypothesis[77]

By mid-October, the Cuban sites were dangerously close to becoming operative. Only now did President Kennedy and his advisers find themselves in possession of evidence that made the truth all too plain. Resentful though de Gaulle may have been of the Americans, French intelligence passed on some information acquired through its own Cuban network. The Soviet defector Penkovsky delivered some evidence which helped U.S. photoanalysts to identify what they were looking at. Thus the photographic evidence supplied by U-2 spy planes persuaded the CIA, the White House, and the public. On October 22, the president wisely rejected an air strike and announced a blockade to turn back any Soviet ships that might have carried nuclear warheads for the Cuban missiles. Within six days Moscow had backed down, agreeing to crate its missiles and return them to the Eastern bloc.

Even if the handling of the crisis is testimony to the self-control and courage of President Kennedy, it by no means constitutes a glorious chapter in the history of U.S. intelligence. McCone did not enjoy the undying gratitude of his colleagues in government for having been right. Kennedy thought McCone's prediction had been merely accidentally correct, a consequence of his blind anti-Communism. His remark, "you were right all along, but for the wrong reasons," is sufficiently grudging to suggest that the proud Kennedy found it as difficult to forgive someone for being right as for being wrong: McCone later confessed that his relationship with Kennedy had been less "personal" than that which he had developed with Eisenhower. McNamara and Rusk were equally grudging in their acknowledgment of McCone's predictive success. McCone appears to have been rather tactless on the point, constantly reminding colleagues of his feat. McGeorge Bundy reportedly commented, "I'm so tired of listening to McCone say he was right I never want to hear it again." With the CIA discredited for being wrong and its director resented for being right, there was little prospect of a major advance in the Agency's standing.[78]

Another reason for the nonrevival of the Agency's prestige was the failure of its missile crisis postmortem. If McCone had offered a rational explanation for his early suspicions, or if other intelligence officials had with the wisdom of hindsight offered a credible explanation of Soviet motives, the CIA might have climbed in the esteem of U.S. policymakers. Various half-satisfactory explanations have been offered in retrospect: that the Cuban missiles were meant to balance U.S. missiles stationed in Turkey and targetted on Soviet cities; or that the Russians wanted to help Castro fend off CIA attacks; or that the Soviets intended to obtain from the United States a promise not to launch a conventional invasion of Cuba in exchange for withdrawal of the missiles (they succeeded in this aim). As of 1985, however, the typical CIA explanation remained that there was no explanation, that Agency officials had been correct in assuming, in 1962, that it would have been irrational of Russia to confront America's overwhelming nuclear strength. The Russian missile emplacement stemmed from a Russian intelligence miscalculation, namely the assumption that the United States would not seriously threaten to use her strength. The CIA erred only "in assuming that the Soviets would correctly assess the strength of U.S. reaction to such a move."[79]

This kind of assessment was as unconvincing in the 1960s as since for two reasons. First, it was unprovable except by inference. (From the fall of Khruschev, for example, it could be inferred that the Kremlin had punished a mistake—but it occurred two years after the event.) Second, it paid little heed to Soviet strategic doctrine, for in the early 1960s Khruschev was still concentrating on building up Soviet economic strength rather than on a massive nuclear capability. Prosperity was a worthwhile goal in itself, and the Russian leader also wanted the prestige of matching American affluence. Any nuclear war would be so disastrous that atomic parity was a pointless goal. By maintaining even a minimal deterrent (according to Khruschev's early doctrine), Russia could apparently induce America to spend on nuclear weapons extravagantly, perhaps even ruinously. Military bluff, according to this doctrine, could enhance the effectiveness of Russia's relatively small arsenal by showing that the Kremlin was not afraid to act.[80] Among the aggressive gestures of the early 1960s were the construction of the Berlin Wall, and Khruschev's repeated *threats* to use the atomic weapon. An analysis of Soviet strategic doctrine would have suggested that the Cuban missile emplacements were part of this policy of ruble-saving bluster, not, as the CIA argued, evidence of Soviet intelligence error.[81] This would account for the fact that the Russians, while keeping up the pretense of intended secrecy, made no special effort to camouflage their Cuban installations.

The long-term reputation of McCone's CIA has been further stained by its association with an unsuccessful defense strategy. In the Kennedy-Khruschev

period, the United States undertook a massive, one-sided escalation in intercontinental ballistic missile strength.[82] This was not because McCone made the error of
overestimating the Soviet nuclear threat (on the contrary, by the mid-1960s the
CIA was too complacent about Russian strength). McNamara had conceded that
there was no Soviet nuclear lead. The initial object of his strategy was, in fact, to
increase U.S. strength to the point where a nuclear war would be winnable at a
limited cost to the United States even if the Russians struck first with a surprise
attack. There were three drawbacks to his strategy. First, the United States missed
an opportunity to negotiate arms reductions with the Soviet Union from a position
of strength (though it must be conceded that a very persistent effort would have
been required, for the Soviets were reluctant to negotiate from a position of
weakness). Second, the strategy did not work: McNamara eventually had to
concede that the increase in U.S. preemptive firepower could not reduce U.S.
casualties to an acceptable minimum. Third, Soviet planners responded in due
course with a substantial weapons push of their own. The failure of McNamara's
strategy could not be blamed on the CIA alone. But it did reflect one of the inherent
weaknesses of the Agency in being the product of noncollation of intelligence on
enemy and U.S. strength. And regardless of the merits of the case, the CIA became
closely associated with a national security strategy that was expensive and self-
defeating.[83]

The assassination of President Kennedy on November 22, 1963, further impaired public faith in the Agency, especially when conspiracy theories began to
circulate about revenge motives arising from the CIA's own assassination plots
against foreign leaders. In reality, the Agency's involvement in the assassination of
Dominican tyrant Rafael Trujillo on May 31, 1961, had been peripheral if it
existed at all. Again, though President Kennedy and Hilsman authorized and
encouraged the removal of South Vietnamese president Ngo Dinh Diem, McCone
twice vetoed plans to assassinate him, and Diem's murder on November 2, 1963,
was a local affair.[84] And even though the Agency did plan to assassinate Lumumba
and Castro, it was preempted in the first case and frustrated in the second, and
there is no hard evidence that Castro plotted a revenge killing. In view of the
murky record regarding Agency intent, however, it is not surprising that rumors
flew about to the detriment of the CIA's moral standing.

The CIA's golden age was over by 1961, when the Bay of Pigs fiasco followed
hard on the heels of Kennedy's initial shake-up. The Agency recovered a little of its
former standing under McCone and the years of its worst ignominy were still some
way in the future. Nevertheless, the overall picture for the Kennedy years is one of
substantial loss of prestige. The Cuban missile crisis and the failure of strategic
doctrine contributed to the process, and the interaction of covert operations with
the death of a president rubbed on a raw nerve for many years to come.

8

PRESIDENTIAL
NEGLECT
LBJ
and the
CIA
to June 1966

Good relations and mutual respect be-
tween the White House and the CIA are necessary to the proper functioning of U.S.
intelligence. Eisenhower had achieved that good relationship. Kennedy shook up
the intelligence process, then punished the CIA's leading officials in a demoralizing
fashion for the Bay of Pigs fiasco. Johnson made things worse, for he neglected
intelligence and showed little respect either for the CIA or for the concept of
neutral analysis which it enshrined. The consequence of neglecting the CIA and
ignoring its analytical product depends, of course, on the quality of the Agency's
analysis of the topic at hand. But, by disregarding or suppressing the CIA's
accurate evaluations of the progress of the Vietnam War, the White House undoubtedly insured that the nation floundered ever more deeply into a quagmire
that sapped America's strength and prestige.

Why did President Johnson neglect the CIA and treat its product with such
contempt? One factor that preyed on his mind was his suspicion that the CIA had
something to do with the tragic event in Dallas that had made him president. He
had no firm grounds for fear. Nonetheless, as ignorance and rumor can be more
disturbing than certainty, it is understandable that, in the light of unanswered
questions about Kennedy's assassination, the new president should feel some
trepidation about the CIA's past and future roles.

The left-wing, pro-Castro leanings of Kennedy's assassin, Lee Harvey Oswald,
did suggest there was something to investigate. The fact that Dallas nightclub
owner Jack Ruby shot Oswald dead during a jail transfer two days after Oswald's

own fatal act made thorough investigation into Kennedy's murder at the same time more difficult and, in light of such suspicious circumstances, more necessary. But the presidential commission which, under Chief Justice Earl Warren, inquired into the assassination, came up with what some people considered a whitewash: the conclusion that Oswald had acted alone. Unsatisfactory ballistic evidence (How many guns were used? Was there more than one assassin, making it a conspiracy?) fueled speculation—speculation which, many years after the event, prompted a House Select Committee on Assassinations to conclude that there had indeed been a conspiracy.[1]

Johnson's fear was that the CIA's assassination plots against foreign leaders had provoked the revenge or preemptive killing of Kennedy, and that his own life might be in danger for this reason. The intensity of this fear is a matter for speculation. According to Johnson's memoir *The Vantage Point* (1971), it was his concern about Castro's possible revenge motive that had prompted him to set up the Warren Commission.[2] The CIA's Richard Helms confirmed Johnson's original concern, but differed as to its source and intensity: Johnson "had some kind of belief or conviction . . . that because President Kennedy had been in a sense responsible for *Diem's* demise, he in turn was assassinated himself."[3] Helms added: "I didn't know whether this was just like the fly fishermen flick over the water to see if he has any takers, or whether he really believed it."

Johnson's suppression of the very investigation he had authorized lends credence to Helms's suggestion that he did not fully believe in the conspiracy theory. Others, too, were less than keen on bringing to light every relevant detail. Crime-busting attorney general Robert Kennedy did not want the public to know about Mongoose, his contacts with the Mafia, or for that matter his brother's philandering with Judith Campbell. J. Edgar Hoover had no desire to see exposed the FBI's preassassination investigative incompetence in relation to Oswald and other matters. Chief Justice Warren pushed aside Helms's suggestion that Oswald, who had defected to the Soviet Union for a while, might be connected to the KGB. This was partly because he was "tired and frayed," partly because of White House pressure—for Johnson wanted the voters to forget about Kennedy with the approach of the 1964 presidential election, and to concentrate their minds on the virtues of the new man in the White House. Continued speculation could in any case be damaging to the administration and to public confidence in government. As soon as Oswald was shot, Hoover had told Deputy Attorney General Nicholas Katzenbach that something would have to be "issued so we can convince the public that Oswald is the real assassin." Katzenbach told Johnson that speculation would have to be "cut off." Johnson told the Warren Commission to wind up its inquiry.[4]

It is clear that Johnson did not give overriding priority to his assassination fears; nonetheless, the Secret Service (the federal agency charged with the protection of the president and his entourage) received a major increment to its budget.[5] Furthermore, more than three years after Kennedy's death, Johnson was still sufficiently worried to respond to a March 1967 newspaper story that Castro may have instigated the murder of President Kennedy in response to the CIA's attempts on the Cuban leader's own life. He ordered Helms (by now director of the CIA) to initiate a new inquiry. The CIA's inspector general, Jack Earman, prepared a secret report. This detailed the CIA-Mafia link and the attempts to get rid of Castro.[6] Evidence cited in the report fell far short of proof that the CIA was responsible for Kennedy's death. But nagging suspicions about this possibility were a psychological factor that probably inhibited Johnson in his relations with the CIA. It is beyond doubt that, had the CIA not engaged in assassination plots in the first place, such suspicions would not have arisen and this particular cause of White House-CIA mistrust would not have existed.

At the same time, there were other factors of both smaller and greater significance that caused Johnson to mistrust or neglect the CIA. Perhaps of relatively small significance is the fact that Johnson believed the Agency had been one of the several forces aligned against him at the 1960 Democratic convention, when he had lost the presidential nomination to Kennedy.[7] Like Nixon, he suspected the CIA of playing at politics and favoring its own, the Ivy League man. More important than this, however, was Johnson's determination to succeed, where Kennedy had failed, in pushing through domestic reforms. In 1964 and 1965, especially, the former Senate majority leader managed to persuade Congress to pass some of his "Great Society" measures, including the Civil Rights, Economic Opportunity, Medicare, Medicaid, and Voting Rights acts. Like Franklin D. Roosevelt, he concentrated so much on domestic matters in the first part of his presidency that he neglected foreign affairs, including foreign intelligence.

When he did turn his attention to Southeast Asia, Johnson did so with an angry resentment that clouded his judgment and dulled his receptiveness to sound intelligence advice. To "that bitch of a war" in Vietnam, as he put it, he sacrificed "the woman [he] really loved," the Great Society.[8] Anxious to win the war quickly, embittered by having to fight it at all, and keen to show he was a good Cold Warrior in spite of his "socialistic" domestic reforms, Johnson proved deaf to cautionary advice, whether from George Ball of the State Department or from the CIA. So, in spite of the fact that Johnson devoted increasing attention to foreign policy from 1965 on, the CIA's status and credibility continued to decline, for its estimates, being at variance with the premises which underpinned U.S. conventional military escalation in Vietnam, were ignored.

Other factors, too, sapped confidence in the CIA and discouraged influential people from allying with the Agency as its senior officials fought to maintain their position within the Washington bureaucracy, in the realm of democratic debate in Congress and elsewhere, and as an independent influence on the White House. These factors made it politically feasible for the president to disregard intelligence estimates, so the process was a vicious circle, with the CIA being weakened from both sides—the situation being serious enough to induce McCone's resignation from the directorship in April 1965. Among those factors that merit consideration in the period up to McCone's resignation are residual foreign distrust, incompetence and overaggressiveness in intelligence collection, and a determination to press on with certain covert operations that were offensive in principle to American public opinion.

There can be little doubt that there remained a residual foreign distrust of the CIA and therefore of America in the wake of the Kennedy presidency. This distrust disturbed U.S. diplomats, and senior Agency officials recognized the need to do something about it. In January 1964, director John McCone planned a visit to Bonn, Madrid, London, and Paris. In the fall, his deputy director for intelligence Ray Cline was to follow up this European venture with visits to Taipei, Tokyo, New Delhi, Ankara, Athens, and Lisbon. The plan was to give the visits "low key" publicity—not enough to provoke anti-CIA, anti-American demonstrations, but sufficient to show that the Agency was doing a good intelligence job. The touring officials were to "brief" foreign leaders on U.S. perceptions of Soviet economic performance and the Chinese detonation of an atomic bomb. McCone was to "provide and elicit" information to bolster allied consensus, backing up a recent appeal by Secretary of State Dean Rusk for NATO unity.[9]

Bonn welcomed the announcement of McCone's visit unreservedly, and the director was to get along famously with Franco when he arrived in Madrid and talked about Cuba and other Communist problems. But the U.S. ambassador in London was more cautious when he received news of the proposed visit: there would certainly be sensationalist reference in the press to the presence in Britain of the "U.S. master-spy," and the visit should definitely be kept very low key.[10] In France, where memories still lingered of the CIA's alleged attempt to overthrow de Gaulle, the diplomatic reaction was sharpest of all. The ambassador there was the formidable Charles E. ("Chip") Bohlen, survivor of the Roosevelt camp, of a smear campaign by Joe McCarthy, and of a spell at the Moscow embassy. Bohlen was an admirer of the CIA in its performance of its main function, watching the Soviet Union, but he reacted with muted fury to John McCone's proposed visit.[11] It was "not entirely clear . . . whether his trip has special White House approval or [is] merely his own idea." The veteran diplomat confessed "some concern at head of intelligence agency visiting chiefs of government, especially here in France." He warned that "low key" releases in Washington would not inure the CIA against "considerable publicity here in France."[12] The problem was that the French were pursuing a unilateralist foreign policy. Just before McCone's arrival they recognized Red China, and they were on the verge of withdrawing from NATO (though the final breach did not occur until the spring of 1966). Bohlen at first suggested the cancellation of McCone's visit, and then agreed to it only on the condition that the CIA director did not request a meeting with de Gaulle and limited himself to an innocuous agenda in meetings with other officials.[13] Bohlen had clearly joined the growing number of American public servants who regarded the CIA as a diplomatic liability.

According to former CIA officer Patrick J. McGarvey and also his fellow intelligence veterans Victor Marchetti and John D. Marks, the Agency lost standing in the 1960s very largely because of its embarrassingly overaggressive espionage. "Intelligence," McGarvey claimed, "seems to be creating almost as many dangerous situations as it brings to the attention of the President." He thought the U-2 episode in May 1960 had wrecked the impending summit. Later in the decade, the spy ship USS *Liberty* strayed too close to the shore during the 1967 Arab-Israeli war, suffering an Israeli air strike and thirty-four American deaths; in 1968, the North Koreans captured another American spy ship, the USS *Pueblo*; in the following year, the North Koreans shot and brought to ground an American reconnaissance plane. McGarvey argued that the most momentous event of all, however, was the skirmish on the night of August 2, 1964, between the destroyer *Maddox*, part of a U.S. electronic espionage unit, and some North Vietnamese vessels—for Johnson, concealing the true purpose of the U.S. naval presence, used the incident to secure from Congress the Gulf of Tonkin resolution, mandating his escalation of the war in Vietnam. According to this line of reasoning, then, intelligence incidents had become the chief source of CIA-triggered problems.[14]

McGarvey's observations are helpful to a limited degree only. The real significance of the 1964 Gulf of Tonkin incident is not that it was an embarrassingly overaggressive piece of espionage, but that it gave rise to a controversial bit of presidential opportunism that happened to involve a spy ship. While other episodes listed by McGarvey were undoubtedly embarrassing to the United States and in a minor way dented the CIA's standing even if the Agency was not always directly involved, there is little evidence that any serious-minded person in the United States wanted a less aggressive espionage policy. McGarvey's opinion is nonetheless revealing in its emphasis on intelligence as opposed to operational incidents, for in the Johnson administration the view that in due course prevailed was that covert operations required cosmetic rather than surgical treatment.

Senior officials on the intelligence side of the CIA did take a critical view of covert operations, but only from a narrow perspective. In June 1964 the Board of National Estimates approved a report in which senior analyst Willard C. Matthias singled out clandestine operations as a danger to world peace, but blamed these operations on the importunings of Third World leaders. Matthias had high hopes for detente and the liberalization of Soviet society; he believed that the chief threat to superpower relations lay in developing countries' plots to involve Russia and America in their affairs: "Individuals and groups calling themselves Castroists or Communists might stage revolutionary attempts or initiate guerilla movements, not on the orders of Moscow, [Peking], or Havana, but in the hope of gaining their support. Similarly, individuals and groups may organize or execute plots to gain U.S. support." Matthias forecast that a "consequence of this disorder and of the inhibitions upon open involvement is likely to be an increase in clandestine activities designed to influence the course of events in a desired direction or to block similar activities by other powers." Matthias worried about this, though he offered the consolation that covert operations were relatively cheap.[15]

In 1965 Sherman Kent—still serving as director of the office of national estimates—took a similar approach in a report on Portugal's African colonies, Angola
and Mozambique. Up to a point, his report was sound in its cautions and predictions. He said that Portugal faced no immediate threat from left-wing guerillas but
that the situation might change upon the death of the dictator Salazar. (In the
event, following Salazar's death in 1970, both countries did indeed become independent and had acquired "Marxist" regimes five years later.) In his 1965 report
Kent went on to observe that African nationalists hoped the United States would
treat Portugal harshly, "which they believe would alter the situation swiftly and
possibly propel them to power. During this period they will continue both to
importune and to criticize the West, and the U.S. will remain a principal target of
nationalist fulminations."[16]

This vision of the United States and the CIA struggling helplessly in the grip of a
few African guerilla leaders was based on a particle of truth, but little more. It is
possible that Matthias and Kent were attempting to minimize the "cowboy"
influence by suggesting that the tail (manipulative foreigners) was wagging the dog
(the gullible purveyors of American clandestine power). Whatever their reasoning,
they failed to focus attention on two important factors: the hostility of the Third
World in general to U.S. clandestine operations and the effect of those operations
on domestic public opinion.

In the absence of effective counterargument, the Johnson administration authorized large-scale covert operations. In Chile, the objective was to build an already
firmly democratic nation into a shining model of conservative prosperity which
would put Castroism in the shade. At the same time, there was a desire to prevent
the nationalization of the Chilean components of American multinational corporations, notably the Anaconda Copper Company and International Telephone and
Telegraph. The CIA had started to subsidize the activities of the Christian Democratic party in 1962. In 1964, the Special Group (renamed the 303 Committee in
June) set out to assist Eduardo Frei, the Christian Democratic candidate, in the
presidential election of that year. It approved a grant of $160 thousand to help the
Christian Democrats help slum dwellers, and a subvention of $3 million for the
manipulation of the media to ensure the defeat of the socialist candidate, Salvador
Allende. Aiming at women in particular, the CIA ran a scare campaign through its
secretly controlled newspapers and other media, with images of Soviet tanks and
Cuban firing squads pervading its propaganda. By June 1964, one CIA-funded
group was issuing twenty-four daily radio newscasts in Santiago alone. One of the
main disinformation themes encouraged and paid for by the CIA was that Allende
received funds from abroad. On September 4, the Chilean voters chose Frei as their
president.[17]

Details of the CIA's intervention in the 1964 Chilean election did not leak out
until later, so there was no scandal at the time. Project Camelot, in contrast, yet
again brought America into disrepute abroad, and in addition sparked some
ominous expressions of domestic discontent. This project was the brainchild of the

army's special operations office, which issued a preliminary planning report in August 1964. In December of the same year, the office issued a document describing the project. The object was to devise a "general social systems model" to help with the prediction and prevention of disorder in "the developing nations of the world," especially in Latin America. The language of the document—it referred to "nation building" and the "counterinsurgency program of the U.S. Government"—suggests a continuing faith in the prescriptions of Edward Lansdale.[18] The focus of the project, though, was academic, with a projected expenditure on research programs of one to one-and-a-half million dollars annually: "the largest single grant ever provided for a social science project," claimed one authority.[19]

According to Project Camelot's critics, the CIA helped to finance various Camelot research projects by organizing grants via "sundry 'front' foundations or 'pass-throughs' created with covert government funds."[20] Though the Agency's involvement was in fact marginal, Project Camelot so strongly resembled what people assumed the CIA did that opprobrium stuck to the Agency anyway. As early as September 1964, the *New York Times* had begun to fulminate at the CIA's use of front foundations, commenting in the wake of a Senate subcommittee disclosure: "What evidence can American professors or field workers present to prove they are not engaged in underground activities when it is known that CIA is using its money to subsidize existing foundations, or is creating fictitious ones?"[21]

On April 22, 1965, the distinguished Norwegian pacifist Johan Galtung publicly turned down a Project Camelot research grant and denounced the program. At the time, he was a visiting scholar in Chile, and Project Camelot achieved instant notoriety in that country. The left-wing press, still frustrated by lack of proof of the widely suspected CIA involvement in the 1964 election, pounced on the Galtung revelation. President Johnson's military intervention against democratic-liberal forces in the Dominican Republic in the week following Galtung's gesture further inflamed anti-American feeling in Chile, as elsewhere in Latin America. In spite of the fact that Project Camelot had earmarked relatively little money for Chile, the newspapers in that country were awash throughout the month of May with wild spy tales and stories of academic outrage at being unwittingly recruited by the clandestine machinery of Yankee imperialism. Frei as well as Allende felt obliged to denounce Project Camelot. The chairman of the Chilean House of Representatives special investigatory committee concluded that the project "has not been conceived to try to solve the problems of hunger in Latin America, only to avoid revolution."[22] Local U.S. ambassador Ralph A. Dungan demanded and obtained the cancellation of the project.[23]

The Camelot affair spelled danger for CIA domestically, too. This was in part because it threatened to alienate an articulate section of society, academia. Disclosures about the project made life difficult for Americans who wished to conduct research abroad and to persuade foreign scholars to trust and cooperate with them. The project also seemed to constitute an improper invasion of academic freedom by agencies of the federal government. As one scholar put it in his lecture to the American Anthropological Association in November 1965, Camelot threatened "the right to investigate freely, to think freely, and to write freely."[24]

Furthermore, opinion was changing outside academia. In their book *The Invisible Government*, journalists David Wise and Thomas Ross had recently alerted Americans to the way in which CIA affected the lives of Americans. The *Washington Post*, *New York Times*, and *St. Louis Post-Dispatch*, formerly so supportive of the CIA, could now be relied on to take the offensive. (Conversely, the formerly critical *Chicago Tribune* had started supporting the CIA.) Senator J. William Fulbright attacked the CIA over Camelot in a way that suggested that oversight advocates in Congress were now rebels with a cause. In one article for the *St. Louis Post-Dispatch*, he pointed to the divisive moods affecting America's campuses, with some professors and students protesting against the Vietnam War, but other academics accepting government funds to conduct "ponderous studies" whose "opaque language" failed to disguise their objective, which was to stop all revolutions whether bad or good.[25]

The new criticism of the CIA differed from earlier protests about its predictive shortcomings (Bogota, Korea) or operational failings (Bay of Pigs) in that it focused on points of principle. As those points of principle were connected with the self-interest of some Americans (academics not on CIA support), they were politically potent. The CIA's covert operations were in danger of becoming a 1960s cause. For this reason, potential allies and defenders of the Agency in the press, in the Congress, and in the Washington bureaucracy held back for fear of being contaminated. Increasingly short of support, the Agency's leadership found it difficult to command respect.

Matters came to a head for John McCone in April 1965. For some time the CIA director had smarted from President Johnson's neglect. Some of his colleagues had remarked on his absence from the president's influential Tuesday luncheon meetings. McCone complained that whereas he had seen Kennedy weekly, he was seeing Johnson on a need-to-meet rather than regular basis. This irregularity was harmful not just to the relationship between Johnson and McCone, but also to McCone's Washington standing. As Helms later put it, "there is a feeling loose in the land that unless you're in the President's presence a good deal you don't have any influence on him."[26]

LBJ now asked his White House staff to determine how many times, since becoming president, he had met McCone or conversed with him by telephone. The answer he received on April 25 was eighty-nine meetings and fourteen telephone conversations.[27] Thus he had met McCone more than once a week on average, even if he had not afforded him the privilege of a regular audience. On the basis of this evidence, the CIA director was exaggerating the degree of presidential neglect. Perhaps, indeed, it is an indication of his conservative instinct that he now compared Johnson unfavorably with Kennedy, whereas previously he had compared Kennedy unfavorably with Eisenhower.[28] According to McCone's critics, he was too ambitious, wishing to influence policy and even to form a policy troika with the president as chief and the CIA director and secretary of state enjoying parity under him.[29] Thus McCone wilfully misconstrued the nature of the Tuesday luncheon meetings, which were about policy and rarely touched on intelligence matters.[30] According to this view, McCone's ambitions led him to ignore the dangerous effects that policy advocacy could have on the objectivity of CIA analysis, and his resignation stemmed from his overblown idea of his own importance.

But McCone robustly defended his position, and his point of view merits serious consideration. Insisting that the CIA should always be kept "at the apex" of America's large intelligence community, McCone argued it had an exceptional legitimacy: it was the world's only intelligence organism, with the single exception of its West German counterpart, which had been established and scrutinized by a democratically elected legislature.[31] He was right in his appreciation that democratic legitimacy was essential to the proper standing and efficiency of a U.S. intelligence organization—and that the CIA was the only U.S. foreign-intelligence organization which had that legitimacy. Other points, too, might be adduced in his defense. Although policy bias can impair objectivity, an appreciation of policy requirements is necessary to useful estimates, as intelligence theorists Wilmoore Kendall and Sherman Kent had earlier observed. By the same token, policy determined without due reference to intelligence can go badly awry. Chester Cooper, the CIA veteran used by Kennedy in a liaison capacity and retained by Johnson, later remarked on the fact that Johnson's autobiography *The Vantage Point* "contains not a single reference to a National Intelligence Estimate." In Johnson's day, he recalled, "in-depth analyses were far from best sellers."[32] Had intelligence findings been a regular item at the Tuesday luncheons and had McCone been in attendance, it is quite possible that President Johnson's foreign policy would have followed a wiser course.

There is no reason to suppose, it is true, that greater CIA involvement in policy would have solved every problem: like other branches of the intelligence community, for example, the Agency failed to predict the progressive escalation in Soviet production of SS-9 intercontinental ballistic missiles that began in 1965.[33] But it was surely worth fighting for the principle of a foreign policy based on neutral intelligence—and, in April 1965, one important illustration of this point was at hand.

Looking at the Vietnam War in their clinical way, senior CIA analysts had by April developed a skepticism about America's role—a skepticism which later events justified, and a skepticism which McCone had quite rightly conveyed to the president. No doubt CIA officials could be accused of bias in opposing conventional military escalation, for that escalation alienated local people whose support was essential to the "nation-building" efforts favored by Lansdale (whose Vietnam counterinsurgency activities were by now overshadowed by U.S. Army action). Be that as it may, cogency underlay the CIA's opposition when Johnson announced phase one of "Rolling Thunder" in February 1965. The objective of this bombing campaign was to destroy North Vietnam's system of logistic support for the Viet Cong insurgent movement in the South.[34] The CIA assessment of the likely result was not alarmist, and it failed to predict North Vietnam's response of infiltrating regular troops into the South under the cover of secrecy. The Agency did warn, however, that bombing would not stop Viet Cong attacks, that Russia and China would compete to help their Vietnamese comrades, and that North Vietnam might in anticipation of international sympathy evoked by the bombing, "decide to intensify the struggle."[35]

Early in April, President Johnson authorized U.S. Marine units stationed in South Vietnam to engage in offensive combat operations against the Viet Cong. An advocate of the all-or-nothing approach, McCone denounced this as a half-measure, especially with respect to the incremental nature of Rolling Thunder: "We must look with care to our position under a program of slowly ascending tempo of air strikes. With the passage of each day and each week, we can expect increasing pressure to stop the bombing. This will come from various elements of the American public, from the press, the United Nations and world opinion." McCone went on to predict that North Vietnam and her allies would exploit foreign and U.S. opinion and "build up the Viet Cong capabilities by covert infiltration," and he recommended that ground escalation should not be ordered unless accompanied by all-out aerial attack.[36] The White House's disregard of such warnings confirmed once again, and in a vital case, the administration's indifference to intelligence. With public opinion substantially supportive of Johnson's Vietnam policy and in the absence of powerful allies who would rally to his cause, McCone had to accommodate or resign. He resigned.

By mid-April, the president was ready to announce McCone's successor. This was Vice Admiral William F. ("Red") Raborn, a political supporter of Johnson's from Texas. His aunt—Miss Mamie of Wichita Falls—summed up his qualities when she wrote to the president soon after his appointment, stating facts that would not be "in the FBI files." Her nephew was a patriot whose aircraft carrier had been hit, in World War II, by a Japanese suicide pilot, with dreadful loss of life. She had "never seen such a change in a man." He determined to devote himself to a deterrent so convincing such tragedies could never happen again. He subsequently worked on the submarine-launched Polaris missile system "like a man possessed," incurring a heart attack like the president himself, whom "we all down here in Texas especially" so admired.[37]

Though Johnson now had his own man in Langley, the CIA's impact on the president's thinking remained slight. Raborn's successor as director, Richard Helms, noted that the admiral attended the Tuesday luncheons "only once or twice" during his spell with the Agency.[38] Within the CIA, critics complained that Raborn failed to be a true leader of their organization. Not surprisingly, the disillusioned McCone thought him "an unfortunate choice." He conceded that the admiral was a "hard-driving, technical man." But he thought him ill equipped to act the parts of the "operational manager" and "college president" in an agency populated by hundreds of projects and thousands of university graduates. Some CIA veterans thought Raborn had been chosen for his proven ability, while director of the Polaris program, to "muster support" in Congress. This was a quality that may well have appealed to a legislative veteran like Johnson, yet it failed to command unqualified respect in the CIA. Furthermore, the new director was thought to be a yes-man. In February 1966, he confirmed this impression when he told Senator Fulbright and the Senate Foreign Relations Committee, with underlining for extra force: "*Let me assure you—and I say this with the strongest of conviction and emphasis—U.S. intelligence agencies do not make policy.*"[39]

The Dominican crisis immediately made enemies for Raborn—enemies within the CIA for being overcompliant, and in the White House for not being compliant enough. The trouble arose from an attempted countercoup, beginning on April 24, in favor of Juan Bosch. The only politician since Trujillo's murder to have commanded popular support (60 percent of the votes in a 1962 election), Bosch had lasted only ten months as president before being deposed by a conservative military junta. Though Bosch was no Communist, hardline U.S. officials thought him too weak to be able to stand up to totalitarian challenges if once again installed in office. Ambassador John B. Martin assured Washington that there were at least fifty Communist or Castroist leaders among the pro-Bosch forces in the 1965 rebellion. Raborn took over at the CIA on April 28, just as the Dominican crisis reached boiling point, and, with little time for preparation, he had to face up to an intelligence problem that proved too much for him.

The problem arose from the two opposing types of political pressure affecting LBJ, both illustrated in a memorandum to the president by his assistant and close advisor, Jack Valenti. On the one hand, if "Castro-types" took over in the Dominican Republic, it would be a blow to Johnson's credibility just when his Great Society plans were coming to fruition; the president also reportedly worried that domestic support for his conventional escalation in Vietnam would wither away if he showed himself irresolute in the Dominican crisis.[40] On the other hand, an all-night teach-in at the University of Michigan had recently inaugurated the student protest movement against the Vietnam War. Even though that protest movement commanded only minority support, the student constituency to which it appealed had been militant over other issues like civil rights and free speech and was important to the Democrats. Valenti insisted that U.S. intervention in the Dominican Republic, if undertaken at all, would have to be on a demonstrably sound basis: "Show *indisputable evidence* that Castro-types are in charge. This cannot be *just* a statement. Raborn must have *pictures, names*, a full *dossier*."[41]

Johnson did not ask Raborn for his assessment before sending in twenty thousand marines and backup forces to ensure the defeat of the pro-Bosch rebellion. He telephoned the new director to inform him of his decision and to request the backup evidence. Deputy director for intelligence Ray Cline overheard the admiral's response: "Aye, aye sir!"[42] Raborn attempted to produce the required evidence but the result was, according to one CIA veteran, a "mishmash."[43] From

LBJ's point of view, his new man had failed to comply with what appeared to the president to be a reasonable request. From Cline's perspective, the CIA was now under supine leadership.

During the rest of his brief directorship, Raborn tried to make amends and to restore the prestige and standing of his agency. To handle future crises of the Dominican type, he established an operations room which could cut through the Agency's internal, compartmentalizing, barriers to get at the truth quickly. On July 19, he wrote an emollient letter to LBJ thanking him for selecting a CIA employee to serve on the U.S. Tariff Commission which did "great honor to this Agency and to me personally" and defending the quality of Agency personnel: 80 percent of the top fifty people "have at least one advanced degree; about one third have two or more degrees; and 10% hold doctorates." Furthermore, Raborn said, he was improving the CIA's facilities for drawing on external academic, industrial, and scientific expertise.[44] The reply, which Johnson personally drafted, betrayed the president's attitude: "I have told you before but I cannot repeat too often my hope and insistence that we must make every possible fresh, imaginative effort to get the best out of the talent assembled at the Agency . . . I know you are not a man to rest on laurels of the past—and we really don't have many laurels in the intelligence field."[45]

Johnson's advisers persuaded him to scrap the letter and replace it with a more diplomatic one.[46] Events nonetheless seemed to conspire to perpetuate the hemorrhage that was slowly draining the CIA of its prestige, standing, and self-respect. In October, Singapore's prime minister Lee Kuan Yew initiated an embarrassing scandal. The Malaysian Federation had recently expelled Singapore; the new sovereign state therefore had to establish itself in the international community, and this at a time when internal Malay-Chinese racial tensions were becoming acute.[47] Apparently in an attempt to rally African and Asian support for his country, and, no doubt, to boost his own internal standing, Lee Kuan Yew now told the story of the three-million-dollar bribe CIA officers had offered him in 1961. Inept American denials only furnished him with an opportunity to threaten further disclosures about "putrid and grotesque" U.S. clandestine operations, and Secretary of State Dean Rusk had to issue a humiliating confession and apology. The *New York Times* attacked the CIA, claiming the Agency was alienating Asian friends—not only the prime minister of the nation at "the hub" of Western defenses in Southeast Asia, but also others with similar grievances, including Prince Norodom Sihanouk of Cambodia and General Ne Win of Burma.[48]

The CIA fought back, issuing to the press an impressive document called "The Soviet and Communist Bloc Defamation Campaign." The general thesis of this twenty-page analysis of Soviet tactics was that the CIA was in the frontline of U.S. national security policy and was therefore "the prime target of Soviet disinformation and defamation operations" planned by the KGB's Ivan Agayants in conjunction with the Soviet leadership. The document cautioned the credulous about attacks on the CIA. Its authors warned that Soviet disinformation was increasing in sophistication and, with the backing of lavish funds, was now affecting new areas: Southeast Asia, Africa and the Near East. The document's compilers took their cue from Allen Dulles's public-relations techniques, for they quoted reassuring, heartwarming Soviet attacks on successive directors of the CIA: McCone was "the servant of the uncrowned kings of America, the Rockefellers"; Raborn would be an even "more successful accomplice" of the "American imperialists."[49]

On September 28, White House officials noted that the CIA's pamphlet had achieved "wide press attention."[50] For their part, the CIA's officials remained alert to the continuing necessity of restoring the Agency's reputation. For example, they tried—in vain—to track down the source of an October story that the FBI was to regain its Latin American empire at the CIA's expense.[51] More spectacularly, they released the notes and private memoranda of Oleg Penkovsky. In these, the Russian defector warned the West to beware of Soviet propaganda and deception, described the "misinformation" techniques of USSR military intelligence (the GRU), listed KGB front organizations such as the USSR Ministry of Culture, and supplied horrific details of Communist interrogation techniques, including the use of rats.[52] The CIA entrusted the job of improving a translated version of Penkovsky's writings to a *Newsweek* editor, and *Newsweek* made a hero of the spy: he had knowingly risked detection, the magazine claimed, by sending Kennedy a vital message at the height of the Cuban missile crisis: "Soviet nuclear forces not in a state of readiness"; this led to Penkovsky's detection and execution by firing squad in May 1963. The Soviet media obligingly (though perhaps doubly disingenuously, if Penkovsky's own thesis is to be believed) denounced the Penkovsky account as a "mixture of anti-Soviet invention and slander."[53] The *Washington Post* serialized the edited Penkovsky writings prior to their publication by Doubleday as *The Penkovsky Papers*.

But the tide was running too strongly against Raborn's CIA for such propaganda to be fully effective. Anti-Raborn stories were rife in Washington (according to one, he believed KUWAIT to be a codeword not a place, and demanded a decryptification). Joseph Kraft told *Washington Post* readers in November that there was nothing very substantial about the stories except the fact that they were being told, but added that the admiral was a "Babbitt," and a mimetic as opposed to incisive intelligence officer. In January 1966, Clark Clifford—still interested in intelligence and a grey eminence in the Johnson administration—informed McGeorge Bundy that the Foreign Intelligence Advisory Board was "genuinely and deeply worried about the leadership problem in CIA," and Bundy suggested to the president he might consult Clifford to see about a change.[54]

Ray Cline's departure in the spring of 1966 was a further blow to Raborn. The deputy director for intelligence had admired McCone and thought Raborn a poor replacement. He told both Clifford and Bundy that the admiral would have to go and, according to *Esquire*, waged a war of leaks and character assassination.[55] But there was more to his resignation than personality differences. In his partly autobiographical account of the CIA's history, Cline indicates that he had organized an "objective analysis" of Rolling Thunder, and that he associated himself with the pessimistic findings of this, and other Agency studies, on the Vietnam War's progress. Because the "CIA was the bearer of bad tidings throughout the Vietnam war," he and the Agency were at odds with Secretary of Defense McNamara and other hawks who predominated in the Johnson administration. Not surprisingly, President Johnson assumed that Cline's impending departure was a policy protest. He complained the intelligence director was "running out" on him.[56]

Even more ominous than Cline's resignation was the manner of his departure. Instead of making a clean break with the Agency, he decided to step sideways and down, becoming station chief in Germany. By this stratagem, Cline hoped to evade the president's wrath and possible dismissal. Upset at Johnson's blunt assessment of the reason for his departure, he told the president on March 2 that he just wanted to recharge his batteries through a tour of duty in Europe. Choosing his words carefully, he said he strongly supported the president's policies, "especially in facing up to the tasks and dangers before us in Southeast Asia."[57] These words fall short of an explicit endorsement of Rolling Thunder or ground escalation in Vietnam, but on the other hand they signify Cline's compliance, which is partly explained by Cline's career profile and ambition. After Harvard, Oxford, and a desk job with the OSS, he had worked on the operational as well as intelligence side of the CIA and was clearly a potential director; furthermore, his career had been almost entirely with the OSS and CIA, and he had nowhere else to turn for a job (he was a trained historian, but, as universities were becoming ever more wary of the CIA, academia was no haven).[58]

Cline probably drew his own conclusions from CIA history. Successive presidents had allowed three directors (Hillenkoetter, Dulles, and McCone) to depart under a cloud. Irrespective of the merits of the case, it seemed that the president, as the repository of democratically conferred sovereignty, had to emerge the unconditional victor in any clash with an intelligence chief—let alone one of his deputies. Cline's learning of this lesson sounded the death knell of the CIA's influence on the Vietnam war. After his departure, other CIA leaders behaved in like fashion. They did not stop commissioning objective assessments of the war's progress, but they did relax their efforts to insure that those assessments had some influence on policy. Their attitude both reflected the CIA's loss of standing and contributed to a further decline in that standing, a decline that made the Agency less effective than it should have been.

Following Cline's resignation, Raborn tried to restore his dented image as leader of the intelligence community, and for a while LBJ supported him. On March 3, after Johnson's special assistant Bill Moyers had invited Raborn to "come over and talk things over," the director sent across a written defense of his record. He emphasized his improved management techniques, his delegation of important tasks to Richard Helms, his science and technology upgrading, his "24-hour Operations Center," his development of a "Vietnam Task Force," and his public relations efforts. Moyers sent a copy of Raborn's letter to William S. White, the

New York Times's Senate correspondent, saying "our mutual friend [the president] wanted you to see that despite the Georgetown clatter, Raborn is making progress at CIA."[59]

But the supportive consensus in government, the media, and Congress which had seen Dulles through thick and thin in the 1950s had lost its former strength. In the Senate, Eugene McCarthy was leading a renewed campaign for congressional oversight. McCarthy came from the mold that produced so many of the CIA's critics. He represented a state that, with only the seventeenth largest population in the Union, was relatively weak in terms of political power brokerage—though Minnesota did, in fact, breed considerable political talent that included Harold Stassen, Hubert Humphrey, and Walter Mondale, as well as McCarthy. McCarthy sought the limelight conferred by attacks on the CIA because he was ambitious for himself and his principles (he became a "dump Johnson" peace candidate in the 1968 Democratic primaries). He had recently joined the Senate Foreign Relations Committee, whose chairman, the formidable J. William Fulbright, had earlier been a supporter of executive privilege but now shared his desire to assert the congressional prerogative of participation in foreign affairs. McCarthy had introduced oversight measures as a congressman in the 1950s, and he secured a debate on the issue in the Senate immediately after the Bay of Pigs. He had opposed McCone's nomination in 1962 on the ground that McCone would meddle in policy matters. On January 24, 1966, he had introduced a resolution providing for investigation by the Senate Foreign Relations Committee of all U.S. intelligence activities. Although McCarthy and his supporters were still a minority in Congress, the CIA's disarray under Raborn meant they had to be taken seriously.[60]

Attacks on the CIA in other quarters did nothing to restore the Agency's fortunes in the spring of 1966. One such attack appeared in the April issue of *Ramparts*, a West Coast magazine of Catholic provenance and radical inclination whose staff were already known for their opposition to U.S. participation in the Vietnam war. The *Ramparts* story focused on Michigan State University, where a number of students had recently been arrested for protesting the war. *Ramparts* revealed that the CIA had paid the university $25 million to hire five Agency employees to train South Vietnamese students in covert police methods. The mainstream U.S. press now pounced on the issue, revealing that other universities, including the Massachusetts Institute of Technology, had similar CIA contracts. The *New York Times* disgorged the contents of its CIA dossier in a five-part series that focused on the Agency's political bribery, blackmail, organization of coups d'etat, and election fixing in Asia, Africa, and Latin America.[61]

The foreign press took up the hue and cry. In London the *Daily Telegraph* saw hope in a stronger congressional watchdog committee, but the equally conservative *Daily Express* suggested the CIA had "so tarnished the American image that it ought to be abolished entirely." The most hostile response was in South Asia, where distorted accounts suggested that the CIA was running U.S. foreign policy and supplying up to 75 percent of local embassy staffs.[62] These press distortions sometimes reflected local circumstances—Communist affiliations, for example, or Indian suspicions of U.S. secret collusion with Pakistan. They also, however, reflected foreign reliance on U.S. sources. The anti-American, anti-CIA Indian writer Natarajan was as revealing as he was mischievous when he wrote in the preface of a 1952 book "my thanks are due to the United States Information Service for its generous, if unwitting, co-operation."[63] The free American press was not just a potential source of security leaks but also a potent source of anti-CIA and therefore anti-American propaganda. Its concentration on that colorful target, dirty tricks, gave a misleading picture of the main functions of the CIA and also of the Agency's power within the U.S. foreign-policy establishment.

The fuss over the CIA's covert conspiracies to dominate the world threatened to undermine U.S. foreign policy. A worried White House commissioned, and on May 5 received, a United States Information Agency report on foreign press reaction to the *New York Times* series, a matter of some importance at the time, as American troops were pouring into Southeast Asia in the tens of thousands.[64] The president was clearly bent on cosmetic solutions and the neutralization of opposition rather than on modifying U.S. covert operational or Vietnamese policy. With neutralization in view, on May 19 the CIA's deputy director Richard Helms supplied the White House with a report on *Ramparts* personnel. He conceded the magazine's Christian origin and the fact that its editor-in-chief, Edward M. Keating, was a "Catholic layman." He then went on to dwell on the magazine's expanding readership, its support for the antiwar movement, and its objections to the way in which the CIA was allegedly "deciding policy and manipulating nations." Though Helms failed to produce evidence of foreign funding of the *Ramparts* exposé, he reported that "at least two" of the magazine's staff were "active Communists."[65]

The 1966 *Ramparts* investigation was one of several low points in the relationship between the CIA and American democracy. Because of police-state fears in the 1940s and the consequent ban on the CIA's domestic operations, there was an inexperienced, amateurish quality about its investigation of the domestic protest movement. Even the FBI, which helped with the *Ramparts* inquiry, had concentrated so long on Communists that its agents could understand no other form of protest. The upshot was that neither agency alerted the president to the fact that the protest movement was genuine and indigenous. The *Ramparts* affair shows, moreover, how the CIA had been driven into the lair of its predator, the president. Helms defensively equated criticism of CIA covert operations with criticism of the Vietnam war, thus identifying himself and the CIA as the president's loyal retainers in spite of a record of White House disloyalty to the CIA. The Agency came to be ever more reliant on presidential protection because, by defending a war in which its analysts had little faith, and by using illegal means to do so (the investigation of U.S. citizens protesting the war), the CIA further alienated potential support in Congress.

Congressional anger soon reached such a pitch that the president once again removed his protection from the CIA. On May 17, the Senate Foreign Relations Committee had reported favorably on Eugene McCarthy's January oversight resolution. On May 25, majority leader Mike Mansfield, fearing "a procedural wrangle and a bitter fight," proposed a compromise whereby the director of the CIA would still report to subcommittees of the Senate Armed Services and Appropriations Committees but would also appear before a three-man Foreign Relations subcommittee.[66] Raborn opposed the additional oversight and interceded with the president via Walt Rostow (Bundy's successor as national security advisor), complaining that Fulbright would demand information on sources and methods. Clifford of the president's Foreign Intelligence Advisory Board joined the opposition: echoing the sentiment of his former boss President Truman he said Senate committees should not be more fully briefed—"Because they leak!"[67] In the Senate, armed services chairman Richard B. Russell fought to retain the privileges of the existing intelligence subcommittees, on both of which he sat.

Ever since 1964, however, when Congressman Wright Patman had revealed CIA involvement in eight American philanthropic foundations, there had been concern on Capitol Hill about the Agency's domestic incursions.[68] Fulbright wanted to know about possible abuses of domestic groups, and whether the international academic exchange scheme named after him—the "Fulbright awards"—had been used as cover for CIA activities (the answer is apparently no).[69] Mansfield wavered between his 1950s determination to create an oversight mechanism and the necessity of holding together the Democratic majority in Congress. But he, too, expressed resentment, at what he alleged was the CIA director's relative candor with the nonelective President's Board, compared with his secrecy before Congress. He reminded President Johnson on June 6 that Russell and his friends refused to admit more members to either of the existing Senate subcommittees, and predicted a press furor "both at home and abroad" if nothing were done.[70]

Johnson had too long neglected foreign intelligence—at first casually, and later willfully. His reluctance to listen to the CIA and his reluctance to reform its practices alike undermined its standing and stimulated the demand for congressional oversight. But Johnson would not surrender to demands for an oversight committee that his predecessors had rejected, that his advisers opposed, and that would be privy to the true state of affairs in Vietnam. Instead, he resorted to the by-now traditional tactic of designating a scapegoat. Raborn would have to go. In his June 8 resignation letter, the admiral recommended his deputy as successor: "Importantly, Mr. Helms has the approbation of the U.S. media as well as the Congress. He commands respect in State circles as well as foreign intelligence circles."[71] In this indirect manner, Raborn delivered a fitting epitaph on his own tenure, and confirmed that a major problem now faced the CIA, that of winning respect and approval.

9

HELMS, JOHNSON, AND COSMETIC INTELLIGENCE

In 1967, *Ramparts* magazine published revelations that forced President Johnson to pay heed to the Agency and also gave him a golden opportunity to establish new guidelines for the CIA and to restore the Agency's standing. But the president opted, instead, for a cosmetic fix. Then, having "saved" the Agency, he demanded its loyalty on the Vietnam issue. His demand produced further cosmetic exercises, including an attempt to discredit political protest against the war and the suppression of dissent within the CIA. As if this were not enough, the repressive tenor of the Johnson administration appears to have had a stultifying effect on other aspects of CIA analysis. The Johnson White House did not encourage the CIA's personnel to take an imaginative and independent approach. In the last three years of LBJ's presidency, the CIA's analysts failed to draw attention to the Soviet effort to achieve nuclear parity.

At first, Raborn's departure on June 30, 1966, seemed to promise better things for the CIA. Raborn had come to constitute an obstacle to self-respect, so his resignation was good for morale. Furthermore, Richard M. Helms, the new director, commanded respect within and outside the Agency. Helms was acceptable within the Agency because he was the first hundred-percent intelligence professional to win the directorate. A native of Pennsylvania, he had spent two years in high schools in Switzerland and Germany before graduating from Williams College in 1935. He worked as a journalist in Germany—interviewing Hitler and appreciating his anti-Soviet viewpoint—before joining the OSS to begin his lifetime service to U.S. intelligence.[1] This career profile inspired trust and confidence within the CIA, though it also meant that Helms was dependent on his Agency job and therefore on the president, as he would have nowhere else to go if dismissed.

Outside the Agency, the press saw Helms as the man who could handle Congress and especially Fulbright, who remained suspicious of the CIA's nonaccountability to any elective body. Helms tried to reassure Congress that the CIA was not part of a policymaking conspiracy. Prior to his confirmation by the Senate Armed Services Committee on June 23, 1966, he pledged that the CIA would "devote itself to intelligence work and leave policy making to others."[2] According to Helms, Johnson realized that there was congressional antipathy to the idea of CIA policymaking, and was "not keen" on the idea himself: "On no occasion in all the meetings I attended with him did he ever ask me to give my opinion about what policy ought to be pursued by the government." He defended Johnson's method of working out policy through Tuesday luncheon meetings which excluded the CIA.[3] His agreement to such procedures may have stemmed less from conviction than from an instinct for political survival vis-à-vis both president and Congress. Whatever the reason, his compliance contributed to an American catastrophe in Southeast Asia.

Though in mid-1966 Senator Russell of the Armed Services Committee had believed it would be necessary to "spread the gore" in a debate in order to "win big" and crush the intelligence oversight proposal, congressional-CIA-White House relations gradually improved by the end of the year. The president's counsel Harry C. McPherson elicited from Russell and Everett Dirksen (the Republican Senate leader) a promise that the White House would be kept out of the fight.[4] In an effort to mollify the opposition, Russell emphasized the importance of President Kennedy's reform that had placed local CIA people under the control of ambassadors and the secretary of state.[5] Then, in January 1967, he invited three members of the Senate Foreign Relations Committee, Fulbright and Mansfield included, to sit on the Armed Services CIA subcommittee. The invitation was for one congressional session only and did not imply that a precedent had been set, though the precedent was nevertheless followed for a while. Thus, face had been saved all round. The reformers had achieved defeat in the guise of victory, and the CIA seemed to have weathered the storm.

On February 14, the *New York Times* and *Washington Post* ran a full-page advertisement that ended the complacency of those who imagined the CIA issue might just go away. The advertisement was for an article in the next issue of *Ramparts*, the West Coast magazine which had been for some time under federal scrutiny. The ten-thousand-word article would expose the relationship between the CIA and the National Students' Association (NSA). A "case study in corruption of youthful idealism," it would show how the Agency used students to spy, and how it exploited private institutions as conduits for secret funds.

The *Times* and the *Post*, obviously prepared for this moment, plastered their front pages with backup stories of their own, and for several days the readers of these and other newspapers feasted on a spate of disclosures. The NSA, it now seemed plain, had engaged not just in Cold War propaganda, but in espionage, too. Its officers supplied the CIA with information about their fellow students in foreign countries and about the "political situation among student organizations abroad."[6] According to the NSA's own investigator, Harvard Divinity School student Samuel W. Brown, the CIA had recruited its youthful agents through blackmail and bribery. One of the inducements offered was draft deferment. It is in fact true that General Lewis Hershey of the Draft Board had secretly volunteered this arrangement for many years; at the time of disclosure in 1967, it was a particularly inflammatory issue on the nation's campuses because of the Vietnam war and the recent abolition of student deferments. NSA president W. Eugene Groves noted the sensitivity of the issue in a letter to Douglass Cater, Jr., a White House staffer who had worked with the Department of Health, Education, and Welfare. Groves defended, to Cater, his failure to put the lid on the disclosures; he could accomplish little in the teeth of "a growing disaffection, not simply with the current administration, but with the processes of national government itself."[7]

The *Ramparts* article had serious implications for America's image abroad, as it dwelled on the foreign activities of the NSA as well as other CIA-subsidized organizations such as the Congress for Cultural Freedom. But the revelations in the magazine and in the press also affected a wide spectrum of domestic opinion. Here, the CIA was in two senses the victim of an excess of democracy. First, 1940s fears of an American police state had led to the legislative ban on the Agency's domestic activities, which would otherwise have been perfectly legal. Second, Senator Joe McCarthy's attacks on overt information and propaganda programs drove them into the CIA's clandestine embrace—where, not surprisingly, they became tainted with ruthless methods originally devised for other purposes.

Though much attention focused on the NSA, revelations about other CIA domestic activities were sufficiently wide-ranging to provoke general concern. For example, the 983,000 American teachers who belonged to the National Education Foundation learned that this and its international counterpart had received CIA money via the Vernon Fund. Outside the educational realm, it transpired American businessmen and labor union officials had worked for the CIA—a disclosure which in turn played into the hands of student radicals who believed that labor had been sucked into the military-industrial complex. More shocking still to those nurtured on belief in the freedom of the press was the fact that the American Newspaper Guild had received just under one million dollars in CIA subsidies since 1961, for use abroad in combatting the Communist-dominated International Organization of Journalists. In yet another sphere, the president of the American Political Science Association declared himself "sickened and alarmed" by CIA stories, when it emerged that two of his fellow officers had received secret funds via Agency conduits. The fact that those two officers (Evron M. Kirkpatrick and Max M. Kampelman) were, as the *Washington Post* put it, "close friends" of Vice

President Hubert Humphrey, made it even more imperative for the administration to respond to mounting congressional pressure for reform.[8]

There can be little doubt of the intensity of that pressure. On the day the scandal broke, eight congressmen wrote to President Johnson demanding an "immediate investigation at the highest level." As on several occasions in the past—and in the future—fear of a possible importation of police-state methods to the domestic scene underlay their suspicions of the CIA: "This disclosure leads us and many others here and abroad to believe that the CIA can be as much a threat to American as to foreign democratic institutions." In a similar vein, Senator Mansfield declared that the CIA had never told the Russell committee of its NSA secret subsidies, and he denounced the practice as a "move toward big brotherism." The domestic aspect of the affair ensured that Gene McCarthy's voice—this time he demanded a new committee to investigate the CIA's domestic as well as foreign activities—would be joined by a chorus of support, and that the support would be bipartisan. On the Democratic side of the House, for example, the Education and Labor Committee chairman Carl Perkins demanded an investigation, while in the Senate the Republican Barry Goldwater, horrified at the CIA's apparent subsidization of liberal causes, attacked the Agency's determination "to finance socialism in America."[9]

The CIA's defenders in Congress took a less gloomy view and disagreed with Fulbright's contention that the defeat of previous oversight proposals could now be seen to have been "tragic." Congressman William H. Bates of Massachusetts, ranking Republican on the House Armed Services Committee, made light of the matter when journalists accosted him and his wife on their way into town for dinner: "It's Hallowe'en. I mean Valentine's Day." Senator Russell said his committee *had* known about the NSA subsidies, that "we got more for the dollar out of this," and that talk about the impairment of academic freedom was "just a load of hogwash." There was still support, then, on which the Johnson administration could build. The usual avenue of escape, however, namely to blame the CIA and fire its director, did not on this occasion offer itself. Backing up Senator Russell in his defense of the Agency, Stuart Symington ominously noted that "everybody should realize that the policies of CIA are not set by the Agency. They operate under instructions." Details in *Ramparts* and associated news coverage made it clear that more would be required than a diversionary swipe at the Agency or the invocation of the "circuit-breaking" mechanism.[10]

Much of the responsibility for handling the *Ramparts* affair fell on Nicholas de B. Katzenbach, the official who had advised Johnson in 1964 to "cut off" speculation about the Kennedy assassination. Now Undersecretary of State, and Acting Secretary when news of the impending disclosures reached the administration on February 12, Katzenbach's first thought was once again to suppress information: "we will volunteer nothing," one of his aides instructed in an internal memorandum on February 15.[11] The White House, for its part, on the next day issued an official disclaimer, stating that President Johnson had been "totally unaware" of the student subsidies.[12] The press was so incredulous of this statement, however, that the administration now invented another tactic, which one might describe as "flashback." The assumption behind flashback was that the assertion of every president's complicity would be more effective than an implausible denial of the current president's complicity. Helms later claimed that when Russell and Robert Kennedy stated that all four presidents since Truman had authorized clandestine subsidies, "it immediately stopped the congressional attacks."[13]

The flashback technique did help to achieve the desired cosmetic effect, yet it was not sufficient to do this in itself. President Johnson had to set up an inquiry. Its three members were Katzenbach (in the chair), Helms, and Health, Education, and Welfare Secretary John Gardner. Just after its announcement, the journalist James Reston castigated Johnson for dealing "not with the problem but with the politics of the problem." Reston did, however, come up with a suggestion that Katzenbach and the administration were to take seriously. He declared that America needed its own equivalent of the British Council. Through the British Council, London subsidized overtly, and with an ambience of almost fossilized respectability, precisely those types of activity in which the CIA had been obliged to become involved to the embarrassment of the Johnson administration. Surely the British model could be followed in this instance? Senator Edward Kennedy embraced the British Council approach. So did Vice President Humphrey, who, in spite of darker press innuendo about his CIA associations, had a year earlier tried unsuccessfully to disentangle the NSA's finances from the CIA's. Clearly, this was a propitious time for the establishment of possible new guidelines for the CIA.[14]

But Helms was reluctant to accept new controls, whether by Congress or through executive decree. In his view, the *Ramparts* scandal did not really damage the CIA or the American image abroad. At the end of February, he sent Johnson's advisor Walt Rostow for his "delectation" an item to indicate the contrary. It was a letter from Morrill Cody of the Paris Bureau of the Radio Liberty Committee to the RLC's headquarters at East 42d Street, New York. Cody had recently attended one of Ambassador Bohlen's receptions and spoken to a man named Jorgensen, head of the American Department at the French Foreign Office. Jorgensen declared himself impressed at the CIA's utilization of educators and others: "We never believed the Americans were so clever." Had the Americans arranged these disclosures "purposely to impress us?" He admitted he was teasing, but said he really did think the Americans "*formidables*." Having delivered himself of that verdict, "he turned to the waiter and ordered another scotch."[15]

Indeed, a certain cynicism already prevailed in at least a few European circles. Simone de Beauvoir's 1954 novel *The Mandarins* had hinted at the naivete of a fictional editor (reputedly Camus) who refused both dollar and ruble secret subsidies but unwittingly received funds from Nazi-tainted sources.[16] Perhaps not everyone followed the story of the 1964 Patman exposure of eight CIA proprietaries, or credited the authenticity of E. Howard Hunt's 1965 novel *Return from*

Vorkuta ("The 'X Foundation,' Mr. Ward?" "Cover will provide the name"), but the Camelot affair had had worldwide press coverage.[17] Taking stock in September 1967 of the British fuss over the *Ramparts* affair, the caustic English journalist Malcolm Muggeridge professed astonishment that anyone could have imagined that the London magazine *Encounter* and its sponsor the Congress for Cultural Freedom could have been financed other than from U.S. government sources. "Those interested in matters of the kind" would have assumed all along that the U.S. Treasury paid not just for *Encounter*, but also for *Preuves*, *Tempo Presente*, and *Der Monat*: "Who else would be fool enough to finance them?" The fact that the CIA channeled the money "was just an American peculiarity." Muggeridge personally objected merely to the cultural, as opposed to political effects of literary interventions by a government agency. "In France, Italy and West Germany the *Ramparts* disclosures have caused," he maintained, "scarcely a ripple."[18]

On the basis of such evidence, one might argue that Europe was not surprised or upset by the *Ramparts* disclosures, and that there was no need for a rigorous new set of guidelines for the CIA's secret propaganda operations. But the truth is that Muggeridge would not have written as he did except against the background of a British outcry, while Jorgensen, if he is to be taken seriously at all, was at least surprised.[19] The *Ramparts* disclosures were the most comprehensive of their kind so far, and the dramatic culmination of a process which by now was having a cumulative effect. They upset potential supporters of the United States at a time when an international boom in American studies promised a deeper understanding of U.S. aspirations, but also when the unpopular Vietnam war was already pulling the nation into the abyss of contempt. Producing his book *The Anti-Americans* (1967) after a tour of the world, journalist Thomas B. Morgan concluded that "our postwar interventionism," especially by the CIA, was the prime cause of U.S. unpopularity (followed, in his ordering, by the "race crisis," the Vietnam war, memories of McCarthyism and Kennedy's assassination, and "the tragic inadequacy of our global economic policies"). In 1968, Claude Julien published a book that was a veritable diatribe against the CIA's cultural activities; he regarded the Agency as a key element in American "imperialism." His views carried some weight, for he was chief of the foreign affairs bureau of France's most respected newspaper, *Le Monde*.[20]

While CIA leaders had in the past warned Americans and citizens in allied countries to beware of Soviet propaganda designed to dissolve the unity of the West, there can be little doubt that the 1967 crisis was homebred. Still, as one might expect, Communist publicists avidly fastened on the scandal. The East German historian Julius Mader issued a *Who's Who in CIA* (listing 3,000 U.S. nationals but omitting, perhaps in a pathetic effort to delude counterintelligence, major figures like James Angleton, William Colby, and Cord Meyer), followed in 1970 by a *Yellow List* of CIA cover organizations.[21] The American Communist George Morris in his *CIA and American Labor: The Subversion of the AFL-CIO's Foreign Policy* (1967) rehearsed the story of the connections between Jay Lovestone, George Meany, and the CIA, and he warned that U.S. organized labor had become, in the 1960s, the Agency's Trojan horse in Africa.[22]

The *Ramparts* disclosures stimulated a major wave of revulsion in the Third World. Chester Bowles, who had advocated the abolition of the CIA in 1961 and was now ambassador to India, claimed that the 1967 revelations "hurt us throughout the world, particularly in India, where we had developed especially close and extensive relationships with Indian universities and with individual scholars, none of which were in any way connected with intelligence operations." Bowles conceded that Soviet bloc propaganda was further inflaming Indian opinion. Nonetheless, the CIA's actions had caused Indians to suspect every one of their countrymen who had links with, or favorable opinions of, the United States. Although Bowles may have been a little jaundiced in his opinion of the CIA, there is no reason to doubt his judgment in this case. In the wake of the *Ramparts* scandal, the Indian journal *Seminar* accused America of "academic colonialism." Indira Gandhi, prime minister of India from 1966, treated the CIA as the pariah of international politics and as a direct threat to Indian self-determination and democracy.[23]

Similar reactions occurred in every Third World continent. In October 1967, Bolivian forces put to death the Argentinian revolutionary Ernesto "Che" Guevara, who had been trying to arouse the poverty-stricken tin miners. With the world's press now poised to attack the CIA on any and every front, it was only a matter of time before the former Bolivian Interior Minister, Antonio Arguedas Menietta, recounted how the CIA had bribed him to falsify stories of the charismatic leader's death. Menietta's confession led to savage denunciations in the U.S. press and renewed fears about the effects of the CIA's actions on world opinion.[24] These fears were justified: in 1970 Gregorio Selser, an academic banished from his native Argentina for expressing socialist opinions, published *La CIA en Bolivia*. Selser based his account on stolen Bolivian military documents, on Guevara's "diary," and on further *Ramparts* disclosures. He alleged that the CIA had arranged the Guevara assassination.[25] In the meantime, yet another *Ramparts* disclosure had made known the CIA's penetration of the American Society for African Culture as a means to the manipulation of emergent African nationalist leaders.[26] There seemed no end to the repercussions of the sensational story first advertised in February 1967. At a moment when it needed foreign understanding, support, and counsel, America was losing the confidence both of its allies and of emergent leaders in the nonaligned and Third World nations.

The full extent of the damage did not, however, become plain to American policymakers until it was too late. In 1967, the year when effective remedial action might have been taken, a number of factors obscured the urgency of the *Ramparts* scandal's effect on foreign opinion and domestic confidence. These included the operation of other phenomena stimulating anti-Americanism, the intangibility of opinion and its effects, and the confusing complexity of various reactions in different parts of the globe. Not only the Gaullists and Lee Kuan Yew, but also

Indira Gandhi and various African and Latin American leaders, attacked the CIA mainly to boost their own internal prestige; sometimes, they were publicly critical, while secretly supportive, of certain CIA operations.[27] Such opportunism obscured the underlying hostility without which the opportunism itself would have been inoperable. More important than all these factors, however, was President Johnson's development of a siege mentality that made him blind to the issues that gave rise to the celebrated "credibility gap" during his administration.[28]

Because he underestimated the significance of the *Ramparts* affair, Johnson resorted to half-measures designed to limit the short-term damage. At first, the administration promised that the Katzenbach inquiry would take into account additional revelations in the press showing the CIA had been involved with more than just the NSA. Also, after receiving a letter from his vice president endorsing the British Council proposal, Johnson conceded in a press release that "there may now be other methods for supporting important United States objectives." However, he turned down a Mansfield suggestion that, in order to calm public opinion, the Katzenbach committee be augmented to include "members drawn from Congress and the public at large." (Showing himself insensitive to the people most offended by the *Ramparts* scandal, Mansfield had proposed as a public member Clark Kerr, the University of California president who had clashed with the students' Free Speech movement in Berkeley.) Johnson explained that enlargement would mean delay, and that quick action was needed to quell adverse publicity. Katzenbach accordingly issued his report on March 29—after an interval only just long enough to allow the appearance of some proper research.[29]

An interim report to the president on March 17 had in the meantime alerted Johnson to a split on the Katzenbach committee and made it plain that at least one senior official wanted thorough reform: John Gardner demanded a ban on covert subsidies to private, voluntary, and educational institutions, with "virtually no leeway at all" allowed to the CIA. Helms opposed Gardner's recommendation, wanting more flexibility. Johnson in the event chose a policy that recognized the principle of restraint without committing him to its implementation. As Katzenbach put it, "we ought to *try* to achieve a flat ban, but without handcuffing the Administration or the United States Government, whatever the future danger."[30]

To look into the requirements of organizations soon to be stripped of covert funds, Katzenbach recommended a new committee. Secretary of State Dean Rusk assumed the chairmanship of this committee, which included a student, Senator Fulbright, and representatives of both public and private interests. Though Katzenbach had, in announcing his findings to the press, invoked the example of the openly and publicly funded British Council, he and the Rusk committee looked at other options, too. One was private subsidization of hitherto CIA-financed enterprises. The other, "where overriding national interests so require," was the continuation of secret CIA subsidies.[31]

The salient feature of the Katzenbach reform was its cosmetic, stopgap character. The government made no serious effort to emulate the open-finance methods of the British Council. Ironically, therefore, the United States, with its exceptionally open system of government at home, retained relatively secret methods abroad. Nor—as Humphrey had earlier discovered in trying to make the NSA independent of CIA subsidies—was private philanthropy equal to the task. The Congress for Cultural Freedom, it is true, won support from the Ford Foundation, now presided over by the former overseer of clandestine CIA dispensations, McGeorge Bundy. But the NSA was one of those organizations that had become useless as cover and could attract no philanthropy, so it simply had to do without.[32]

In other cases, it was business as usual. The State Department found a loophole in its own declared policy of not secretly subsidizing private foundations: it justified the CIA's continuing secret payments to *public* organizations, even if those organizations masqueraded as private bodies. Thus, the CIA continued to pay for the Free Europe Committee and Radio Free Europe. One authority has suggested that the Katzenbach committee was unaware of the public provenance of Radio Free Europe's funds and of the Radio's continuing eligibility for subsidy; as the Rusk committee's report remained secret until 1971, there was some delay before it became generally apparent that the taxpayer paid for the Radio, and that Katzenbach's guidelines had been less than firm.[33] Little wonder that suspicions continued thereafter: a Senate committee drew attention, in 1976, to the CIA's continued use of "several hundred American academics" and stressed what it perceived as the "narrow" focus of the Katzenbach committee's concern. In 1978, a distinguished journalist protested at a House hearing that the CIA was still being allowed to "destroy the validity of American institutions in order to save them."[34]

The Katzenbach inquiry was, it must be conceded, a turning point of sorts. Its report recognized the principle of restraint in one significant area of covert operations, in a way that promised better awareness of foreign and domestic opinion, yet retained the option of a flexible response to foreign plots against U.S. national security. The report's immediate impact was, however, merely cosmetic. A sufficient number of covert operations of all types continued to make the CIA an increasingly vulnerable target for foreign critics and then for the crusading reformers of the 1970s. Indeed, by promising more than it delivered. the report raised the critics' morale. Even more damaging than this, in the short run, was its effect on White House-CIA relations, for the rescue operation left Helms and his colleagues heavily indebted to the president at a time when they badly needed an infusion of integrity and independence.

But, according to Helms, the Arab-Israeli war soon restored the CIA's standing. LBJ in this case gave the Agency a specific intelligence task to perform and time to do it properly, for trouble had been brewing for a while. Egypt had expelled from the Sinai Peninsula the United Nations force that took over from the Israelis following their 1956 invasion, and had exploited her domination of the Strait of Tiran to blockade the Israeli port of Eilat. Israel feared this would be the prelude to an attack by her Arab neighbors and appealed to the United States for help. For two weeks, the Americans tried to defuse the crisis through diplomacy. Then, on June 5, 1967, Israel launched a preemptive airstrike that destroyed Egypt's air force on the ground and started a war with Syria and Jordan as well. By this time, the intelligence consumer—the White House—had, in the classic manner prescribed by intelligence theorists, phrased its questions for the intelligence producer, the CIA.

Johnson's problem was that, if he entered the war to save Israel, he would incur domestic political wrath (after all, the Republican Eisenhower had used America's weight *against* Israel in the 1956 Suez crisis). He would also alienate the oil-producing and anti-Communist Arabian Gulf states, as well as antagonize world opinion in general. On the other hand, if he stayed out, and if the Israelis were driven into the sea by the numerically superior Arabs, he would lose the springboard of American and especially Democratic strategy in the Middle East. Furthermore, the American Jewish vote—regarded as an important element in some key electoral college states and part of the New Deal Democratic coalition—might be lost to Johnson just as he was beginning to concentrate on his strategy for reelection.[35]

Helms solved Johnson's problem by delivering, on May 26, a special intelligence assessment. He firmly predicted that, should there be a war, Israel would win within a week. This was in fact a remarkably accurate prediction of Israel's victory in the "Six Days War." To put things in perspective, one might add that the Pentagon and West German intelligence also foresaw Israel's triumph—but the State Department and Soviet intelligence did not. Clearly, the CIA assessment was helpful to Johnson for it meant that he could stay aloof from the conflict without incurring the strategic penalties that an Israeli defeat would have brought in its wake.[36]

Many years after the event, Helms still labeled the 1967 prophecy one of his proudest achievements at the CIA.[37] In an interview just after Johnson left office, he explained why the accurate prediction had been important not just to the president and the nation, but to the CIA as well. He claimed that Johnson did not really "understand what intelligence could do for him" until the "events leading up to the June War of 1967." Once he had learned that lesson he promoted Helms: "Starting in the summer of 1967 . . . I was at the Tuesday lunch when there was a Tuesday lunch or the corresponding equivalent." This was important to the CIA director because of his belief that it was necessary to be regularly seen at the president's side, in order to command respect and influence. Thus, Helms claimed that the 1967 prediction achieved for the CIA an improvement in its tarnished image and prestige.[38]

President Johnson no doubt appreciated the accuracy of the CIA's prediction, but Helms appears to have exaggerated the strength of his reaction. The political benefits of doing nothing to help Israel were not clear cut, because the intelligence background to the decision could not be leaked for fear of offending the Arabs:

White House aide Harry McPherson complained that the "American Jewish Community believed that Johnson had done nothing for them; that he was in effect prepared to see Israel suffer terribly."[39] It is far from clear that Johnson's inclusion of Helms in the Tuesday luncheons was a reward for and recognition of the June War predictive achievement. Walt Rostow, Bundy's successor as adviser on national security affairs, had already been urging Helms's inclusion to improve the White House-CIA liaison, and in his memoir he recalled Helms attending "regularly" in 1966.[40] Far from becoming suddenly respectful of the CIA in June, it seems likely that Johnson felt he had the Agency in his pocket since the *Ramparts* affair in February. There must have been a nagging fear in the minds of CIA officials that the president might at any moment punish dissent by invoking the secret findings of the Rusk committee to justify program cutbacks and job losses. Johnson allowed Helms the illusion of satisfactory status not because of one, half-useful, intelligence report, but because he expected the CIA director to be compliant.

In spite of inner doubts, CIA officials went to exceptional lengths, from mid-1967 on, to satisfy the president's ambition for victory in Vietnam. Operation Phoenix exemplified this thrust. The CIA proposed that all U.S. intelligence agencies pool their information on the infrastructure of the Viet Cong, which by this time was running a campaign of terror and intimidation in its bid for power in South Vietnam.[41] The scheme was the brainchild of Robert W. Komer, a former CIA man now on the staff of the National Security Council. William Colby was in charge and responsible for the implementation of the scheme. Though regarded by his critics as an unimaginative, inflexible man all too ready to obey orders, Colby was in reality something of a chameleon, a man for all seasons. A Roman Catholic and the son of a military father, he attended Princeton and Columbia, parachuted into occupied Europe for the OSS, and pursued an "opening to the left" policy in Italy in the 1950s, before running the ruthlessly repressive Phoenix program.

Using Vietnamese personnel, the Saigon-based American directors of Phoenix sought to identify and then "neutralize" Viet Cong leaders on the village level.[42] It is unclear what they meant to signify by "neutralization." One defender of the policy suggests that identified Viet Cong activists were to be "captured, rallied or . . . killed," and that those who died often did so in the course of two-way exchanges of fire.[43] In practice, the nondefinition of alternative means and local outbreaks of mayhem and blood feuding meant that the program degenerated into a counterproductive bloodbath. Though Colby—whose Catholic conscience troubled him less than McCone's—later defended the program as being "well within moral limits," he admitted in a 1971 congressional hearing that the number killed was as high as 20,000.[44] Although Vietnamese personnel did most of the killing, the program ran contrary to the principle of indigeneity so dear to counterinsurgency theorists: one of them later observed that Phoenix was "entirely American and largely the initiative of the CIA."[45] The Agency was using methods in which its theorists had no faith, to fight a war in which its analysts did not believe.

In another Vietnam-related program, the Agency acted not just against the better judgment of some of its officials, but in violation of its 1947 legislative charter. Its decision to step up its occasional domestic intelligence operations (properly the jealousy guarded domain of the FBI) was the product of many factors, not the least of which was the siege mentality of the president of the United States. In 1966, the Agency had reached a new working agreement with the FBI and produced its calumnifying (though unconvincing) report on *Ramparts*.[46] Following the NSA scandal, the executive itched for more information about its critics: one White House aide suggested in April that "some agency of the government" should be investigating *Ramparts*'s finances (could they be foreign in origin?) in view of its dedication to "smearing the Administration."[47] The contemporaneous race riots also invited suspicion (could they be part of an international conspiracy to discredit the motives behind white boys fighting in Asia?). Establishing the National Commission on Civil Disorders on July 2, 1967, President Johnson called on all departments and agencies of the government to cooperate with its attempts to trace the origins of racial violence, and the CIA in due course supplied twenty-six reports to the commission.[48]

In August 1967, "substantial" White House pressure led to the creation of a special operations group within the CIA's Counterintelligence Staff.[49] The assumption behind this move was that the domestic protest movement against the Vietnam war was being externally orchestrated. President Johnson was by no means alone in entertaining this suspicion. Denouncing Berkeley protestors late in 1964, Clark Kerr had stated that "49% of the demonstrators were followers of the Castro-Maoist line" (the students riposted with a Christmas carol: "Oh come, all ye mindless, Conceptless and Spineless").[50] The problem was largely one of an older generation's incomprehension of the young, the campus students who would actually have to fight the war. At the same time, it is true that the North Vietnamese tried to exploit the disaffection with U.S. policy that already existed not just around the world but in America itself: copies of Hanoi's *Vietnam Courier* were on sale in California by 1966, announcing "great victories" by the Viet Cong and high casualties among U.S. soldiers.[51] After the war was over, Edward Lansdale gave vent to his feelings on this matter: the Americans had "fought battles to finish the enemy keeping tabs by body count," but the Vietnamese Communists had more astutely fought battles "to influence opinions in Vietnam and the world."[52]

The Special Operations Group's task was "to find out [the] extent to which Soviets, Chicoms [Chinese Communists] and Cubans are exploiting our domestic problems in terms of espionage and subversion." Setting up the unit on August 15, deputy director for operations Thomas Karamessines warned counterintelligence chief Angleton that the contemplated surveillance had "definite domestic counterintelligence aspects." The group's staff was in theory to watch the activities of

American dissidents' foreign contacts, in order to detect and determine the nature of a possible international conspiracy. In practice, the group grew (eventually numbering fifty-two) and took on new functions. Its members spied on Americans and, in the illegal operation called Chaos, compiled files on 7,200 U.S. citizens.[53]

The group found nothing to suggest that the mounting unrest was other than spontaneous and indigenous. Helms told President Johnson on November 15 there was "no evidence of any contact between the most prominent peace movement leaders and foreign embassies, either in the U.S. or abroad." He enclosed a report based on intelligence from several agencies and coordinated by the CIA. This report described Tom Hayden and other sworn enemies of Johnson's war policy as "tireless, peripatetic, full time crusaders."[54] Commenting on the state of affairs, Helms said the CIA was "woefully short of information about the protestors."[55] It is probably true that the CIA was hampered in its investigation by relative inexperience in the domestic field, and by the confusingly rapid turnover in student organizations which baffled the FBI as well as the Karamessines team. It is possible that Helms, accustomed as he was to the CIA's numerous operations to fabricate "indigenous" movements in foreign countries, too readily assumed that enemy powers would be intriguing within America and, having had this expectation dashed, felt doubly disappointed.

The main reason, though, why Helms considered the lack of information "woeful" had little to do with performance and expectation. Rather, the dearth of evidence would be so unwelcome to the president, whose wishes and even prejudices the CIA director was prepared to gratify, because proof of the perfidy of LBJ's opponents would have been good news: it would have boosted Johnson's popularity at a time when he was starting his campaign for reelection. But the CIA director was even more petrified by the prospect of conveying to Johnson some really bad news, namely that U.S. troops were unlikely to achieve their expected, politically timely breakthrough against the Viet Cong. Agency analysts and therefore Helms himself knew perfectly well that U.S. bombing and groundfighting tactics were doing little to destroy the military threat posed by Vietnamese Communist forces. If they had forced the administration to take cognizance of this fact, for example by alerting Congress, then America would have been able to withdraw from the war or, perhaps, change its tactics and win it. But, after the buffeting of recent years and especially the *Ramparts* affair, Helms and his colleagues were by now almost reflexively compliant to the wishes of the president. Helms did not alert him to the true state of affairs until it was too late.

The CIA's analysts were consistently pessimistic in their appraisals of two aspects of the Vietnam war. One was the bombing campaign. In 1965, phase one of Rolling Thunder had aimed at destroying North Vietnamese logistic support for rebels south of the 1954 demarcation line. A second phase of the highly accurate, B-52 saturation bombing campaign destroyed about 70 percent of North Vietnam's petroleum storage facilities in the summer of 1966. Phase III, beginning with the lifting of the monsoon season in the spring of 1967, inflicted widespread damage on industrial targets in North Vietnam, for example, electricity, steel-producing, and cement-manufacturing facilities, and coastal commercial installations.[56] The escalating bombardment inflicted impressive damage that showed up well in briefing photographs. However, one CIA assessment after another suggested that the bombing did not impair the flow of men and materials into South Vietnam. In fact, there were strong indications that U.S. attacks stiffened North Vietnamese morale and stimulated retaliation in the form of increased support for insurgency in the South. Nobody in the Johnson administration seemed to be asking questions about North Vietnamese morale and likely responses to U.S. escalation, and Helms refrained from speculation of a type that would have made him unpopular in the White House.[57]

CIA analysis was, secondly, pessimistic on the subject of enemy strength. Led by the American commander in Vietnam, General William C. Westmoreland, the advocates of escalation argued that Viet Cong fighting strength was relatively modest at around 270,000, and declining fast as U.S. forces inflicted crippling casualties. Buoyed up by such hopes and yearning for a victory that would win votes in the forthcoming election, Johnson allowed Westmoreland more and more troops until the number of Americans under arms in Vietnam had reached 549,000 by April 1968. Yet the CIA had for some considerable time been in a position to counsel caution. Toward the end of 1965, the Agency assigned Sam Adams the job of estimating enemy strength. He received little encouragement and worked alone on the project until early 1968. But Adams—a young Harvard graduate descended from a Revolutionary patriot and distantly related to President John Adams—had the ability and self-confidence to come up with a startlingly different appraisal of Communist strength. Tied to conventional thinking even when opposed by a largely guerilla enemy, Westmoreland and his advisers had excluded from their calculations of enemy strength about 300,000 guerilla-militia. By December 1966, Adams had already concluded that Viet Cong strength was closer to 600,000 than the 270,000 of the official estimate. To Adams's horror, however, his superiors ignored his report, tried to suppress it, and made no effort to place it on the desk of the president.[58]

Not every senior member of the Johnson administration was oblivious to the possible flaws in U.S. policy. On June 17, 1967, Secretary of Defense Robert S. McNamara, incipiently troubled by the course of events, commissioned a "History of U.S. Decision-Making Process on Vietnam Policy." Later dubbed the "Pentagon Papers," this top-secret compilation of military, CIA, and other documents ran to forty-seven volumes by its completion in May 1968. It showed that CIA analysts, and sometimes experts in the Pentagon, too, had long questioned some basic premises of U.S. policy—for example, the domino theory and the invincibility of conventional U.S. ground and air strength. By the fall of 1967, McNamara was a skeptic. When his pleas for a cutback in the Rolling Thunder campaign fell on deaf ears, he offered Johnson his resignation. His departure infuriated the president but the announcement did not precipitate a debate, for McNamara slipped quietly into the presidency of the World Bank and concealed from the public his tardily conceived doubts about the war he himself had helped to escalate. CIA pessimism therefore failed to have an impact either directly or through the disenchanted secretary of defense.[59]

In February 1968, the Viet Cong and their northern allies achieved what the CIA had failed to accomplish, the destruction of the faulty premises behind Johnson's Vietnam policy. Beginning on the first of that month, they launched the famous Tet offensive. The nature and timing of the offensive (guerilla infiltration of the cities in the monsoon season) had been anticipated by some analysts both in the CIA and the military.[60] But the heavily televised fighting and casualties shocked most Americans back home. There seemed to be a desperate need for a revision of U.S. official estimates of enemy strength. Military spokesmen tried to retrieve their position by pointing to the unquestionable punishment imposed by the U.S. counterattack, which killed forty thousand of the Viet Cong and their supporters.[61] But their efforts were to no avail. The Communists had pricked the bubble of American impregnability. Johnson could no longer peddle the illusion of imminent victory backed up by cosmetic estimates of enemy strength.

Having previously been a potential embarrassment to be swept under the carpet, the figures compiled by Sam Adams had suddenly become too dangerous to ignore. With the Tet campaign two weeks old and Communist fighting strength by now self-evident, Helms testified before the House Appropriations Committee. His testimony was supposed to be secret but it gave rise to a *Denver Post* story by the former CIA critic, Thomas B. Ross. The journalist said Helms had given the appropriations committee "a frank account of the agency's Vietnam position." Ross claimed that a "high state of tension" had developed between the White House and the CIA over the Agency's "steady pessimistic assessments of the Vietnam war." The White House—especially, he thought, the "optimistic" Walt Rostow—was bullying the CIA. In fact, the House watchdog committee feared that in consequence there would be "a reduction in the flow of intelligence from the agency," for the "White House, CIA split on Vietnam Prospects" meant, according to Ross, that "key CIA officials are worried about their jobs."[62]

Helms strenuously denied the authenticity of the Ross story in a memorandum to the president, and Johnson sent an insultingly hostile rebuke to the *Denver Post*'s editor, who had up till then been a friend of his.[63] In one sense, Helms and Johnson were justified in their denials. There had, indeed, been no White House-CIA split. Stories about this split smacked of self-preservation on the part of Agency officials who could foresee an impending Democratic defeat at the polls over the issue of the war. Because of the overdeferential attitude that Ross had correctly noted, the CIA challenge to White House premises on Vietnam had come too late—too late for the politically doomed president, too late for the compromised Agency, and too late for the nation.

By the end of March, the president knew that, in spite of the brave U.S. military counteroffensive, the Viet Cong had landed him in serious political trouble. On the advice of the new secretary of defense, Clark Clifford, he called on the counsel of a senior advisory group known as "The Wise Men." The group included State Department Vietnam skeptic George Ball, as well as other knowledgeable and hitherto less critical old hands like McGeorge Bundy and Robert Murphy. The Wise Men took into account the relative inefficiency of the Phoenix program as well as the Adams figures in reaching their majority verdict that the United States should reduce its commitment in Vietnam. According to Clifford their opinion "really shook the president," who at first claimed that "somebody had poisoned the well."[64] He summoned Helms to find out what he, George Carver, and other CIA officials had told the Wise Men, and Helms now informed the president in full of the grim truth. On March 31, having been run close by peace candidate Eugene McCarthy in the New Hampshire primaries and with the Gallup Poll showing him to be increasingly unpopular, LBJ withdrew from the presidential race. He also called a halt to the bombing of North Vietnam, and a few days later removed General Westmoreland from his command post in Vietnam.[65]

Since 1968, there has been considerable debate and recrimination about the CIA's Vietnam estimates. In 1975, the Republican congressman Paul M. McCloskey, who had been a noted foe of the Vietnam war, told President Ford he had unearthed some documents which proved the White House had suppressed the CIA's views. This "command influence" was unhealthy, and the Vietnam estimates episode demonstrated it was "imperative that the intelligence estimates of CIA not be screened by policy-makers." McCloskey assumed that the American democratic system provided an intrinsically sound mechanism for the conduct of foreign affairs, but that the executive had arrogated to itself too much power, especially that power which attaches to information. Helms, on the other hand, saw things more in terms of personality. He believed that national security affairs adviser Walt Rostow had helped "the President to reinforce his impressions." According to McNamara's Pentagon Papers study, it was the president himself who "seized upon" Westmoreland's optimistic reports. But Sam Adams, who resigned in disgust the day before the Tet offensive began, blamed the Agency itself: Helms knowingly signed the military estimate of Viet Cong strength, "along with its doctored numbers."[66]

Helms and the CIA can be defended on two grounds. First, they were "not asked," in the words of one scholar, to supply an alternative perspective—and the tasking of the Agency was, by common consent, an executive prerogative.[67] Second, one might argue by analogy with Allen Dulles's reticence, in his day, over the apocryphal nature of the "missile gap," the defense being that it is unwise to push a valid argument too hard if the likely consequence is your removal from the conference table in the future. This is precisely the point made by John Huizenga, chief of the Soviet affairs group within the CIA's Office of National Intelligence: "In doing Estimates about Vietnam, the problem was that if you believed that the policy being pursued was going to be a flat failure, and you said so, you were going to be out of business. In expressing such an opinion you would lose all influence."[68] Yet there was a difference between the Dulles and Helms predicaments: Dulles held his silence when evidence was sparse and guesswork might have led to death and suffering for millions of Americans, while Helms kept quiet when there was clear evidence about a problem on the other side of the Pacific.

The truth is that CIA officers were suffering from a kind of collective anomie, from a paralysis of the will and intellect. The departures, in rapid sequence, of Dulles, McCone, and Raborn had been depressing evidence of parlous standing and shaky independence. The Rusk committee, first, and then disagreements over Vietnam threatened job losses throughout the Agency, not just at the top. If the *Ramparts* affair had been humiliating, the presidential rescue operation was even more so. It was all too tempting for the CIA's leadership to protect the extra jobs created through acquiescence to the Vietnam situation, and to thus avoid angering the president. The atmosphere was just not conducive to imaginative analysis and dissent.

The demoralized Agency's failure to communicate the message about Vietnam led to expensive reverses that adversely affected U.S. prestige, the economy, Johnson's career, and the status of the presidency itself. Where the Agency was concerned, the failure was self-perpetuating. Internal disillusionment with the war and with the suppression of truth accelerated the demoralization that had made the CIA compliant in the first place. Eventually, another factor compounded the problem: a number of CIA employees—Patrick McGarvey in 1972, then Victor Marchetti, Sam Adams, Philip Agee, Frank Snepp, and Ralph McGehee—turned to apostasy, listing Vietnam as a major cause of their defections.[69] With the exception of covert operations, no other issue caused a comparable degree of disaffection within the Agency. The sorry story and consequences of the suppression of the Vietnam estimates therefore had a particularly debilitating effect on an already vulnerable CIA.

The psychological climate within the Johnson administration and within the CIA probably contributed to another serious intelligence failure, the underestimation of Soviet nuclear strength in the 1960s. As early as 1962, at least one Soviet strategist had been openly suggesting the desirability of a massive nuclear buildup.[70] By the mid-1960s, the two superpowers were in the process of exchanging strategic doctrines, the United States settling for a balance-of-terror concept called MAD ("mutually assured destruction") but the Soviet Union opting for a "war-waging" capacity based on nuclear superiority. In the two-and-a-half-year period to September 1968, for example, the Soviets tripled their launching capacity for intercontinental ballistic missiles. Each year, the CIA dutifully reported the increase in Soviet missile-launching capacity. But Helms and his advisers did not foresee, and therefore did not warn McNamara and Johnson, that the upward *trend* would continue and might constitute a threat to U.S. national security. Until 1965, McNamara harbored the illusion that the Soviets would accept a continuing nuclear inferiority. In the later 1960s, a new conviction took root in U.S. policymaking circles, namely that the Soviets aimed at missile parity and no more. Thus a Defense Department "posture statement" in January 1968 reflected CIA reasoning that a recent doubling in Soviet missile-launching capacity indicated a desire to catch up, and that a leveling-off in the Soviet effort could be expected. By 1970, it was plain to the Nixon administration that the Soviet Union had stolen a march on America with regard to numbers of missiles deployed—and that the CIA had failed to supply a warning in spite of being in possession of most of the necessary technical information.[71]

The causes of the CIA's underestimation of the Soviet weapons buildup have been the subject of intense debate. According to CIA veteran Patrick McGarvey, Defense Intelligence Agency officials regarded its civilian rival as being composed of "fuzzy-headed liberals."[72] By the 1970s, when details of the underestimate had become widely known, it was an article of faith among conservatives that dewy-eyed liberalism and gullibility about Soviet intentions caused the CIA gaffe and allowed the Soviet Union to steal a dangerous lead.[73] During the neoconservative ascendancy in the 1980s, the Soviet defector Golitsyn claimed the West had fallen victim to Kremlin-KGB disinformation. The gullible CIA was directly at fault, added influential publicist Edward Jay Epstein, while others even suggested that counterintelligence chief James Angleton had been a Soviet "mole."[74] But these attacks on the CIA were speculative, opportunistic, and partisan. The Agency's "liberal" reputation was largely a myth, and even the myth properly belonged to the 1950s more than to the 1960s. The CIA's analysts were, in reality, constantly on guard against Soviet deception.

The CIA proved vulnerable to self-deception, not to KGB plots. Its analysts were the prisoners of the recent past and of current U.S. strategic doctrine. In the recent past, the Agency had—until after the 1960 election—gone along with the "missile gap" theory about the then-mythical Soviet superiority. In the words of one historian, "having been stung once, members of the intelligence community became cautious about raising unnecessary alarms."[75] This led the analysts to be overskeptical of the implications of the Soviet buildup. Current U.S. strategic doctrine also led the analysts astray, for they too readily assumed the Soviets would behave just like the American leadership. McNamara was keen on establishing a stabilizing balance of power, so the Russians must be thinking along the same lines (in fact, they were by the mid-1960s intent on reversing the earlier U.S. missile lead). The Americans were considering the development of more advanced weapons, such as antiballistic missile systems and missiles carrying several individually-targettable warheads. The CIA knew enough to doubt the efficacy of the Russians' carefully monitored research along similar lines, yet it failed to foresee that they would eschew high-technology "quality" systems in favor of quantity— the mass-production of SS-9 intercontinental ballistic missiles. In other words, the CIA had again succumbed to mirror-imaging.[76]

Retrospectively, students of the intelligence problem came to agree that mirror-imaging had been a serious problem, but they offered differing explanations for it. One explanation was that technocrats, the "prudent professionals," had taken over the running of the Agency, edging out the human factor—the historians and other Soviet experts who would have been able to distinguish Russian from American intentions.[77] Les Aspin, a Democratic congressman from Wisconsin and member of the House Select and Permanent Select Committees on Intelligence from 1974 to 1981, offered a different perspective. Mirror-imaging had, he argued, led to overestimates as well as underestimates of Russian strength. It arose partly from the intrinsic inscrutability of Russian society, which Churchill had described as a "riddle wrapped in a mystery inside an enigma." But Aspin also stressed that in his opinion "many of the intelligence community's problems stem from the weakened condition of Soviet studies in U.S. universities," so the problem was not that the CIA picked the wrong people, but that they had nobody to recruit.[78]

Persuasive though the mirror-imaging thesis is, it describes the intellectual mechanics of error, rather than the failure in willpower that led to the underestimate. Whatever the state of academic Soviet studies, there can be little reason to doubt the effect of low status and low morale both on recruitment and on the performance of existing employees. One academic consultant on Soviet affairs noted that "during the period of disenchantment with the Vietnam War, the Board of Estimates found it increasingly difficult to recruit graduate students for its Office of National Estimates."[79] McGarvey said that serving CIA officers were afraid their careers would be adversely affected if they offered dissent, that Helms wished to be surrounded by "yes-men." He thought the Agency already contained men who had been "beaten to a moral pulp by their profession," and that the Southeast Asian crisis made things worse.[80] Another authority concurred in saying that there had arisen the specter of the "intelligence briefer with a golden voice and not much else."[81] President Johnson, already burdened with several billion dollars of extra expenditure on the Vietnam War, simply did not want to know that massive additional expenditure would be required to keep ahead of the Russians in the arms race—so nobody told him. When Huizenga noted officials' reluctance to query assumptions about Vietnam for fear they "would lose all influence," he might just as well have been speaking of his own section in the ONE, the Soviet affairs group. There is no evidence to suggest that the true Soviet estimate was suppressed, but there is a great deal to support the view that it was no longer considered worthwhile to ask politically embarrassing questions about the cosmetic intelligence required by the Johnson administration.

The 1960s intelligence underestimates helped the Soviet Union to achieve a psychologically important numerical, if not qualitative, nuclear-missile parity with the United States. In itself, this was no disaster. It encouraged the Americans to go to the negotiating table in the Nixon presidency, to try to achieve an arms control agreement that would protect the U.S. national security and economy more effectively than any new weapons system. It reassured the Russians that they would no longer appear to be negotiating from a humiliating position of weakness, so they, too, sat down to bargain seriously with the result that the two sides reached a historic agreement. Ironically, therefore, the achievement of a strategic arms limitation treaty had stemmed from an intelligence error.[82]

But exposure of CIA deficiencies led in due course to bitter criticism of the 1960s Agency as well as deep suspicions about detente. The critics often went too far, for one can see, even in the later Johnson years (1966–68), some incipient improvements in the CIA's effectiveness. The post-*Ramparts* Katzenbach committee of inquiry at least subscribed to the principle of restraint in the case of covert operations; Helms's briefing of the president on the true state of affairs in Vietnam may have been too late but at least it pointed to an ultimate return to reality; disaffection within the Agency was demoralizing in the short run but ultimately stimulated constructive discussion and reform. Yet there can be no quarreling with the fact that the Agency reached its performance nadir under LBJ. By comparison, the reform-laden 1970s, though regarded by some Agency diehards as the low-point in CIA history, were years when U.S. intelligence began to redeem itself. First, however, the CIA had to navigate the treacherous waters of the Nixon presidency.

10

NIXON, KISSINGER, AND THE FRUITS OF MANIPULATION

President Nixon and his foreign-policy adviser Henry Kissinger exploited the CIA's lack of stature for their own ends. These ends, the achievement of a more stable relationship with the Soviet Union and the general strengthening of the prospects for peace, were admirable. Their manipulation of intelligence in pursuit of the overriding goal is therefore defensible both morally and pragmatically. Yet the Nixon-Kissinger techniques inevitably produced bitter as well as mellow fruits, and the CIA was left, in 1974, with an even lower standing than at the start of Nixon's presidency. This is important because, after the Nixon era, respect for the intelligence community and its findings would be a necessary ingredient in peace diplomacy; the slump in the CIA's prestige was unfortunate from this point of view. Nevertheless, even at the end of the Nixon presidency, the prospects for intelligence were by no means entirely gloomy, for the nation had at last been shaken from its complacency. Nixon's concern with peace in the short run may well have imperiled future arms agreements, but it may also have accidentally engendered the spirit of intelligence reform.

White House manipulation of intelligence with a view to the achievement of a strategic arms limitation treaty was not the only cause of the continuing atrophy in the CIA's standing in the Nixon years. Covert operations in Southeast Asia and elsewhere undermined domestic faith in the Agency, as did the critical climate of the day. Indeed, Congress was going through one of its assertive, anti-executive phases, with several of its members eager to pounce on every detectable CIA misdemeanor. The press was in a complementary muckraking frame of mind and in full cry over the Watergate scandal. Leakers inside the Agency and disillusioned apostates outside it fed the host of newspaper reporters who eagerly awaited their revelations.

While all these factors mattered, none was so important as the White House's determination to subordinate the CIA. Whereas Nixon manipulated the Agency, it is clear that he was also prejudiced against it. In an early address to "top personnel" at Langley, he issued warnings:

> I surveyed the field [before rehiring the existing leadership]. I checked the qualifications of all the men, or, for that matter, any woman who might possibly be Director of the CIA. That could happen.
>
> I saw the number of women outside of this organization. You have plenty of opposition.
>
> . . . this organization has a mission that runs counter to some of the very deeply held traditions in this country and feelings, high, idealistic feelings, about what a free society ought to be.

The newly installed president went on to praise the CIA as "one of the great instruments of our Government for the preservation of peace, for the avoidance of war," but few among his audience could have failed to detect the carefully understated element of distrust and menace in his remarks.[1]

When, therefore, Nixon manipulated the CIA, he was capitalizing on his own natural bias. Neurotic persecution feelings underlay that bias. For example, he was unable to justify his assertion that the Agency conspired against him in the 1960 election. He also clung to a similar, largely irrational suspicion that the American social elite was pitted against him. Henry Kissinger recalls his intervention with the president to prevent him from dismissing CIA Director Richard Helms at the start of the administration: "Even more than the State Department, Nixon considered the CIA a refuge of Ivy League intellectuals opposed to him."[2] There can be little question concerning Nixon's continuing doubts about the competence and loyalty of CIA personnel. He was to complain that "those clowns out at Langley" failed to warn him of important developments, such as the impending fall of the Sihanouk government in Cambodia. Bitterly recalling the CIA's desertion over Watergate, he was to observe that the "CIA protects itself, even from Presidents."[3] In a nation whose population was shifting to the South and West and was no longer predominantly "Anglo-Saxon" in composition, Nixon represented an increasingly powerful if not always rational reaction against the "Eastern Establishment." It is ironic that the CIA bore the brunt of his suspicions at the end of a decade when the "Prudent Professionals" had begun to make inroads into the Agency at the expense of the older socio-educational elite.

In spite of his distrust, Nixon made an effort to get along with the CIA. In May 1969, for example, he tried to establish a bridgehead within the Agency by installing his own man as deputy director for central intelligence. Marine Corps General Robert E. Cushman, Jr., had been assistant for national security affairs to Vice President Nixon, 1957–61. President Nixon emphasized the bond of loyalty between him and the new number two by attending Cushman's swearing-in ceremony on the White House lawn and by singing his praises in a short speech.[4]

Several considerations prompted Nixon to seek a working relationship. Common sense, reinforced by his experience as vice president, told him that he needed a foreign-intelligence service, and his political instincts restrained him from trying to replace the CIA, a maneuver that would only have produced a welter of scandal and recrimination. Nixon believed that the CIA could not only be neutralized as a potential enemy, but also be made compliant to, and even a useful instrument of, his will, by means of making the Agency's officials conscious of their dependence upon his support. He could see, furthermore, a certain mutuality of interest, notably the existence of common political enemies, that would tend to bind the CIA to him.

Like his predecessor in the White House, Nixon thought he would be able to cement the CIA's loyalty by "saving" it from Congress: on February 3, 1969, just two weeks after Nixon's inauguration, Senator Fulbright established a troublesome ad hoc subcommittee on United States security agreements and commitments abroad. The Democratic senator from Missouri, Stuart Symington, was its chairman. A product of the Truman stable, Symington was committed to the principle of central intelligence and had supported the CIA during the 1967 *Ramparts* scandal. But he had also publicized the mythical missile gap in the 1960 election (when Kennedy considered him a possible running mate) and, on several occasions, had criticized the CIA's Soviet estimates for being "soft."[5] Symington could also be relied upon to rake over the embers of Vietnam-related decisions. It came as no surprise when, on September 19, 1969, he attacked the "cloak of secrecy" that had obscured American efforts over five years in Laos, and announced an investigation into the matter. His committee became a notorious source of leaks and, at the end of October, the *New York Times* ran detailed articles on the "secret war in Laos," revealing that Green Berets on contract to the CIA had, from time to time, led Meo operations.[6]

Helms was furious about the Symington attack and spoke with exceptional vehemence about it. For one thing, he resented armchair criticism of men who were "living in the boonies, a long way from Broadway," and who were doing "a superb job," even if "one or two of them" might have "got off the reservation at some time or other." Secondly, it was wrong to blame the CIA alone: "the whole government worked together with CIA in the lead." Above all, Helms resented Symington's hypocrisy, for the senator had known about the operation all along: when, in 1969, he "got up and started talking about a 'secret war,' he knew far better than that."[7] Kissinger agreed with this view—the "issue was not to obtain the facts—they were widely known—but to induce the government to confirm them publicly."[8] This was no doubt the case, for the Senate's Democrats, now being in opposition to a Republican administration, wished to publicize embarrassing issues that previously they had helped obscure. One factor that may have motivated Symington in particular was that he was up for reelection in 1970 and had to show he was no "patsy." At the same time, it is probable that he was unaware of the *extent* of U.S. involvement until 1969, when a couple of his new subcommittee staff members visited military installations abroad and told him about it.[9]

Regardless of Symington's true motivation, the Laos controversy gave Nixon an opportunity to make common cause with the CIA. From Nixon's point of view, the revelations were an attack on executive privilege and an attempt to harm Republican prospects in the 1970 midterm elections, as well as an unjustifiable attack on the CIA and on administration policy. He resorted to the same "flashback" technique that Johnson had used during the *Ramparts* affair. The White House instructed the CIA to show that the Laos operation had started under the Democratic presidency; the Agency had briefed no fewer than sixty-seven Senators on the CIA's Laotian "secret" war since 1963.[10] Letting another opportunity for covert operational reform slip by, Nixon demonstrated his loyalty to the CIA in the expectation of reciprocal favors.

As a prelude to their manipulation of intelligence, Nixon and Kissinger first set out to establish control over the CIA, and they were more difficult to resist because they made such a formidable team. The president had a brilliant, intuitive grasp of domestic politics flawed only by his neurotic personality; his national security affairs adviser had complementary abilities in the foreign policy sphere. Both men were erudite about international politics. They were agreed on the need to control national security policy through the National Security Council. The revival of this institution, however, did not entail a return to the style of the 1950s: the CIA was to occupy a lower rung on the national-security bureaucracy ladder and commanded less respect.

It soon became evident that Kissinger would exert extraordinary influence. Notably, a debate raged in 1969 between the CIA's analysts and the powerful combination of Kissinger and Defense Secretary Melvin Laird. The Pentagon argued that the Soviets were developing accurate, independently variable, multiple missile warheads and a "first-strike" capability to deal a knockout nuclear blow. Agency analysts, having conceded the Soviet missile buildup and having themselves warned of the multiple-warhead danger, now wrote sober—and, it transpired, accurate—estimates indicating that the new Soviet technology was inferior to that of the United States and would take time to develop. John Huizenga believed the Pentagon was exaggerating Russian prowess because it wanted Congress to approve its "Safeguard" antiballistic missile system.[11] Kissinger's support for Laird appears to have been partly a maneuver to win control over estimating procedures and policy, and partly an early attempt to put chips on the table which could be used in bargaining with the Russians. Conditioned as he was by encounters with President Johnson, Helms simply offered continuing loyalty and cooperation.

At first sight, the compliant behavior of the CIA director might seem to have won gratitude, consideration, and even respect from the White House, for, at last, Nixon implemented a Vietnamization policy. Against the backdrop of huge anti-war demonstrations in the fall of 1969, the president cleverly claimed that a "silent majority" nonetheless backed him, then announced that the fighting of the war would be handed over to the Vietnamese. The size of the Vietnamese armed forces increased to over one million; the Americans played their part by supplying the new army with modern weapons and by continuing the undercover Phoenix program aimed at the elimination of the Viet Cong infrastructure.[12]

The change in American policy might seem to be a concession to CIA philosophy in two respects. First, the United States was at last taking steps to extricate itself from direct involvement with a foe whose strength the Agency had long recognized. Second, the reliance on indigenous anti-Communists was congruent with the covert-operational doctrine of the 1950s. General Lansdale (whose presence as senior liaison officer at the Saigon embassy, 1965–68, had been only reluctantly tolerated by local military and civilian personnel), rather plaintively made this point in a paper called "A Comparison: Viet Nam & the Philippines." In the paper, he mercilessly attacked the heavy-handed U.S. military presence of the mid-1960s:

> To a Vietnamese farmer or villager, there usually were some Americans on the scene or close by when military or civilian representatives of the Saigon government appeared. Regardless of the kindly behavior, the hard-working habits, or the open generosity in fulfilling local needs which were exhibited so often by so many of these Americans, none of them was a Vietnamese. He was a foreigner, in a land where everyone not from that immediate locality was suspect. It didn't take much skill for the Communist cadre to exacerbate the inbred suspicions of the Vietnamese and ascribe ulterior motives to the American presence.[13]

The change in American policy meant a planned reduction in U.S. ground force level, and it might seem to have been reflective of the philosophy advocated by Lansdale and others. Yet, it should be borne in mind that Kissinger needed no instruction from the CIA on the principle of indigeneity—the subject of his advice to the Psychological Strategy Board in 1952. Nor is it likely that Nixon was, as he later hinted, specially influenced by CIA doctrine and persuasion. Rather, he was conscious of the fact that the draft was the chief goad to student protest against the Vietnam war. As he had based his political appeal on the law-and-order issue, he did not wish to give way to disorderly protest: "Under no circumstances will I be affected whatever by it," he declared in the fall of 1969.[14] For Nixon, the attraction of Vietnamization was that it would, by bringing the boys home, undercut a major source of domestic discontent and make political surrender unnecessary. Furthermore, while the policy change may have been consistent with advice from some CIA people in the past, it was not implemented in conformity with counterinsurgency doctrine. It was military not civilian in character, it was accompanied by bombing and other policies not calculated to win the hearts and minds of the Vietnamese people, and it carried no prospect of democratic government. Vietnamization was the product of American democracy and the ploy of a president in control of his bureaucracy, rather than a step toward Asian democracy arising from CIA persuasion.

Nixon's determination to control the CIA had a considerable impact because, in spite of his bluster about "high idealistic feelings," he saw undercover methods as a useful arm of U.S. policy. While his distaste for the Ivy League, Georgetown set was real enough, he was much more interested in intelligence affairs than his predecessor. His sense of urgency communicated itself to his officials, and Kissinger, in particular, needed no second invitation to institute stronger control. On February 17, 1970, National Security Decision Memorandum 40 established the Forty Committee to oversee the CIA's covert operations. This successor to the Special Group and the 303 Committee was composed of the deputy secretaries of State and Defense, the chairman of the Joint Chiefs of Staff, and Richard Helms, with Kissinger in the chair. The memorandum did not set up guidelines for the conduct of covert operations, a move which would have removed too much discretionary power from Nixon and Kissinger. Nor, according to Kissinger, did it pass the initiative to the White House, which only in rare instances requested specific operations.[15] But the memorandum did state which operations should go before the Forty Committee for scrutiny: those costing more than $25,000, those designed to support political or military groups, those which were economic, paramilitary, or counterinsurgent in character, and, above all, those which were politically sensitive.[16] The purpose of the memorandum was not, therefore, to reform the principles governing covert operations, but, rather, to exert tighter White House control over such operations in the future.

There can be little doubt that White House control over the CIA was effective, even though shortly after the issuance of the memorandum there occurred two events which led critics to claim, in retrospect, that Nixon and Kissinger had failed to establish such control. In neither case, however, does the evidence confirm that the Agency's leaders were defying the White House. The first event arose from Nixon's February 14, 1970, directive that "all existing toxin weapons," as well as supplies of toxin not required for research, should be destroyed.[17] The CIA disobeyed this order with respect to its own supplies in Fort Detrick, Maryland. The reason is unclear. Helms later claimed that an oral command for destruction had been issued, and that Agency employees were trained to accept such commands as "orders written in blood."[18] But Nathan Gordon, the CIA scientist in charge of the chemical program, said he never received the order. There does seem to have been a genuine misunderstanding: as Gordon pointed out, Nixon's directive was a general order aimed largely at military stockpiles and designed to prepare the way for the United States to become a signatory of a new United Nations-sponsored treaty on chemical and biological weapons. The CIA received no specific, reinforcing directive from the newly formed Forty Committee, and its leadership, though fully aware of Nixon's aims, was guilty of negligence rather than deliberate disobedience.[19]

The second event that gave some people the impression that the CIA was rampaging out of control was the March 1970 deposition of the Cambodian head of state, Prince Norodom Sihanouk. He had been democratically elected, and his overthrow by Marshal Lon Nol threw Cambodia into a period of bloody anarchy and foreign intervention. But Sihanouk, in spite of professions of neutrality, had tolerated territorial incursions by the neighboring North Vietnamese while condemning U.S. bombing missions against them, so his departure was welcome news to U.S. government officials. Sihanouk entitled his 1973 book-in-exile *My War with the CIA*. His assumption that the CIA "particularly" was behind the Lon Nol coup, as well as Nixon's angry surprise at the news of Sihanouk's removal, encouraged some to believe that the Agency may have operated on its own initiative. Yet while the CIA did operate in Cambodia, and while there, as elsewhere, local CIA officers probably took an option on the opposition, there is no evidence to confirm that Sihanouk was correct in his allegation. Rather, like other politicians in the aftermath of the Bay of Pigs, he exploited popular fears of CIA machination to boost his nationalist image—as the champion of "our modest aims of living our own Cambodian way of life within our own national boundaries." For when Sihanouk wrote his book he still had political ambitions; in 1975, in fact, he returned as head of state for a short while before handing over the government to Peking-orientated Communists. Ambition colored Sihanouk's account; the CIA leadership appears not to have organized the 1970 coup at all, let alone on its own initiative.[20]

Far from indulging in maverick behavior, Helms did his best to please Nixon over Cambodia. With the pro-American Lon Nol in place, Nixon authorized, in April 1970, a groundforce invasion of Cambodia with the declared objective of finding and destroying what was presumed to be North Vietnam's military headquarters. The attack carried the danger that it would provoke a North Vietnamese retaliatory invasion, and in any case, it proved to be an ineffective move against a nonexistent target. Just before the attack, a CIA analysis had pointed to the impracticability of the proposed invasion. In his desire to placate Nixon (who knew the raid was risky but wanted a sideshow to satisfy the hawks while he withdrew more U.S. troops from South Vietnam), Helms suppressed the CIA analysis. For this reason among others, Huizenga later accused Helms of "gross interference" in the intelligence process.[21] The episode illustrates, in cameo, Nixon's manipulation of intelligence with an overriding peaceful goal in mind— but at a cost to the CIA's self-respect and standing.

The CIA proved equally responsive to Nixon's proddings over Chile. The Agency already had a program of covert action there, and multinationals such as the International Telephone and Telegraph Corporation, as well as politicians, were demanding action to frustrate the Chilean socialists' plans. But, as Kissinger records, Nixon took the rare step of proposing Chile as an agenda item for the Forty Committee.[22] The president was determined to prevent the accession to power of the socialist Salvador Allende. In June 1970, he overruled Assistant Secretary of State for Latin America Charles Meyer's objections to operations which would lead to a "further tarnishing [of] America's image in Latin America."[23]

In spite of continuing CIA activities, Allende won a plurality in Chile's presidential election on September 4, 1970. Annoyed and disappointed, Nixon now told Helms to step up the CIA effort. The CIA director scribbled a subsequently famous note to remind him of the president's instructions: "$10,000,000 available, more if necessary—full time job—best men we have—game plan—make the economy scream."[24] Subsequently the CIA did spend eight million dollars. Additionally, it issued estimates confirming the strength of the opposition in Chile. Because of compartmentalization, however, the authors of the estimates did not know about the Forty Committee-CIA program, and, in the words of a 1975 Senate staff report, they assessed the "durability of opposition sectors" in ignorance "of covert American funding of precisely those sectors."[25] The CIA's cooperation with Nixon over Chile therefore sprang from the Agency's organizational structure, as well as from the spirit of compliance.

By the 1970s, the CIA needed a good shakeout, an airing of grievances, and a reexamination of its role and working methods. This is precisely what happened in due course, one of the reasons being the development of tension between some of the lower ranks and the top officials of the Agency. Helms's continuing cooperation over Southeast Asia provoked considerable dissent and incipient rebellion. His assistance in the stepping up of illegal domestic operations was another deeply divisive factor.

In June 1969, White House aide Tom C. Huston had told the CIA of Nixon's wish that the aims of Operation Chaos be more broadly construed. Helms acceded to the request, and Chaos developed to encompass CIA penetration of domestic protest groups, an expanded CIA mail-opening program, and an extension of the National Security Agency's program of international communications intercepts. This initial expansion of Chaos was so disturbing to some Agency officers that, as revealed in a 1972 CIA Inspector General report, they voiced protests.[26] In 1970, undeterred by and perhaps unaware of the discontent, Nixon approved the "Huston Plan," which set up central evaluation of information on domestic dissent collected by the FBI, CIA, NSA, and DIA. FBI Director J. Edgar Hoover, though so often accused in the past of infractions against civil liberties (and deeply enmired in his own attempts to discredit American dissenters), protested to Helms at the illegal nature of powers now contemplated for the CIA.[27] Helms pressed on with the Huston plan, but at a cost to Agency morale that may be deduced from his attempts to reassure employees: "We're not trying to do espionage on American citizens in the United States, and we're not tapping telephone lines," he told them in a "State of the Agency" speech on September 17, 1971.[28]

But Nixon was in no mood to rein in. On the contrary, he was developing the siege mentality and taste for draconian methods for which he became notorious. He was particularly angry when Daniel Ellsberg, a defense consultant turned war critic, leaked the Pentagon papers to the *New York Times*. Starting on June 3, 1971, the newspaper serialized a selection of excerpts from this secret, governmental study of the Vietnam decision-making process. Nixon had good cause for annoyance. The papers, and especially the selection published in the *Times*, credited the CIA with remarkable prescience over the Vietnam war and showed up the politicians in a poor light. The Eastern Establishment, it seemed, had struck again.[29]

There was a further danger that the sensational leak would prove to be a psychological release, starting a deluge of further revelations. It was, in fact, after the Pentagon papers example had been set, that a number of former CIA officers set their Vietnam grievances in print. Patrick McGarvey, who had worked for the CIA in Saigon in 1964–65, started the process with his 1972 book *CIA: The Myth and the Madness*. In this balanced if carelessly compiled publication, McGarvey described the suppression of CIA analysts' criticisms of Defense Intelligence Agency and White House assumptions underpinning the extension of the war to Laos and Cambodia. Thus, Marchetti, Agee, Adams, Snepp, and McGehee were to follow suit with their own, more biting criticisms wholly or partly occasioned by the Vietnam War. Nixon's anger at the Pentagon papers leak and his fear that it would be "a signal to every disgruntled bureaucrat" were therefore well founded, even if his response was extreme.[30]

Just after the *New York Times* started its serialization, Nixon took action which, after considerable delay, was to produce a long-overdue CIA defiance of presidential judgment. The story began when Nixon instructed his domestic adviser and confidant, John Erlichman, to set up a unit to plug leaks, and to examine the Ellsberg case specifically. With an election year approaching, Nixon also wanted, as he later put it, "ammunition against the antiwar critics, many of whom were the same men who, under Kennedy and Johnson, had led us into the Vietnam morass in the first place."[31]

Erlichman assigned Egil "Bud" Krogh to head the leak-plugging unit known as "The Plumbers." Former FBI man G. Gordon Liddy helped Krogh, as did onetime Kissinger aide David Young. But the most colorful member of the group was former CIA operative and sometime novelist E. Howard Hunt. At the time, the selection of Hunt seemed appropriate. He had only recently retired from the CIA—on April 30, 1970. Though his speciality had been covert political operations, his new employers blithely assumed he knew all about clandestine operational techniques. He appeared to be sound ideologically, for he deplored Kennedy's support of the "democratic left" in Latin America, and he believed the "Eastern Establishment" had aided and abetted Ellsberg in leaking the Pentagon papers.[32] He was intensely loyal to Nixon and, once hired, even went so far as to forge a cable in an unconvincing attempt to pin Diem's murder on Kennedy.[33]

In spite of his inexperience in such matters, Hunt took charge of the arrangements for an infamous burglary. The plan was to enter the office of Ellsberg's psychiatrist, obtaining evidence to tarnish the reputation of the leaker without leaving a trace of the break-in. In the event, Hunt's team found nothing of interest and bungled the cover-up. Misleadingly, the circumstances of this abortive operation later created the impression of official CIA complicity, for Hunt approached Nixon's man in the CIA, deputy director Robert E. Cushman, and obtained a favorable response:

> HUNT: I've been charged with quite a highly sensitive mission by the White House to visit and elicit information from an individual whose ideology we aren't entirely sure of, and for that purpose they asked me to come over here and see if you could get me two things: flash alias documentation, which wouldn't have to be backstopped at all, and some degree of physical disguise for a one-time op—in and out.
> CUSHMAN: I don't see why we can't, no.[34]

Furthermore, three other CIA veterans, as well as Gordon Liddy, accompanied Hunt when he entered the psychiatrist's office over the Labor Day weekend of 1971.[35] There, however, the CIA association ends, however much abuse the Agency later suffered on account of its imagined wrongdoings. The Ellsberg affair was, in fact, one of a string of events that alerted not just the CIA rank and file, but also the hitherto loyal leadership, to the dangers that would be involved in unswerving obedience to future White House instructions.

Yet, the process of redemption was painfully slow. A renewed sense of mutual interest in the face of a common foe continued to bind Nixon and Helms together, for the critics of the CIA in Congress were renewing their attack. They were stung by the fact that John Stennis, Russell's successor as chairman of the Armed Services Committee, dealt with the problem of overinquisitive additions to his CIA subcommittee (as arranged in the 1967 compromise) by the simple expedient of holding very few meetings, in fact, none at all in 1971 and 1972. With the oversight avenue closed, disaffected senators turned to the more drastic tactic of trying to block the CIA's funds. In July 1971, Senator George McGovern, the Democratic presidential candidate in 1972 and a noted dove, signaled a possible campaign issue by trying to force public disclosure of the CIA's budget. Senator Symington tried in the same month to halt CIA expenditures for U.S. operations in Laos, and in September he attempted to limit the annual expenditure of the intelligence community to $4 billion. Though all these attempts failed, they were a clear signal to Nixon and Helms that they could ill afford to fall out.[36]

At this point, Senator Clifford P. Case entered the lists. Case was a legislator of some stature, having successfully battled corruption in New Jersey. The bill he introduced in July prohibited the use of funds to pay for U.S. paramilitary operations in Cambodia, "especially" by the CIA. His proposal became law in December.[37]

For Nixon, this reverse was more than a blow against his policy in Southeast Asia. It was an early indication of a general and bipartisan revolt against over-weaning executive power. As he was to discover, worse was to come: The Case-Zablocki Act of 1972 insisted on congressional review of executive agreements; the War Powers Act of 1973 prohibited the president from waging war for more than sixty days without congressional approval; in 1974 Congress defied the president by placing an arms embargo on Turkey, following that country's inva-sion of Cyprus. From the president's point of view, then, the Case law of 1971 was a premonitory shock. It was the first legislation adverse to CIA interests since the Agency's formation in 1947; but the law also demonstrated the CIA's dependence on protection by the politically potent president.

By the spring of 1972, two additional issues tightened the CIA's bondage to the White House. One of these issues was the running controversy over Radio Free Europe. Senator Case knew of the CIA connection through his assistant John D. Marks, who had worked in State Department intelligence until the Cambodian invasion prompted him to resign in disgust. When Case exposed CIA financing of Radio Free Europe and Radio Liberty and demanded open State Department funding with a budgetary limit of $30 million for 1972, Fulbright joined in the attack, calling the radios "outworn relics of the Cold War." So did Senator Frank Church, who had been angered by the discovery that the CIA had secretly financed his own activities in Idaho via the Crusade for Freedom. These senators were annoyed because the CIA still seemed to be financing private voluntary organiza-tions in breach of the recommendations of the 1967 Katzenbach committee.[38] The timing of their attack was ironic, even implausible: they were complaining about Cold War tactics just when Nixon—in China, Vietnam, Russia—was trying to reduce conflict and tension. Nonetheless, the CIA leadership had to take notice, and had to hope for White House support.

The administration fought back with the Jesuitical observation that Radio Free Europe was "not an educational or private voluntary organization," and by releasing the hitherto secret text of the Rusk report commissioned by the Demo-cratic Johnson administration, with its recommendation that the CIA should continue to finance the radios.[39] Then, in March 30, 1972, Nixon signed a com-promise measure arranging temporary financing for the radios together with an investigation by a special commission into longer-term arrangements.[40] Though not ideal, the arrangement saved the day for the CIA, while deepening its indebted-ness to the president.

When Nixon remarked he had "protected CIA Director Richard Helms from a lot of things," he cited as a leading example the Marchetti case—the second issue that bonded the CIA to the White House in the spring of 1972.[41] Prior to his disillusionment and resignation from the Agency in 1969, Victor Marchetti had worked for the CIA for fourteen years, as an expert on the Soviet military and antiballistic missile systems until 1966, then in the office of the director. On March 12, 1972, it came to the attention of Langley that Marchetti was planning a book about the CIA's activities. An outline fell into the Agency's hands, indicating that the work would be much more critical than the McGarvey book. This would be the first deeply critical publication by a veteran, and in fact marked the start of the "whistle-blowing" campaign by apostates whose first-hand observations gave their accounts greater plausibility than those by outsiders. Helms viewed the situation with such gravity that he made a direct appeal to President Nixon for help.[42]

The threatened publication of the Marchetti book seemed to epitomize the clash between democratic values and the requirements of an effective foreign-intelligence service. If the book were somehow suppressed, this would infringe perhaps the most cherished right guaranteed by the U.S. Constitution, that of free speech. The political penalties of free speech suppression might well be great, too, as the fate of the Federalist party in the 1800 election had demonstrated. But, argued the proponents of the CIA case, publication would damage national security, embarrass foreign political leaders who had helped the Agency and America, imperil the lives of CIA officers and secret agents, and impair the effectiveness of U.S. intelligence.[43]

Opponents of the book were partly motivated by fear of the unknown, for they had not seen a full draft. The text in fact turned out to be less embarrassing than the later book by CIA veteran Philip Agee, whose *Inside the Company* (1975) contained an appendix naming CIA officers, agents, contacts, and front organizations in Latin America.[44] Yet the opponents had seen enough to realize that Marchetti's *thesis* was offensive. Marchetti argued that the Agency placed too little emphasis on intelligence, engaged in too many counterproductive and irresponsible covert operations abroad and at home, and had developed a "cult of intelligence" based on the mystique of secrecy.[45] Those who opposed publication did so partly because they resented Marchetti's criticism of their own roles and partly, no doubt, because they were affected by the very mystique which Marchetti attacked.

In the absence of an American equivalent of the British Official Secrets Act, the administration pursued a policy of civil court action. Like all CIA employees, Marchetti had signed a contract promising not to divulge national-security secrets. Therefore, he could be required to delete certain passages upon pain of prosecution. Joined as co-author in the fall of 1972 by Case's assistant John D. Marks, Marchetti did complete *The CIA and the Cult of Intelligence*. But prosecution delayed publication until 1974, and even then minus "168 deletions demanded by CIA."[46] Some of the deletions, for example about well-known proprietaries, are now known to have been trivial. Others, for example about continuing subsidization of youth organizations, concealed malpractices. Still others may indeed have protected genuine national-security secrets.[47] But, whatever the merits of the last point, Nixon clearly felt that, by authorizing peacetime censorship, he had taken a risk—and he expected a great deal from the CIA in return.

The CIA leadership remained loyal to the White House long enough to ensure that no politician could sabotage the U.S.-Soviet strategic arms limitation agreements. In 1971, Kissinger had negotiated with the Russians an accord to restrict construction of antiballistic missile systems. Then in May 1972, the two sides agreed to set upper limits on the number of nuclear-tipped missiles each could hold. The Soviet Union was to have 1,600, considerably more than the 1,054 held by the United States. On the other hand, because the United States had a technological lead with regard to independently targetable multiple warheads, the Americans would have at their disposal twice as many deliverable nuclear bombs as the Russians.

Kissinger's tactics in securing the 1971–72 arms-limitations agreements (SALT I), were, as he had always anticipated they would be, manipulative. For he had long been convinced that it would be necessary to adopt a Machiavellian approach. In his *Nuclear Weapons and Foreign Policy* (1957), he had urged the need to "strike a balance between the requirements of organization and the need for inspiration." He saw in Washington's bureaucracy an obstacle to the formation of intelligent strategy: "Against the Politburo, trained to think in general terms and freed of problems of day-to-day administration, we have pitted leaders overwhelmed with departmental duties and trained to think that the cardinal sin is to transgress on another's field of specialization." When, in the pursuit of his higher goal, Kissinger set out to manipulate government institutions including the CIA, he was acting according to his egocentric, antibureaucratic precepts.[48]

As Kissinger pursued his arms-control policy, he knew that his successive goals each had a corresponding intelligence need, such needs relating, in every case, to public opinion and the democratic process. Though the negotiations were highly complex, Kissinger may be seen to have had three, successive, goals. At first, it was necessary to encourage a U.S. arms buildup in order to show American hawks that Henry Kissinger was tough, and in order to create bargaining chips to be used in negotiation with the Russians. By planning an antiballistic missile system, the United States would be creating hypothetical assets to be used as such chips. "Regrettably," Kissinger later recalled, "this insight was not widespread."[49] To persuade Congress and other opinion leaders to go along with the plan, the administration had to exaggerate the threat posed by Russian missiles and the speed with which the Soviets would develop and deploy multiwarhead launchers. That was why, to Huizenga's dismay, the CIA's more accurate estimates had to be discredited.

Once the Russians had been brought to the negotiating table and reached an agreement, the administration had to aim at a second goal, public reassurance. Kissinger had always been aware of the problem of verification and had more than once grilled CIA officials regarding their competence to monitor that process, but in 1972 he kept quiet, for the administration now had to minimize the Russian threat. "You cannot come up here," protested Senator Henry Jackson, "when you are demanding a weapons system with one line and then when you are trying to justify a treaty take an opposite line."[50] Yet Kissinger could and did do that, and succeeded. At this point, he was assisted not only by the CIA's current malleability, but also by the fact that the agreements he negotiated were consistent with Agency thinking, which suggested that Soviet nuclear might was insufficiently formidable to preclude the possibility of advantageous agreement.

When, however, Kissinger pursued his third goal—the defense of SALT I in retrospect with a view to possible negotiation of SALT II—an area of disagreement opened up, for CIA analysts spotted some Soviet infractions of the 1971–72 agreements. Now, as the House of Representatives' Pike Report later revealed, Kissinger exploited his dominant position to hush up the evidence, and to prevent the CIA from identifying weaknesses in the 1971–72 agreements with the USSR.[51]

By the time of the mid-1970s flap over intelligence, an influential body of critics had realized that Kissinger had been disingenuous both in his method of achieving SALT I and in his method of building up that agreement as a shining triumph and building-block for further Russo-American negotiations. A group of Republican congressmen later complained that under Kissinger's aegis "intelligence advice" was being passed "through a screen of policy-making officials." The Democratically controlled Pike Committee similarly described Kissinger's conduct as the "political control of intelligence." By this time, CIA officials were willing to speak out. Edward W. Proctor had been deputy director for intelligence since 1971. One of his predecessors, Ray Cline, supported Proctor when he told the Pike Committee that systematic suppression of intelligence had become routine under Kissinger.[52]

But, for Kissinger and Nixon, the manipulation of intelligence was a means to the enhancement of national security through the propagation of international peace. It is true that SALT I was no blanket solution to the arms race: both sides made qualitative improvements to their weapons systems that soon threatened the logistical stability promised in the 1971–72 agreements. It is also true that when congressmen realized they had been duped by Kissinger's tactics, they became reluctant to endorse updating agreements with the Russians. On the other hand, only political churlishness obscured the fact that Kissinger had achieved the widest-ranging agreement yet with the Russians. By slowing the arms race even to an infinitesimal or purely notional degree, he and his Russian counterparts created the kind of goodwill that militates against holocaust. They achieved a psychological breakthrough, showing that nuclear doom is not inevitable.

It is nevertheless true that intelligence manipulation harmed the CIA. Unjustly, the Agency at first had to suffer the brunt of criticism about the shortcomings of SALT I. When it became manifestly clear that the Agency's advice had counted for little, CIA officials lost caste for that reason, too. It appeared that, whatever the truth of the matter, CIA advice was deficient in quality, weight, or both. All this might seem to indicate that, while the CIA can sometimes give helpful warnings about would-be surprise attacks and can contribute to the stream of analysis flowing into the White House, it can only have a minimal role in the enhancement of national security through arms negotiations.

Yet, a much stronger case can be made to the contrary. After all, one cannot manipulate the truth unless one knows what the truth is—and the CIA was under Kissinger the best source of intelligence on Soviet nuclear strength. Second, manipulation on the Kissinger scale can only work exceptionally, and then only when people are credulous. When Washington (and Moscow) cease to believe that the CIA is a source of objective intelligence taken seriously by policymakers and negotiators, arms-control proposals naturally meet with an uncooperative response. Thus, Kissinger achieved his historic accord with the Russians at the expense of the CIA's standing and potential utility on future occasions.

Because of this, the post-SALT deterioration in White House-CIA relations, instead of damaging the CIA's standing still further, served notice of the start of an Agency revival. Richard Helms, fortified by the realization that he had failed to win White House respect for Agency advice, rebelled over Watergate. The attempt to bug the Democratic party's headquarters in the Watergate apartment complex in Washington, D.C., occurred on June 17, 1972. The reasons for it—was it a simple Republican attempt to find dirt on the Democrats in an election year or a more complicated conspiracy?—remain obscure.[53] The consequences are, however, clear. Once the election was over, more than a score of Nixon's people, including the Plumbers' creator John Erlichman and Attorney General John N. Mitchell, went to prison, while Nixon himself had to resign in 1974 because of the burglary and cover-up. And although ex-Agency man Howard Hunt had hired five of the Watergate burglars (one of them, Eugenio R. Martinez, was still on the CIA payroll as an informer), Helms managed to distance himself and the CIA from Watergate—against the express wish of the president.

To stop the FBI investigation into the affair, Nixon tried to involve the CIA in his cover-up. His plan was for the CIA to stop the FBI by claiming there were national security implications. He also hoped that the CIA background of Hunt and Martinez would point the calumnifying finger away from the White House, and toward the Agency instead: an application of the "fall guy" tactic.[54] Helms refused to cooperate. On November 20, 1972, Nixon, flushed with the success of his run-away presidential reelection victory and unaware that Watergate would develop into a nightmare, summoned the CIA director and told him he was fired.

This was a brutal reminder of presidential power and, because of the continuing determination of Henry Kissinger to control information, the CIA's opportunity for renewed objectivity and independence passed. But between Helms's departure from Langley (February 2, 1973) and Nixon's resignation, events served to confirm in retrospect that the White House-CIA relationship had become strained, which proved an incipient blessing in disguise.

Some of these divisive events were associated with the career of James R. Schlesinger, who succeeded Helms as director. Schlesinger was a Harvard-educated economics professor who had recently served as chairman of the Atomic Energy Commission. At forty-three, he was the youngest-ever director of the CIA. He was vigorous and confident, and he had the advantages of an outsider: freedom from entangling personal loyalties, and an external perspective that helped him perceive what was needed and what was wrong in the intelligence community.

Schlesinger started a program of draconian reform. In an attempt to prune dead wood and give the CIA a new sense of direction, he fired or pushed into early retirement fifteen hundred employees. Of these, one thousand were from the operations side of the Agency, which had always been relatively labor-intensive and, in fact, had been built up to reach record staffing levels to cope with the emergency in Southeast Asia. So there was much more scope for cuts on the operational side of the Agency, especially as, thanks to Nixon's strategy and Kissinger's diplomacy, the Vietnam commitment was at last coming to an end. Nevertheless, in ensuring that the brunt of the Agency's biggest-ever cut fell on the operators, Schlesinger courageously recognized one of the criticisms that had, over the years, done so much to reduce the CIA's standing: its bias in favor of action.

In response to the Ellsberg trial, Schlesinger went further than this. On April 27, 1973, Judge Matthew Byrne, Jr., presiding over the trial of Ellsberg for leaking the Pentagon papers, revealed that Howard Hunt had been involved in the burglary of the defendant's psychiatrist's office. Hunt had by this time been convicted for his role in the Watergate burglary, and Schlesinger, an outsider unfamiliar with CIA secrets, decided to find out what else had been going on that might be contrary to the Agency's legislative charter. On May 9, he and deputy director for operations William Colby drafted a directive asking past as well as current employees to report to the director any illegal activities of which they knew.[55] Colby now set about assembling what came to be known as "The Family Jewels" or "The Skeletons." The former overseer of the Phoenix program set about his task diligently—affected, apparently, by an onset of his Catholic conscience triggered by the death of his daughter in April. In more senses than one, then, Schlesinger seemed to be signaling the end of the era of relatively unfettered covert operations.

Some authorities on intelligence organization have praised Schlesinger for an additional reform.[56] He made a vigorous effort to achieve what had always been expected of a CIA director: guidance and control of the intelligence community as a whole. He took an active personal interest in intelligence problems, especially the crucial question of the strategic balance, about which he knew a great deal. To assist him in his role as director of central intelligence as distinct from director of the CIA, he took on specially selected non-CIA employees. Through these reforms as well as his actions on the operational front, Schlesinger gave the Agency a foretaste of the kind of reinvigorating shake-up it required.

But Schlesinger's intelligence reforms were less effective than they might have been. Many of his colleagues thought they had been introduced for the wrong reasons, in the wrong way, and by the wrong person—for Schlesinger was Nixon's man. He seemed ambitious to use his power to help the president politically, both to secure consent for Nixon's foreign policy and to ensure that the administration would survive Watergate. Schlesinger concentrated intelligence authority in his own hands in such a way that the White House would be even more firmly in control of the informational bases of foreign policy. Notably, he turned his attention to the Office of National Estimates, still largely staffed at the higher levels by OSS veterans, and still referred to as the "Gentlemen's Club." In June 1973, John Huizenga, by this time chairman of the ONE's overseeing board, took involuntary retirement. Thus, in the words of the *Washington Post*'s Lawrence Stern, the administration had "executed a bearer of often unwelcome tidings."[57] By September, the ONE had ceased to function, a development that prompted the understandable reaction that the CIA had lost its objectivity. There was, then, ample scope for questioning the motives behind Schlesinger's reforms.[58]

As for the Skeletons inquiry, who could tell whether Schlesinger would use it to clean up future CIA operations—thus improving the Agency's respectability and standing—or use it to make the CIA, instead of Nixon, the scapegoat for Watergate? Agency feelings on these matters ran so high that there was a possibility of a revolt and of devastating revelations at a time when Nixon was already in deepening trouble over Watergate. When Schlesinger had served only seventeen weeks as director, Nixon made him Secretary of Defense and elevated the more acceptable career intelligence officer, William Colby, in his place.

Schlesinger's reforms were therefore little more than a dubious foretaste of improvements to come. The events of Nixon's last year in office confirmed that there had been no drastic improvement in intelligence guidelines or performance. Partly as a result of CIA measures undertaken in response to Nixon's request, conservative revolutionary forces in September 1973 overthrew Chile's democratically elected socialist government and killed its leader, Allende. In Latin America, this produced bitter attacks on the CIA and the United States.[59] Elsewhere, as well, the event revived anti-Americanism of the Bay of Pigs/*Ramparts* dimensions. In India, for example, Prime Minister Gandhi diverted attention from domestic economic problems by claiming that the CIA was attempting to overthrow her, too: an opportunistic claim but one that emphasized once again the prime role of excessive covert operations as a liability to American diplomacy.[60]

With Chile a likely goad to major domestic criticism, the CIA once more needed to earn White House protection and a reputation for sound intelligence work. This was not to be, and not only because of Watergate's enfeeblement of the presidency. The nonprediction of the Syrian-Egyptian attack on Israel on October 6, 1973 (the Yom Kippur war) underlined the CIA's continuing unreliability in the prediction of surprise attacks. The Agency had collected a mound of information on Egyptian intentions but, in a failure reminiscent of previous shortcomings, had not picked out the crucial indicators that should have provided adequate warning. Kissinger's secretiveness and determination to manipulate information contributed to the recurrence of another failing: poor White House-CIA liaison on which problems should be looked at closely, and how. These failings meant that America, having been caught unawares, had to go to Israel's assistance with military supplies. As one CIA Middle Eastern veteran put it, this "resulted in an Arab boycott of petroleum shipments to the United States and its armed forces overseas," leaving

"NATO incapable of defending Western Europe, and the U.S. unable to fight a global war by conventional means."[61] The boycott furthermore damaged the economies of the United States and her allies—compounding the inflationary effects of the Vietnam war and weakening the West's will to spend adequately on military defense.

Against the background of such events, of a spate of damaging revelations, and of a manipulative White House, CIA people could be forgiven for believing that their fortunes were at an all-time low and sinking lower. White House intelligence manipulation had, of course, nurtured one mellow fruit, SALT I. But that same manipulative process had produced a bitter fruit for the CIA, its much-impaired standing in the policymaking process. Even worse for those who would be at the center of the storm, the Agency was on the eve of a particularly traumatic shake-up.

Yet, from the calmer perspective of later years, it is possible to see in the developing drama itself the seed of a sweeter fruit, the promise of intelligence improvement. In the nation at large, there was a dawning realization that the CIA was not the prime source and instigator of all evil. In 1975, it is true, the myth that the CIA was a "rogue elephant" out of control gained brief currency. But already, in 1974, a House report had cleared the Agency of complicity with the Plumbers.[62] Watergate served the useful function, furthermore, of jolting senior intelligence officials from their supine posture and torpid acceptance of the status quo. It would be an overstatement to say there was a spirit of rebellion. Rather, it would be accurate to say that, inside the Agency as well as in the media and Congress, there were now people who wished to clear the air, establish new guidelines, and reestablish the CIA's integrity and standing. To the establishment of the day, these questioners were pests. To posterity, they will appear more in the guise of saviors.

11

DEMOCRACY'S INTELLIGENCE FLAP
Toward
a
New Legitimacy

$\mathbf{A}$merica's democratic process had, in the immediate postwar period, delayed the setting up of an agency for central intelligence. Then, beginning in 1947, the same democratic process established the CIA's legitimacy and standing. By the early 1970s, however, a questioning spirit had returned. Confidence in and within the Agency was already at a low ebb after a decade of poor White House-CIA relations, the inadequate mid-1960s estimates, and the exposure of some overambitious covert operations. Now, critics both motivated and protected by democratic ideals launched a renewed attack on the Agency's undercover operations at home and abroad. These covert-operations critics helped to ensure that, between the fall of 1974 and the start of 1976, the CIA became the leading political issue before the nation. The relationship between democracy and intelligence came to the fore in public debate as never before or since.

Meanwhile, a differently motivated set of critics mounted a renewed challenge to the CIA's Soviet estimates. Like those who criticized operations, they were partly concerned with the historical record. Their main worry, however, was about the Agency's current competence to assess the nature and degree of the Soviet threat. Once again, such critics claimed, the analysts were underestimating. For the CIA, the double dose of criticism—from estimates hawks as well as operational doves—was bewildering. Caught in the complex ideological cross fire that reached its greatest intensity in 1975, the Agency's leaders struggled to respond to apparently separate and divergent, yet sometimes overlapping critical constituencies.

The effect of the attacks on the CIA was, according to one of its supporters, that they "nearly destroyed its effectiveness at home and abroad."[1] Director William Colby complained that he had to spend most of his time defending the Agency, instead of running it.[2] Congress placed restrictions on covert operations, and the White House ended, at least temporarily, the Agency's supremacy in the all-important field of Soviet estimates. Thus, a plausible case can be made for the view that the Agency was hamstrung and deprived of its proper status. Yet, this dismal opinion cries out for correction. For one thing, the Agency's operations in Iraq and Angola in 1975 suggest that it was far from restrained, even in the short run. More importantly, the vigorous, open, and democratic debate about the CIA had a valuable educative effect in the longer term. By creating a greater understanding of the role and problems of intelligence, as well as by stimulating some organizational and behavioral improvements, the debate laid the foundation for a new legitimacy.

The prospects for both the Republican administration and the CIA looked gloomy on August 9, 1974, the day when Nixon resigned. Executive government was in disgrace. Nixon's successor, Gerald R. Ford, did not carry the authority of a nationally elected official: Nixon had appointed him vice president following the revelations of corruption that had forced Vice President Spiro Agnew to resign in October 1973. Yet, in spite of these handicaps, Ford was determined to stem the dual hemorrhage of secrets and presidential authority.

Ford's attempt to stop the informational flow reflected his natural inclinations. He had always defended the right to privacy—not in the radical sense that individuals should be defended from the prying methods of the FBI, but in the conservative sense that public officials should be allowed their secrets. From 1957 to 1965, he had sat on the intelligence subcommittee of the House Appropriations Committee, taking pride in being a member of the small and then-watertight group of congressmen privy to some of the CIA's secrets. He was close enough to the CIA to defend Dulles over the Bay of Pigs. He sat on the Warren Commission, informed on its activities to the FBI, then defended the findings of the commission. Thus Nixon had selected a reliable man to be vice president. Ford, indeed, obliged by putting pressure on members of the House Banking and Currency Committee to withdraw support from the committee's iconoclastic Democratic chairman, Wright Patman, who had spotted the way in which Republican money had financed the Watergate burglary and wished to press on with the inquiry.[3]

Neither could Nixon and Kissinger have faulted Philip W. Buchen on matters of discretion. One of the "Michigan Mafia" that entered the White House with Ford, Buchen was the new president's legal counsel and his leading adviser on the political aspects of intelligence affairs. A paraplegic since youth, Buchen more than made up for his own disability by fighting hard for Ford, the "determined, handsome man" to whom he was devoted.[4] He constantly counseled the president to be discreet, to keep his political ambitions and strategies secret. When Vice-President Ford headed the Domestic Council on the Right to Privacy, Buchen was its executive director. According to Ford, in May 1974 Buchen had used his strategically placed office to form a "sub rosa" team to work on the transition to a Ford presidency (Ford claimed he did not know about this plan until the last moment). As part of the deal, Ford agreed that the Nixon presidential archives—950 reels of tape and 46 million pieces of paper which contained information that was embarrassing to Ford and the CIA as well as to Nixon—should be treated as the outgoing executive's personal and private property. Second, on September 8, 1974, Ford pardoned Nixon for his presidential crimes. Ford presented the pardon in the light of a need for rapid healing: "You can't pull a bandage off slowly." Buchen already had his eye on the 1976 election.[5]

At first, it seemed as if the Ford tactic of clamming up might succeed. Following the resignation trauma, he had enjoyed a honeymoon period with Congress and the press. He had inherited from Nixon the redoubtable Henry Kissinger—now secretary of state as well as national security affairs adviser. It was just possible that Kissinger, through his diplomatic skills and by manipulating intelligence in a continuing shroud of secrecy, might redeem the Republican administration through new achievements, for example a further strategic arms limitation treaty.

Without having to make concessions, the administration and its supporters in Congress survived the first wave of assaults over the intelligence issue. These began on September 8, 1974, when the *New York Times* and *Washington Post* published the text of a confidential letter from Michael J. Harrington of Massachusetts to his fellow Democratic congressman, House Foreign Affairs Committee chairman Thomas Morgan. Harrington reminded Morgan that CIA director Colby had told the House intelligence subcommittee earlier in the year about the Agency's involvement in Chile in the three years prior to the fall of Allende. Nixon and Ford had continued to deny U.S. involvement and congressmen like Fulbright had thwarted legislative investigation for fear of damaging Henry Kissinger's diplomacy. Now, however, with Chile's democracy dead, an investigation was imperative.

The Harrington leak contributed, as *Newsweek* put it, to the "fire storm over the Nixon pardon."[6] Senator Walter Mondale of Minnesota was particularly scathing about President Ford's contention that Allende, not the CIA, had been the real threat to democracy in Chile: "Congress and the press will no longer tolerate hogwash," he declared.[7] Keeping up his barrage, Harrington complained about the State Department being "almost . . . a benign patsy to events that are initiated and executed by CIA"; in a letter to Ford, he said that the Chile episode would have a disastrous effect on world opinion, and appealed to the president to end his defense of covert operations.[8] However, the administration responded by barring Harrington from further access to the files of the House Armed Services CIA oversight subcommittee, chaired by Lucien Nedzi. The administration could find at least some solace in the fact that while a mere 18 percent of a sample quizzed in a

Harris Poll supported the CIA's intervention in Chile, only 29 percent opposed it. The majority in Congress, furthermore, fell into line. When Congresswoman Elizabeth Holtzman and Senator James Abourezk tried to cut off secret operations funding, Idaho's senator Frank Church spoke out successfully against an absolute ban.[9]

In December 1974, events occurred that ended Ford's ability to control the intelligence issue and set off protracted attacks on the CIA from both defense hawks and operational doves. One of these events was a parting of ways between Colby and his counterintelligence chief, James Angleton. Following an interview with the CIA director on December 17, Angleton quit his job effective December 31, 1974; his three senior aides followed him into retirement. Angleton departed because of policy differences with his boss. Though Angleton had himself cultivated center as well as conservative elements in Italy, he was known to be critical of Colby's "opening to the left" policy in that country and elsewhere. Neither did Colby and Angleton see eye to eye on the question of CIA organization. Compartmentalization in the interest of security was fundamental to Angleton's theory of counterintelligence. His critics thought his fears of penetration verged on the paranoid. (Perhaps the most notorious example of his alleged paranoia was his belief that the British prime minister Harold Wilson may have been working for the Soviets.) Uncompromising counterintelligence officer that he was, Angleton believed in acting on the assumption that such suspicions might be justified, just in case they were. Colby found this irritating, especially as Angleton's stress on compartmental divisions seemed to threaten the geographic demarcations favored by himself.[10]

In his December 17 interview with Angleton, Colby told his colleague of a short-term factor which made it desirable that his departure should be imminent. Seymour Hersh, an investigative journalist who had won the Pulitzer prize in 1970 for his exposure of the My Lai massacre in Vietnam, was about to publish a story on the CIA's illegal domestic surveillance activities. Presidents Johnson and Nixon had, of course, ordered these activities. But, in time-honored tradition, there would be a search for a CIA scapegoat. As counterintelligence chief, Angleton would be an obvious candidate. The best course would be for Angleton to resign preemptively, so that his departure would appear unconnected with the Hersh story. To Angleton's horror, Colby added that he was going to submit to an interview with Hersh, in order to confirm the story and clear the air. Giving Angleton very little breathing space, Colby did talk to Hersh on December 20. Though his decision to do so may have helped restore faith in the Agency in the long run, in the short term it confirmed Angleton's worst fears. Angleton, the CIA, and the executive branch of government were plunged into immediate disrepute.

For Hersh's December 22, front-page story was now more explicit and authoritative than it might otherwise have been. Its first paragraph proclaimed: "The CIA, directly violating its charter, conducted a massive illegal domestic intelligence operation during the Nixon Administration against the anti-war movement and other dissident groups in the United States." The Agency had also used prohibited methods, burglary, telephone tapping, and mail opening, in pursuit of its permitted counterespionage duties. These methods had commenced in the 1950s, but Hersh concentrated on the Nixon administration. As a *New York Times* editorial put it, "yet another conspiracy under the Nixon Administration to defy the law and infringe the constitutional rights of American citizens has now sprung into the open." Hersh's report revealed how, at its height, the CIA's domestic program had entailed the keeping of files on some ten thousand U.S. citizens. The authenticity of his story was taken for granted long before the CIA confirmed its main points in a July 1975 press release.[11]

The Hersh story shocked public opinion and played into the hands of the covert-operational doves. Americans naturally worried more acutely when the CIA's activities affected U.S. citizens. Once alerted, they were more sensitive to what the Agency might be doing abroad, for its foreign actions might, after all, be turned inward one day, especially as its officers seemed impervious to the obligations of law. Because of this symbiotic relationship between anxieties over domestic and foreign operations, covert-operational doves experienced a new lease on life.

Shortly after the Hersh exposé, the covert-operations critics won a major victory with the passage of the Hughes-Ryan Amendment to the Foreign Assistance Act. This measure required the president to report any nonintelligence CIA operations to relevant congressional committees, including Foreign Relations (Senate) and Affairs (House), "in a timely fashion." The amendment's critics believed it to be a prime example of democratic excess. Senator Goldwater later estimated that it obliged the CIA to brief 50 Senators and 120 congressmen on sensitive issues. He complained that security leaks in 1975 could be traced to this fact, notably in the case of the CIA's covert operations in Angola. But the amendment's sponsor, Iowa Democrat Senator Harold F. Hughes, believed it to be "only a beginning" in the process of controlling "cloak-and-dagger operations," and in 1976 a congressional report depicted congressional control over covert operations as "still limited," particularly as the law did not require prior notification of such endeavors.[12]

The Hughes-Ryan Amendment was the first serious congressional attempt to curb the excesses of the covert operators, excesses which had tarnished the image of America and the CIA alike. Its conservative critics overlooked several points. First, the White House is often more leaky than Congressional committees. Second, at the time of passage the proliferation of leak-prone, intelligence-orientated congressional committees had not yet occurred. Mansfield and Fulbright were, in fact, still pressing for a single joint intelligence oversight committee.[13] Had they succeeded in late 1974, the CIA could have been accountable to just one, relatively discreet committee. Still another point missed or ignored by the conservatives was that the hue and cry over leaking secrets was to a great extent the alarmed protest of covert operators whose activities might not survive public scrutiny, as the case of Angola was to demonstrate. For these reasons, there might appear to be greater substance to the contention that the amendment did not go far enough. Still, there can be no doubt that it signaled congressional intent to curb both the president and the CIA. The amendment showed a disillusioned world that it might yet be possible, in America, to lay down secret-operations guidelines in the interest of probity.

The Hughes-Ryan Amendment of December 30, 1974, was just the first signal of what would dominate the ensuing year's politics. Intelligence had taken over from Watergate as the stick with which to beat the allegedly power-mad White House. Political controversy over intelligence became a time-consuming preoccupation of White House staff, of Congress, and of top CIA officials. The press, already in a rampant mood following the part played by *Washington Post* journalists in bringing down the Nixon administration, was in peak muckraking form. A survey of the leading 137 newspapers in the United States (with a combined readership of 28 million) reveals the CIA to have been the prime theme of 227 editorials in the calendar year 1975. In the calendar year 1970, there had been no such CIA-dominated editorials at all.[14]

CIA director William Colby's tactic in the face of this pressure was to make selective disclosures. His disclosures seemed inexplicable to some of his colleagues, who could not understand why the ruthless manager of the 1960s Phoenix program had suffered such a strong infusion of apparently irrational morality. Yet Colby later explained his actions in perfectly logical terms: "I had to . . . educate the Congress, press, and public. . . . The Agency's survival, I believed, could only come from understanding, not hostility, built on knowledge, not faith."[15] There was logic, too, in the way in which he had made his original disclosures to Hersh. While he exonerated the Ford administration by saying that domestic snooping had now stopped, he made it clear that the order for illegal actions had come from the White House, not Langley, and invited support from a Democratic Congress by concentrating on the malfeasances of the Republican, Nixon administration.

With both national-security and political considerations in mind, President Ford was reluctant to go along with the policy of disclosure. Following the Hersh story, Colby showed him a list of infractions, and Ford later claimed to have supported the CIA director's "decision to tell the truth."[16] But throughout the year of the intelligence flap he pursued a policy of proclaimed candor and actual secrecy. To this end, he established on January 4, 1975, a Commission on CIA Activities Within the United States, usually known after its chairman, Vice-President Nelson Rockefeller.

The Rockefeller Commission was a "blue ribbon" affair designed to deflect more serious criticism and investigations. Among its eight members were four Harvard men and such pillars of the establishment as C. Douglas Dillon, chairman of the Wall Street banking firm that bore his name, and formerly Secretary of the Treasury in the Kennedy and Johnson administrations.[17] Rockefeller, it will be recalled, had helped keep Eisenhower's secrets from prying eyes—and at least one of his commissioners thought the subject of the investigation merited little serious attention: Ronald Reagan, retiring on January 6 after eight years as California's governor and now with his eye on the presidency, said he had strenuous speaking engagements and would have to miss some of the commission's meetings. True to his prediction, Reagan missed three out of the Commission's first four weekly sessions.[18]

The executive order which established the Rockefeller Commission fixed a narrow remit: the commission was to determine whether any CIA employees had broken U.S. law. The narrow, domestic focus of the inquiry was designed to inform people on greater authority of what had already been leaked to the press. According to Colby, Rockefeller objected to being told too much: "Bill, do you really have to present all of this material to us?" Furthermore, from the White House perspective, the Rockefeller inquiry seemed a reasonable justification for turning down further demands and queries. This was Philip Buchen's argument when the White House considered a resolution requesting a copy of the list of infractions Colby had shown the president. Buchen told House Armed Services Committee chairman Melvin Price of Ford's view that to ensure "the protection of important defense and foreign relations information," access to such documents should be limited to the Rockefeller inquiry, which would make available to Congress the "essential facts."[19]

Having elicited a satisfactory response from the administration, Colby now demonstrated his loyalty to Ford by resorting to the flashback technique which had been used by the Democrats themselves in the 1967 *Ramparts* scandal. On January 15, he revealed that the Democratic president Johnson, not the Republican president Nixon, had initiated the CIA's controversial research into domestic dissidence.[20]

The Senate responded on January 27 by voting eighty-two to four to create the Select Committee to Study Governmental Operations with Respect to Intelligence Activities, the size of the majority indicating that many senators saw the issue of intelligence in Constitutional rather than in partisan terms. The initial budget of the Select Committee was to be $750 thousand spread over nine months, and the investigation turned out to be one of the largest ever conducted by the Senate. While its original mandate was mainly domestic, it was also empowered to look at the issue of executive control over the CIA, the desirability of congressional oversight, and covert intelligence activities abroad.[21]

The major impact of the Select Committee owed much to the personality of its chairman, Frank Church—indeed, it is usually known as the Church Committee. President Ford did not mince words in alluding to the senator in his memoir: "The Church probe was sensational and irresponsible—Church made no secret of his presidential ambitions—and it was having a devastating impact on morale at the CIA."[22] President Johnson had also noted Church's presidential ambition, and Church perhaps shared with earlier CIA critics the perception that the publicity stemming from speeches on intelligence could help compensate for derivation from a relatively small state, Idaho being the ninth smallest in the Union.[23] At the same time, political style and principle governed his behavior. He had grown up admiring Idaho's senator William E. Borah, whose isolationist approach and oratorical excellence he was to emulate. He had long been aggrieved at the CIA's domestic trespasses, long concerned about the Agency's effect on U.S. diplomacy: as a member of the Senate subcommittee that debated the Bay of Pigs fiasco in April 1961, he had demanded a "full briefing" in view of the "immense influences" the CIA and the military were exerting on policymaking, at the expense of the State Department.[24] While there can be no doubt that Church was politically ambitious, he also offered a serious, principled critique of the CIA, and his committee's work, though demoralizing at the time, contributed to its revival in the long run.

In the first six months of 1975, President Ford tried to contain the intelligence debate. He hoped the existence of the Rockefeller inquiry would calm the nation's fears. When Church requested documents to assist his committee's inquiry, notably Colby's reports to the president based on Schlesinger's Family Jewels probe, the president, having promised cooperation in principle, stalled.[25] Ford was successful up to a point, managing at least to forestall further legislative curbs on the CIA's freedom of action. However, the intelligence crisis deepened, not only because of pressures from Congress and the media, but also because of the proddings of the president's own conscience as Ford learned more about the issues involved. By the summer of 1975, therefore, Ford was prepared to accept some reforms.

On February 19, the House of Representatives established its own Select Committee on Intelligence. This made President Ford nervous because a few of the committee's members were known to be highly critical of the CIA. In the event, the committee's chairman, Lucien D. Nedzi, proved sluggish in his conduct of his inquiry. He had previously chaired the House Watergate-Ellsberg inquiry which helped exonerate the CIA with respect to those events, and in the past, he had, as chairman of the House Armed Services intelligence subcommittee, been privy without demur to various CIA covert operations. Unruffled by criticism inside his committee and in the media, he proceeded slowly.

By far the most explosive revelation of the first half of 1975 came from an unexpected quarter, the president himself. At a White House luncheon for senior *New York Times* editors, he explained why it had become necessary to launch the Rockefeller inquiry. Were the task left to people less responsible than the vice-president and his blue-ribbon team, dreadful disclosures might be made about every president since Truman. "Like what?" asked one editor. Ford, in a state of moral shock following Colby's latest briefing, replied, "like assassinations."[26] Thus, Ford sparked a morbid and sensational national debate that lasted several months. The journalist Daniel Schorr, who had been present at the meeting and first leaked the news in a CBS broadcast on February 28, noted one of the reasons behind the public outcry: "The wave of assassinations that cut down, in less than a decade, President Kennedy, Senator Robert F. Kennedy, Martin Luther King, Jr., Medgar Evers, and Malcolm X troubled Americans deeply, making them wonder if this alien aberration was becoming a feature of American life."[27] Foreign and domestic transgressions were now so closely linked in the public's perception that an injury to an alien seemed equally threatening to Americans. As Linda Charlton put it in the *New York Times*, the malaise about domestic spying had "now spread to include the CIA's permitted function abroad."[28]

Though shocked by what he had learned about assassination plots, President Ford pressed on with his policy of political containment. On March 17, it is true, he confirmed his intention of looking into the assassination issue. Buchen said the Rockefeller Commissioners would now "(1) ascertain whether the charges of assassination plots have a basis in fact and involve unlawful domestic CIA activities and (2) determine whether existing safeguards would prevent activities of that nature in the future regardless of whether they might involve domestic or foreign conspiracies." So, in one respect at least, it seemed that the commission would now investigate a foreign-intelligence problem and suggest new guidelines. Ford and Buchen, however, were acting on the advice of the commission's executive director, David Belin, and Belin was a man of proven discretion—he had been counsel to the summarily concluded Warren Commission. Buchen's memorandum explained that, once the Rockefeller inquiry had completed its investigation into assassinations, Belin "should advise the President of the outcome, through me [Buchen], and then it can be decided whether the subject should eventually be included as an integral part of the Commission's final report or whether it may call for an earlier submission to the President and possible immediate Presidential action."[29] Given the protraction of the commission's period of investigation caused by the inquiry's widened scope, it was just possible that the furor would die down and that Buchen could limit the outflow of damaging secrets.

American newspapermen ensured that this would not be the case. The *Washington Post* led the way with stories about CIA involvement in plots against the lives of Lumumba, Trujillo, and Castro; Lansdale told the *New York Times* about Robert F. Kennedy's involvement in the anti-Castro plots; *Time* magazine followed up with a story on Castro's revenge motive and the assassination of President Kennedy. Speculation reached new heights when an unknown assassin shot dead Sam Giancana before he could testify to the Church Committee on the Kennedy administration's Howard Hughes connection and vendetta against Castro.[30]

Even now, there were some glimmers of hope for Ford and Buchen. Church would clearly have to tread warily in light of the Kennedy brothers' role as Democratic icons. Furthermore, press reaction to CIA stories was by no means uniformly hostile, as is demonstrated by the effects of the *Glomar Explorer* leak. On his second day in office, President Ford had authorized a disguised vessel of this name to raise from the bed of the Northern Pacific the remains of a sunken Russian submarine. The decision was potentially controversial because the operation was expensive, and because the *Glomar Explorer* was leased from Howard Hughes, by now doubly controversial because of his alleged involvement in bribing the Nixon administration to protect his illegal Las Vegas gambling enterprises. Yet, Ford's decision was certainly defensible in terms of national security, for the submarine would yield valuable naval and intelligence secrets. When the *Los Angeles Times* broke the story regardless of national security considerations, veteran intelligence journalist Hanson W. Baldwin denounced the front-page article as "one of the most damaging and irresponsible leaks in United States intelligence history," and he bitterly rebuked the "self-serving politicians" behind the CIA flap.[31]

As intended, the Rockefeller Commission's main, domestic findings and recommendations satisfied a good number of the CIA's milder critics. The *Report* confirmed the existence of operation Chaos and of a CIA computerized list of 300 thousand citizens and organizations, and it revealed that President Nixon had tried to use CIA records for political ends. It noted that such domestic infractions had been uncharacteristic of the CIA's general conduct, but, it nevertheless recommended firm measures to reduce the likelihood of future abuses, including a joint oversight committee and a greater measure of frankness about the Agency's finances. Commenting on all this, a *New York Times* editorial stated "there is probably no better answer."[32]

But the *Report*'s release did not quell the storm. Some were upset that Ford made public only a part of the Rockefeller findings. Others noted the proposed legalization of certain domestic counterintelligence activities, and the recommendation that a harder line be taken with leakers than with the malefactors whose activities had been leaked.[33] Above all, there was dissatisfaction over the assassination issue. The *Report* did contain a chapter on the Kennedy assassination allegations, but ignored the Castro revenge motive in favor of an inquiry into possible infractions of U.S. law, concluding "there was no credible evidence of any CIA involvement."[34] All the major news networks noted that the issue was being handed to the House and Senate committees for further investigation, and Rockefeller himself conceded the point.[35] In the week following Ford's presentation of the *Report* in a news conference, incoming White House correspondence confirmed that a majority of Americans wanted more disclosures.[36]

President Ford was against further disclosures. Instead, he now prepared his own reform plan. On August 16, he ordered the immediate implementation of twenty out of the Rockefeller Commission's thirty recommendations. He dug his heels in over budget disclosures and procrastinated on congressional oversight, but he ordered internal CIA measures for improved supervision and efficiency, a higher degree of restriction on domestic counterintelligence activities, an outright ban on mail opening, a partial destruction of Chaos files in the near future, a speeding-up of declassification procedures, and an end to wiretaps, tax espionage, and the testing of drugs on unsuspecting guinea pigs (one of the more sensational spring revelations).[37]

There can be little doubt that, by the late summer of 1975, President Ford was trying to think constructively about CIA reform. His efforts were a tribute to the effectiveness of the democratic debate then going on, even if Ford still recoiled from open debate. The president realized, for one thing, that the Agency's standing would have to be restored. One of the recommendations of the Rockefeller Commission had been that the CIA directorate should be filled by "individuals of stature, independence, integrity," not necessarily recruited from within the Agency. Such persons should be able to "resist improper pressure and importuning, whether from the White House, within the Agency or elsewhere."[38] In response to this, and to pressures within his own party, Ford devised a plan to reduce Henry Kissinger's influence on the intelligence process—a plan he was to put into effect in the fall.

Additionally, President Ford realized that, if the CIA's covert operations were to continue without the familiar counterproductive effects, a restraining doctrine or set of criteria would be needed. By September, critics were demanding to know why the CIA had intervened in Chile but was doing nothing to bolster Portugal's fledgling democracy, then facing both fascist and Communist threats. Ford responded with an implied doctrine. He defended the CIA's activities against Allende's Chile on the ground that Allende's measures had threatened a long-established democracy; by the same token, CIA methods were not called for in Portugal, which was only just beginning to emerge from the long shadow of fascism.[39] Ford's analysis is clearly vulnerable to the counterargument that the CIA, not Allende, had been the main threat to Chilean democracy. On the other hand, Ford recognized the need for covert operational restraining guidelines—in contrast to the time-honored congressional position, which was to lay down guidelines merely concerning which operations Congress wished to scrutinize. Secretive and calculating though he may have been, Ford had a claim to being a genuine CIA reformer.

Few such consoling thoughts, however, entered the minds of senior CIA officials in the summer of 1975. Colby's remark that the CIA director had become a public relations man did not mean that all of the CIA's several thousand employees were engaged in nothing other than the preparation of congressional testimony and press releases. It is, however, true that paralysis and demoralization affected the prime area of the director's responsibility, intelligence.[40]

The intelligence shortcomings of the CIA in 1975 should not, of course, be exaggerated. The Agency was still superior in resources and expertise to any of its competitors in the United States or other Western countries. When the Soviet diplomat and U.N. undersecretary general Arkady Shevchenko defected to the West in December, supplying Soviet position papers pertaining to SALT II negotiations, he turned to the CIA—still the most trusted, as well as most competent, Western foreign-intelligence agency.[41] Nevertheless, independent investigators agreed that the CIA's intelligence standing was too low, and that for this reason its impact on strategic policy was too weak. The Rockefeller commissioners had wished to boost the "stature" of the CIA director. Reporting later in June after three years' labor, the Commission on the Organization of the Government for the Conduct of Foreign Policy, which had concentrated on intelligence matters under the chairmanship of Robert Murphy, recommended that the CIA director be given greater status in the White House and in the intelligence community.[42]

Following the dismantling of the Office of National Estimates in 1973, the CIA spoke with less concerted authority. Colby had himself helped to set up a substitute system of uncoordinated national intelligence officers, each with responsibility for a special area or field: Africa, the Soviet Union, Science and Technology, Economics, and so on. These officers did not have staff assigned to them, but were supposed to draw on the resources of the entire intelligence community. By implementing this arrangement, Colby had helped to weaken the OSS-Ivy League Old Guard and furthered Kissinger's divide-and-rule objectives. At the same time, Colby, just as much as the CIA's critics, had contributed to the undermining of his own authority as the nation's chief foreign-intelligence officer. For example, in 1975 Colby convinced the National Security Council that the nation's next generation of spy satellites should have an enhanced telemetry collection capability (the ability to pick up radio and other signals from foreign missile systems), but Defense Secretary Schlesinger argued for better photo reconnaissance instead, and Colby won no support from Congress.[43]

Although there was a growing consensus behind the need for a revival of the CIA's estimating independence and authority, serious disagreements prevented that development from taking place. These extended beyond mere recriminations about spineless CIA leadership, Kissinger megalomania, or congressional irresponsibility. The Agency ran into trouble both for underestimating Soviet military expenditure and, paradoxically, for being so suspicious of Soviet intentions with regard to SALT I compliance. To create SALT II bargaining chips via increased U.S. military expenditure, Kissinger now wished to foster an image of relentless Soviet buildup: "When we build weapons, they build; when we stop, they nevertheless continue to build."[44] At the same time, Kissinger wished to preserve the pristine image of SALT I specifically and arms negotiations generally by stifling stories about Soviet noncompliance.

The CIA was also under attack from a more traditional source, the military establishment and its conservative allies. In August, the president's Foreign Intelligence Advisory Board chairman George W. Anderson, Jr., wrote to Ford proposing a system of "competitive analysis": an alternative team would go through the strategic evidence at the CIA's disposal and produce its own conclusions.[45] The CIA's analysts would therefore lose their supremacy, and national estimates their unity. With reference to the all-important Soviet estimate, therefore, diverse critics insisted that the CIA was not doing its job. Their complaints held back the revival in CIA authority that a growing number of people wanted.

Notwithstanding the requirements of the Hughes-Ryan Amendment, the CIA was by no means as emasculated on the covert operational side as it was in the realm of intelligence. Indeed, the Agency as a whole displayed a misplaced vigor—showing more signs of life on the operational than on the analytical level. While many old, established clandestine operations continued without scandal, the CIA

also refrained from interrupting enterprises that were remarkable for their impru-
dence in a year of heightened political activity. One of these was the Kissinger-
inspired supply of clandestine aid to Kurdish rebels in Iraq. The left-wing, pan-
Arab government in Iraq was unpalatable to Washington, and also in dispute with
America's ally, Iran. The CIA therefore funneled secret aid to Iraq's rebellious
Kurds via the shah's officials. But the shah turned out to be more interested in
boundary disputes than in ideology. Influenced by a favorable territorial settle-
ment, by the Kurds' poor performance in Iraq, and by fear of Kurdish rebellion
within his own country, Iran, the shah suddenly cut off aid. The CIA had to
abandon the resultant 200 thousand Kurdish refugees, leaving another "nation-
building" effort in shreds, and itself at the mercy of its critics.[46]

Undaunted by the turn of events in Iraq, the Forty Committee authorized, in July
1975, a CIA mission to Angola. That country was in a state of turmoil following
the collapse of Portuguese colonial control. Kissinger and his colleagues aimed to
ensure a conservative victory in the developing civil war. The CIA put John
Stockwell in charge of the operation. Stockwell had grown up in Africa and had
put in years of enthusiastic service in the marines and the CIA. By 1975, however,
he was disillusioned. The CIA's covert operators, he observed, constantly invented
schemes to stay in business. He believed the CIA was governed by cynical objectives, and, in Africa, by rivalry with the KGB rather than a regard for local
circumstances. He thought that Kissinger had no understanding of the problem in
Angola and was merely throwing money at it, that Kissinger escalated U.S. aid in a
way that brought in the Russians and Cubans (the official U.S. position was that
America was *responding* to external influence), and that Kissinger and CIA officers
treated the Hughes-Ryan Amendment contemptuously by lying to congressional
committees about South African involvement on the American side. The Angolan
enterprise was not, then, in the control of a true believer, and it does indeed bear
the marks of an automatic superpower rivalry with little regard to local welfare
and aspirations. Worse still, from the American viewpoint, the CIA-backed factions were losing their war by the end of the year, and the CIA intervention was
becoming a potent source of black African anti-Americanism.[47]

In Australia, meanwhile, the CIA's covert operations had become a serious
threat to U.S. national security. In 1968, the United States and Australia had
reached an agreement: America would develop, on a desert site called Pine Gap,
electronic eavesdropping facilities which, along with similar assets in Iran, would
monitor Soviet missile testing and other military activities; Australia would receive, in exchange for the consequent risk of automatic attack in case of war, the
benefits of continuing U.S. friendship and military protection. The CIA had rou-
tinely penetrated Australian labor unions that might have the capability of crippling the Pine Gap facilities and other U.S.-Australian defenses through strikes or
other disruptive action.[48] The Australian authorities had not objected to this. But
in 1972, after twenty-three years of unbroken conservative rule, Australia elected a
Labor prime minister, E. Gough Whitlam.

From the outset, CIA right-winger Angleton had been aghast at the election of a socialist premier to lead a close ally, intelligence partner, and important "power base in the Far East."[49] Distaste for Whitlam spread within the Agency when the Australian leader pulled his nation's forces out of South Vietnam and condemned America's 1973 bombing of Hanoi. In Australia, there were suspicions that U.S. listening posts in Pine Gap, Narrungar, and North West Cape had been used, without Canberra's approval, to prosecute the Southeast Asian war; CIA officials in Australia and the United States were afraid that Whitlam would seek to dismantle U.S. intelligence facilities in his country, and they secretly expressed the wish to see him go. In the aftermath of Whitlam's attempt, in 1972, to shake up Australia's intelligence services, followed up in 1973 by an Australian government raid on the headquarters of its own foreign-intelligence service (which cooperated with the CIA), the provocation seemed great. Rumors now began to circulate about CIA subsidies to Australian opposition parties.[50]

Though ideologically moderate, by 1975 the Whitlam government had earned a stormy reputation for a number of reasons quite independent of the intelligence issue: for example, the prime minister had provocatively called for the abolition of royally conferred knighthoods. Then, on November 2, Whitlam alleged that the CIA was funding the conservative opposition National Country Party. This started a further political tempest, but it was as nothing compared with the uproar when, on November 11, the Queen's governor-general in Australia, Sir John Kerr, dismissed the democratically elected Whitlam government and replaced it with a conservative administration headed by Malcolm Fraser.

To some of America's critics in Australia, Whitlam's dismissal was a CIA "coup." In spite of much subsequent debate, it is still unclear what CIA did or did not do to Australian politics in 1975. For the critics, Kerr's former links with intelligence and with the Congress for Cultural Freedom, and, above all, the CIA's history of involvement in coups in Chile and elsewhere, were proof enough. The absence of convincing evidence did not really matter, for suspicion alone proved the undoing of the U.S.-Australian security link. One American analyst of the aftermath of the Whitlam dismissal noted that, in consequence of the outcry against it, the United States would no longer be able to depend on automatic Australian consent to Pine Gap, "one of the last reliable means of verifying any Soviet-American strategic arms accord."[51] America did, in fact, turn to other, more expensive, means of verification. The CIA's reputation for excessive covert operations had once again cost America dearly.

Congress, to whom the investigatory initiative had passed in June, was aware of the CIA's continuing covert operations and of their costs. Some members, at least, were determined to draw blood. In July, Otis G. Pike had taken over from Lucien Nedzi the chairmanship of the now-enlarged House Select Committee on Intelligence. Pike, a conservative Democrat from Suffolk County, New York, at first seemed an unlikely gadfly. As a Marine Corps pilot in World War II, he had flown 120 Pacific zone combat missions. A patriot to the core, he supported the U.S. role in the Vietnam war to the last moment. His very patriotism, however, in the event drove him on to seek the root of the CIA's troubles. The Pike committee report in due course excoriated the hypersecrecy of Kissinger and Ford, suggested that the CIA's covert operators were propping up dictatorships, listed CIA intelligence failures, claimed Congress had been misled about the total cost of foreign and domestic intelligence, and included a further attack on Kissinger under the heading "SALT—Political Control of Intelligence."[52]

The Pike inquiry attracted enormous criticism and many dubbed it irresponsible. In the telling words of a Church Committee staff member, the senator from Idaho was able to use the Pike investigation as a foil: "The object of the exercise was to prove we were not Pike."[53] By the spring of 1976, Pike seemed to be thoroughly discredited: the left-wing Italian journalist Oriana Fallaci described him as a failed conservative hero.[54] Those who condemned him explained their attitude by pointing to the leak-prone nature of his inquiry—even his final report fell into the hands of lower Manhattan bohemian journalists and appeared in the *Village Voice*. Yet the real reason for the bitter reactions was not the leaks themselves, but the painful nature of their subject matter. It was Pike's uncompromising and seemingly partisan agenda that made him unpopular in Washington; at the same time, that agenda helped both to broaden the CIA debate and to focus attention on vital matters such as the manipulation of intelligence.

Church, meanwhile, was trying to keep his inquiry responsibly nonpartisan, partly because of an inbuilt statesmanlike instinct, partly because the Senate as a whole had backed his committee, partly, no doubt, because he was ambitious.[55] His problem was that, in order to retain the loyalty of Democratic politicians, he had to defend Democratic administrations; in order to preserve the appearance of being nonpartisan, however, he also had to refrain from concentrating his fire on Republican administrations. In a posthearing press briefing on July 18, he arrived at his solution with the oft-quoted statement: "The agency may have been behaving like a rogue elephant on the rampage." This statement convinced Daniel Schorr that Church was now "obviously nursing presidential dreams."[56]

Shrewd though it may have seemed at the time, Church's statement had three disadvantages. First, it is clearly untrue that the CIA had operated in defiance or independently of White House instructions; Church soon began to look very foolish for having made the statement. Second, the statement alienated the vast majority of CIA employees and veterans, encouraging them to close ranks against congressional meddling and even to ally with Church's foes. Third, it revealed to Church's Republican opponents a chink in his armor: in spite of statements to the contrary, he was afraid to rake over the direct White House authorizations issued during the Kennedy administration.[57] A *Washington Star* reporter noted in September that "an ambitious fellow like Church" did not want to be "the intrepid investigator who pointed the finger and cried assassin at the martyred John F. Kennedy and Robert F. Kennedy." OSS veteran and Export-Import Bank chief

William J. Casey drew President Ford's attention to Church's desire "to get over his CIA inquiry without embarrassing the Kennedys."[58]

Ford read Casey's letter, but kept his silence on the Kennedy-assassination issue, perhaps realizing that Church would have to deal with it anyway, and certainly obeying his own instinct for silence as well as the counsel of Kissinger and Buchen.[59] Aggressive informational demands from and revelations by the Pike committee only reinforced the adminstration's determination to retain control over intelligence secrets. On September 11, for example, the Pike committee made public part of a secret study of the 1973 Yom Kippur war that criticized not just the intelligence community's performance, but also Kissinger's unreceptiveness to intelligence warnings. A few days earlier, Ford had set up a powerful new group to deal with intelligence problems. Including Kissinger, as well as Colby and Buchen, it met daily, and with the president twice a week.[60] Following Pike's leak, Schlesinger, Kissinger, Buchen, and Rockefeller warned Ford that, with an election year coming up, "any veto [on information] in the name of national security will be portrayed as a repressive act," but Kissinger added in a later, personal memorandum that Pike had challenged "the President's constitutional responsibility to conduct foreign affairs and protect the national security of the United States."[61]

By comparison, the executive's relationship with the Church committee was characterized by compromise, or, at least, competitive cooperation. The White House, for example, agreed to feed the senators information on any one of six covert operations which it nominated. The senators chose Chile.[62] Buchen was still obstructive, asking for scrutiny of the case law on the Nixon tapes which might justify the withholding of White House evidence pertaining even to the agreed area of Chile.[63] But the Church committee did review a considerable volume of evidence on Chile and on other matters within its remit. Its hearings formed a pile two feet high. Senator Church proudly noted that the assassination investigation alone involved nearly one hundred witnesses and yielded eight thousand pages of testimony, comparing in size with the whole of the Watergate inquiry.[64]

Buchen failed when he attempted to block publication of the interim assassination report.[65] The Church committee was therefore able to help to clear the air and to restore confidence in relation to this issue, as well as several other issues it publicly investigated and reported upon. On some grounds, it is true, the committee may be faulted. For much of the time, the senators confined themselves to a moralistic exposure of abuses, instead of aiming at the heart of the intelligence problem. When they did address themselves to the CIA's foreign-policy role, they concentrated on procedure, rather than on how to secure optimal foreign-intelligence performance in the context of a democracy. Yet, it cannot be doubted that the Church inquiry, in addition to restoring a measure of public confidence, both increased and widely disseminated the sum total of American wisdom on intelligence.

Be that as it may, some time elapsed before the administration resolved its immediate politico-intelligence crisis. Aware of the gravity of the situation, President Ford tried to hasten the end of the crisis. He executed a maneuver designed to be a genuine reform, on the one hand, and a preemption of further attacks, on the other. The background to the maneuver was his perception of Henry Kissinger's unpopularity. Additionally, the president had noted the Rockefeller Commission's recommendation that the standing of the CIA director should be restored. In his "Hallowe'en Massacre" of November 2, 1975, he made Kissinger step down from his job as national security affairs advisor, though allowing him to continue as secretary of state. This move limited Kissinger's opportunities for dominating the intelligence process, giving the CIA director room to breathe, and, potentially, to assert himself in policymaking circles. Ford had broken the link (in the person of Kissinger) between intelligence overlord and policymaker, the very link which, the critics had pointed out, militated against objective and independent CIA analytical input to foreign and strategic policy.

Kissinger's demotion was also, of course, an appeasatory gesture toward that official's critics. Ford, no doubt with half an eye on the 1976 presidential election, was anxious to divest himself of old liabilities. In the interest of creating a fresh image, he also installed, as part of his massacre, a new defense secretary, Donald Rumsfeld—and nominated a new CIA director, George Bush. Currently America's representative in Peking, Bush had previously served as a congressman, as U.S. ambassador to the United Nations, and as chairman of the Republican National Committee. He could be expected to sweep with a new broom at the CIA and yet be diplomatically and politically sure-footed. Bush did not disappoint his supporters, and Ford's cabinet reshuffle did eventually help to restore confidence in the Agency.

The "Massacre" failed, however, to put an immediate end to the intelligence crisis. Senator Church denounced Bush's appointment as political.[66] More seriously, the unrepentant Kissinger launched into another fight with Congress. His difficulties on this occasion arose from the Pike committee's demand to see consultative documents on covert operations since 1961, Forty Committee documents since 1965, and documents pertaining to the Soviet Union's compliance or noncompliance with the Strategic Arms Limitation Treaty since May 1972. The Pike committee issued seven subpoenas on November 7, 1975, and a week later cited Kissinger for contempt when he withheld the SALT documents. Buchen in desperation resorted to the flashback tactic recommended earlier by William Casey: he offered Pike Forty Committee documentation for the period 1961–64, as well as for the subsequent period; in other words he threatened further exposures of the activities of the Kennedy administration.[67] Clearly, the half-sacrifice of Kissinger had failed to halt the running battle between Congress and the White House.

Worse, from Kissinger's point of view, was to come. By December 10, when the House dropped its contempt proceedings against him, the Pike committee had obtained, in the words of its report, "volumes of SALT intelligence materials."[68] As

Kissinger had foreseen, the inevitable leaks further damaged his reputation. One senior official claimed that Kissinger had kept Ford in the dark about CIA evidence of gross Soviet treaty violations. The *Chicago Tribune* warned that Kissinger was leading the nation into further SALT negotiations "that may be booby-trapped."[69] Such suspicion and uncertainty demonstrated, of course, that the nation needed a foreign-intelligence agency capable of offering an authoritative finding, but, in the short term, the prevailing distrust continued to make things difficult for all concerned in the policymaking process.

In November-December 1975, it must have seemed that there would be no end to the CIA's travail. On October 31, President Ford had warned Senator Church that publication of materials handed over in confidence by the executive would be a breach of trust, a blow to U.S. prestige, and "may endanger individuals."[70] So long as Congress confined itself to past events like the Castro plots and the Chile affair, such dangers would be at least relatively containable. But, early in November, the Australian story broke and Pike began to probe into the CIA's current antipodean operations.[71] Then, thanks to a report by the indefatigable Seymour Hersh, news leaked of the ongoing Angolan operation. The cynicism of the day is reflected in one of Joseph Heller's novels: "Gold . . . learned in Washington that the CIA was recruiting mercenaries to fight in Africa. He learned this at breakfast from his morning newspaper when he read: CIA DENIES RECRUITING MERCENARIES TO FIGHT IN AFRICA."[72] In December and January, respectively, the Senate and House voted to cut off funds for the CIA's covert operation in Angola. Senator Richard Clark and his supporters argued that the "Clark Amendment" was an attempt to forestall an anti-American backlash in Africa. Yet they offered no general philosophy on covert operations. As the CIA's Cord Meyer put it, the amendment went through because the nation had been "traumatized by Watergate and Vietnam."[73]

In spite of the Clark amendment, it suddenly seemed, at the very end of 1975, as if the effects of the trauma were going to wear off, with the CIA's critics, instead of the Agency itself, being put into the dock. One underlying cause was the revival of the Cold War—to which, in a circular process, the decline of the CIA's estimating reputation had contributed. A further, cumulative, factor, was the onset of boredom in a public satiated with sensationalism. A more immediate event was the assassination of Richard S. Welch, CIA station chief for Greece. Three men gunned this official down as he stepped from his car outside his Athens home on December 23. They escaped apprehension, so it is still unknown whether they struck at Welch for his activities in Latin America, or in support of Lebanon's Phalangists, or for his opposition to EOKA-B Cypriot terrorists, or for some other reason.[74] What is ascertainable is the effect that the murder had on the CIA debate at home.

Pro-CIA partisans blamed Welch's death on Agency critics who had irresponsibly released too much information. Philip Agee's book *Inside the Company* had recently blown the cover of many of his former colleagues in Latin America; Theodore Shackley, the CIA's clandestine chief in that region, had had to end the covert careers of a number of officers as a result.[75] The Welch affair was a perfect opportunity for a counterblow, for, prior to the murder, the radical quarterly *Counterspy* had not only named Welch as a CIA "agent," but also given his Athens address. In reality, the significance of this may not be great. Mader's *Who's Who in CIA* had much earlier, in 1967, named Welch.[76] Stockwell ridiculed in general terms the CIA's efforts at cover: "People would come up to you at cocktail parties in a foreign country and say, 'Hey, what's the CIA up to?'" Welch, furthermore, had incautiously moved into his predecessor's house in a city where CIA security was notably lax. Regardless of all this, Welch's death produced a patriotic reaction. He received a hero's funeral at Arlington National Cemetary, and a named fellowship in his honor at his alma mater, Harvard University.[77]

By this time, friends of the CIA were mounting a defensive campaign. In May 1975, David A. Phillips, the CIA's Western Hemisphere chief, had retired at the age of fifty-two with the express purpose of defending the Agency. He formed an Association of Former Intelligence Officers and, with other CIA veterans like Ray Cline and Harry Rositzke, launched an educative program in defense of the Agency's record. One of Phillips's aims was to convert Congress to be once again the "absolute salvation of CIA."[78] By early 1976 Congress was, in spite of its passage of the Clark amendment, in a receptive mood. On January 29, the House voted to suppress the Pike Report. When the report was leaked to the *Village Voice* via Daniel Schorr, the House Ethics Committee initiated legal proceedings against Schorr, which it eventually dropped but which nonetheless signaled the change in mood. Analysis of the media confirms the point. In 1976, media network news devoted more attention to leaks than to revelations, while the time allocated to all aspects of the CIA issue was almost halved, compared with 1975.[79]

Although the CIA had survived the "year of intelligence" and was beginning to recover its good name, on January 26, 1976, it suffered a sharp blow to its standing as the nation's leading foreign-intelligence service. On that day, Robert F. Ellsworth, recently appointed deputy secretary for defense with responsibility for intelligence, endorsed the "competitive analysis" system earlier demanded by George W. Anderson and his supporters on the president's Foreign Intelligence Advisory Board. Defense Intelligence Agency experts had been arguing that CIA analysts, misled by the complexities of dollar-ruble conversion rates and by the supposition that Russian tanks and other military items cost just as much to produce as their more sophisticated U.S. equivalents, had underestimated likely Russian arms procurement. Ellsworth was one of those who believed such underestimates had occurred because of liberal bias and preoccupation with covert operations. In spite of his weakened position, Colby had held out against the campaign for competitive estimating, but the appointment of Ellsworth at Defense and of the conciliatory Bush at the CIA helped tip the balance the other way. The administration resorted to its A-Team, B-Team stratagem.[80]

Under the scheme which Bush put into effect, the CIA's usual Soviet experts made up the A-Team. His competitive, B-Teams were made up of three groups of outside experts who were to examine Soviet air defenses, missile accuracies, and strategic objectives—all with full access to the raw materials at the disposal of the A-Team. The strategic-objectives B-Team in due course became known as *the* B-Team, because its hawkish findings attracted so much publicity. Harvard's Russian historian Richard E. Pipes was the chairman of this B-Team. Pipes was a critic of detente. He believed the Russians were insincere when they pretended to agree with the nuclear strategy known as *mutually assured destruction.* They were committed not to balance-of-power, mutual-deterrence, arms-reduction strategy, but to a war-winning philosophy combined with deception about their real motives. The CIA had lost its ability to use history to judge these motives, and it was dominated to a lamentable degree by civilians and scientists: "The Soviet *nomenklatura* (the ruling elite of the Communist party), very experienced in taking advantage of the weaknesses of its victims, brilliantly exploited the political innocence of American scientists."[81] The appointment of Pipes meant that the CIA's Soviet analysts had not only lost their supremacy, but lost it to someone with views markedly different from their own.

The B-Team generated considerable publicity for the view that the Soviet Union was determinedly trying to steal a march on the United States in the arms race. The cumulative picture was, indeed, less than reassuring. Johnson's CIA had suppressed evidence of Viet Cong strength; Kissinger had stifled reports of Soviet violations of SALT; the CIA had underestimated the Soviet missile buildup at one point in the 1960s and had now, apparently, done the same for Soviet expenditure to such a degree, that the Soviet Union might well be capable of quicker-than-expected deployment of new missiles with multiple warheads. Under pressure, the CIA began to revise some of its estimates, stating early in 1976, for example, that the Soviets spent eleven to thirteen percent of their gross national product on defense (nearly triple the U.S. percentage), not five to seven percent as previously stated.[82] Similarly, the CIA accepted some highly optimistic *Soviet* estimates of Soviet economic investment.[83] In due course, CIA Soviet estimates settled down— but, in the meantime, the prospects for SALT II had diminished, and the Agency had suffered a further setback to its authority, and to its utility in the defense debate.

That setback was, however, more apparent than real. President Ford had not wholeheartedly endorsed the contemporary critique of the CIA's estimates, and he had implemented the A-Team/B-Team proposal largely in order to appease the Republican party's "Superhawks." Neither had he forgotten the Rockefeller recommendation about boosting the stature of the CIA director. He was furthermore aware of the Church committee's view that the director should have greater access to the decision makers, and he was still responsive to the Pike committee's widely shared conviction that Kissinger should have less power. So he followed up his Hallowe'en Massacre with a series of further proposals for reform and, on February 18, a new executive order on intelligence that would govern the CIA under its new leadership (Bush had taken over on January 30). He created the Committee on Foreign Intelligence to report to himself as chairman of the National Security

Council—with the Defense Department represented, but with Bush in the chair. At the same time, Ford replaced the Forty Committee with a five-man Operations Advisory Group. Its composition was not unusual: senior representatives of the White House, State, Defense, the military, and the CIA. But perceptions are important: the *U.S. News and World Report* claimed the new arrangement rescued covert operations from Kissinger's domination. The CIA veteran and partisan Ray Cline thought the February reform package as a whole rendered it "unlikely" that the Agency director would be "again . . . reduced by willful policy officials to silent acquiescence in practices, procedures, or intelligence judgements he considers fundamentally wrong."[84]

Ford's proposals clearly bore his own stamp, not least in the case of his futile call for an official secrets act along British lines. At the same time, his proposals were a well-judged political response to the congressional inquiries of the past year. He outlawed assassination as an instrument of American policy—a most unusual step, even for a democracy. To guard against future misunderstandings, he listed the CIA's domestic duties. He proposed that there should be a new and more explicit legislative charter to define the Agency's functions overall, and he conceded to Congress the principle of a joint oversight committee.[85]

The Church committee's *Final Report* came out on April 26—officially, and with congressional blessing. In some respects, for example in its plea for enhanced authority for the director of central intelligence, the committee merely confirmed the wisdom of reforms Ford had already implemented or proposed. In others, notably the demand for publication of a "National Intelligence Budget," the committee ran into a familiar stone wall. In one important area, the committee left an open agenda. It applauded the president's ban on assassinations, but also—in a rare expression of senatorial philosophy—outlined possible further restraints on covert operations: there should be a statute to prohibit the subversion of democratic governments, and to outlaw clandestine support for repressive regimes that disregarded human rights. Here, then, there was scope for further agreement with a president who had already tried to theorize about the CIA's role in relation to foreign democracies, and who was himself in favor of a legislative charter. Ideally, there would be no more Guatemalas, no more Chiles, much less foreign opprobrium, much more domestic respect for the CIA. Congress took no immediate steps to regulate covert operations. But the Senate (in May) and the House (in July) set up separate, permanent intelligence oversight committees—an arrangement which fell short of the joint committee proposal, but seemed to hold out the prospect of greater discretion and responsibility, which might in turn win support for further reforms.[86]

CIA employees and veterans understandably look back with anguish to the year 1975, a time when they went through fire. Considered more coolly, however, the "year of intelligence" appears in a more positive light. Attacks of the "rogue elephant" type were painful for a while but, in the process of being debunked, they actually helped the Agency. The CIA emerged from its trial with a refurbished reputation. The crisis inspired the most extensive debate ever undertaken on the role of intelligence in a democracy, and on the relationship between the two. The result was a wider comprehension of the CIA and its work—a valuable, if incomplete educative process that more than compensated for the discomfiture and demoralization of CIA personnel at the time. Many people now agreed on the need for covert-operational guidelines, for the relegitimization of objective intelligence, and for enhanced status for the CIA director. Democracy had triumphed over the impediments of secrecy, partisanship, and opportunism.

12

RESTRAINED INTELLIGENCE AND THE HALF-WON PEACE

The CIA found itself restrained in two ways during the Carter administration (1977–81). First, it had less freedom to conduct covert operations. For a while, this restriction helped the Agency by making it more respectable. But then events occurred, notably in Iran, which hastened a change of opinion on the subject, so that the American people began to demand more action of precisely the type they had previously condemned. Second, the CIA was unable to exert an optimal degree of influence on American strategic policy. The problem no longer stemmed primarily from strained White House-CIA relations. On the contrary, President Carter wanted to believe in the CIA's capacity to underwrite the viability of SALT II. This time, the trouble arose from a change in the public mood toward the Soviet Union and from a popular distrust of CIA's estimates. The new discontent over covert inaction fueled this distrust of the CIA's Soviet estimates, based as it was on a common, uniting principle, that the Agency was "soft" on Communism.

The election of James E. ("Jimmy") Carter alarmed those who thought that the CIA was already too tightly controlled. He was an outsider who regarded Washington's bureaucracy and secrecy with suspicion, and he had been carried into office on the crest of a wave of disillusion created by Watergate, Vietnam, and the CIA. As Carter later recalled, he had been "deeply troubled" by governmental deception about foreign policy, and by the "CIA's role in plotting murder and other crimes."[1] He chose as his vice-presidential candidate Walter Mondale (who had done better in the Democratic primaries than Church, who was ill). Mondale thought that the CIA had brought the United States into disgrace: "Almost anything bad that happens in this world is attributed to the CIA."[2] He installed himself in the West Wing of the White House, where he acted like a zealous policeman.[3] Mondale secured the appointment of David I. Aaron as deputy assistant for national security affairs. Ray Cline complained that Aaron used his position to block "unseemly clandestine proposals," and that Mondale himself was hypersensitive about infractions of civil liberties and "was flatly against any exercise of covert capabilities to influence events abroad."[4]

The Carter team's CIA policy was in fact less extreme than the critics claimed. Barely a month after taking office, Carter refused to confirm or deny that the CIA had on one occasion bribed King Hussein of Jordan. Certain covert operations were "legitimate and proper," even in peacetime, and should not be revealed. He was "shocked" to discover how many people the CIA had to brief on its operations.[5] As for Mondale, he had already declared in the primary season that "a strong intelligence base" was essential "to control nuclear and conventional arms," and that he found himself "in the unhappy position of not being able to take the stand that U.S. covert action should be banned."[6] His protégé Aaron was so far removed from banning covert operations that he later testified in their favor.[7] Furthermore, Aaron's boss in the White House, national security affairs assistant Zbigniew Brzezinski, opposed "strict restrictions on CIA activities" and wanted to "revitalize" the Agency's foreign operations.[8] Critics of Carter's CIA policy therefore overlooked the way in which he balanced both his opinions and his staff, even if it is true that the administration was at first reluctant to launch adventurous covert operations.

In spite of his moderation, Jimmy Carter found himself perilously close to being out of touch with public opinion on the CIA—a failing he could ill afford if he wished to command support for his foreign policy. One problem was that public opinion was moving in a hawkish, conservative direction. Indeed, it had taken exceptional circumstances, the Vietnam-Watergate-CIA affairs, to project into the White House a man whom the electorate would otherwise have deemed too soft. But Carter's CIA problems arose also from his administration's tactics, especially in the case of the Agency's director.

Carter provoked controversy by dismissing the Republican appointee, CIA director George Bush. This was the first time that a president had applied the "spoils of office" principle to the CIA directorship; what made matters worse was that Bush had won the affection of the Agency's employees. Nor did Carter's initial choice for Bush's successor restore the doubters' faith. Theodore C. Sorensen had served in the Kennedy administration, walked with JFK on the South Lawn after the Bay of Pigs defeat, and seemed the right man to conjure up the Kennedy mystique without blabbing about Mongoose.[9] Some senators, however, attacked him as a former conscientious objector who had breached confidential information in his laudatory book on Kennedy. Sorensen withdrew, Bush's deputy

E. Henry Knoche had to serve as acting director from January 20 to March 9, and, as one critic put it, the office of director "had been symbolically politicized."[10]

Carter next turned to Admiral Stansfield Turner, then serving in Naples as commander of the South European flank of NATO. The president remembered Turner from his days at the Naval Academy, when they had been classmates. Carter and Turner had both applied for a Rhodes scholarship to Oxford University, with Turner being the successful candidate who traveled to England. Having been commandant of the U.S. Naval War College, Turner brought to the CIA the very qualities that many believed necessary in an Agency director: exceptional technical competence and the ability to manage an academic community.

It was to be Turner's misfortune—as well as Carter's and the CIA's—that the new director earned the reputation of being unsympathetic to people. A Christian Scientist who took hot water with lemon for breakfast, he seemed to exude an inappropriate personality. He early gave offense by dismissing Knoche, the long-serving Agency professional who had stepped into the breach when senators challenged the Sorensen nomination. Soon, too, he was bickering with Brzezinski, especially about access to the president. Brzezinski, himself a prickly character, found fault with some of the CIA's estimates, while Turner thought the national security affairs adviser had a naive faith in covert operations. Turner turned out to be a tough advocate of his point of view, and a bureaucratic battler determined to assert his authority not only within the White House, but also over the National Security Agency and other vital components of the intelligence community. While these were admirable traits from one perspective, from another they merely confirmed the impression that Turner was willing to trample on people.[11]

The degree to which Turner had alienated even some of his own employees came to light in the wake of a round of personnel cuts on October 31, 1977. The cuts were the latest in a series that had affected the operations division, in particular, since the heyday of paramilitary activity in Vietnam. When Turner took over, the operations division had already declined to 4,730 from a peak of 8,000 employees. The Ford administration had planned a further reduction of between 1,200 and 1,400, mainly aimed at headquarters staff in Langley, Virginia. Former director James Schlesinger, architect of the major 1973 cuts, told Turner that the Agency was still overstaffed, and the admiral was horrified to learn that people were "walking the corridors" at Langley, looking for something to do. Turner decided a smaller number should go, but that the run-down would occur quickly to minimize the duration of unpleasantness. Attrition accounted for most of the 820 released in a two-year period, but Turner forced 147 into early retirement, and he fired seventeen.[12]

The timing of this latest "Hallowe'en Massacre" followed the same principle as earlier ones—it occurred midway between elections and on the eve of the congressional recess, giving less opportunity for politically motivated leaks and recriminations. Nevertheless, the cuts met with a stormy reaction. Associate director for operations Theodore G. Shackley resigned in protest. He accused Turner of virtually annihilating the "clandestine service," of "destroying morale throughout the CIA," and of failing "to grasp the significance of the human factor."[13] The press seized on this last point. Turner, it appeared, was a cold, "teetotaling" technocrat who sent out two-sentence pink dismissal slips without a word of praise for men who had in some cases spent their whole careers in the service of their country. Smitten by nostalgia at the departure of such colorful characters as Teddy Roosevelt's descendant Campbell James (who spoke with a British accent and wore a tiger tooth on a chain), *Newsweek*'s reporters quoted an unnamed source: "Intelligence used to be poker—what did the other guys have. Now it's chess; we know his pieces and where they are located—we need to know his intentions." This was a hurtful point, as the CIA was already under fire for investing in technology at the expense of humanists who might be able to predict the workings of the Russian mind.[14]

Turner defended himself against what he believed were misleading press stories. He had aimed his cuts at bureaucrats, he declared, not at men in the field.[15] He did envisage a contraction of covert operations to a point where there would no longer be a need for a doctrine of "plausible deniability"; but he intended to keep a small paramilitary capability, and to use it for purposes which could be publicly acknowledged, notably counterterrorism.[16] Turner's policy is, indeed, defensible. Stories that linked his cold personality to personnel cuts and to neglect of the human factor in the estimating process were glib and muddled. Throughout his tenure, Turner did his best to operate the CIA in a manner that enhanced the credibility of Carter's main foreign policy goal, the achievement of a further arms accord with the Russians.

If Turner had run the CIA in the unbridled manner favored by some hawks, he would have encountered damaging criticism from those who still remembered the excesses in Cuba, Chile, and elsewhere. President Carter himself gave a lead to such critics: on January 24, 1978, he issued an executive order that strengthened Turner's authority over the intelligence community but also listed restrictions that took up eight pages of the twenty-six-page document. *Time* labeled the restrictions "extensive and severe."[17] In fact, the prohibitions—on assassination, drug experiments, and other malpractices—were not new, but their restatement served notice to the CIA that restraint was still required.

Congress, too, remained a source of actual and potential criticism by restrictionists, in spite of the fact that the newly formed intelligence committees were trying hard to be respectable. In an effort to establish their own legitimacy, members of the Senate Intelligence Committee, under Daniel Inouye's chairmanship, took a responsible approach. The committee was select and bipartisan. This meant that the Senate leaders chose its members (eliminating freakish membership on the basis of chance seniority), and that the governing party, the Democrats, had a majority of only one, irrespective of the number of seats they held in the Senate as a whole. The committee's first annual report on May 18, 1977, had noted that U.S.

intelligence agencies were operating under the proper control of the CIA director and were accounting to Congress in a satisfactory manner on covert operations. The House Intelligence Committee, made permanent in July 1977 under the chairmanship of Edward P. Boland, similarly appeared to be set on a less controversial course than its 1975 predecessor. Though it was not bipartisan (there were nine Democrats to four Republicans), Boland was a close friend of House Speaker Thomas P. ("Tip") O'Neill, who wished to keep the Democratic administration on an even keel and to curb the outspoken critics in his own party.[18]

Yet, in spite of these good omens, the criticism continued with enough vigor to serve as a caution to CIA officials. Nineteen-hundred-seventy-eight opened with one set of House hearings on the CIA and the media, and closed with another on assassinations. Though in favor of open government to the greatest degree compatible with national security, Turner risked confrontation with the House committee by telling them bluntly there was some "sources and methods" information he would never, in any circumstances, reveal.[19] Continuing approval by the Senate Committee clearly depended on good conduct in the area of covert operations. Furthermore, the Senate committee busied itself with its new charter for the CIA. This need not have been a document of reprimand. Indeed, it could have confirmed the relegitimization of the Agency—according to CIA veteran Joseph B. Smith, respectability had always been a problem for CIA officers and their families; a document drafted in sympathetic language might well have helped to build up morale within the Agency, as well as the CIA's standing in government circles.[20] But, in the event, the Senate committee compiled a cumbersome, 263-page draft bill containing extensive domestic and other restrictions. Thus, the CIA was still encountering suspicion, even from responsible and informed senators.

The Foreign Intelligence Surveillance Act of October 25, 1978, is further evidence of the continuing urge to curb the CIA and other U.S. intelligence agencies. It legalized the use of wiretaps and bugs in suspected cases of foreign espionage, terrorism, and sabotage; however, it allowed such electronic surveillance only after the case-by-case issuance of federal warrants by newly created special judges.[21] From start to finish, then, 1978 was a year of suspicion and restriction. It would have been foolish for Carter to authorize a major adventure, and Turner was only being prudent in winding down his capacity at that particular time.

Yet, by the end of 1978, some of the critics had the air of breaking in a tame pony. The Senate's proposed charter seemed excessive and unnecessary and met with a scornful reception. Even before the traumatic events in Iran and Afghanistan that transformed public opinion on covert operations, a change of heart was taking place. In 1974, opinion polls had indicated that only 43 percent of those asked supported CIA intervention in the internal affairs of foreign countries. By November 1978, the figure had climbed to 59 percent.[22] An attitudinal shift was about to take place. Whereas, previously, the CIA's covert operations had brought the Agency into disrepute, now its inability to launch such enterprises began to appear as a serious weakness.

The upheaval in Iran hastened this process. On January 16, 1979, the shah, dying of cancer, unable to face mounting economic problems and domestic turbulence, and loaded with riches to finance his family's exile, fled the country. The revolution sparked criticism of the CIA for two reasons. First, its intelligence had not been good enough to alert U.S. policymakers to the impending crisis. Second, the CIA lacked the covert capability either to prevent the fall of an important ally, or to limit the damage to American interests in the wake of his departure.

The controversy over the relationship between covert operations and the loss of Iran as an ally was no mere tempest in a teacup. Oil-rich Iran was a source of wealth to American multinational corporations—more so, indeed, than other nations like Vietnam into which Washington had poured far greater resources. And Iran was even more important in another sense. In the north of the country, the United States maintained two radar installations called Tackman I and II. These monitored the Soviet missile test launch site six hundred miles away at Tyuratam. The Iranian revolution forced America to abandon Tackman I and II. Because continuing scandal about the CIA's alleged intervention in Australian politics had made possible the return of a Labor government there and the subsequent dismantling of the Pine Gap facilities, verification of SALT II was problematic and confirmation of the new agreement, therefore, less likely.[23] If the CIA was responsible for the loss of Tackman and the possible loss of Pine Gap, then it had damaged rather than helped the U.S. intelligence effort.

The first point to be made in the CIA's defense is that its covert operations, whether excessive, inadequate, or just right, were in the 1970s and always had been authorized by the White House. The second point is that the particularly virulent anti-American strain in the Iranian revolution fed on long-term CIA excesses, not on the Agency's short-term failure to hatch plots of expediency. The Iranian revolution of the 1970s was Moslem and fundamentalist, profoundly antipathetic to Communism and potentially a threat to the stability of southern regions of the Soviet Union, where many Moslems lived. If they had been left to their own devices earlier, the Iranians might have accomplished social change without becoming enemies of the United States in the process. But they vividly remembered the 1953 coup and the CIA's role in it. The acronym "CIA," displayed on so many of the street demonstrators' placards, encapsulated Iranian anti-Americanism; for six years after the revolution, Iranian students obsessively reconstituted CIA documents that the Tehran embassy staff had shredded during the crisis, publishing the results as vivid testimony to American perfidy. President Carter might have delayed the Shah's fall by authorizing CIA action in Iran, but CIA restraint was correct for it was too late to repair the damage of the 1950s.

On the other hand, Carter's CIA did fail to give adequate warning of the crisis. In August 1977, it had predicted that there would be "no radical change in Iranian political behavior in the near future," and in August 1978 it had noted that the country was not "even in a 'prerevolutionary' situation."[24] Brzezinski had complained to the president about the poor quality of intelligence, and Carter issued a rebuke on November 11. The rebuke leaked to the press, and, as principal White House aide on Iran Gary Sick noted, this caused a flurry of defensive maneuvers that only impeded intelligent guesswork about future events in Iran.[25]

These defensive maneuvers were only one of the reasons for the Iran intelligence failure. Another was the fact that Iran watchers had become impervious to probability. The shah had survived for a long period in spite of personal and military aggrandization, permissiveness in defiance of a puritanical people, vicious repression through the CIA-supported intelligence agency SAVAK, gullibility in dealings with U.S. businessmen, and general incompetence. The improbability of his survival in the past created expectations of his survival against equally improbable odds in the future, and it so dulled anticipation of the coming revolution. This circumstance did not affect the CIA alone. U.S. military attachés in Tehran had complacently concentrated on selling American weapons to the Iranian government instead of on what only polite fiction denied was their real job, spying. Thus, there was no alternative source of warning, no rival, military assessment to stir the CIA from its slumber. A House Intelligence Committee report identified yet another cause of the CIA's predictive failure, poor White House tasking of the Agency in relation to Iran.[26] The nonprediction of change in Iran sprang, then, from a variety of factors, not all of them the prime fault of the CIA. In further extenuation of the failure of Carter's CIA, it may be said that the Agency had never been capable of predicting every significant event in every significant country. This was, of course, paltry consolation for the hapless Carter, who was given little opportunity to react quickly or to save face.

In 1979, attitudes toward the CIA continued to change, both in Congress and elsewhere. This change affected foreign policy, domestic politics, and, in due course, the CIA itself. Opinion began to gravitate toward support for a mythical CIA. The properties of this mythical CIA were that it was located in the past (somewhere between the mid-1940s and the mid-1960s according to the storyteller); it was indispensible and a "miraculous" achievement by a nation which had naively neglected intelligence before the OSS; it rarely failed with its estimates; it would achieve significant objectives through major covert operations; it commanded absolute loyalty to America; and it conducted effective counterespionage. This conservative idea of a "golden past" was a blend of hallucination and truth, a blend so potent that it made people impatient with the real CIA of 1979. Their impatience meant trouble for Carter and Turner at the same time that it meant support for the advocates of a stronger foreign policy backed by a restored CIA.[27]

By 1979, there were mounting fears that America was, through an overfastidious application of democratic principles, undermining her own security in the face of Soviet espionage. Debate on the Foreign Intelligence Surveillance bill revealed that William Kampiles, a former CIA employee, had sold the KGB a technical manual on the CIA's satellite surveillance system. Though the American Civil

Liberties Union and its allies secured the inclusion, in the act, of safeguards against electronic surveillance, the Kampiles case helped to turn the tide. When the White House Intelligence Committee's subcommittee on legislation began a series of hearings early in 1979, its chairman Morgan Murphy declared that there were too many restrictions on the intelligence community, and he summoned witnesses who testified against the overprotection of citizens' privacy.[28]

In April 1979, further details of the Andrew Lee–Christopher Boyce story appeared in the *New York Times*, encouraging the reaction against open government and fanning suspicions that the CIA was no longer impenetrable. Lee and Boyce had been convicted of espionage in 1977. Attention had then focused on Boyce's motive for spying—his discovery, via signals traffic, of the CIA's involvement in Australian politics. But, in April 1979, there was little talk of this, or of the effects of the CIA's covert operations on Australian politics, Pine Gap, and U.S. national security. Instead, advocates of stronger counterintelligence directed discussion to the significance of Lee's and Boyce's confessions that they had received $80 thousand from the KGB in return for satellite secrets.[29] The perils of clandestine intervention were forgotten in the midst of a sudden clamor to guard the nation's secrets.

Toward the end of 1979, two events occurred that sharply reminded the nation of the need to retain, at whatever level and in whatever form, at least some kind of covert operational capability. On November 4, a revolutionary mob stormed the U.S. embassy in Tehran, which the new Iranian leader, Ayatollah Ruhallah Khomeini, had called a "nest of spies." Khomeini's followers held fifty-three of the embassy staff hostage. This act of state terrorism screamed for a clandestine rescue operation but the CIA was incapable of mounting one.

Then, in Christmas Day and in the ensuing Christmas week, the Soviet Red Army poured into Afghanistan and occupied the capital, Kabul. The Russians' objective was to stabilize a government which was already Communist, but faction ridden. CIA veteran Cord Meyer declared that they also wished to set in motion "a pincer movement closing on the Persian Gulf . . . , with Ethiopia forming one prong and Afghanistan the other." Brzezinski believed that the Russians would attempt to gain access to the Indian Ocean by promoting the independence of adjoining Pathan areas in the western Pakistani province of Baluchistan. But the Russians found themselves bogged down by the fierce resistance of Afghan Moslem fundamentalists and guerrilla fighters, the *mujahidin*, who eventually tied up more than 100 thousand Soviet troops. Here, it seemed, was an opportunity for the CIA to foster local nationalism in the manner prescribed by 1950s covert-operational doctrine. Instead, President Carter seemed to waver as not only Afghanistan, but also Angola, Ethiopia, and South Yemen teetered on the brink of Communism. The image was emerging of a weak president who had further restrained a CIA which already bordered on inertia.[30]

Against this background, President Carter was forced in January 1980 to withdraw the SALT II treaty from the floor of the Senate, where a changing mood indicated likely defeat. The signing ceremony for the agreement had taken place in Vienna in June 1979. Each side had agreed to the principle of nuclear parity, to forswear new destabilizing weapons systems, to eschew deployment of larger numbers of intercontinental missiles or missiles with greater destructive power (the multiple warheads problem unresolved in SALT I), and to limit the number of short-range, ground-hugging "cruise" missiles to 1,320 on each side. The Soviet and American negotiators also established the framework for further negotiations, or SALT III, which would lead to mutual nuclear arms reductions. Finally, there were new monitoring arrangements which would help with verification of mutual compliance. Article XV, for example, recognized the legitimacy of satellite sur-veillance, insuring U.S. spy satellites against destruction. SALT II also stopped telemetric encryptification, or the coded scrambling of radio emissions which supplied U.S. intelligence with information on the operating characteristics of Russian missiles and other weapon systems.[31]

Carter's failure to achieve the two-thirds majority necessary to this treaty's ratification in Congress did not spring entirely from disenchantment with the performance of the CIA. Russian aggression in Afghanistan and elsewhere in-creased U.S. suspicions of Soviet intentions. The president's handling of inflation made people think of him as ineffectual and insupportable for reasons quite independent of intelligence (though, even here, there were grumbles that the CIA had not forecast the problems that OPEC would pose for oil supplies and prices). Furthermore, the CIA was not the only U.S. intelligence agency which could be faulted, and a whole plethora of government bureaus were involved in SALT: to name but a few, there were the National Security Council with its SALT Working Group and SALT Backstopping Committee, the Arms Control and Disarmament Agency with its special SALT staff, and the SALT Support Group and SALT Task Force within the Defense Department.[32]

On the other hand, Turner did preside, in his capacity as director of central intelligence, over the intelligence community's SALT Steering Group, and the CIA had its own SALT support staff.[33] The Agency was deeply involved in the arms negotiations process, and, of greater importance politically, both critics and sup-porters of SALT afforded importance to the CIA's role. The CIA's standing at a given time was thus both an indicator of and an influence on Carter's ability to carry the nation with him in his dealings with the Russians.

It is therefore significant that the Agency continued to come under fire, while SALT negotiations were in progress, for underestimating Russian capabilities in a number of ways. For example, a team of defense analysts in 1979 attacked a 1978 economic report by the National Foreign Assessment Center, the Carter admin-istration's name for the CIA intelligence directorate. The center's economists had argued that a downturn in the rate of Soviet economic growth would soon occur, constraining the Kremlin's defense policy options. But their critics argued that increasing use of technology would put Russian defense expenditure ahead of America's by a ratio of 3:2 before the year 2000, even if it consumed no more than the present rate of 12 percent of gross national product.[34] In the meantime, the B-Team point of view, ably expounded in the magazine *Commentary* and elsewhere by Richard Pipes, still commanded support: In the light of past deceptions, how could one trust Russian intentions about the future? It was in this climate of doubt that CIA critics speculated plausibly about the causes of the Agency's weakness: dovish pro-Soviet bias, preoccupation with covert operations, poor staffing reflecting recruiting bias, or the poor state of Soviet studies on American campuses.[35]

The strength of the case *against* Pipes, though, made much of this speculation redundant. In February 1978, a Senate report on the A/B-Team experiment had rejected the idea that the CIA showed a dovish bias.[36] Two years later, the House Intelligence Committee listened to a respected consultant's scathing indictment of the methodology of the historian who advocated an examination of Russian statements instead of statistics, but then selectively used only the statements that bolstered his point of view.[37] Pipes refused to consider seriously the evidence that Russian advocates of aggressive, war-winning strategy may have been just one faction among several.[38] Nor did he and his supporters pay heed to the possibility that Soviet leaders may have been concealing their weaknesses, not their strengths, in spinning their webs of deception. Pipes was on record as saying that America should "press for superiority" to force the Russians to "accept realistic terms, and not insist on perfect parity."[39] A new generation of American "MX" missiles was under consideration and might achieve precisely that purpose; Pipes and his supporters did not wish to undermine Americans' will to pay for superior bargaining chips. For understandable reasons, Pipes had put his faith in a weak case.

Defenders of the administration's SALT policy had also fought to a standstill those who questioned the CIA's ability to verify Soviet compliance. These fears had arisen from worries about Russian deception, suspicion that Soviet disinformation was now being enhanced through the presence of moles within the CIA, and, of course, the loss of the Iranian test-monitoring facility. As early as 1977, Admiral Turner's critics had pounced on his speeches in favor of SALT II, arguing that he was partisan rather than objective: how, then, could he be trusted on verification?[40] In April 1979, Turner admitted it would take four to five years to develop full alternative systems to the capability lost in Iran, an admission, it seemed, that verification would now be impossible even if it had been feasible in the past. However, he explained that only partial replacement of the Iranian facility would be necessary for SALT II verification, and that this could soon be achieved.[41] SALT II itself provided for additional monitoring and opened the door to still further negotiations on the same subject. The Senate Intelligence Committee issued a report on October 5, 1979, which indicated that SALT II monitoring arrangements were satisfactory.[42] The opponents of SALT II and critics of Carter's CIA lost the argument on verification.

It was the CIA's relatively poor image, not its inadequate strategic estimates performance, which contributed to the senatorial demise of SALT II. That relatively poor image derived from historical factors, notably Kissinger's manipulation of estimates and verification intelligence. It also derived from misperceptions—for example, in 1979 a groundless but sensational allegation that the CIA had failed to observe the presence in Cuba of what turned out to be a harmless Soviet training brigade contributed to senatorial procrastination over SALT II. It was little consolation for those who worried about such cases when, early in 1980, the National Foreign Assessment Center's director said it was "an unexpected achievement" if the CIA at any phase in its history guessed right "50 percent of the time."[43] By this time, events in Iran and Afghanistan had crucially undermined the Agency's image. As a result, then, of several factors having little to do with arms control in themselves, the CIA had insufficient authority to command overwhelming faith in SALT II through its objective imprimatur.

Yet, the CIA's standing—because of recent reforms, and because its Russian specialists put a good case well—was higher than it had been in the Johnson-Nixon years. For this reason, Carter was able to agree with the Russians on informal compliance with the provisions of SALT II. The case for compliance was sufficiently good, and the support for the CIA sufficiently strong, for him to do so with impunity, and both sides stuck to the agreement until December 1986. The CIA had at least contributed to a half-won peace.

If, however, SALT II were to move along its planned route toward SALT III and nuclear reductions, there would have to be a dramatic upsurge of confidence in both Carter and the CIA. The president recognized this. In a forlorn attempt to generate such confidence, he began to genuflect in the direction of the conservatives' mythical CIA. On January 16, 1980, he stated that "we must tighten our controls on sensitive government information and we need to remove unwarranted restraints on America's ability to collect intelligence."[44] Not long after this, Admiral Turner testified before the Senate Intelligence Committee on the need to curb the Hughes-Ryan restriction: "The administration believes that the requirement for reporting of significant anticipated intelligence activities, including special activities or covert operations, is unnecessary, improper, and unwise." Senator Daniel P. Moynihan wryly remarked "Carter has now discovered that it is *his* CIA!"[45]

Carter was attempting to move along, preemptively, with the conservative tide. This tide was ebbing strongly away from the high-water mark of mid-1970s reforms. The Intelligence Oversight Act of 1980 required that the CIA notify only the Senate and House intelligence committees of proposed covert actions, not the eight committees so privileged under the now repealed Hughes-Ryan amendment. Looked at from one point of view, this was a sensible arrangement that reduced leaks and confirmed the mid-1970s achievement of oversight by making it more respectable. Looked at in a different way, it reflected the late-January prediction by Senate majority leader Robert C. Byrd that "this will be a security-minded Congress." Further hearings and legislation confirmed the senator's point, notably the

Classified Information Procedures Act, which arranged for the protection of classified information in trial proceedings.[46]

Nor was Congress the only branch of government disposed, in 1980, to temper the radicalism of the mid-1970s. The Supreme Court decided in *United States v. Snepp* against the author of the book *Decent Interval* (1977), a criticism of the arrangements for U.S. withdrawal from Vietnam. Frank Snepp's story of American abandonment of former CIA agents in Vietnam did not disclose classified information, but he did publish it without clearance from the Agency, in abrogation of his CIA contract. The Court's finding reversed the *United States v. Marchetti* decision of 1972, according to which the CIA's "secrecy oath" infringed First Amendment rights. Snepp had to surrender his royalties. From now on, CIA apostates published at their peril.[47]

Carter's attempt to move with this tide was not out of character, for at the very beginning of his presidency he had expressed dismay at the degree of openness about CIA affairs. But in the eyes of a growing number of critics, he had been too slow to emphasize the need for increased security and greater effectiveness. It was not reassuring that his apparent change of heart occurred in an election year. The abortive Iranian rescue attempt in April 1980 only seemed to confirm his continuing ineffectiveness. The airborne attempt to pluck out the hostages was a military mission; its failure was an instance of military incompetence rather than presidential or CIA ineptitude.[48] Nevertheless, there remained the questions of whether a stronger CIA might not have run a more effective operation itself, or whether it might have provided the military with better intelligence and local help through its secret agents on the ground.[49] As the hostages continued to languish in their Iranian confinements and as election day approached, such questions became burning issues.

Whereas Jimmy Carter won votes in the 1976 presidential election by promising to restrain the CIA, Ronald Reagan won support in 1980 by saying he would loosen the restrictions. In February, George Bush showed well in the Republican primaries having supported "moves to beef up the CIA."[50] He proved no match for Reagan later in the year, but the ultimately victorious Republican candidate recognized the former CIA director's electoral appeal by adopting him as his vice-presidential running mate. Reagan was by now promising to "unleash" the CIA. "How can we unleash the agency when it hasn't yet been leashed?" asked one former National Security Council official, pointing out that Carter was already authorizing undercover operations for counterintelligence purposes and to fight terrorism and narcotics trafficking.[51] But the Republicans had identified a winning campaign issue. The detailed "National Intelligence" plank of the July 1980 Republican platform asserted that the Democrats had impaired the efficiency of the intelligence community and underestimated Soviet strength. Responding to the "strong national consensus" that had emerged, a Republican administration would "seek to improve U.S. intelligence capabilities for technical and clandestine collection, cogent analysis, coordinated counterintelligence, and covert action."[52]

The advocates of operational restraint went down to defeat on November 4: not just President Carter, but others like third-party candidate John Anderson, and Senators Church and Bayh. The result was a blow to the prospects of a SALT III, and, by the same token, to the prestige of Carter's CIA. Yet, by promising to deliver their conception of a stronger CIA, Reagan and his supporters seemed to be holding out hope for the 1980s. They would unleash the covert operators against a background of sympathetic public opinion, and thus somehow bolster the Agency's standing in the intelligence field. The latter undertaking promised a sound strategic policy in the future, and a sure foundation for further arms-control agreements with the Russians.

13

IGNORING
THE CREDIBLE
The CIA
in
the 1980s

The mid-1970s exposures reduced fears that had been based on ignorance of the CIA. Reforms in the Ford and Carter presidencies further reassured the critics and were sufficiently far-reaching to suggest the need for a halt to new restrictions and a loosening of some old ones. Against this background, the election of President Reagan promised a reincarnation of the mythical CIA of the 1950s. And, sure enough, the Agency's prestige did escalate and hold good for the first six years of the new administration. White House-CIA relations were better than ever before, with the Agency director occupying a cabinet seat. There were hiccups in CIA-congressional relations, it is true, setbacks which served notice of the serious trouble that lay in the future. But, for the time being, periodic legislative gripes only reassured the nation that the CIA remained under proper supervision.

Yet, in qualitative terms, the Agency still had not won the standing that should be the due of a competent foreign-intelligence service. While few objective analysts seriously challenged the credibility of the CIA's estimates by comparing them adversely with earlier performance or with the accomplishments of rival intelligence agencies, the Reagan administration chose to ignore the credible on a number of occasions. Its reactions to intelligence on the shooting down of a Korean airliner, Nicaragua, and the Soviet military threat are reminders of the dangerous fact that, in matters of state, truth is often a pawn to fiction.

The CIA was already well on its way to recovering its prestige by the time Ronald Reagan entered the White House. The campus radicalism of the Camelot-*Ramparts*-Vietnam era had died down and it was no longer imprudent for Agency recruiters to enter university precincts or place job advertisements in academic journals.[1] One indication of the return of the old mystique, indeed, is that a record 9,200 men and women applied for 1,458 CIA jobs in 1980; by the mid-1980s, the Agency was receiving about 150 thousand inquiries annually.[2] Reinforced by CIA veterans pursuing a second career on campus, university professors began to offer courses of instruction on intelligence: there were few such courses before 1980; by 1985 there were fifty-four courses wholly devoted to intelligence, and the subject formed a component of many others. Serving officers turned up at academic conferences, wearing "CIA" badges, to deliver learned papers. A spate of publications also appeared on the CIA and allied subjects, contributing to that wider public awareness and sympathy which is so necessary to the Agency's effective operation in its democratic context.[3]

In the period between his election and assumption of office, Reagan busied himself with the work of his transition team. David M. Abshire, chairman of the Center for Strategic and International Studies at Georgetown University, supervised the team's review of State, Defense, and the CIA. A subgroup working on the CIA contained another Georgetown academic, Roy Godson, as well as three staff members from the Senate Intelligence Committee and three Agency veterans. Ray Cline, also by now a Georgetown professor, described the prospects for CIA "revival" as "almost a miracle."[4]

At first, the transition team seemed a major threat to the CIA as then constituted. One of its outline reports labeled the Agency "elitist" and self-serving. Its leaders were "leftist-orientated." Its Legislative Counsel Fred Hitz had cooperated with the White House in "selling SALT II," which, of course, the president-elect claimed to be unsound. The same report contained a list of intelligence failures, including the CIA's "general and continuing" incompetence in judging future Soviet economic and military performance and its "consistent gross misstatement of Soviet global objectives." There was pressure from a minority within the transition team for the breakup of the CIA and its replacement by new agencies for analysis, counterintelligence, and covert operations: reportedly, there was also a demand that every senior officer should be dismissed.[5]

In spite of their ominous pronouncements, however, the transition team offered indications and hope of a revival in CIA prestige. While they saw the CIA's "dangerous condition" as the "fundamental problem confronting American security," they also saw the Agency as "the keystone in achieving a reversal of the unwise policies of the past decade." Though contemptuous of director Stansfield Turner, they endorsed one of his main goals, the upgrading of the CIA's technical capabilities. They demanded a stepping-up of high-technology surveillance facilities both at ground level (to compensate for losses in Iran), and at altitude. Prophetically, in light of the *Challenger* disaster in January 1986, they criticized America's reliance on a single spy-satellite launch system: "A failure of the space shuttle could be disastrous for the entire technical intelligence collection effort."[6]

As in the past, their main solution for bad intelligence was more intelligence; the prospect of more money could not but raise Agency morale and prestige. As for the proposal that the CIA should be dismembered or purged, Reagan simply looked the other way. Unlike President Carter, he realized it was "his" CIA from the outset, even if it was imperfect. Wanting no quarrel with the Agency, he saved it from the jackals of his own pack, appointing, as a signal of intent, a new director who was firmly convinced of the merits of central intelligence organizations.

William J. Casey contributed to the image if not to the substance of renewed integrity and standing for the CIA. He had acquired his faith in centralized, coordinated intelligence while serving with the OSS in London. During the War he had been close to his fellow Irish-American Wild Bill Donovan, and had, as he put it, analyzed "the structure of the British and European intelligence services for General Donovan's initial paper urging President Roosevelt and the Joint Chiefs of Staff to develop a peacetime central intelligence agency." In London, Casey said, he had commanded "virtually all the intelligence, paramilitary and research personnel."[7] His OSS experiences therefore inclined him to support an agency that combined analysis with action. His goal was to improve American intelligence, not to reshape it drastically.

In some ways, Casey was equipped to do the job. He had been in and out of government in the course of his long career as a New York lawyer (he was already sixty-seven years of age when he started in his post at Langley). He had dealt with Congress since 1947 on behalf of various government departments, often abrasively, but also showing an instinct for good public relations. He was a member of the Murphy Commission and had drafted the intelligence section of its 1975 report, which recommended that the CIA should change its name to the Foreign Intelligence Agency but should remain intact with enhanced status. He had also served on the President's Foreign Intelligence Advisory Board until Carter abolished it on the ground that its members were overenamored of covert operations. He was therefore fitted to become a high-status CIA director who would boost the Agency's covert-operational capability: President Reagan confirmed his importance by giving him, in a foreign-policy reorganization on February 25, 1981, parity with the secretaries of state and defense.[8]

Nonetheless, a number of serving and former intelligence officers found fault with Casey. The director's education at Fordham University, the Catholic University of America, and St. John's University had not equipped him to understand the complexities of high technology. Instead, he had a literary bent and was a keen amateur historian. Though he had been an efficient campaign manager for Reagan in the 1980 election, he was absentminded and sometimes incoherent, earning the nicknames "Spacey" and "Mumbles" and sparking speculation about a biography to be called *The Man Who Never Was*.[9]

Still, Casey had the apparently winsome advantage of being a boss who would bring more money, jobs, and promotions to the Agency, truly a welcome contrast to the days of Schlesinger and Turner. His appointees basked in the reflected glow of bureaucratic success, and none more so than Robert M. Gates. When Casey promoted the thirty-eight-year-old Gates to be deputy director for intelligence in January 1982, the appointment promised glittering achievement. Gates had taken his doctorate in Russian and Soviet history from Georgetown University. He joined the CIA in 1966, served on the National Security Council staff as a nuclear weapons specialist under both Republican and Democratic presidents from 1974 to 1979, and then was national intelligence officer for the Soviet Union under Turner. Ostensibly, Casey, who saw the president twice a week, would be able to pass on the findings of a brilliant young analyst who had bipartisan blessing.

In reality, the Casey-Gates relationship presented a two-fold problem. For one thing, Gates disagreed with some of the premises behind Reagan's strategic thought: he believed, for example, in the beneficial effects of SALT II. Second, Casey did not press such divergent views upon the president. Observers remarked on Gates's loyalty to his superiors, and on Casey's willingness to tolerate dissent on the one hand, and to misrepresent intelligence findings, on the other. One MIT professor suggested it was useful for the CIA to be led by a hawk like Casey: "They want to be perceived as being on the right so that they will be left alone."[10] But the upshot was that, under Casey and Reagan, important aspects of U.S. foreign policy followed a course contrary to that suggested by intelligence findings. While, therefore, Casey projected an image of increased prestige and respectability, the Agency's restored standing was, in some significant ways, an illusion.

One of the Reagan administration's objectives was the strengthening of American counterintelligence. The curtailment of Soviet espionage activities would save billions of dollars by protecting the integrity of existing defense systems. By protecting itself against penetration and agents of disinformation, the CIA could enhance the accuracy of its Soviet estimates. The open advocacy and implementation of such measures would also, in theory, enhance the CIA's credibility and the likelihood of public support for prospective arms agreements. To pursue the counterintelligence avenue toward the establishment of confidence in the estimating process, however, the administration had to erode the very open-government measures that had helped restore confidence in the 1970s, when "police state" fears had been widespread.

A Republican majority in the Senate and on its intelligence committee augured well for President Reagan's counterintelligence proposals. Senator Barry Goldwater, the committee's new chairman, had been the leading pioneer of those conservative policies which Reagan took to the White House, and he supported the notional CIA Reagan had in mind. Dissenting from the Church committee's *Final Report* in 1976, Goldwater had insisted on the retention of a covert operational capability to give the president "a range of actions short of war to preserve the free world and to thwart the global ambitions of Communist imperialism." Assuming the intelligence committee chairmanship in January 1981, the senator from Arizona said, "I think the CIA is going to find a very cordial reception here."[11]

From the latter remark, one might assume that the oversight mechanism had become tame and meaningless, a mere continuation of the acquiescent committee system of the 1950s. In fact, this was far from true. Having blazed an uncompromising conservative trail at the expense of his own presidential ambitions, Goldwater was disinclined to tolerate slack behavior in the beneficiaries of his earlier efforts. Nor was he, for that matter, an automatic champion of the CIA, which he had periodically criticized in the 1950s and 1960s for what he perceived to be left-wing tendencies. He wanted the CIA to have a military director and had opposed Casey in favor of Admiral Bobby R. Inman, director of the National Security Agency (who in the event became deputy director of the CIA under Casey). In the summer of 1981, Goldwater and his allies forced Casey to remove his choice to head the operations directorate—Max Hugel, an old crony of Casey's under suspicion for alleged business irregularities.[12] Clearly, the 1970s oversight reform had not been in vain. Nevertheless, Goldwater remained committed to the principle of a strong, wideranging intelligence organization: as he put it in 1983, "intelligence has always been a vital force in the history of our country."[13] Not only Goldwater, but also a majority in the Congress, now believed that counterintelligence would have to be strengthened.

In March 1981, a press leak revealed details of a draft executive order designed to restore some of the CIA's powers to operate domestically. The counterintelligence measures aimed particularly at Moscow-directed terrorism. Predictably, there was a hostile reaction. American Civil Liberties Union director Ira Glasser claimed the proposed executive order "resurrected and legalized most of the worst abuses revealed during the Nixon administration." Inman threatened to resign. The Senate Intelligence Committee's Democratic vice-chairman Daniel P. Moynihan wanted to know why the administration was again making an issue of the CIA, "just when it was getting back to work."[14] The Soviet media claimed that the CIA was itself running terrorists throughout the world. But a Senate committee on terrorism tried to show, with the assistance of the Georgetown academic stable, that the Soviet Union was involved in "a worldwide network of terrorism."[15] The attempted assassination of President Reagan on March 30, 1982, strengthened the security-consciousness of the nation, especially when rumors began to circulate that a five-man hit squad from Moslem, revolutionary Libya was inside the United States with orders to finish the job. Against this background, Reagan issued his executive order on December 4. The order confirmed some old restrictions, such as that on CIA-sponsored assassinations, but in other ways gave effect to the president's promise to "unleash" the CIA. Notably, the order allowed the CIA more scope to spy at home and to follow up the domestic dimensions of foreign problems with which it was concerned.[16]

The administration now sought passage of an Intelligence Identities Protection Act. This would protect Agency employees against disclosure of the Philip Agee type and encourage potential Soviet defectors: one Oleg Penkovsky, said the CIA's former chief of Soviet operations John Maury, "is worth a hundred Ph.D.s."[17] Goldwater supported the bill, which proposed legal penalties for those who named names in a deliberate attempt to harm the U.S. intelligence effort.[18] Goldwater denied that First-Amendment rights would be impaired. According to the Senator, the measure was "a clear signal that U.S. intelligence will no longer be fair game for those members of their own society who wish to take issue with the existence of CIA or find other motives for making these unauthorized disclosures."[19] In June 1982, Congress passed the Intelligence Identities Protection Act by overwhelming majorities.

Some opponents of the counterintelligence initiatives thought that they threatened American liberties: the *Nation* detected in Reagan's approach "a profound contempt for the values underlying the Constitution."[20] Others decried what they believed was paranoia: when Inman resigned the deputy directorship in June 1982, it was reportedly because he refused to believe the Soviet Union had "orchestrated a massive deception" which could only be overcome through "all-source" countersurveillance, including spying through electronic devices and by other means, on U.S. citizens.[21] Opposition was formidable enough to delay moves to secure CIA exemption from the provisions of the Freedom of Information Act. Statements to the effect that the First Amendment was "only" an amendment had driven civil libertarians to fury.[22] In his angry defense of the exemption, Goldwater was driven to allege that the media propagated "lies and distortions" about "our entire intelligence family."[23] There were delays and holdups in Congress. Finally, however, a limited exemption went through in October 1984. The Reagan-Casey-Goldwater initiatives to tighten security had therefore succeeded in attracting considerable support.

They were less successful in stopping Soviet espionage. One case that came to light after the new legislation was the treason of Karl Koechner. Trained by Czech intelligence, Koechner posed as an anti-Communist refugee, gained U.S. citizenship, and joined the CIA, betraying several names to his Eastern bloc controllers. Clearly, the Agency was no longer (if it ever had been) impenetrable. In 1985, there emerged the facts in the case of U.S. Navy Chief Petty Officer John A. Walker, who for fifteen years sold to the Soviet Union secrets whose betrayal seriously compromised the security of NATO hunter-killer submarines operating in the strategic routes between Greenland, Iceland, and Scotland. "U.S. CATCHES THE BRITISH SPY DISEASE," ran one London headline. The following year, the FBI first questioned and then allowed to escape Edward L. Howard, who had worked for Russian intelligence between 1981 and 1983, yet had been slated for CIA assignment in Moscow; the Senate Intelligence Committee concluded that American counterintelligence was uncoordinated and incompetent. The heightened security-consciousness indicated by Reagan's 1981 executive order and by subsequent legislation was not, then, a definitive answer to the KGB. On the other hand, it may have contributed to the exposure of existing spy rings, and it was symptomatic of a restored faith in the intelligence community's mission to pursue foreign spies without endangering American civil liberties.[24]

President Reagan's fulfillment of his campaign promise to revive covert operations was another symptom of the political climate of the 1980s. But the CIA's expanded efforts—especially in Nicaragua—did not occur against a background of 1950s-style tranquility. The international reaction was hostile. The Congress was only reluctantly supportive and was a constant source of trouble, with many members critical on moral, diplomatic, and Constitutional grounds. Additionally, there were objections to the administration's manipulation of intelligence with regard to operations. These objections were especially serious because they emphasized the fact that the administration was ignoring some of the best advice of the very Agency it was trying to boost.

In December 1981, President Reagan had agreed to increase annual foreign-intelligence spending from $6 billion to $20 billion by the end of his first term. The nation's intelligence budget reportedly expanded faster even than the rapidly escalating Pentagon spending. The operations directorate had access to the money, though the personnel contractions of the pre-Reaganite years made it difficult to expand quickly. Because recruitment and training were slow processes, clandestine services director John Stein rehired on short-term contracts some eight hundred of the covert operations veterans who had retired or been released between 1977 and 1980. With a reported one thousand field operatives consequently at its disposal, the CIA now launched over a dozen operations classified as "major" (congressional watchdogs defined these as costing over five million dollars, or designed to overthrow a foreign government, or both). *Newsweek* speculated that the CIA was spending money in Central America, Afghanistan, Iran, Libya, Ethiopia, Mauritius, and Cambodia.[25]

The trouble in Nicaragua had its origin in events half a century earlier. In 1934, upon the U.S. Marines' withdrawal after long periods of occupation, civil guard sergeant Anastasio Somoza seized power. Somoza invited to Managua the guerrilla leader Cesar Augusto Sandino, but instead of proceeding with the promised peace talks, the civil guards murdered Sandino. In 1961, a group of Nicaraguans formed the Sandinista National Liberation Front. In June 1979, they finally brought to a close the nepotic rule of the Somoza family, setting up instead a Sandinista government.

The Reagan administration initially explained its clandestine intervention in Nicaragua as an attempt to stop the Sandinistas from overthrowing the pro-United States regime in nearby El Salvador. In January 1981, just before Reagan took office, the U.S. embassy in San Salvador reported an attack on El Salvador by Nicaraguan commandos. The next month, the State Department published a "White Paper" purporting to document Nicaraguan support of Salvadoran revolutionaries.[26] Events in Southeast Asia had in the past decade given the domino theory a renewed respectability; America's U.N. ambassador Jeane Kirkpatrick pointed to the presence of two thousand Cuban military advisers in Nicaragua, and she broadened the interventionist argument by claiming that Nicaragua had become a surrogate for Soviet-Cuban imperialism throughout Central America.

The departments of state and defense employed an additional strategic justification for action in a pamphlet aimed primarily at European opinion. According to the pamphlet, 45 percent of U.S. foreign trade passed through Gulf ports, and 55 percent of U.S. crude oil imports came through, or sailed adjacent to, the Caribbean. From Gulf ports would sail 60 percent of NATO resupplies and reinforcement material needed in the first two months of a European war. The militarization of Nicaragua was part of the "Soviet strategy to increase pressure on the United States in the Caribbean Basin."[27]

In November 1981, President Reagan endorsed a plan that offered support to private businessmen in Nicaragua, but also set up a covert and paramilitary operation with an initial budget of nineteen million dollars. The purpose of the plan was to force the Sandinistas to change course politically, or, failing that, to replace them with a government more congenial to U.S. policymakers. Some of the methods used, such as the stirring up of the Miskito Indians in armed insurrection, reminded critics of events in Laos twenty years earlier.[28] But the CIA's main instrument was the "Contra" movement. Various opponents of the Sandinista government, known collectively as the Contras, mounted guerrilla attacks on their native country from bases in neighboring Honduras and Costa Rica. Some of the Contras represented genuinely independent viewpoints. For example, Edgar Chamorro, leader of the largest Contra faction, was proud of his descent from a family which had produced several pre-Somoza national leaders, some of whom opposed U.S. intervention in the 1920s. To Nicaragua's foreign minister, however, the Contra attacks were "a war sustained, financed and organised by the CIA."[29]

Members of Congress were uneasy about the Nicaraguan operation. Some critics on the Hill worried, in *Newsweek*'s words, about the "diplomatic danger that secret missions always pose." Others suspected that congressional oversight was retreating into the realm of convenient fiction. "We are like mushrooms," declared Norman Mineta of the House Intelligence Committee, "they keep us in the dark and feed us a lot of manure."[30] In December 1982, Congress issued an unmistakable warning when it passed an amendment sponsored by the chairman of the House committee, Edward P. Boland. The Boland amendment prohibited the CIA from arming Contras "for the purpose of overthrowing the government" of Nicaragua.[31]

The administration responded with policies of evasion and propaganda. Its spokesmen advanced the view that the CIA was merely harrassing, not "overthrowing," the Sandinista government. In Central America, the Agency relied, with few exceptions, on contract employees and on the efforts of the Contras themselves, thus at least abiding by the letter of the congressional restriction in the sense that its own officers did not become directly involved. In breach of the Lansdalean precept of indigenous initiative as well as of congressional instruction, however, the Agency directly orchestrated and controlled the flow of funds and weapons. To avoid detection and criticism, the administration arranged for cash and arms transfers via foreign conduits. By October 1983, for example, Casey and a White House official had induced Israel to arrange weapons support for the Nicaraguan rebels.[32]

The White House official in question was a lieutenant-colonel on secondment from the marines: Oliver North. As a platoon leader in the Vietnam war, North had won a Silver Star and two Purple Hearts. He served Reagan as deputy to the president's national security affairs adviser and deputy director for political-military affairs on the National Security Council. In due course, the war hero assumed an important role in organizing major, internationally channeled assistance to the Contras. Undertaken in defiance of Congress, this venture reflected in equal measure North's dedication and his naivety about the likely potential consequences. But, for the time being, Congress, and perhaps even the highest officials in State, remained ignorant of his activities.

George P. Schultz, at any rate, felt free to launch a thoughtful propaganda offensive. The secretary of state responded to foreign and domestic criticism of the CIA's activities with a statement of general principle on February 23, 1983. "We do not seek destabilization," he claimed. Like President Ford, he stressed instead the role of U.S. covert action in propping up endangered democracies, and "to counter the substantial efforts by the Soviets and their allies to spread their oppressive system throughout the world." Schultz went on to elaborate on the Ford doctrine: "Our support for democracy should not be hidden; we should be proud to be seen to provide it."[33] This was not the same as saying (like Katzenbach in 1967) that the CIA should stay out of trouble by handing over secret schemes to overt agencies. Instead, Schultz had in mind open justifications of schemes whose operational details would remain secret. Thus, he sought to end one of the traditional disadvantages of covert action, the difficulty of justifying publicly what one publicly denied doing. Open justification of some of the CIA's covert activities became a hallmark of the administration's style. Foreign observers began to comment on the CIA's "world-famous 'covert' aid" and to note President Reagan's efforts "to revive the more positive image of the CIA as a covert (but not too covert) crusader for democracy."[34]

Although the public-relations exercise was fairly successful in terms of domestic opinion, substantial elements in Congress remained dissatisfied. In May 1983 a House Intelligence Committee report concluded that continuing U.S. support for the Contras was playing into the hands of the Sandinistas—and "it hurts the CIA."[35] Thus, although the full extent of White House plans to circumvent congressional intent was hardly guessed at, there was already serious discontent. Boland, in particular, was furious. Unaware of the role of the White House in secret Contra funding, he claimed that the CIA was once again "almost like a rogue elephant." In House Intelligence Committee hearings on oversight in September, he sought to broaden the scope of his amendment, demanding "some way for Congress to be in on the takeoffs as well as the crash landings of covert operations."[36]

In 1984, the White House and the CIA experienced a foretaste of the serious trouble that was later to break out over the secret funding of the Central American conflict. Early in the year, the administration authorized increased CIA support for Contra groups in Costa Rica and Honduras. Indeed, Nicaragua's army chief of staff Joaquim Cuadra claimed that the CIA had backed an eight-thousand-man invasion of his country from bases in Honduras.[37] In a further operation which the Reagan administration later acknowledged, the CIA mined Nicaragua's main ports. The mining action was in breach of international law, and the Nicaraguan government eventually won its case against the United States at the international court in The Hague. Domestic critics did not need to wait for the outcome of the case before pillorying the CIA for yet again bringing the United States into disrepute. By its action in Nicaragua, the CIA had even alienated some avid supporters of the anti-Communist crusade, especially by failing to notify Congress: an eighty-one-page briefing to the Senate Intelligence Committee on March 8 contained only one sentence on the mining.[38] Edgar Chamorro, the by-now disillusioned Contra leader who had earlier helped the Agency lobby for money, declared that "the CIA men didn't have much respect for Congress."[39] Republican Senate Intelligence Committee chairman Goldwater, though formerly an opponent of covert operations oversight, wrote a highly publicized letter to Casey saying he was "pissed off." The CIA director had to apologize and stop the mining operation.[40]

Meanwhile, discontent had been building up within the Agency over the administration's disregard for intelligence estimates. Political reactions to an event in 1983 had fueled apprehension within the wider intelligence community on this point. The event was the Russians' downing of a South Korean jumbo jet with the loss of 269 lives. The jet had been on a civilian flight, but had strayed off course over the Sakhalin peninsula, entering sensitive Soviet military airspace. The National Security Agency indicated that the Soviet generals who ordered the shootdown had genuinely believed, at the time, that the jumbo was a spy plane. But the Reagan administration ignored this credible intelligence data about Soviet beliefs and insisted, in its public pronouncements, that the Russians had murdered innocent people in cold blood. The Soviet leadership engaged in similarly unfounded rhetoric, claiming that the CIA had callously risked innocent lives by sending a civilian flight on a spy mission. Yet, U.S. analysts could not fail to note the apparent dissonance of reason and rhetoric in the case of their own leaders.[41]

In relation to Central America, a new group of CIA apostates argued that the U.S. public was being deliberately deceived. Very early in the Reagan administration, Ralph McGehee, who had worked with the CIA from 1952 to 1977, had claimed the operations directorate was being "pressured" to produce studies proving Cuban-Soviet paramilitary imperialism. He now speculated that the alleged Nicaraguan commando raid on El Salvador, CIA's casus belli in 1982, may have been an Agency deception operation. In 1984 David MacMichael, a contract analyst for the CIA between 1981 and 1983, confirmed the spuriousness of the

Salvadorean rationale, revealing there had been no arms shipments from Nicaragua to El Salvador since April 1981.[42]

In May 1984, senior Latin American analyst John Horton resigned from the CIA. He repeated the allegation that intelligence reports were being censored to suppress doubts about the intensity of the left-wing threat in Central America. In any case, he averred, Carter and Reagan were indisposed to listen to intelligence people because they had "run against Washington and the federal government," and "in their arrogance they overestimated their own talents." In June, the transfer of deputy director for operations John Stein to the post of CIA inspector general seemed to confirm Horton's analysis, in being the administration's way of dealing with a man who believed that intensification of the CIA effort would provoke more Cuban support for the Sandinistas. The cumulative evidence suggests that when the administration did not wish to listen, it cut off its ears. It is in this sense that the CIA, in spite of its apparently restored status, lacked the standing due to a competent intelligence agency.[43]

In October 1984, with the election campaign in full swing, a story broke that seemed ideally suited to the ambitions of the Democratic presidential candidate and long-time critic of covert operations, Walter Mondale. Journalists obtained a copy of a Contra manual, *Operaciones Sicológicas en Guerro de Guerrillas*, or psychological operations in guerrilla warfare. The manual gave instructions on kidnapping, terror bombing, blackmail, and, apparently contravening Reagan's 1981 executive order, on assassination. The author, John Kirkpatrick, was a CIA agent who dressed in black in order to inspire the cult of death—in Chamorro's words, "a character out of a Graham Greene novel" who "drank too much and cried all the time."[44] President Reagan said the manual was the work of a contract employee, not a CIA officer, and there have been suggestions since that its function was to regulate existing savagery, not to propose new ideas. Nevertheless, Mondale and his running mate Geraldine Ferraro attacked the notion that "refining the murder techniques of Central Americans will advance our national interests."[45]

In 1976 the Democrats had played the intelligence card and won a presidential election, and in 1980 the Republicans had done the same. But when Mondale and Ferraro tried a similar tactic in 1984, it proved of no avail against a hugely popular incumbent with a patriotic image. Fifty-nine percent of the votes cast on November 6 went to the president. Though many other factors contributed to Reagan's reelection, the voters' verdict could now be presented as, among other things, an endorsement of the administration's use of the CIA as an aggressive Cold War weapon. Against an encouraging background, the White House and the CIA made efforts to step up covert operations.

One of the CIA's new programs was to supply Afghan anti-Communist rebels with Stinger ground-to-air missiles. Congress reportedly supplied the money for this through a secret appropriation; there was certainly widespread approval of clandestine efforts to inhibit Soviet expansion. Thus, the Republican Senate and the Democratic House voted in June and July to end the Clark amendment, enabling the CIA to send aid to conservative rebels in Angola; Stinger missiles were once again a leading item of equipment. There was, however, some unease about the Angolan operation. According to internal CIA leakers, Casey first had to replace a senior Africa analyst who believed the continent's troubles stemmed from indigenous problems like poverty and inadequate education—not from Soviet subversion. There was also some unhappiness in the House. In November, Foreign Affairs Subcommittee on Africa chairman Howard Wolpe attacked White House-CIA plans to escalate the Angolan conflict.[46]

There would have been a much greater outcry had the administration not succeeded in keeping secret, for the time being, its maneuvers to supply Iran with war material. Iran was anxious to obtain weapons because its war against Iraq had taken a heavy toll in munitions as well as lives since its start in 1980. But, in arranging supplies of those weapons, America was in breach of her own policies: of her declared neutrality, and of the arms boycott of Iran which the United States had prescribed for itself and forcefully urged on its allies on the grounds that Iran fomented international terrorism.

Several factors prompted U.S. policymakers to launch their apparently muddled Iranian initiative. One was the need to revive American influence in a crucial strategic area. Another was a fear that the Iranians would turn to the Soviet Union for support (in May 1985, a senior CIA analyst gave credence to this danger, though the Agency discounted his report in the following year). The hostage issue was a further factor that weighed heavily with President Reagan, mindful as he was of the role it had played in the 1980 election. Between March 1984 and June 1985, the Hezballah terrorist group, which had links with the Khomeini regime, kidnapped several American hostages in Beirut, Lebanon. One of these was the CIA's local station chief, William Buckley. Casey, as well as the president, was upset at this—as much because of personal anguish over Buckley, presumed to be dying under torture, as because of the fear that Buckley would inevitably give away CIA secrets in the process. By July 1985, Casey was confronting fellow cabinet members Schultz and Weinberger in his fight for measures to increase U.S. "leverage" in Iran. In August, after negotiations in which Oliver North played a prominent part, President Reagan approved Israeli sales of U.S. weaponry to Iran, with the United States resupplying Israel to make up that country's resultant munitions deficits. By January 1986, the president was ready to authorize direct sales to Iran in exchange for Iranian influence in releasing U.S. hostages.[47]

Although these details did not emerge until later, Congress was already uneasy about the secret doings of the administration. In particular, Congress blew hot and cold over the Contra issue. Just before taking over the chairmanship of the Senate Intelligence Committee in January 1985, Minnesota's David Durenberger told the *Minneapolis Star and Tribune* that "the responsible people in the agency" wanted nothing to do with the Nicaraguan operation, and Casey had "no idea that his agency [was] going down the tubes" over the issue. In April, Congress cut off all U.S. aid, humanitarian as well as military, to the Contras. Subsequently Congress allowed some nonlethal aid, but by March 1986, the Contras faced a total dearth of official U.S. aid. Only after a protracted debate did Congress in October authorize $100 million (of which $70 million were for military use)—and soon thereafter scandals erupted that confirmed earlier misgivings.[48]

Outside Congress, too, the CIA issue refused to lie down. A survey of the leading newspapers in the United States reveals that in 1985 the Agency was the prime theme of 103 editorials. This number was considerably smaller than the 227 in 1975, but large enough to indicate continuing concern and discussion.[49] Abroad, CIA operations in Nicaragua (for so they continued to be perceived) remained an embarrassment to the United States. While the majority of people in Costa Rica, Honduras, and El Salvador saw Nicaragua with its inflated armed forces as a threat to their security, Latin American support for CIA operations was not forthcoming.[50] Argentina (having earlier, when under military dictatorship, helped funnel CIA funds) had by now returned to the democratic fold. Its new, elected leadership opposed U.S. support to the Contras, as did the presidents of Peru, Colombia, and Mexico. The June 1986 World Court ruling against U.S. aid to the Contras left America isolated from the very legitimizing, legal framework its statesmen had, in the past, sought to nurture.[51]

The CIA's major covert operations as they affected Nicaragua and other countries had contradictory effects on the Agency itself. They did enhance Reagan's image as an anti-Communist hero, and some of the strength that derived from that image passed on to the CIA via the president's friend and ally, William Casey. At the same time, the operations were a running sore that eroded respect for the CIA as a whole amongst potential supporters of its more narrowly defined intelligence work. Indeed, the operations seemed to indicate both a misunderstanding of world politics and a willingness to manipulate the truth at will.

The debate over the CIA's role in Nicaragua was damaging not merely in itself, but also because it distracted attention from a more important issue, the administration's scant attention to the significance of the Agency's Soviet estimates. Casey and Robert Gates had introduced some intelligence reforms in line with the Reagan campaign promise to make the CIA more effective than it had been in the Iranian and other crises. They set up a "Weekly Watch Report" to monitor foreign trouble spots, and they ranked countries both according to their potential instability and according to their importance to American interests.[52] In October 1983, *Newsweek* reported that the reformed CIA's predictions had been "early and accurate on important matters."[53] The ascendancy of Gates at the intelligence directorate should have been particularly reassuring, as he was so eminently equipped to understand the problems of Soviet analysis. What could not have been foreseen was that such an ambitious young man would, while remaining politically loyal, "frequently" tell "Casey and the Reagan Administration things they did not want to hear."[54]

Gates's stand took place against the background of long-term divergences between CIA and military estimates. In the aftermath of the B-Team jolt, the CIA had accepted some of the Defense Intelligence Agency's positions, without, however, ceasing to voice its independent and relatively objective point of view. In 1979, for example, the DIA claimed that the Soviet SS–18 missile carried fourteen warheads, in violation of the penciled SALT II agreement, but the CIA insisted that the missile had no more than the permissible ten. Gates brought the Soviet-estimate debate to life when, in 1983, he stated that the Defense Department was exaggerating the volume of Soviet military expenditure.[55] His statement was a triple blow to the assumptions behind Reaganite defense policy. First, it seemed to cast doubt on the assumption that the Russians had aggressive motives and were moving ahead in the arms race. Second, it undermined the assumption that a massive increase in U.S. defense spending was necessary—notably on a space-based antiballistic missile system, the Strategic Defense Initiative ("Star Wars")—to force the Soviets to the bargaining table or, failing that, to supply America with a partial defensive shield by the twenty-first century. Finally, Gates's challenge invited a reexamination of the assumption that the Reagan administration could and should win votes by creating jobs via defense outlays that more than compensated for cutbacks in domestic programs and a large budget deficit.

What Gates challenged was the administration's contention that Soviet defense expenditure had increased at a relentless four to five percent annually since the base year 1965. Gates had already made the unwelcome suggestion, in 1982, that the SALT II agreement had slowed down Soviet weapons procurement. His 1983 statement that Soviet expenditure stagnation had set in around 1976 soon found support. In January 1984, a separate NATO study agreed with and substantiated Gates's findings. In March, a national intelligence estimate discredited the defense lobby's claims in another area. In 1978, the CIA had gone along with the view that SS–18s and SS–19s were twice as accurate as previously thought. This meant that they could destroy U.S. missiles even if they were shielded in concrete silos. Therefore, the defense lobbyists were entitled to their new generation of mobile missiles, the MX system, or its even more modern successor, the Midgetman. But, with the CIA exerting a more confident influence, the 1984 estimate reduced Soviet accuracy by a factor of one-third.[56]

Partly because 1984 was an election year, but also because of their general indisposition to credit embarrassing evidence, administration officials turned a deaf ear to CIA estimates. Defense Secretary Caspar W. Weinberger dismissed the 1983 CIA Soviet-expenditure report as "irrelevant" on the grounds that the Russians were building more powerful weapons even if their overall defense spending had lost its former momentum.[57] Once the president's reelection campaign was under way, he arranged a Pentagon press conference to defend the premises behind Reagan's policy. At the press conference, defense officials reported an overall Soviet military spending increase of three to four percent for 1982–83, and, in the same period, an increase of five to ten percent in major weapons-system procurement. Like some of its predecessors, the Reagan administration was undermining the findings of its objective and supposedly superior intelligence service, the CIA, by using figures from a subjective source.[58]

With the election safely over, Gates reiterated his implicit critique of Defense Department estimates and administration policy in secret testimony to the joint congressional trade, finance, and security economics subcommittee. Before 1976, he said in his November 21 statement, total Soviet defense spending increases had indeed averaged four to five percent annually; since then, however, the growth rate had stagnated at around two percent per annum. This was a slower rate than hitherto assumed, and considerably smaller than the annual percentage increases in U.S. defense expenditure. In January 1985, a DIA official admitted to the same subcommittee that the Soviet arms industry had shifted to a lower gear in the mid-1970s. In February, the subcommittee released Gates's now-declassified testimony. The subcommittee's ranking Democrat, Senator William Proxmire of Wisconsin, declared, "It is time for Washington to take official notice that Soviet military procurement has been stagnant for the past seven years and to stop acting like nothing has changed."[59]

In February 1985, other events occurred which suggested that the CIA's analysts should be listened to after all. A panicky lawyer dropped William C. Westmoreland's suit, brought against Sam Adams and CBS for alleging the general had conspired to "suppress and alter critical intelligence" on Viet Cong strength. The publication of Arkady Shevchenko's Breaking with Moscow also seemed to vindicate the analysts even with regard to one of their more controversial periods, for the Russian defector and former United Nations official claimed he had supplied the CIA with Soviet arms negotiations details and "fallback provisions" between 1975 and 1978, when SALT II was in gestation. The neoconservative intellectual Edward Jay Epstein suggested that Shevchenko may have been a "dangler," or KGB disinformation agent, also that the 1985 book was a CIA publicity stunt comparable with the Penkovsky Papers. But why, asked Shevchenko's editor, should Reagan's CIA whitewash Carter's CIA and the SALT II negotiations? For all its Byzantine twists and turns, the Shevchenko story helped to rehabilitate the CIA via the intelligence route, adding force to Gates's demurrals.[60]

As Gates was a loyal and ambitious member of the administration, he was under pressure to minimize the differences between the CIA's intelligence directorate on the one hand, and Defense and the White House on the other. In March 1985, the Pentagon obtained from him and issued from its own press office a statement that his cautionary testimony had been "misread and misused," and that Russia's outspending of America on "far more" weapons than the Pentagon could deploy was an "awesome fact."[61] But Gates could not effectively paper over cracks that at times seemed more like a yawning gulf between administration rhetoric and the truth as perceived by the CIA's specialists. In the course of his tenure at the intelligence directorate, CIA analysts effectively challenged defense experts not only on Soviet missile accuracy and expenditure, but also on Soviet silo hardness, the size of previous Soviet test explosions, and the range of the Soviet Backfire bomber.[62]

In the summer of 1985, two reports appeared which undermined the stated case for U.S. military buildup. One was the earlier technical study of the accuracy of the 360 SS—19 missiles by now deployed by the Soviet Union. The other, an unclassified national intelligence estimate, was similarly deflationary in dismissing the notion that the Soviet Union was on the brink of nuclear "breakout" or superiority. Soviet weapons systems could not reliably destroy U.S. ground-based missiles, could not knock out American military satellites, and would not pose a threat to U.S. nuclear-armed submarines until after the year 2000. The intelligence directorate's findings provided consistently cold comfort for congressional and administration hawks.[63]

Leading Republican loyalists, accordingly, did not feel warm toward the intelligence directorate. In November, Senate Intelligence Committee chairman Durenberger castigated its performance. He singled out the CIA's predictive failures in three main areas, the Philippines (where the eventual downfall of President Ferdinand Marcos should have been foreseeable), with respect to the emergence of Moslem fundamentalism, and regarding "the energy factor." More seriously, he charged that the Agency lacked "guidelines" for collecting information about the Soviet Union. Having no "sense of direction," its analysts had in fact failed to understand the Russians. In striking contrast to most earlier students of the intelligence problem, members of Durenberger's committee contemplated a reduction in the standing of the CIA director, and they looked at the proposal that the president's national security affairs adviser should assume the role of tasking the CIA and evaluating the effectiveness of its analyses within the context of the policymaking process.[64]

Early in 1986, the administration had an opportunity to do something about the Gates problem. John N. McMahon, deputy director of the CIA since 1982, had been under attack for some time. McMahon was a long-term skeptic on the matter of covert operations. His reputed opposition to the CIA's provision of ground-to-air missiles to Afghan rebels (what if they fell into the hands of the wrong fundamentalists?) sparked a letter-writing campaign aimed at his removal. When he resigned from the number two post in February, Reagan nominated Gates to replace him. The Senate Intelligence Committee unanimously approved and acclaimed the nomination after Gates had testified that covert action was all right "as long as it is taken within a broader context." On the face of it, the administration had removed a potentially troublesome official, McMahon, and replaced him with a man who, according to the press, could be relied upon to guide the CIA into smoother waters. The fuss over covert action, however, obscured a more important, and much more deftly accomplished, goal—the removal by mellifluous means of the man who had restored an awkward credibility to the intelligence directorate.[65]

The administration's determination to ignore the CIA's deflationary Soviet estimates had grave consequences. Instead of using the estimates to counter hawkish arguments against arms agreements with the Russians, Reagan's team formulated policy in a way that encouraged people to believe in the danger of approaching Soviet strategic superiority. They repeated the tried, tested, and apparently proven tactic of exaggerating the Soviet threat in order to obtain U.S. weapons procurements, with a view to using the procurements as bargaining chips in future negotiations. But, by the 1980s, various American generals and politicians had cried wolf too often for informed observers to accept such exaggerated claims at face value. Congress voted more money for Reagan's arms proposals because of the electoral popularity of his tough, poker-playing style, not because the president presented a credible case.

Popularity, however, did not compensate for poor credibility. Perceptions of White House disregard for and manipulation of intelligence were all too plain—in regard to El Salvador, Nicaragua, and the Korean airplane, as well as the Soviet Union. Revelations, in October 1986, about recent White House attempts to destabilize the Libyan government through disinformation in the Western media, did nothing to reassure people that they could expect truth from the administration.[66] Widespread skepticism within informed circles in the United States both mirrored and influenced foreign opinion. Distrust of American intentions grew in Western Europe, where several countries tried to rid themselves unilaterally of nuclear responsibilities. Most important of all, the Russians proved reluctant to negotiate. The Soviet Union had, in Mikhail Gorbachev, a new leader with the courage to compromise, for he regarded the arms race as an obstacle to internal reforms, as well as a menace in itself. Yet, at the 1986 Reykjavik summit meeting, he could not bring himself to trust the Americans, particularly because of their insistence upon the right to pursue the Strategic Defense Initiative. (Gorbachev's reasonableness was nonetheless to contribute to the 1988 superpower agreement to eliminate medium-range missiles. Ironically, that popular achievement carried with it the danger of enshrining the respectability of White House intelligence manipulation which in truth constituted a threat to peace and security.)

Failure to inform Congress about important developments seemed to confirm that the administration lacked evidential justification for its conduct, and the sorry story of the Iran-Contra scandal did nothing to reverse this impression. On November 4, 1986, the press lifted the veil of secrecy from the U.S.-Iran arms sales. Then, on November 25, there began to emerge details of another conspiracy. Colonel North, it transpired, had long solicited money to help the Contras, both from private sources and from foreign governments. Furthermore, anticipating the absolute curtailment of congressional financial support in March 1986, he had arranged for the transference to Contra groups, via concealed Swiss bank accounts, of profits made from the Iran arms sales. Casey tolerated the diversion, delighting in the "sting" whereby an enemy (the Ayatollah) funded a friend (the Contra). Casey, North, and others privy to the initiative had planned to keep Congress, including the intelligence committees, in the dark about this and other similar ventures. In the event of exposure, North was to have been the "deniable link."[67]

The Reagan White House's response to the Iran-Contra affair was no less palliative or cosmetic than those of previous administrations. There was talk of "rotten apples," as in the past of "rogue elephants"; Casey's death in May 1987 made it safer to assert that he, North, and other conspirators had operated without the knowledge or authorization of the president; as North's loyal secretary Fawn Hall had destroyed some of the key evidence, congressional investigators found it difficult to prove otherwise.[68] The flashback technique was another time-honored device that reappeared during the Iran-Contra affair: the State Department released documents showing that the Democratic Carter administration had seriously considered an arms-for-hostage exchange with the Iranians.[69] Reagan also appointed a "pet" commission of inquiry which, like the Taylor, Katzenbach, and Rockefeller investigations into earlier scandals, was meant to preempt more damaging probes. The members of this inquiry, the Tower Commission, were former senators John Tower (chairman) and Edmund Muskie, and former national security adviser Brent Scowcroft.

At the end of the commission's deliberations, Senator Tower soothingly dismissed the Iran-Contra episode as an "aberration."[70] His inquiry, however, did not turn out to be a whitewash. Its report criticized the president for incompetence, urged the development of a better set of "guidelines" for covert operations, and recommended the compilation of an "institutional memory" at the National Security Council, so that there would not be yet another repetition of the mistakes of the past. It also demanded greater respect for objective intelligence.[71] This last conclusion was similar to that reached by the joint House-Senate investigation chaired by Hawaii's senator Daniel K. Inouye, a veteran of the 1970s inquiries. The congressional report offered strictures on the president and the CIA, especially for ignoring procedural guidelines whereby oversight committees should have been kept informed. At the same time, in a view parallel to that held by the Tower commission, the Inouye panel accused the CIA, and especially Casey, of manipulating intelligence in a way that subverted "democratic processes."[72] The Inouye panel's accusation was particularly serious, as it drew upon evidence which showed that informational manipulation had occurred within the Agency itself. This clearly undermined the Agency's standing: perhaps the CIA was no longer an objective source of intelligence, and should not be trusted.

The Iran-Contra affair lowered America's prestige and that of its allies. It left Western antiterrorist policy in tatters. It injected paralysis and obsessive self-justification into the White House. Its implications went beyond the local crises in Iran and Nicaragua. Not least among its various consequences was its effect on the career of Robert Gates. Reagan nominated Gates to be the new director of the CIA when Casey fell ill. But, after initial enthusiasm for the nomination, Congress became suspicious of Gates's failure to blow the whistle in a timely fashion on the Iran-Contra affair. Like a number of other CIA officials, Gates had chosen to remain ignorant of potentially embarrassing information, lest he should be obliged to testify about it later. In the words of the Inouye report, he was one of those who "consciously" chose "to avoid knowledge," thus turning "upside down the CIA's mission to collect all intelligence relevant to national security."[73] The tragedy is that, earlier, Gates had so courageously insisted on the dissemination of knowledge which had cast doubt on some of the more extravagant claims about Soviet might. Though embarrassing to the administration at the time, his efforts had contributed to that restoration of confidence between the superpowers which illuminated, if only fleetingly, the later stages of the Reagan presidency. But, in March 1987, Gates fell victim to the consequences of the Iran-Contra dissimulation which he had failed to expose. Reagan withdrew his nomination, and gave it instead to FBI director William H. Webster, a specialist in counterespionage.

With Gates discredited, the sins of the operators had once again been visited upon the analysts. The United States lacked, in its arms negotiations with the Soviet Union, the benefit of respected CIA counsel. While this was by no means the only difficulty in the way of a permanent series of confidence-boosting agreements, it was a significant obstacle. There was still a crying need for an objective intelligence source of sufficient standing to compel respect in the White House and Congress, and, belief, at home and abroad, in the reasonableness of U.S. strategy.

CONCLUSION

The CIA's recurrent lack of proper standing by no means indicates that the Agency's history is one of unmitigated failure. On the contrary, as Barry Goldwater said in 1980, in many intelligence controversies "the finger should have been pointed at Presidents and not the intelligence group."[1] The various people who say that the CIA has been the world's best postwar foreign-intelligence agency are not wide of the mark.[2] One rival claimant to the honor, the British service, has suffered from Communist penetration and contracted with Britain's financial and geopolitical decline. As for the KGB and Soviet military intelligence, it may be said without deprecating their determination or competence that because of America's open society they have had a much easier task to accomplish.

With regard to the CIA's problems, lack of proper standing is not the only point that should be considered. The Agency has been prone to some of the weaknesses that affected some of its rivals, too. Its failure to predict Soviet missile emplacements in Cuba and to account for the move in retrospect indicated a scarcely unique incapacity to escape from the framework of one's own strategic assumptions. The CIA's mirror-imaging in the mid-1960s, which contributed to nonperception of the Soviet missile buildup trend, is a graphic if transient instance of the Agency's being in the grip of a universal failing: as the Americans rewrote Shaw, why can't a woman be more like a man?[3]

While the American democratic process helped the CIA in some ways—supplying free-ranging ideas and a quality-enhancing critique, for example—it also contributed some distinctive problems. One of these was an obsession with crisis prediction. To protect the Roosevelt-New Deal image, the Democrats had to dwell on predictive failure at Pearl Harbor, and on the necessity of inventing an agency that would guard against surprise attack. This gave rise to the extravagant expectation that the CIA would be able to foresee every crisis, an expectation that gave an inappropriate skew to the Agency's tasking and led to inevitable disappointment on account of the inevitable predictive failures (or sometimes, when the White House needed a scapegoat, *alleged* predictive failures). Because successive presidents continued to stress crisis prediction in the belief that voters rewarded quick responses rather than long-term solutions, preemption of surprise events remained a high priority for the CIA. In fairness, it should be added that this was, from Bogota to Tehran, an important goal, and that the Agency had its irrefutable failings. One of these was an overreadiness to assume, or at least to connive at the myth, that Communists lay behind every potentially embarrassing crisis. That assumption sprang from one of modern American democracy's salient features, virulent antisocialism. It also reflected intellectual laziness: It was dangerously convenient for the CIA's masters to blame Moscow and Peking for student disorders in the 1960s and acts of "state" terrorism in the 1980s, instead of undertaking the exhausting task of studying the myriad factions and complex ideologies really involved.

Democratic sentiment, or at least its libertarian component, underpinned another source of CIA weakness, its restriction to foreign work. The "American Gestapo" fears that produced a division of labor between the CIA and FBI were not, it is clear in retrospect, a temporary, post-Holocaust aberration of the 1940s. American antipathy to state espionage, secrecy, and intrusiveness had historical roots and continues to the present day. The CIA-FBI division, its effects exacerbated by CIA-FBI rivalry and noncooperation, impaired counterintelligence and, therefore, the CIA's reputed—and perhaps actual—resistance to KGB penetration and deception. Even more seriously, the domestic proscription prevented the CIA from making combined or "net" estimates of Soviet and American capabilities and strategies, as the Agency did not evaluate the U.S. side of the picture. The creators and perpetuators of the CIA never effectively answered Wilmoore Kendall's point that its intelligence stopped "at the three mile limit;" they never devised a means of unbinding the intelligence directorate in a way that would not revive fears of an American police state. This shortcoming left the politicians and vested interests more scope to weave their fantasies and implement their delusions.

The CIA's noninvolvement in net estimating at least helped its officials observe one of the golden rules of their profession, the separation of intelligence from policy. There is no general substance in the often-voiced charge that the Agency's elite were biased in a liberal-left-dove direction and influenced U.S. strategy in accordance with that bias. In a few specific cases like the Bay of Pigs operation, it is true, senior officials did reach subjective and erroneous conclusions about schemes to which they were committed. But the separation of evaluation from policy advocacy was on the whole strict. Even the intelligence oversight committees observed the rule. In the course of the 1980 House hearings on "The Role of Intelligence in the Foreign Policy Process," Congressman Boland and Senator Goldwater both stressed that the intelligence committees oversaw the intelligence process only; the Foreign Affairs and Foreign Relations committees then discussed the implications of intelligence for policy.[4]

This scrupulously observed distinction reflected the assumption that appointed officials in the CIA should leave policymaking to their elected masters. Just as important, from the viewpoint of the theorist, is the fact that it helped to preserve the objectivity of U.S. foreign intelligence. Yet, as Sherman Kent and other intelligence theorists have pointed out, there must be interaction between policy and intelligence if each is to be effective. This interaction has tended to break down not only because policymakers have ignored intelligence, but also because they have not asked the right questions. One of the saddest features of the CIA's history is the inadequacy of the White House's approach to the tasking job. Some presidents have, by chance and inclination, been more equal to the challenge than others: Eisenhower stands out in this respect. But others have been apathetic, ignorant, opportunistic, or manipulative. Successive attempts at bureaucratic reform have done little to counter this human factor. (*Double* tasking, with the CIA asking a few questions of its own and supplying continuity from one administration to another, is one experiment that has gone begging.) Presidential ignorance and exploitation of the intelligence process stemmed, in part, from absence of pressure from a general public largely uneducated in intelligence affairs. The public's often easy tolerance of presidential abuse of intelligence both reflected and contributed to the low standing from which the CIA has periodically suffered.[5]

Adventurer though he may have been, "Wild" Bill Donovan had been correct in his perception, during World War II, that an American central intelligence organization which lacked bureaucratic standing would be useless. In wartime conditions, he established the OSS's reputation by linking it to daring covert operations. In the peacetime era, however, the CIA's covert operations often had a reverse, destabilizing effect on the Agency. What made things worse was that, under pressure from the White House, the CIA often ignored those principles of covert activity—notably the encouragement of genuinely indigenous tendencies—that Lansdale and others had established. A recognized set of restraining guidelines would have improved matters. But congressional guidelines by and large safeguarded democratic oversight, instead of establishing behavioral ground rules. Executive guidelines helped in some respects, as in the case of Ford's banning of assassinations. Yet, there has been no formalization, or bipartisan approval of, some of the more thoughtful executive doctrines: Ford's justification of secret operations to prop up democracies, or Schultz's potentially self-limiting plea for openly justifiable secret operations. Thus, resort to excessive clandestine practices has remained a liability to American diplomacy, and a repellent to U.S. politicians who might otherwise be inclined to champion the intelligence directorate in its recurrent battles to establish the truth.

If White House abuse and excessive covert operations have undermined the CIA's credibility and standing, so has intelligence mythology. For reasons that had more to do with American society than with the CIA itself, conservative and hawkish critics repeatedly denounced the Agency as liberal, elitist, soft on Communism, and prone to underestimate Soviet strength. The Agency did, of course, suffer from the shortcomings and fallibility of all human institutions. Conservative critics referred selectively to its past lapses to build up a mythology that, by the Carter administration, impaired the CIA's standing and contributed to the non-ratification of SALT II.

Yet another factor contributing to the periodically low standing of the CIA and some of its estimates has been supine Agency leadership. The dismissals of Hillenkoetter and Dulles contributed to an atmosphere of nervousness. McCone's resignation because of White House neglect of intelligence might have served warning of the possibility of similar, principled actions in the future, but it was too low-key and isolated to seem other than a defeat. Thereafter, leading officials dared not oppose abuses of the intelligence process—notably in the cases of the Vietnam War, of the SALT I negotiations, and of the premises behind the Star Wars program. There has never been a conspicuous, high-level, resignation-in-protest from the CIA.

For these various reasons, the CIA's standing has suffered from time to time—declining in the 1960s and early 1970s, recovering in some ways from 1975 on, but then plunging in Reagan's second term, and never achieving for the Agency's estimates the authority that they usually deserve. In one conspicuous case, Kissinger's achievement of SALT I, the consequent manipulation of intelligence actually contributed to a positive and peaceful goal. But there are limits to human trust and gullibility; intelligence manipulation has more often than not threatened national security and the prospects for world peace. Therefore, the question of the CIA's standing invites close attention—and it cries out for redress.

★
ABBREVIATIONS
USED
IN THE NOTES

ACLS	Records of the American Council of Learned Societies, Library of Congress, Washington, D.C.
AMHI	U.S. Army Military History Institute, Carlisle Barracks, Pennsylvania.
AWD	Allen W. Dulles Papers, Seeley G. Mudd Library, Princeton University, Princeton, New Jersey.
CDJ	C. D. Jackson Papers, Dwight D. Eisenhower Library, Abilene, Kansas.
CHM	Charles H. McCall Files, Gerald R. Ford Library, Ann Arbor, Michigan.
CMC	Clark M. Clifford Papers, Harry S. Truman Library, Independence, Missouri.
CNOTS	Secretary of the Navy and Chief of Naval Operations Top Secret Files, 1945, Navy Section, National Archives, Washington, D.C.
DDE	Dwight D. Eisenhower Library, Abilene, Kansas.
EAA	Eben A. Ayers Papers, Harry S. Truman Library, Independence, Missouri.
EGL	Edward G. Lansdale Papers, Hoover Institution Archives, Independence, Missouri.
FE	Ferdinand Eberstadt Papers, Seeley G. Mudd Manuscript Library, Princeton University, Princeton, New Jersey.
GME	George M. Elsey Papers, Harry S. Truman Library, Independence, Missouri.
GRDS	General Records of the Department of State, National Archives, Washington, D.C.
GRF	Gerald R. Ford Library, Ann Arbor, Michigan.
HDS	Harold D. Smith Papers, Harry S. Truman Library, Independence, Missouri.
HIA	Hoover Institution Archives, Stanford, California.
HST	Harry S. Truman Library, Independence, Missouri.

HWB	Hanson W. Baldwin Papers, Yale University Library, New Haven, Connecticut.
JFK	John F. Kennedy Library, Boston, Massachusetts.
JVF	James V. Forrestal Papers, Seeley G. Mudd Manuscript Library, Princeton University, Princeton, New Jersey.
LBH	Lewis B. Hershey Papers, U.S. Army Military History Institute, Carlisle Barracks, Pennsylvania.
LBJ	Lyndon Baines Johnson Library, Austin, Texas.
LC	Library of Congress, Washington, D.C.
MMHB	Modern Military Headquarters Branch, National Archives, Washington, D.C.
NA	National Archives, Washington, D.C.
NLC	New Left Collection, Hoover Institution Archives, Stanford, California.
NSC	National Security Council.
NSCT	National Security Council Papers, Harry S. Truman Library, Independence, Missouri.
NSFJ	National Security Files, Lyndon Baines Johnson Library, Austin, Texas.
NSFK	National Security Files, John F. Kennedy Library, Boston, Massachusetts.
NUL	Records of the National Urban League, Library of Congress, Washington, D.C.
OFHM	Office Files of Harry McPherson, Lyndon Baines Johnson Library, Austin, Texas.
PPF	Post Presidential Files, Harry S. Truman Library, Independence, Missouri.
PRO	Public Records Office, London.
PSB	Records of the Psychological Strategy Board, Harry S. Truman Library, Independence, Missouri.
RAC	Rose A. Conway Files, Harry S. Truman Library, Independence, Missouri.
SGM	Seeley G. Mudd Manuscript Library, Princeton University, Princeton, New Jersey.
SIR	Samuel I. Rosenman Papers, Harry S. Truman Library, Independence, Missouri.
SJS	Stephen J. Spingarn Papers, Harry S. Truman Library, Independence, Missouri.
SWS	Sidney W. Souers Papers, Harry S. Truman Library, Independence, Missouri.
WBS	Walter Bedell Smith Papers, Dwight D. Eisenhower Library, Abilene, Kansas.
WDL	William D. Leahy Files as chairman, Joint Chiefs of Staff, 1942–48, R.G. 218, Modern Military Headquarters Branch, National Archives, Washington, D.C.
WHCF	White House Central Files, Presidential libraries.
YUL	Yale University Library, New Haven, Connecticut.

NOTES

Chapter 1
THE LESSONS OF AMERICAN HISTORY

1. The founders and shapers of the CIA had, of course, learned a variety of lessons from the past, so any attempt to generalize necessarily obscures some important distinctions. Among the more important founders discussed in this and the succeeding chapter are President Harry S. Truman, Navy and Defense Secretary James V. Forrestal, Office of Strategic Services Chief William J. Donovan, the two directors of the CIA's predecessor the Central Intelligence Group, Sidney W. Souers and Hoyt S. Vandenberg, and congressional figures like Senator Chan Gurney and Representatives Clare Hoffman and Clarence Brown.

2. The CIA's founders, listed in the preceding note, were necessarily advocates, too. Strictly speaking, some additional advocates were not founders of the Agency: among them, the Republican brothers John Foster and Allen W. Dulles, respectively Secretary of State and CIA director in the 1950s, and the journalist Hanson W. Baldwin. The original advocates, including the Dulles brothers and Baldwin, naturally defended the Agency later on. Newcomers joined, augmented, and succeeded these apologists as the years passed: for example, Ray S. Cline, a deputy director of the CIA in the 1960s, and David A. Phillips, founder in 1975 of the pro-CIA lobby, the Association of Former Intelligence Officers. While it is possible to generalize about the views of the CIA's supporters, it should be borne in mind that the Agency is not an ideologically rigid institution, and that it has been justified for a variety of, and sometimes even contradictory, reasons.

3. Dulles, *The Craft of Intelligence*, pp. 35, 47; Cline, *CIA*, pp. 26, 27.

4. Unless otherwise stated, the following section on U.S. intelligence history is based on Jeffreys-Jones, *American Espionage*, a book on the period 1898–1947 which also supplies a prefatory sketch of U.S. espionage prior to 1898.

5. Wriston, *Executive Agents*, p. 296.

6. On Hoover's "Watergate," see Dorwart, *Conflict of Duty*, pp. 3–5.

7. David Kahn, "United States Views of Germany and Japan in 1941," in May, *Knowing One's Enemies*, pp. 476, 500–501.

8. Troy, *Donovan and CIA*, pp. 11–12.

9. Jeffreys-Jones, *American Espionage*, pp. 163–65. See also Troy, *Donovan and CIA*, pp. 13, 170, and Smith, *Shadow Warriors*, p. 105.

10. Brown, *The Last Hero*, p. 37.

11. Bradley Smith, *Shadow Warriors*, pp. 38–39.

12. Thomas F. Troy, "CIA's British Parentage—and the Significance Thereof," paper presented at the tenth annual meeting of the Society for Historians of American Foreign Relations, Aug. 3, 1984, and kindly supplied by its author; John H. Godfrey, "Intelligence in the United States," July 7, 1941, CAB 122/1021 S4206, PRO, kindly supplied by Bradley F. Smith in the first instance, and later reproduced in Smith, "Admiral Godfrey's Mission to America, June/July 1941," *Intelligence and National Security*, 1 (Sept. 1986): 441–50, at 445–50; Troy, *Donovan and CIA*, pp. 38–39.

13. Troy, *Donovan and CIA*, p. 56.

14. Troy, *Donovan and CIA*, p. 423.

15. Troy, "British Parentage," p. 8.

16. S. Theodore Felstead found much to criticize even after the start of the war: Felstead, *Intelligence*, p. 14. For more recent criticisms, see Hinsley, *British Intelligence*, 3; and Donald Cameron Watt, "British Intelligence and the Coming of the Second World War in Europe," in May, ed., *Knowing One's Enemies*, pp. 237–70. The historian Wesley K. Wark has periodized the performance of British intelligence between 1933 and 1939. At first, British analysts underestimated German strength; then, they exaggerated German strength and became overpessimistic; only in 1938–39, on the eve of war, did they begin to supply a balanced and realistic picture: Wark, *The Ultimate Enemy*, pp. 225–40.

17. Godfrey, "Intelligence," pp. 3, 6 (original pagination); Watt, "British Intelligence," p. 270; Andrew, *Secret Service*, pp. 448–86.

18. See Patrick Beesly, *Very Special Intelligence: The Story of the Admiralty's Operational Intelligence Centre, 1939–1945* (London: Hamish Hamilton, 1977) and *Very Special Admiral: The Life of Admiral J. H. Godfrey* (London: Hamish Hamilton, 1980); Ronald Lewin, *Ultra Goes to War* (London: Hutchinson, 1978) and *The American Magic: Codes, Cyphers, and the Defeat of Japan* (Harmondsworth: Penguin, 1983); and Bradley Smith, *Shadow Warriors*, pp. 36, 37, 46, 103.

19. Sir William Stephenson, "The Story of OSS," printed as an appendix in H. Montgomery Hyde, *Secret Intelligence Agent: British Espionage in America and the Creation of OSS* (New York: St. Martin's, 1982), pp. 248, 260; Malcolm Muggeridge quoted in Smith, *OSS*, p. 163.

20. In reply to a barb by Lewis Mumford, see Kirkpatrick, *The U.S. Intelligence Community*, p. 174.

21. Cline, *CIA*, pp. 21, 41.

22. Roberta Wohlstetter, *Pearl Harbor: Warning and Decision* (Stanford: Stanford University Press, 1962), p. 399; Kahn, "United States Views of Germany and Japan," pp. 500–501.

23. Troy, *Donovan and CIA*, p. 427.

24. See Bradley Smith, *Shadow Warriors*, p. 417.

25. See Jeffreys-Jones, *American Espionage*, pp. 175–76.

26. "Report on the Covert Activities of the Central Intelligence Agency" (Sept. 30, 1954), p. 22, in unnumbered box, MMHB, NA. President Eisenhower had commissioned General James Doolittle to inquire into the CIA's efficiency and produce this report.

27. Bradley Smith, *Shadow Warriors*, p. 361.

28. David A. Walker, "OSS and Operation Torch" (M.Sc. diss., Edinburgh University, 1985), pp. 61, 62, 66, 71. For a synoptic version of Walker's findings, see his "OSS and Operation Torch," *Journal of Contemporary History* 22(October 1987): 667–79.

29. Bradley Smith, *Shadow Warriors*, p. 361; Robin W. Winks to R.J.-J., June 3, 1985. See also Winks, *Cloak and Gown*, p. 35.

30. Bradley Smith, *Shadow Warriors*, pp. 348, 349, 359.

31. At the Washington Disarmament Conference of 1921–22, codebreaking experts attached to the American "Black Chamber" passed on to U.S. negotiators details of Japanese bargaining tactics, helping America obtain a favorable deal on naval tonnage ratios: David Kahn, *The Codebreakers: The Story of Secret Writing* (New York: Signet, 1973), pp. 176–77. This episode did not, however, lead to a widespread use of intelligence for arms control purposes.

32. See the book by the CIA's longest-serving director, Dulles, *The Craft of Intelligence*, pp. 35, 47, as well as Cline, *CIA*, pp. 26, 27.

33. In President Washington's day, if a person brought you "intelligence" of such and such an event or person, he simply delivered news or information. By the 1940s, the word meant more than that. It meant information which had been evaluated. In the 1960s, the term *intelligence* covered a wide range of CIA services. Harry E. Ransom, a leading academic observer and critic of the CIA, wrote: "Such services can only be justified by stretching the meaning of the term [intelligence], admittedly a common practice": *The Intelligence Establishment*, p. 86. According to one 1980s definition, the word *intelligence* referred to four integrated activities engaged in by a full-service agency like the CIA: spying, counterintelligence, evaluation, and covert action (Roy Godson and Richard Shultz, "Foreign Intelligence: A Course Syllabus," *International Studies Notes*, 8[Fall-Winter 1981–82]:5). Robert R. Bowie, head of the CIA's National Foreign Assessment Center in the late 1970s, offered the narrower definition, "knowledge and analysis designed to assist action," while the diplomatic historian Ernest R. May proposed the further refinement "knowing one's enemies": Bowie quoted in the introduction to May, ed., *Knowing One's Enemies*, p. 3.

34. Jeffreys-Jones, *American Espionage*, pp. 107–8, 114–15.

35. Melosi, *The Shadow of Pearl Harbor*, p. 144. The classic revisionist studies are Charles A. Beard, *President Roosevelt and the Coming of the War, 1941: A Study in Appearances and Realities* (New Haven: Yale University Press, 1948), and Charles C. Tansill, *Back Door to War: The Roosevelt Foreign Policy, 1933–1941* (Chicago: Regnery, 1952).

36. See chapter 2.

Chapter 2
THE BIRTH OF THE CIA

1. [Anne Karalekas], "History of the Central Intelligence Agency," in "Supplementary Detailed Staff Reports on Foreign and Military Intelligence" (Final Report of the Select Committee to Study Governmental Operations with Respect to Intelligence Activities, 5 Books, Book 4), *Senate Report*, 94 Cong., 2 sess., no. 94–755 (April 23, 1976) (hereinafter "Karalekas History"), p. 7. Anne Karalekas's historical report has also appeared as Karalekas, *History of the Central Intelligence Agency* (Laguna Hills, Calif.: Aegean Park Press, 1977).

2. Souers to Eberstadt, June 5, 1946, folder "1945–1946; 1948–1949: Central Intelligence Agency," Box 31, FE.

3. Memo, Leahy to Secs. War and Navy, Sept. 19, 1945, enclosing memo for the President, RG 80, folder 21, Box A8, CNOTS.

4. Memo, Samuel Murray Robinson to Forrestal, Oct. 4, 1945, RG 80, folder 21, Box A8, CNOTS.

5. Pettee, *The Future of American Secret Intelligence*, pp. (ix), 4–7, 39, 44, 49, 67, 115.

6. Penciled sheet attached to Donovan memo, Aug. 25, 1945, folder "OSS. Donovan—Intelligence Services," Box 15, RAC.

7. On OSS ambitions and intelligence failures in North Africa, see Walker thesis, "OSS and Operation Torch," p. 49. Murphy was a career diplomat who helped Donovan and later endorsed some of the CIA's covert operations—unlike some other high-ranking State Department officials.

8. "Substantive Authority Necessary in Establishment of a Central Intelligence Service," enclosed with Memo, Donovan to Roosevelt, Nov. 18, 1944, folder "OSS. Donovan—Intelligence Services," Box 15, RAC.

9. Troy, *Donovan and CIA*, p. 235.

10. "Labor's Rebuff by UNCIO at San Francisco," Memo, Donovan to President, June 21, 1945, folder "OSS. Donovan—Chronological File June-August, 1945," Box 15, RAC.

11. "Remarks by Major General William J. Donovan at Overseas Press Club Dinner," Feb. 28, 1946, carbon copy of typescript in Box 31, FE. Faulty grammar as in typescript.

12. Troy, *Donovan and CIA*, p. 445.

13. Bradley Smith, *Shadow Warriors*, p. 399.

14. Memo, Roosevelt to Donovan, April 15, 1945, and letter, Donovan to Truman April 30, 1945, both in folder "OSS Donovan—Intelligence Services," RAC, Misc. WHCF, HST.

15. Memo, Biddle to Truman, April 20, 1945, RAC, Misc. WHCF, HST.

16. Transcript, George M. Elsey oral history interview, Feb. 10, 1964, by Charles T. Morrissey, p. 6, HST.

17. There was a change in emphasis between George M. Elsey's original pencil notes on Clifford's statement ("Mr. Clifford pointed out that it was the Pres. original intent *not* to create a new agency," Elsey's emphasis) and his final report for the file: Clifford "pointed out that it was not [last word inserted in Elsey's hand] the President's original intention that a new agency ["not" deleted at this point] be created," July 17, 1946, file on central intelligence, GME.

18. Truman to Morse, Feb. 22, 1963, PPF Sec. Off. File, folder "Central Intelligence Agency," HST.

19. Memoirs discussion, March 12, 1954, PPF Memoirs File, folder "1954, March 12," HST.

20. Memo, Biddle to Truman, April 20, 1945, RAC, Misc. WHCF, HST.

21. Transcript, George M. Elsey oral history interview, July 10, 1970, by Jerry N. Hess, p. 461, HST.

22. Max Lowenthal, *The Federal Bureau of Investigation* (New York: William Sloane, 1950); Souers interview, Dec. 16, 1954, PPF Memoirs file (Associates), folder "Souers, Sidney, Dec. 15–16, 1954," p. 24, HST.

23. Transcript, Lewis Hershey oral history interview, May 7, 1975, by Robert Elder and James Hattersley, p. 26, LBH.

24. Smith diary, July 6, 1945, HDS.

25. Harry S. Truman, "Truman Deplores Change in CIA Role," *Evansville Courier*, Dec. 21, 1963.

26. Smith diary, Sept. 5, Dec. 11, 1945, HDS.

27. Note on off-the-record press conference, April 18, 1946, kept by White House assistant press secretary Eben A. Ayers, general file, folder "Intelligence Service," EAA.

28. Harry S. Truman, *Memoirs*, 2 vols. (Garden City, N.Y.: Doubleday, 1955 [1], 1956 [2], 1, *Year of Decisions*, p. 99.

29. Transcript, Walter Trohan oral history interview, Oct. 7, 1970, by Jerry N. Hess, p. 62, HST.

30. Thomas F. Troy, "Knifing of the OSS," *International Journal of Intelligence and Counterintelligence* 1, no. 3 (1986):97–100, 102–06. See also Troy, *Donovan and CIA*, p. 258; Harris Smith, *OSS*, p. 363.

31. Memo, Donovan to JCS, Feb. 15, 1945, folder "OSS Donovan—Intelligence Services," RAC, Misc. WHCF, HST.

32. Troy, *Donovan and CIA*, p. 256; Donovan, *Conflict and Crisis*, p. 198.

33. Trohan oral history, p. 16.

34. Troy, *Donovan and CIA*, p. 281.

35. *Washington Times-Herald*, June 12, 1947; *Chicago Tribune*, June 15, 1947; Les K. Adler and Thomas G. Paterson, "Red Fascism: The Merger of Nazi Germany and Soviet Russia in the American Image of Totalitarianism, 1930s–1950s," *American Historical Review*, 74(1970).

36. Troy, *Donovan and CIA*, p. 463.

37. James F. Byrnes, *Speaking Frankly* (New York: Harper, 1947), p. 243.

38. McCormack's plan, and his advocacy of it on the radio and elsewhere, are described in a memo from Souers to Clifford, Dec. 27, 1945, folder "Central Intelligence Agency/NME," CMC.

39. "Comparison of JCS Plan and State Department Plan," n.d., folder "Central Intelligence Agency/NME," CMC.

40. Acheson, p. 157.

41. Acheson, *Creation*, p. 160.

42. Joseph Anthony Panuch, assistant to Donald Russell, assistant secretary for administration in the State Department, quoted in Acheson, *Creation*, p. 162. According to future high-ranking CIA official Sherman Kent, "conservatives" in State supplied the opposition: Kent, *Strategic Intelligence for American World Policy*, p. 113.

43. Andrew Jackson May, May 14, 1946, quoted in Acheson, *Creation*, p. 161.

44. *New York Herald Tribune*, April 25, 1946; *New York Times*, April 23, 1946.

45. Acheson, *Creation*, pp. 159, 161.

46. Donovan, *Conflict and Crisis*, p. 268.

47. Memo, Souers to Clifford, Dec. 27, 1945, folder "Central Intelligence Agency/NME," CMC.

48. For a summary of the main proposals, see McCormack's memo to Harold Smith, Jan. 10, 1946, folder "Intelligence," SIR.

49. "Directive Regarding the Coordination of Intelligence Activities," a draft dated Aug. 1, 1945, modified, and forwarded for President Truman's consideration on Jan. 1, 1946, folder "National Intelligence Authority," CMC.

50. Donovan, *Conflict and Crisis*, p. 26; *St. Louis Post-Dispatch*, May 11, 1947, Feb. 29, 1948.

51. Translation from July 30, 1949, issue of Madrid's *Pueblo* in NSC file, SWS.

52. Editorial, *Washington Post*, Dec. 8, 1952.

53. Comment, written in Truman's hand and initialed by him, on first page of transcript of Souers interview, Dec. 15, 1954, PPF Memoirs file (Associates), folder "Souers, Sidney, Dec. 15–16, 1954," HST.

54. Yergin, *Shattered Peace*, pp. 216–17; Souers interview, Dec. 15, 1954, PPF Memoirs file (Associates), folder "Souers, Sidney, Dec. 15–16, 1954," p. 20, HST; Gosnell, *Truman's Crises*, p. 286.

55. Truman to Wayne Morse, Feb. 22, 1963, PPF Sec. Off. File, folder "Central Intelligence Agency," HST.

56. Memo, Robinson to Forrestal, Oct. 4, 1945, RG80, folder 21, Box A8, CNOTS.

57. Memo, Donovan to Truman, Sept. 6, 1945, folder "OSS. Donovan—Chron. File, Sept. 1945," RAC, Misc. WHCF, HST.

58. Souers interview, Dec. 16, 1954, PPF Memoirs file (Associates), folder "Souers, Sidney, Dec. 15–16, 1954," p. 22.

59. Memo, Souers to Clifford, Dec. 27, 1945, folder "Central Intelligence Agency/ NME," CMC.

60. "Foreign and Military Intelligence" (Final Report of the Select Committee to Study Governmental Operations with Respect to Intelligence Activities [the "Church Committee Report"], 5 Books, Book 1), Senate Report, 94 Cong., 2 sess., no. 94–755 (April 26, 1976), p. 102; Cline, CIA, p. 44.

61. "Clifford and Vandenberg were the sources of this column" was written in Elsey's hand on a Krock item clipped from the New York Times, July 16, 1946, folder "Central Intelligence," GME.

62. Note in Elsey's hand, attached to ibid.

63. Memo, Clifford to Vandenberg, July 12, 1946, and Elsey's paraphrase of Clifford's statement to Vandenberg in Elsey, "Memorandum of conversation on 8 January 1947," both in folder "Central Intelligence," GME.

64. Memo, Elsey to Clifford, March 14, 1947, folder "Central Intelligence," GME.

65. Truman to Morse, Feb. 22, 1963, PPF Sec. Off. File, folder "Central Intelligence Agency," HST.

66. Elsey's initialed handwritten note of Clifford's remark, Aug. 2, 1947, folder "Central Intelligence," GME.

67. Fahy memo, Dec. 18, 1945, in Office of Military Government Papers, quoted in Tom Bower, Blind Eye to Murder: Britain, America and the Purging of Nazi Germany—A Pledge Betrayed (London: Granada, 1981), p. 250.

68. Memo, Eddy to Acheson, n.d., RG 59, Decimal File 1945–1949, 811.20/2–547, GRDS.

69. Braden to Fahy, Feb. 5, 1947, 811.20/2–547.

70. Fahy memoranda, Feb. 7, 24, 1947, 811.20/2–2447.

71. Washington Post, March 4, 1947; March 21, July 27, 1950.

72. Dulles to Gurney, April 25, 1947, reproduced in Senate Committee on Armed Services hearings on S.758, March 18–May 9, 1947, reprinted in Grover S. Williams, ed., Legislative History of the Central Intelligence Agency as Documented in Published Congressional Sources (Washington, D.C.: Congressional Research Service of the Library of Congress, 1975), p. 44.

73. Dulles memo, in Williams, Legislative History, p. 47. This memorandum was also reproduced, in its entirety, in Ransom, The Intelligence Establishment, Appendix A, pp. 257–63.

74. Dulles memo in Williams, Legislative History, p. 46.

75. Donovan, Conflict and Crisis, p. 305.

76. Brown in the course of Forrestal "Statement," House Committee on Expenditures hearings on H.R. 2319, April 2–July 1, 1947, reprinted in Williams, Legislative History, pp. 88–89.

77. Senate hearings in Williams, Legislative History, p. 29.

78. Donovan, Conflict and Crisis, pp. 151, 272; exchange between Bridges and General Carl Spaatz during Senate hearings, mentioned in Durward V. Sandifer to Fahy, March 26, 1947, R.G. 59, Decimal File 1945–1949, 811.20/1–145, GRDS.

79. Congressional Record as reproduced in Williams, Legislative History, p. 138.

80. Ibid., p. 146.

81. The text of the relevant section of the National Security Act is conveniently reproduced in Leary, The Central Intelligence Agency, pp. 128–30.

Chapter 3
THE MISTS OF BOGOTA

1. Pforzheimer quoted in Tom Braden, "The Birth of the CIA," p. 11.

2. Dulles testimony in United States Congress, House, 80 Cong. 1 sess., Committee on Expenditures, "National Security Act of 1947," *Hearing*, June 27, 1947, pp. 22, 25–27, 28. Witnesses in the secret hearing were originally identified as Mr. A through Mr. F, Dulles being Mr. B. In 1982 at the request of Congressman Robert McClory, the transcript was released, the names supplied, and the modified document republished.

3. Senate hearings in Williams, *Legislative History of the Central Intelligence Agency*, pp. 31–32.

4. Dulles to Bruce, June 27, 1947, folder "Central Intelligence Agency 1947," Box 29, FE.

5. Rhodri Jeffreys-Jones, "W. Somerset Maugham: Anglo-American Agent in Revolutionary Russia," *American Quarterly* 28(Spring 1976): 90–106; Leonard Mosley, *Dulles*, pp. 9, 14, 16.

6. Corson, *The Armies of Ignorance*, pp. 116, 295–96.

7. Karalekas History, p. 11, and Mosley, *Dulles*, p. 240.

8. *New York Herald Tribune*, March 4, 1951; Karalekas History, p. 11.

9. See, for example, Baldwin, "Intelligence–IV," *New York Times*, July 24, 1948.

10. Frank Wisner quoted in Mosley, *Dulles*, p. 343.

11. See Corson, *Armies of Ignorance*, pp. 292–93.

12. Cline, *CIA*, pp. 119, 128; Karalekas History, p. 11.

13. Rositzke, *The CIA's Secret Operations*, pp. 12, 23.

14. Hillenkoetter memo, Aug. 8, 1947, folder 129, Box 20, R.G. 218, WDL.

15. "Russian intentions," enclosed with Hillenkoetter memo cited in note 14.

16. Ibid.

17. Evaluation of "Russian intentions," Aug. 8, 1947, enclosed with Hillenkoetter memo.

18. All quotations from Laqueur, *A World of Secrets*, pp. 111–12.

19. This viewpoint persisted into the 1980s. In August 1984 journalist Tad Szulc reported that "a recently completed U.S. intelligence study" pointed to the incompetence of American intelligence agencies in monitoring Soviet atomic research, 1940–49: Szulc, "When the Russians Rocked the World," London *Times*, Aug. 28, 1984.

20. Herken, *The Winning Weapon*, pp. 231, 379 *n* 34.

21. "The Death of Philippine President Roxas," CIA Special Evaluation No. 30, April 16, 1949, File 129, Box 20, RG 218, WDL.

22. "Clandestine Air Transport Operations by U.S. Citizens and U.S. Owned Aircraft in Areas Outside the U.S.," June 1, 1948, and Hillenkoetter memo, Dec. 13, 1948, both in File 129, Box 20, RG 218, WDL.

23. "Political Parties in Israel," CIA intelligence Memo No. 108, Dec. 28, 1949, file "NSC/CIA(S-11)—Intelligence Memoranda. Dec. 1948–Dec. 1949," Box 2, NSCT.

24. "Resignation plans of Generalissimo Chiang Kai-shek" (Memo, signed by Hillenkoetter), Dec. 16, 1948, File 129, Box 20, RG 218, WDL. On the predictability of a Kuomintang collapse by the fall of 1948, see Nancy B. Tucker, *Patterns in the Dust: Chinese-American Relations and the Recognition Controversy, 1949–1950* (New York: Columbia University Press, 1983), pp. 59–60 and passim.

25. Snow, *Red Star Over China*, p. 102, n. 1. The book sold twelve thousand copies in the first four weeks: see Jerry Israel, "Mao's 'Mr. America': Edgar Snow's Images of China," *Pacific Historical Review* 47(1978):107–22.

26. Secretary of State Dean Acheson's 1949 view, quoted in David McLean, "American Nationalism, the China Myth, and the Truman Doctrine: The Question of Accom-

modation with Peking, 1949–50," *Diplomatic History* 10(Winter 1986):36. The State Department's "China White Paper," published in the same year, stated the same view.

27. Donovan to Forrestal, Aug. 14, 1947, Box 73, JVF.

28. Quotation from ibid. See also, Rogow, *Forrestal*, p. 334.

29. William D. Leahy, *I Was There* (London: Victor Gollancz, 1950), pp. 152–70. For a glimpse of Vichy tactics, see Roger Austin, "Surveillance and Intelligence under the Vichy Regime: The Service du Contrôle Technique, 1939–45," *Intelligence and National Security* 1(January 1986):123–37.

30. Quoted in Rogow, *Forrestal*, pp. 334–35.

31. See Rogow, *Forrestal*, p. 332.

32. Forrestal to Donovan, Oct. 9, 1947, Box 73, JVF.

33. Alfred McCoy, *The Politics of Heroin in Southeast Asia* (New York: Harper, 1972), pp. 31, 38, 42, 44.

34. Donald R. Whitnah, "United States Information Agency," in *Government Agencies*, ed. Donald R. Whitnah, The Greenwood Encyclopedia of American Institutions, vol. 7 (Westport, Conn.: Greenwood, 1983), p. 554.

35. Bradley Smith, *Shadow Warriors*, p. 180.

36. Karalekas History, p. 29.

37. George F. Kennan's testimony to the Church committee, Oct. 28, 1975, quoted in Karalekas History, p. 31.

38. Ford quoted in the *San Francisco Examiner*, Sept. 16, 1976. An analysis of U.S. interventions in "pro-Western" democracies and elsewhere in the period 1965–75 appeared in United States Congress, House of Representatives, Select Committee on Intelligence, *CIA: The Pike Report* (London: Spokesman, 1977), p. 16.

39. NSC 1/2, Feb. 10, 1948, quoted in Smith, "The Fear of Subversion," p. 140.

40. Faenza and Fini, *Gli americani in Italia*, pp. 10, 28, 180.

41. Corson, *Armies of Ignorance*, pp. 295–98.

42. Powers, *The Man Who Kept the Secrets*, pp. 35ff; Holt and Van de Velde, *Strategic Psychological Operations*, p. 183. See, also, Radosh, *American Labor*.

43. Colby, *Honorable Men*, p. 109; Copeland, *Without Cloak or Dagger*, p. 11.

44. Hoover Commission finding reported by Joseph and Stewart Alsop, *Washington Post*, Dec. 2, 1948.

45. Dewey quoted in Stephen J. Spingarn, "A Basic Program for the Vitalization of the National Defense Establishment Organization (and its lower echelons) relating to Overseas Counter Intelligence . . . Addendum of April 16, 1948," p. 23, folder 1, Box 1, SJS; *Washington Post*, April 9, 1948.

46. William M. Simms, "Straight Story of the Revolt in Colombia," *Washington News*, April 21, 1948.

47. Spingarn, "Basic Program. . . . Addendum," p. 23.

48. Duncan Aikman, "Fanatical Colombian Rightists Share Good Part of Blame," *PM*, April 20, 1948, text in Folder 1, Box 1, SJS.

49. "Functions of Central Intelligence Agency," typescript of a hearing before the intelligence subcommittee of the House Committee on Expenditures, April 15, 1948, p. 2, file "NSC/CIA—Memos to Director—1948," Box 3, NSCT.

50. Spingarn, "Basic Program . . . Addendum," p. 23.

51. Spingarn, "Basic Program . . . Addendum," p. 25; Marquis Childs, "Uncoordinated Security," *Washington Post*, April 22, 1948; "Functions of Central Intelligence Agency," pp. 11, 12.

52. Trask, "The Impact of the Cold War," p. 280.

53. *Washington News*, April 17, 1948.

54. George T. Mazuzan and J. Samuel Walker, *Controlling the Atom: The Beginnings of Nuclear Regulation 1946–1962* (Berkeley: University of California Press,

1984), pp. 11–12; memo, John R. Steelman to President Truman (including excerpt from Devitt's April 21 speech), April 24, 1948, OF Box 1656, File 1290–B, "Central Intelligence Agency," HST.

55. Wilmoore Kendall, "The Function of Intelligence," *World Politics* 1(1948–49):549. On Kendall, see Hilsman, *Strategic Intelligence*, p. 123.

56. See, for example, the comments by the military historian Walter Millis in Millis, ed., *The Forrestal Diaries*, p. 427.

57. Charter of the Organization of American States (signed April 30, 1948), in James W. Gantenbein, comp. and ed., *The Evolution of Our Latin-American Policy: A Documentary Record* (New York: Columbia University Press, 1950), pp. 855–71, at p. 859; Walter LaFeber, *Inevitable Revolutions: The United States in Central America* (New York: Norton, 1984), pp. 93–98.

58. Spingarn, "Basic Program . . . Addendum"; Karalekas History, p. 29.

59. For the text of NSC 10/2, see Thomas H. Etzold and John L. Gaddis, eds., *Containment: Documents on American Policy and Strategy, 1945–1950* (New York: Columbia University Press, 1978), pp. 126–28.

60. Kim Philby, *My Silent War*, p. 158.

61. Hunt, *Undercover*, p. 66.

62. Memo, Robert Blum to Souers, Jan. 19, 1948, file "NSC/CIA—Memos to Director—1948," Box 3, NSCT.

63. Mosley, *Dulles*, p. 246; Spingarn, "Memorandum for File on SJS CI Program," May 10, 1948, Folder 2, Box 1, SJS.

64. Dulles quoted in Laqueur, *World of Secrets*, p. 311.

65. Quotations from the abridged text in Leary, ed., *The Central Intelligence Agency*, pp. 137, 140.

66. Baldwin, *The Price of Power*, p. 215; Baldwin, "Intelligence-I . . . V," *New York Times*, July 20, 22, 23, 24, and 25, 1948.

67. Ferdinand Eberstadt Diary, May 6, 10, 15, 1948, and Baldwin to Eberstadt with attached commentary on Eberstadt proposals, March 18, 1949, all in FE.

68. Commission on the Organization of the Executive Branch of the Government (the Hoover Commission), *Task Force Report on National Security Organization* (Washington, D.C.: Jan. 13, 1949), pp. 16, 96.

69. Kent, *Strategic Intelligence for American World Policy*, pp. 99, 100, 102; memo, J. Patrick Coyne to Souers, July 13, 1949, Chronological File, Box 10, NSCT.

70. Kendall, "Function of Intelligence," pp. 548–52.

71. *Washington Times Herald*, June 13, 1948.

72. Williams, *Legislative History*, pp. 135–36, 159, 169.

73. *Washington Star*, June 1, 1949.

74. Karalekas History, p. 31.

75. Mickelson, *America's Other Voice*, pp. 40, 42, 65.

76. Radosh, *American Labor and United States Foreign Policy*, p. 323; *New York Times*, Feb. 17, 1967.

77. Memo, June 1, 1948, in Folder 129, Box 20, WDL.

78. Attorney Irving R. M. Panzer's notes, made in 1980 for the purpose of legal proceedings, on the CIA's classified "History of Air America, 1946–1971," quoted in William M. Leary and William Stueck, "The Chennault Plan to Save China: U.S. Containment in Asia and the Origins of the CIA's Aerial Empire, 1949–1950," *Diplomatic History* 8(Fall 1984):363. See also, Leary and Stueck, "Chennault Plan," pp. 349–50, 353–54, 353n16, 357, 367; Marchetti and Marks, *The CIA and the Cult of Intelligence*, pp. 149–60; William M. Leary, *Perilous Mission*, pp. 110, 200.

79. Philby, *Silent War*, p. 160.

80. Andrew, *Secret Service*, p. 493.

81. Souers to Truman, Dec. 27, 1963, file "Correspondence. Harry S. Truman," Box 1, SWS.

82. Souers interview, Dec. 16, 1954, PPF Memoirs file (Associates), Folder "Souers, Sidney, Dec. 15–16, 1954," p. 5, HST; Philby, *Silent War*, p. 160.

83. Cline, *CIA*, p. 76.

84. *Foreign Relations of the United States: 1950* 1:237–92.

Chapter 4
SURVIVING McCARTHY

1. Bruce Cumings, "Introduction," in Cumings, ed., *Child of Conflict*, p. 31.

2. Stueck, *The Road to Confrontation*, p. 177; John W. Spanier, *The Truman-MacArthur Controversy*, p. 22; *Washington Post*, July 27, 1950.

3. "The USSR and the Korean Invasion," CIA Intelligence Memo No. 300, June 28, 1950, file "NSC/CIA(5): Memos for Director—1949 [sic]," Box 3, NSCT.

4. Ambrose, *Ike's Spies*, p. 170.

5. Senator Joseph C. O'Mahoney as quoted in Stephen Pelz, "U.S. Decisions on Korean Policy, 1943–1950: Some Hypotheses," in Cumings, ed., *Child of Conflict*, p. 130.

6. CIA National Intelligence Estimate, "Chinese Communist Intervention in Korea," Nov. 8, 1950, *Foreign Relations of the United States, 1950*, 7:1102. See also, Harry Temple, "Deaf Captains: Intelligence, Policy, and the Origins of the Korean War," *International Studies Notes of the International Studies Association* 8(Fall-Winter 1981–1982):19; Roger Hilsman, *Strategic Intelligence and National Decisions*, p. 89; Stueck, *Road to Confrontation*, pp. 243, 254.

7. Memo, "Probable Soviet Reaction to Full-Scale U.S. Mobilization," Walter Bedell Smith to NSC, Dec. 11, 1950, Gen PSF, Box 114, Folder "Central Intelligence Agency," HST.

8. Walter Bedell Smith, *My Three Years in Moscow*, pp. 309, 324.

9. U.S. Senate, Hearing, Executive Session, "Nomination of Lieutenant General Walter Bedell Smith to be Director of Central Intelligence Agency," Aug. 24, 1950, Box 3, WBS.

10. Smith to Arthur J. McChrystal, Sept. 26, 1950, Box 14, WBS.

11. Mosley, *Dulles*, p. 369.

12. Tom Braden, "The Birth of the CIA," *American Heritage* 28(Feb. 1977):13.

13. Transcript, Allen W. Dulles oral history interview, May 17–June 3, 1965, by Philip A. Crowl, p. 65, SGM.

14. *New York Herald Tribune*, March 4, 1951.

15. In a 1979 interview with John Bross (formerly director for plans, East European Division, CIA) quoted in Price, *The DCI's Role*, p. 17.

16. Langer, *In and Out of the Ivory Tower*, pp. 210, 212.

17. William L. Langer and S. Everett Gleason, *The Challenge to Isolation: The World Crisis of 1937–1940 and American Foreign Policy*, 2 vols. (New York: Harper & Row, 1952).

18. Karalekas History, p. 18 n12.

19. Karalekas History, p. 31; Price, *DCI's Role*, p. 97.

20. See, for example, Cline, *CIA*, pp. 129, 139–40.

21. Karalekas History, pp. 17–23; Kirkpatrick, *The U.S. Intelligence Community*, p. 29; Bamford, *The Puzzle Palace*, pp. 2–3.

22. "Nomination of Smith," p. 7.

23. Smith to John E. Bierwirth, Aug. 23, 1950, Box 13, WBS.

24. Hook to Smith, Sept. 25, Smith to Hook, Sept. 27, 1950, Box 14, WBS; Steinfels, *The Neoconservatives*, p. 29.

25. Walter Bedell Smith, "Message to the Jewish Labor Committee," Sept. 29, 1950, Box 14, WBS. Also: correspondence, Sept. 12 to Nov. 16, 1950, with Jewish Labor Committee sponsors including Dubinsky and Socialist Party of America leader Norman Thomas, Box 14, WBS, and Memo, "JSE" to Smith, Oct. 30, 1950, on Wisner's introductions to labor leaders Dubinsky, Matthew Woll, George Meany (secretary-treasurer of the AFL, president from 1952, and president of AFL-CIO after the 1955 merger), and Jay Lovestone, Box 13, WBS.

26. *Miami Herald*, Dec. 11, 1950.

27. Lansdale, *In the Midst of Wars*, p. 373 and passim. On Lansdale's employment by the CIA, see W. Bedell Smith to Major General Leland S. Hobbs, Jan. 9, 1951, EGL.

28. Braden quoted in Radosh, *American Labor and United States Foreign Policy*, p. 323.

29. Transcript, John A. McCone oral history interview, Aug. 19, 1970, by Joe B. Frantz, p. 24, LBJ; U.S. National Students Association President William T. Dentzer to John Sherman, Nov. 10, 1951, and NSA Vice-President Avrea Ingram, Jr., to Gordon Gray, n.d. (arrived at PSB ca. Dec. 5, 1951), 080 "U.S. NSA," Box 4, PSB.

30. Rubin, *Paved with Good Intentions*, p. 77.

31. Karalekas History, pp. 36–38.

32. Eisenhower to Doolittle, July 26, 1954, in "Report on the Covert Activites of the Central Intelligence Agency" (the Doolittle Report, Sept. 30, 1954), p. 54, in unlabeled box, MMHB.

33. Doolittle Report, p. 26.

34. See Jeffreys-Jones, "Socio-Educational Composition CIA Elite."

35. Alsop, *The Center*, pp. 228–29, 233.

36. See Jeffreys-Jones, "Socio-Educational Composition CIA Elite," and Gabriel Kolko, *The Roots of American Foreign Policy: An Analysis of Power and Purpose* (Boston: Beacon, 1969), pp. 14, 16–17, 141n6. Nineteen percent of Kolko's "key federal executive appointees" had attended the three elite schools, compared with 28 percent in the CIA leadership sample shown in the appendix.

37. Sixty percent of the Russian experts compared with the CIA's 28 percent: Hugh De Santis, *The Diplomacy of Silence: The American Foreign Service, the Soviet Union, and the Cold War, 1933–1947* (Chicago: University of Chicago Press, 1980), pp. 6–8, 13.

38. Smith, *Portrait of a Cold Warrior*, p. 13.

39. Kolko noted in 1969 that "an increasingly larger percentage" of the "highest federal executives" was now coming from the "non-Ivy League schools": *Roots of American Foreign Policy*, p. 15. In the previous year, Alsop asserted that "real power" in the CIA passed, after the Bay of Pigs (1961) from the "Ivy Leaguers" to the "Prudent Professionals": *The Center*, pp. 228–29. According to one former CIA official historian, Agency officials realized that there was an imbalance and set out to rectify socio-educational anomalies just as, later, the U.S. government as a whole moved toward equal opportunity for blacks and women: Unattributable Source C. However, no figures are available to support these assertions. The CIA appears to have employed blacks in a client capacity rather than as potential top officials and to have debarred women from high positions in much the same way as other federal bureaucracies: see Dan Schechter, Michael Ansara, and David Kolodney, "The CIA as an Equal Opportunity Employer," *Ramparts* 7(June 1968–69):25–33, and David Blundy, "Revolting Women Rattle the CIA," London *Sunday Times*, Jan. 3, 1982.

40. With the exceptions of Kennedy and Ford, every president since 1945 has been an "outsider" in the sense of not having attended an Ivy League school. This factor

appears to have meant more to some (notably Truman, Nixon, and Carter) than to others (especially Eisenhower). None of the leading Senate critics were Eastern establishment: Joe McCarthy, Mike Mansfield, Eugene McCarthy, George McGovern, Frank Church, Walter Mondale, or Barry Goldwater.

41. David Atlee Phillips, *The Night Watch* (New York: Atheneum, 1977), p. 35; Colby, *Honorable Men*, pp. 127–28.

42. Meyer, *Facing Reality*, pp. 50, 53.

43. Steinfels, *Neoconservatives*, p. 30.

44. Mosley, *Dulles*, p. 294.

45. Ambrose, *Ike's Spies*, p. 174.

46. Mosley, *Dulles*, p. 77.

47. Jeffreys-Jones, *American Espionage*, p. 46 and passim.

48. *Washington Post*, Jan. 9 and 27, 1953.

49. Roger W. Jones (director, Legislative Reference, Bureau of the Budget) to William J. Hopkins (White House staff), Sept. 22, 1950, Bill file H.R. 9490, HST; Veto message, Sept. 22, 1950, in Theoharris, ed., *The Truman Presidency*, p. 312.

50. Karalekas History, pp. 39–40.

51. McCarthy quoted in David Caute, *The Great Fear: The Anti-Communist Purge under Truman and Eisenhower* (London: Secker & Warburg, 1978), pp. 45–46.

52. McCarthy paraphrased in Reeves, *The Life and Times of Joe McCarthy*, p. 502.

53. Ambrose, *Eisenhower*, p. 189.

54. Oshinsky, *A Conspiracy so Immense*, p. 324.

55. Braden, *Diplomats and Demagogues*, p. 350.

56. *Chicago Tribune*, July 23, 1953.

57. *Washington Post*, July 13, 1953; *Davenport (Iowa) Democrat*, July 23, 1953.

58. *Washington Star*, July 15, 1953; *New York Times*, July 26, 1953.

59. *Congressional Record*, July 9, 1953, pp. 8583–84; Ambrose, *Ike's Spies*, p. 175; Smith, *OSS*, p. 370.

60. Meyer, *Facing Reality*, p. 71, 77, 79–80.

61. Meyer, *Facing Reality*, pp. 83–84.

62. Dulles, "Off the Record Talk" to Overseas Press Club, May 13, 1954, Box 61, AWD.

63. Smith to Kennan, Sept. 15, Nov. 24, 1950; Kennan to Smith, Sept. 7, 19, 1950, Box 14, WBS.

64. Kennan, *Memoirs*, p. 177.

65. Newfield, *Robert Kennedy*, pp. 78–79.

66. *Baltimore Sun*, Feb. 17, 1967.

67. Braden quoted in Smith, *OSS*, p. 368.

68. Transcript, Roger Hilsman oral history interview, Aug. 10, 1970, by Dennis J. O'Brien, p. 10, JFK.

69. United Press report in *Washington Post*, July 21, 1953.

70. Quotations in Ambrose, *Ike's Spies*, p. 187.

71. Quotations from Hanson B. Baldwin, "Myopia on Intelligence," *New York Times*, June 3, 1954.

72. Oshinsky, *Conspiracy*, p. 325n.

73. *New York Times*, June 3, 1954; Dulles to Baldwin, June 28, 1954, Box 61, AWD; Dulles to Baldwin, July 12, 1954, Baldwin to Dulles, July 19, 1954, both in Box 4, HWB. The *St. Louis Post-Dispatch* (Sept. 23, 1961) was one newspaper that repeated Baldwin's billion-dollar claim, which is now generally taken to be true: see Ambrose, *Eisenhower the President*, p. 395.

74. Baldwin to Dulles, July 6, 1954, Box 4, HWB.

75. Dulles to Arthur S. Fleming, Nov. 16, 1954, Box 61, AWD.

76. Compiled from data in John Costa, *Legislation Introduced Relative to the Activities of the Intelligence Agencies, 1947–1972* (Washington, D.C.: Congressional Research Service, 1972), pp. 3–14.

77. See Harry H. Ransom, "Secret Intelligence in the United States, 1947–1982: The CIA's Search for Legitimacy," in Andrew and Dilks, eds., *The Missing Dimension*, pp. 207–8.

78. Dulles to James E. Mooney, Nov. 14, 1955, Box 68, AWD.

79. See Henry M. Wriston, *Executive Agents in American Foreign Relations* (Baltimore: Johns Hopkins University Press, 1929).

80. Costa, *Legislation Introduced*, pp. 5–6, 11; Ransom, *The Intelligence Establishment*, pp. 167–71; Ransom, "Secret Intelligence," p. 208.

81. Dulles, *The Craft of Intelligence*, p. 235; Ransom, "Secret Intelligence," p. 208.

82. Transcript, Richard Helms oral history interview, Sept. 16, 1981, by Ted Gittinger, p. 8, LBJ.

83. E. J. Applewhite, who retired from the CIA's inspectorate in 1970, stressed the dangers of atrophy in a telephone conversation with the author, Aug. 6, 1983. On the advantages of organizational continuity, see Ernest R. May, "Conclusions: Capabilities and Proclivities," in May, ed., *Knowing One's Enemies*, pp. 533–34.

Chapter 5

THE GOLDEN AGE OF OPERATIONS

1. Transcript in WHCF Name File under Schorr, GRF.

2. "Unauthorized Storage of Toxic Agents," *Hearings before the Select Committee to Study Governmental Operations with Respect to Intelligence Activities of the United States Senate*, 94 Cong., 1 sess., pursuant to S. Res. 21, 7 vols., Vol. 1, Sept. 16, 17, and 18, 1975, pp. 5, 189–90; on the "Health Alteration Committee," see Mosley, *Dulles*, p. 459.

3. Henry S. Commager, "'Intelligence': The Constitution betrayed," *The New York Review of Books* (Sept. 30, 1976), p. 33. Among those who agreed with Commager were foreign service veteran Thomas A. Donovan, the CIA's African specialist John Stockwell, French journalist Claude Julien, and English historian Arnold Toynbee: Donovan, "The CIA Investigation: Asking the Unthinkable?" *Foreign Service Journal* 52(1975):20; Stockwell, "A CIA Trip—from Belief, to Doubt, to Despair," *Center Magazine* 12(1979):20, 28; Julien, *L'Empire américain* (Paris: B. Grosset, 1968), pp. 307, 347–48; Toynbee quoted in McGarvey, *The Myth and the Madness*, p. 32.

4. Hilsman quoted in Blackstock, *The CIA and the Intelligence Community*, p. 14.

5. "Unauthorized Storage," p. 21.

6. Quoted in Gaddis, *Strategies of Containment*, pp. 157–58.

7. Mickelson, *America's Other Voice*, pp. (vii), 26, 27. The penultimate quotation is of Edward W. Barrett, a member, in 1949–50, of the Free Europe Committee which was the conduit for CIA funds to RFE. The last one is of Frank Altschul, chairman in 1950 of RFE's supervisory committee.

8. Edward P. Lilly, "The Psychological Strategy Board and its Predecessors: Foreign Policy Coordination 1938–1953," in Vincitorio, ed., *Studies in Modern History*, pp. 337–53, 353*n*17.

9. Memo, George E. Taylor to Raymond B. Allen, Feb. 3, 1952, 350.05, Box 28, PSB.

10. Lilly, "Psychological Strategy Board," p. 366.

11. My emphasis.

12. W. Y. Elliott to Raymond B. Allen, July 11, 1952, 091 Germany, Folder 1, File 1, Box 6, PSB.

13. Untitled nine-page analysis enclosed with the above letter and signed by Henry A. Kissinger.

14. James E. Miller, "Taking Off the Gloves: The United States and the Italian Election of 1948," *Diplomatic History* 7(Winter 1983):43.

15. Quoted in Ambrose, *Eisenhower: President*, p. 226.

16. Eisenhower, private letter to Lewis Douglass, March 29, 1955, quoted in Gaddis, *Strategies of Containment*, p. 159. Emphasis in the original.

17. David Haight, "The Papers of C. D. Jackson: A Glimpse at President Eisenhower's Psychological Warfare Expert," *Manuscripts* (Winter 1976): 29, 31, 36; "C.D. Jackson," Sept. 25, 1964 (a tribute that appeared in Time, Inc.'s house organ at the time of Jackson's death and was sent in 1975 to Haight at the Eisenhower Library, then kindly supplied to the author), pp. 1, 3; Eisenhower, *The Eisenhower Diaries*, pp. 238, 273; Ambrose, *Eisenhower: President*, pp. 147–48.

18. L. Natarajan, *American Shadow Over India* (Bombay: People's Publishing House, 1952), p. 194.

19. Graham Greene, *Ways of Escape*, p. 163.

20. Graham Greene, *The Quiet American*, p. 20.

21. Steinfels, *The Neoconservatives*, p. 84.

22. Malcolm Muggeridge, "Books," *Esquire* 68(Sept. 1967):12.

23. See J. W. Schulte Nordholt, "Anti-Americanism in European Culture: Its Early Manifestations," and Marcus Cunliffe, "Anti-Americanism as a European Phenomenon," in Kroes and van Rossem, eds., *Anti-Americanism in Europe*.

24. Shackley, *The Third Option*, p. (xiii).

25. "The Death of Philippine President Roxas," CIA Special Evaluation No. 30, April 16, 1948, in Folder 129, Box 20, WDL.

26. Lansdale, *In the Midst of Wars*, pp. (ix), 4, 16, 371–372.

27. On Lansdale's terms of service with the CIA in the early 1950s: W. Bedell Smith to Major General Leland S. Hobbs, Jan. 9, 1951, Box 34, EGL. Allen Dulles later expressed his appreciation for what Lansdale had done "in the Philippines and Vietnam during the period we were working so closely together": Dulles to Lansdale, Nov. 21, 1963, Box 37, EGL.

28. William P. Bundy, "Foreword" to Blaufarb, *The Counterinsurgency Era*, p. (x).

29. Blaufarb, *Counterinsurgency Era*, pp. 32–33.

30. Ambrose, *Ike's Spies*, p. 213.

31. See Solberg, *Oil Power*, pp. 12–13, 192–93.

32. See Rositzke, *The CIA's Secret Operations*, p. 188; Rubin, *Paved with Good Intentions*, p. 82.

33. Acheson, *Present at the Creation*, p. 506.

34. Kermit Roosevelt, *Countercoup* (New York: McGraw-Hill, 1979), p. 6; Ambrose, *Ike's Spies*, p. 197; Rubin, *Paved with Good Intentions*, pp. 77–78.

35. Roosevelt, *Countercoup*.

36. Under threat of litigation, Roosevelt's publishers had to withdraw from sale the original version of the book, re-issuing it later after the deletion of certain references to Anglo-Iranian Oil. See Roosevelt, *Countercoup* (unpurged edition), pp. 7, 107, and Rubin, *Paved with Good Intentions*, p. 385n26.

37. In his autobiographical *Something Ventured* (p. 118), former British intelligence official C. M. Woodhouse confirmed Eveland's account (*Ropes of Sand*, pp. 108–09).

38. Phillips, *The Night Watch*, pp. 42–43.

39. Phillips, *The Night Watch*, p. 48; Leary, *Perilous Mission*, p. 211; Lucien S.

Vandenbroucke, "The 'Confessions' of Allen Dulles: New Evidence on the Bay of Pigs," *Diplomatic History* 8(Fall 1984):373.

40. Immerman, *The CIA in Guatemala*, p. 102; Souers interview, Dec. 16, 1954, PPF Memoirs file (Associates), Folder "Souers, Sidney, Dec. 15–16, 1954," HST, p. 5.

41. Julien, *L'Empire américain*, pp. 330, 333; Ambrose, *Ike's Spies*, p. 223; Schlesinger and Kinzer, *Bitter Fruit*, pp. 23, 91–93, 97.

42. Eisenhower quoted in Phillips, *Night Watch*, p. 51.

43. Corson, *The Armies of Ignorance*, p. 341.

44. Richard Bissell's account quoted and paraphrased in Ambrose, *Ike's Spies*, p. 241.

45. Karalekas History, p. 51.

46. A 1967 CIA memorandum quoted in "Foreign and Military Intelligence" (Final Report . . . Book 1), *Senate Report*, 94 Cong., 2 sess., no. 94–755 (April 26, 1976), p. 52.

47. Gray quoted in Ambrose, *Ike's Spies*, p. 240.

48. Helms quoted in "Foreign and Military Intelligence," p. 46.

49. Rositzke, *CIA's Secret Operations*, p. 239.

50. John Foster Dulles quoted in Divine, *Foreign Policy*, p. 51.

51. Gaddis, *Strategies of Containment*, p. 155.

52. Mickelson, *America's Other Voice*, pp. 98–102; Ambrose, *Eisenhower: President*, p. 444.

53. C. D. Jackson to Allen Dulles, Oct. 9, 1957, July 2, 1958 (with résumé of exchanges with Cord Meyer), Dec. 9, 1958, and May 12, 1959, all in Folder "Allen Dulles," Box 40, CDJ.

54. Ambrose, *Ike's Spies*, pp. 245–51; Lederer and Burdick, *The Ugly American*, pp. 108, 207. The name of one character in *The Ugly American*, Colonel Hillendale, is a composite of Hillenkoetter and Lansdale, and the authors' sympathy with Lansdale's aims and methods may be discerned in the text as well as in correspondence: Lederer to Lansdale, March 1, Oct. 28, 1957, Box 38, EGL.

55. Barron, *KGB*, p. 67; Laqueur, *A World of Secrets*, p. 238.

56. Smith, *Portrait of a Cold Warrior*, p. 163.

57. Donovan, "CIA Investigation," 20.

58. "Foreign and Military Intelligence," Appendix III, pp. 557–62.

59. According to Agency files as interpreted by E. Henry Knoche (deputy director of the CIA, 1976–77): Knoche, "Note for the Director," June 17, 1975, Folder "Central Intelligence Agency 1/1/75–6/30/75," FG 6-2, Subj. WHCF, GRF.

60. Eisenhower quoted in Ambrose, *Eisenhower: President*, p. 507.

61. "Alleged Assassination Plots Involving Foreign Leaders" (An Interim Report of the Select Committee to Study Governmental Operations with Respect to Intelligence Activities), *Senate Report*, 94 Cong., 1 sess., no. 94–465 (Nov. 20, 1975), p. 92.

62. Transcript quoted in Stephen G. Rabe, "Eisenhower and the Overthrow of Rafael Trujillo" (paper at conference of the Society for Historians of American Foreign Relations, June 28, 1985), p. 11.

63. "Alleged Assassination Plots," pp. 14–15, 19, 24–25, 195.

64. Miller, "Taking off the Gloves," p. 54. James E. Miller was an employee of the Historical Office of the Department of State.

65. Transcript, Roger Hilsman oral history interview, Aug. 14, 1970, by Dennis J. O'Brien, p. 11, JFK.

66. Matthias, memo, "Trends in the World Situation," p. 43. Circulating the Matthias memo on June 9, 1964, Sherman Kent noted it had "general Board approval": CIA vol. 1, Agency File, NSFJ.

67. Stockwell, "CIA Trip," 20.

68. The suicides of James Forrestal and Frank Wisner suggest that not every action man is above self-doubt.

69. On the superiority of British to American spy fiction, see Robin W. Winks, *Modus Operandi: An Excursion into Detective Fiction* (Boston: Godine, 1982), p. 66.

70. Some of these files are in the National Archives and the Truman Library, but the largest concentration is in the Allen W. Dulles Papers, SGM: see Boxes 61, 259, and elsewhere.

71. Quoted in Mosley, *Dulles*, p. 6.

72. See Box 61 and elsewhere in AWD for the titles and texts of various addresses.

73. See Box 110, AWD for arrangements to publicize Dulles, *The Craft of Intelligence*.

74. In a conversation on Aug. 6, 1983, E. Fletcher Prouty told the author that he saw a uniformed Hunt working on the Dulles book on a fulltime basis. At the time, Prouty was "Focal Point Officer for contacts between the CIA and the Department of Defense on matters pertaining to the military support of the Special Operations of that Agency": Prouty, *The Secret Team*, p. (vii). Hunt's novels were less effective than they might have been in boosting the CIA's fortunes because they revealed so many of his right-wing prejudices. For an analysis, see Earle D. Davis, "Howard Hunt and the Peter Ward-CIA Spy Novels," *Kansas Quarterly* 10(1978).

75. CIA director Richard Helms was bitter about the way in which some congressmen supported covert operations when they were prestigious and then, later, claimed they had not known about them: transcript, Richard Helms oral history interview, Sept. 16, 1981; by Ted Gittinger, p. 6, LBJ. B. Hugh Tovar, a former chief of the CIA's covert action staff, in 1980 acknowledged "our failure to realize that times had changed" in the 1960s: Tovar, "Strengths and Weaknesses in Past U.S. Covert Action," in Godson, ed., *Intelligence Requirements*, p. 199.

Chapter 6
INTELLIGENCE IN THE GOLDEN AGE

1. *U.S. News and World Report*, March 19, 1954.

2. See James R. Killian, Jr., *Sputnik, Scientists and Eisenhower: A Memoir of the First Special Assistant to the President for Science and Technology* (Cambridge, Mass.: MIT Press, 1977), p. 222, and Price, *DCI's Role*, p. 75.

3. Ambrose, *Eisenhower: President*, pp. 189, 227.

4. Van Slyck quoted in Price, *DCI's Role*, p. 63.

5. Agency veteran Patrick J. McGarvey suggested that "the bromide about 'unsung successes'" was more characteristically a feature of the 1960s, when intelligence failures became more common: McGarvey, *The Myth and the Madness*, p. 15.

6. *U.S. News and World Report*, March 19, 1954.

7. Yakovlev, *CIA Target*, pp. 93–94.

8. Copeland, *Without Cloak or Dagger*, pp. 278–99.

9. Ryan, *Klaus Barbie and the United States Government*, p. 57.

10. See Mosley, *Dulles*, p. 275, and Hugh R. Trevor-Roper's introduction to Höhne and Zolling, *Network*, p. (xv).

11. Erickson, *The Road to Berlin*, pp. 135, 189, 432, 447; Gehlen, *The Gehlen Memoirs*, pp. 164, 204.

12. Gehlen, *Memoirs*, above.

13. Höhne and Zolling, *Network*, p. 308; Powers, *The Man Who Kept the Secrets*, pp. 46, 433n8.

14. Hood, *Mole*, p. 14; Golitsyn, *New Lies for Old*, p. 53.

15. Rositzke, *The CIA's Secret Operations*, pp. 67–69; Hood, *Mole*, p. 13.

16. Price, *DCI's Role*, p. 24; Karalekas History, p. 55.

17. Laqueur, *World of Secrets*, pp. 143–44.

18. Quoted in Laqueur, *World of Secrets*, p. 19.

19. Richard E. Sargent, "The Soviet-American Strategic Competition: The Action-Reaction Process Reconsidered" (Ph.D. diss., University of Edinburgh, 1976), 2 vols., 1:5, 2:766.

20. Laqueur, *World of Secrets*, p. 144.

21. Price, *DCI's Role*, pp. 21–23.

22. Both quotations from Ranelagh, *The Agency*, p. 295.

23. Price, *DCI's Role*, p. 24.

24. Wise and Ross, *The Invisible Government*, pp. 15, 29, and Powers, *The Man Who Kept the Secrets*, p. 117.

25. Freedman, *U.S. Intelligence*, p. 71; Cline, p. 178.

26. Price, *DCI's Role*, p. 23; Laqueur, *World of Secrets*, p. 144.

27. Killian, *Sputnik*, p. 222.

28. Laqueur, *World of Secrets*, p. 117; Ambrose, *Eisenhower: President*, p. 395.

29. Wilbur C. Eveland, *Ropes of Sand: America's Failure in the Middle East* (New York: Norton, 1980), p. 260; Neff, *Warriors at Suez*, pp. 134, 353, 354; Mosley, *Dulles*, pp. 415, 417; Laqueur, *World of Secrets*, p. 122; Ambrose, *Eisenhower: President*, pp. 256–57.

30. Chester L. Cooper, *The Lion's Last Roar: Suez, 1956* (New York: Harper & Row, 1978), p. 248.

31. Neff, *Warriors at Suez*, pp. 134, 353, 354. Dulles later wrote that "U.S. officials" who denied they had been warned about the impending Suez attack were referring merely to the allies' silence, though the "public received the impression" that the CIA had failed—an impression that went uncorrected because the Agency "did not advertise its achievement": Dulles, *The Craft of Intelligence*, p. 166.

32. Laqueur, *World of Secrets*, p. 147.

33. Laqueur, *World of Secrets*, pp. 154, 157.

34. *Reynolds News*, Feb. 22, 1959.

35. Louis J. Halle, *The Cold War as History* (London: Chatto & Windus, 1967), p. 366.

36. Transcript in memo, Stanley J. Grogan (assistant to the Director) to Dulles, Sept. 16, 1959, Box 80. AWD.

37. Grogan memo, above.

38. Dulles, "Memorandum for the Record," Sept. 17, Box 80, AWD.

39. On the Dulles-*Fortune* row: Memo, Hedley W. Donovan to Albert L. Furth, July 24, 1958, Box 40, CDJ. For the full-blown *Fortune* argument, see the Feb. 1957 issue, "A Report on the Soviet Empire," consisting of an editorial and four sections.

40. Allen W. Dulles, "Notes for Talk on Russian Aims and Methods as Seen By C.I.A.; Conference of National Organizations, Atlantic City, New Jersey, March 2, 1959," p. 2, Box 80, AWD.

41. "Statement by Allen W. Dulles, Director of Central Intelligence, to the Subcommittee on Economic Statistics of the Joint Economic Committee of the Congress of the United States, 13 November 1959," p. 25, Box 80, AWD.

42. Victoria Price paraphrasing Dulles's critics in Price, *DCI's Role*, p. 75. See, also, Laqueur, *World of Secrets*, p. 154.

43. Freedman, *U.S. Intelligence*, p. 71.

44. Killian, *Sputnik*, p. 84; James Bamford, "The Spy Plane that Flew into History," *Guardian Weekly*, May 11, 1986.

45. Michael R. Beschloss, *Mayday: Eisenhower, Khruschev and the U-2 Affair* (New York: Harper & Row, 1986), pp. 243, 257.

46. Walter LaFeber, *America, Russia, and the Cold War 1945–1971* (New York: John Wiley, 1972), p. 212; Sargent, "Soviet-American Strategic Competition," 1:345.

47. *New York Daily News*, Sept. 12, 1966; Kirkpatrick, *The U.S. Intelligence Community*, p. 54; Freedman, *U.S. Intelligence*, p. 72.

48. Karalekas History, p. 362; Powers, *Man Who Kept the Secrets*, pp. 127, 362; Verrier, *Through the Looking Glass*, p. 193, 195, 208; Cline, *CIA*, p. 222; Warren I. Cohen, *Dean Rusk* (Totowa, N.J.: Cooper Square Publishers, 1980), p. 159; Prados, *The Soviet Estimate*, pp. 104, 116–18; Freedman, *U.S. Intelligence*, p. 74; Kirkpatrick, *U.S. Intelligence Community*, p. 3.

49. In his scholarly analysis of U.S. intelligence reports in the 1950s and early 1960s, the historian Walter Laqueur suggests that the CIA neglected Soviet open sources until 1960, when the Agency remedied the deficiency: Laqueur, *World of Secrets*, p. 157.

50. Divine, *Foreign Policy 1952, 1960*, pp. 185, 191–92, 216, 257.

51. Transcript, John A. McCone oral history interview, Aug. 19, 1970, by Joe B. Frantz, LBJ, p. 17.

52. Ambrose, *Eisenhower: President*, pp. 598–99. See also Powers, *Man Who Kept the Secrets*, p. 256.

53. Author's conversation with R. Harris Smith (author of a forthcoming Houghton Mifflin biography), Shore Bar, Edinburgh, Oct. 3, 1986.

54. Nixon quoting himself in *The Memoirs of Richard Nixon*, 2 vols. (New York: Warner, 1979), 1:171.

55. Richard M. Nixon, *Six Crises*, pp. 353–54, 354n.

56. Parmet, *JFK*, p. 49.

57. John Pearson, *The Life of Ian Fleming* (London: Jonathan Cape, 1966), pp. 322, 323.

58. Kent M. Beck, "Necessary Lies, Hidden Truths: Cuba in the 1960 Campaign," *Diplomatic History* 8(Winter1984):37, 51; Ambrose, *Ike's Spies*, pp. 309–11.

Chapter 7
PRESIDENTIAL SHAKE-UP

1. Schlesinger, *A Thousand Days*, p. 113; Corson, *The Armies of Ignorance*, pp. 31–32.

2. Author's interview with McGeorge Bundy, Howard Hotel, Edinburgh, May 16, 1984; McGeorge Bundy, "The National Security Council in the 1960s," in Jackson, ed., *The National Security Council*, pp. 276–78; Allen W. Dulles to McGeorge Bundy, Feb. 5, 1961, folder "Congo 1/61–4/61," NSFK.

3. Bowles, *Promises to Keep*, pp. 391–92; Hilsman, *To Move a Nation*, p. 69; Hilsman, *Strategic Intelligence and National Decisions*, p. 177; transcript, Roger Hilsman oral history interview, Aug. 14, 1970, by Dennis J. O'Brien, pp. 4, 6, JFK.

4. Galbraith, entry for March 29, 1961, *Ambassador's Journal*, p. 51.

5. Schlesinger, *Thousand Days*, pp. 381–82; Hilsman, O'Brien interview, p. 4.

6. Hilsman, O'Brien interview, pp. 7, 13; Schlesinger, *Thousand Days*, pp 380ff; Sorensen, *Kennedy*, p. 301.

7. Transcript, John McCone oral history interview, July 26, 1976, by Thomas Soapes, pp. 33–35, DDE; transcript, Chester Cooper oral history interview, May 6, 1966, by Joseph E. O'Connor, p. 4, JFK.

8. Elmer Staatz quoted in Greenstein, *The Hidden-Hand Presidency*, p. 263n39.

9. William Manchester, *The Glory and the Dream: A Narrative History of America 1932–1972* (London: Michael Joseph, 1975), p. 900.

10. Richard M. Bissell, Jr., "Response to Lucien S. Vandenbroucke, 'The "Confessions" of Allen Dulles: New Evidence on the Bay of Pigs'," *Diplomatic History* 8(Fall 1984):380.

11. *Operation Zapata*, pp. 39, 43, 44, 47.

12. Corson, *Armies of Ignorance*, pp. 383–84; Hilsman, *To Move a Nation*, p. 31.

13. See Cline, p. 209, and Hilsman, *To Move a Nation*, p. 31.

14. Transcript, George Decker oral history interview, Dec. 18, 1972, by Dan H. Ralls, pp. 12–14, AMHI. President Kennedy noted that the anonymous leaks reaching the press after the Bay of Pigs seemed to blame everyone except the JCS, from which he deduced that the JCS was the source—implying that the JCS version of events was a self-exonerating one: Wyden, *Bay of Pigs*, p. 305.

15. Manuel Galich, "Playa Giron desde Buenos Aires, hace dos decadas," *Casa de las Américas*, 21 (March-April 1981):55–56; *Executive Sessions of the Senate Foreign Relations Committee* (Historical Series), vol. 131, Pt. 1, 87 Cong., 1 sess., 1961 (Washington, D.C.: GPO, 1984), p. 21; Luis E. Aguilar, "Introduction," *Operation Zapata*, p. (xii).

16. Fidel Castro (Castro Ruz), *Playa Giron, a Victory of the People*, seventy-nine-page text of television address delivered on April 23, 1961 (Havana: Editoriel en Mancha, 1961), pp. 5, 13, 75. See, also, Castro, "The True History of Cuba," together with editorial comment on the article, *Tricontinental* 88:4(1983):14, 20.

17. Szulc, *Compulsive Spy*, pp. 74–75.

18. Tully, *Central Intelligence Agency*, p. 50.

19. Grants story based on National Students' Association sources, *New York Times*, Feb. 15, 1967.

20. Memo, "The Situation in France and Algeria," Allen W. Dulles to the President, April 24, 1961, folder "Algeria 4/24–4/30/61," NSFK.

21. Bohlen, *Witness to History*, p. 479.

22. *The Kennedy Presidential Press Conferences* (London: Heyden, 1978), pp. 102, 108.

23. Tully, *Central Intelligence Agency*, p. 51; Kirkpatrick, *The U.S. Intelligence Community*, pp. 165–68. Tully was guessing at the "inside story" as an outsider; Kirkpatrick was a senior CIA veteran.

24. According to Peter Geismar, the CIA flew Fanon to the United States for leukemia treatment (he died there on Dec. 6, 1961); but the black revolutionary remained thoroughly distrustful of the Agency and refused to cooperate with his CIA interrogator, Ollie Iselin: Geismar, *Fanon* (New York: Dial, 1971), pp. 182–86.

25. "Blame the U.S.: New Jolt for Kennedy," *U.S. News and World Report* (May 15, 1961), p. 84.

26. C. D. Jackson to Allen Dulles, Oct. 9, 1957, in folder "Allen Dulles," Box 40, CDJ; Morris, *CIA and American Labor*, p. 101. The CIA's Wilbur Crane Eveland agrees that in late 1959/early 1960 "the African division was still being organized": *Ropes of Sand: America's Failure in the Middle East* (New York: Norton, 1980), p. 311.

27. In juxtaposition to the Nkrumah case which follows, it is interesting to consider the CIA's dalliance with the socialist, guerrilla-based opposition in Malawi. Information from a May 31, 1983, interview with Andrew C. Ross, a dissident prison chaplain rescued from the clutches of the Malawi authorities and put on a clandestine CIA flight from Zomba to Dar-es-Salaam in April 1965. Ross later became dean of the faculty of divinity at the University of Edinburgh and is a friend of the author.

28. Mahoney, *JFK*, p. 232.

29. Wise and Ross, *The Invisible Government*, pp. 254, 258; Gerard T. Rice, "The American Government's Harnessing of the Overseas Voluntary Spirit—The Peace

Corps," in Jeffreys-Jones and Collins, eds., *The Growth of Federal Power in American History*, pp. 139, 188n24; Mahoney, *JFK*, p. 232.

30. Madelaine G. Kalb, *The Congo Cables: The Cold War in Africa from Eisenhower to Kennedy* (New York: Macmillan, 1981), pp. 379–80.

31. Tully, *Central Intelligence Agency*, pp. 14–15; Blackstock, *The Strategy of Subversion*, p. 288; Wise and Ross, *Invisible Government*, pp. 179–82.

32. *Executive Sessions of the Senate Foreign Relations Committee* (Historical Series), Vol. 13, Pt. 1, 87 Cong., 1 sess., 1961 (Washington, D.C.: GPO, 1984), pp. 313–14 (text of Morse press statement issued on April 27, 1961), 337–84, 387–449, 503–39, 541–68.

33. *Executive Sessions*, pp. 410, 424, 449.

34. "Alleged Assassination Plots Involving Foreign Leaders" (An Interim Report of the Select Committee to Study Governmental Operations with Respect to Intelligence Activities), *Senate Report*, 94 Cong., 1 sess., no. 94–465, (Nov. 20, 1975), p. 51. See also Kalb, *Congo Cables*, pp. 189–90.

35. Schlesinger, *Robert Kennedy*, p. 459; Wyden, *Bay of Pigs*, p. 307; Schlesinger, *Thousand Days*, pp. 262–63; transcript, George Decker oral history interview, Dec. 18, 1972, by Dan H. Ralls, pp. 12–14, AMHI.

36. Schlesinger, *Thousand Days*, pp. 262–63.

37. Wyden, *Bay of Pigs*, p. 311. The account and wording are not significantly different in Alsop, *The Center*, p. 229.

38. Associated Press printout, Aug. 6, 1961, Box 95, AWD; transcript, Richard Helms oral history interview, Sept. 16, 1981, by Ted Gittinger, p. 5, LBJ.

39. Dulles planned and wrote a retaliatory article for *Harper's* magazine, putting much of the blame for the Bay of Pigs failure on President Kennedy. But discretion triumphed and he never published it; see Lucien S. Vandenbroucke, "The 'Confessions' of Allen Dulles: New Evidence on the Bay of Pigs," *Diplomatic History* 8(Fall 1984). See also Bissell, "Response," and Wyden, *Bay of Pigs*, p. 308.

40. Bowles, *Promises*, p. 392. On the impact of the Yew story in official circles and on presidential aide Arthur Schlesinger's reinforcing proposal of CIA abolition, see Hilsman, *To Move a Nation*, pp. 73, 79.

41. Exhibit 7, President Kennedy to Chiefs of Mission, May 29, 1961, in "Covert Action," *Hearings before the Select Committee to Study Governmental Operations with Respect to Intelligence Activities of the United States Senate*, 94 Cong., 1 sess., pursuant to S. Res. 21, 7 Vols., Vol. 7, Dec. 4 and 5, 1975, pp. 137–38. See also, Schlesinger, *Thousand Days*, pp. 381–82.

42. Senator John F. Kennedy quoted in Blaufarb, *The Counterinsurgency Era*, p. 53.

43. Schlesinger, *Thousand Days*, p. 95. The biographer John Pearson took a similar view of *Life*'s inclusion (March 17, 1961) of *From Russia with Love* among Kennedy's ten favorite books: Pearson, *The Life of Ian Fleming* (London: Jonathan Cape, 1966), p. 327.

44. Halberstam, *The Best and the Brightest*, pp. 159–60.

45. Lederer to Lansdale, Oct. 28, 1957, Box 38, EGL.

46. The word "de-Americanization," a variant of the later term "Vietnamization," is taken from the title of Lansdale's undated typescript "The De-Americanization of Vietnam," Box 8, EGL.

47. Kennedy's April 27, 1961, statement quoted in Blaufarb, *Counterinsurgency Era*, p. 54.

48. Taylor, *The Uncertain Trumpet*, p. 6.

49. *Operation Zapata*, pp. 43, 195–96, 277.

50. Helms, Gittinger interview, p. 5; Schlesinger, *Thousand Days*, p. 382.

51. "One of the department's most respected 'old hands'" paraphrased in Harris Wofford, *Of Kennedys and Kings: Making Sense of the Sixties* (New York: Farrar, Strauss & Giroux, 1980), p. 371.

52. Wise and Ross, *Invisible Government*, p. 178n.

53. Blaufarb, *Counterinsurgency Era*, p. 67.

54. Blaufarb, *Counterinsurgency Era*, p. 68; Schlesinger, *Robert Kennedy*, p. 477n.

55. Shannon, *The Heir Apparent*, p. 112; Wyden, *Bay of Pigs*, p. 289; Michael Forrestal interview with Jean Stein in Stein, *American Journey*, p. 205.

56. Schlesinger quoting his own July 1961 memorandum in Schlesinger, *Robert Kennedy*, p. 475. Emphases in the original.

57. Lansdale testimony in "Alleged Assassination Plots," p. 140.

58. Lansdale quoted in Schlesinger, *Robert Kennedy*, p. 480.

59. Peter Collier and David Horowitz, *The Kennedys* (London: Pan, 1984), pp. 368–69.

60. In addition to "Alleged Assassination Plots," pp. 71–90, see Hinckle and Turner, *The Fish is Red*, chapters 2, 4, 5, and passim.

61. After an extensive investigation of President Kennedy's possible involvement, the Church inquiry reported that "there was insufficient evidence from which the Committee could conclude" one way or the other: "Alleged Assassination Plots," p. 263.

62. Kalb, *The Congo Cables*, p. 194; Frederick P. Bunnell, "The Central Intelligence Agency–Deputy Directorate for Plans 1961 Secret Memorandum on Indonesia: A Study in the Politics of Policy Formulation in the Kennedy Administration," *Indonesia* 22(Oct. 1976):153; Philip Agee press stories summarized in Richard F. Grimmett, "Reported Foreign and Domestic Covert Activities of the United States Central Intelligence Agency" (Washington, D.C.: Library of Congress Congressional Research Service, 1975), p. 7; Powers, *Man Who Kept the Secrets*, pp. 169–70; Radosh, *American Labor and United States Foreign Policy*, pp. 399–405. Richard D. Mahoney argues that President Kennedy put the CIA back on the leash in the Congo, and, in the latter part of his administration, built a "durable political center" in that country: Mahoney, *JFK*, pp. 246–47.

63. Powers, *Man Who Kept the Secrets*, p. 226; Helms, Gittinger interview, p. 5.

64. *Washington Post*, Feb. 18, 22, 1967; *Baltimore Sun*, Feb. 17, 1967; Bowles, *Promises*, p. 391.

65. "A New Chief of U.S. Intelligence Takes Over," *U.S. News and World Report* 51(Dec. 11, 1961):20. On the problem which the Oppenheimer case posed for McCone at the AEC, see Charles J. V. Murphy, "Mr. McCone Arrives in Washington," *Fortune* 58(Aug. 1958):113.

66. Cooper oral history, p. 9.

67. Schlesinger, *Thousand Days*, p. 264; Cline, *CIA*, p. 219. According to Powers (*Man Who Kept the Secrets*, pp. 13–14), McCone worried that he might be excommunicated, if word were to leak out that he was involved in attempts on Castro's life.

68. Hilsman oral history, p. 15; McCone, Soapes interview, p. 30; Cline, *CIA*, p. 216.

69. Keith Clark quoted in Price, *DCI's Role*, pp. 66–67.

70. John Bross quoted in Price, *DCI's Role*, p. 64.

71. Karalekas History, p. 73.

72. Karalekas History, pp. 76–77.

73. Karalekas History, pp. 77–78.

74. Author's interview with McGeorge Bundy, May 16, 1984; Alsop, *The Center*, pp. 228–29, 233; Tully, *Central Intelligence Agency*, p. 15.

75. McCone, Soapes interview, p. 54.

76. Ransom, *The Intelligence Establishment*, p. 97. For confirmation of the fall-of-Khruschev lapse, see transcript, John A. McCone oral history interview, Aug. 19, 1970, by Joe B. Frantz, p. 21, LBJ.

77. Allison, *Essence of Decision*, p. 119.

78. Kennedy quoted in Arthur Krock, *Memoirs: Sixty Years on the Firing Line* (New York: Funk & Wagnalls, 1968), p. 380; McCone, Soapes interview, p. 28; McCone quoted in Powers, *Man Who Kept the Secrets*, p. 205.

79. Helene L. Boatner, "CIA's Intelligence Analysis: How Good Is It?" (paper delivered at the annual meeting of the Conference on World Affairs, April 1985, kindly supplied by one of Boatner's CIA colleagues), p. 15. Also, McCone, Frantz, interview, p. 10, and Allison, *Essence of Decision*, p. 190.

80. See Richard E. Sargent, "The Soviet-American Strategic Competition: The Action-Reaction Process Reconsidered" (Ph.D., diss., University of Edinburgh, 1976), 2 vols., 1:8.

81. Sargent, "Soviet-American Strategic Competition," 2:368.

82. Laqueur, *A World of Secrets*, p. 81.

83. See Moulton, *From Superiority to Parity*, pp. (ix)–(x).

84. "Alleged Assassination Plots," pp. 217–19.

Chapter 8
PRESIDENTIAL NEGLECT

1. See Parmet, *JFK*, p. 348. Reviewing later investigations into the assassination, Vaughan Davis Bornet suggests there was only one gunman: Bornet, *The Presidency of Lyndon B. Johnson* (Laurence, Kan.: University Press of Kansas, 1983), p. 21.

2. Johnson, *The Vantage Point*, p. 26.

3. Transcript, Richard Helms oral history interview, Sept. 16, 1981 by Ted Gittinger, p. 18, LBJ. RJ-J's emphasis.

4. All quotations from Epstein, *Legend*, pp. 48, 253.

5. For details, see Rhodri Jeffreys-Jones, "United States Secret Service," in Donald R. Whitnah, ed., *Government Agencies* (Westport, Conn.: Greenwood, 1983), p. 595.

6. Powers, *The Man Who Kept the Secrets*, pp. 198–99.

7. Transcript, John A. McCone oral history interview, Aug. 19, 1970, by Joe B. Frantz, p. 17.

8. Johnson quoted in George C. Herring, "The War in Vietnam," in Devine, ed., *Exploring the Johnson Years*, p. 27.

9. Identical telegrams, Secretary of State Dean Rusk to U.S. embassies in Paris, Bonn, London, Madrid, and Rome, Jan. 11, 1964, CIA Vol. 1, Agency File, NSFJ.

10. McCone, Frantz, interview, p. 20; replies to Rusk from U.S. ambassadors in Madrid (Jan. 14, 1964), Bonn (Jan. 14, 1964), and London (Jan. 15, 1964), CIA Vol. 1, Agency File, NSFJ.

11. Bohlen, *Witness to History*, p. 446.

12. Bohlen to Sec. State, Jan. 13, 1964, folder "CIA, Vol. 1," Box 8, NSFJ.

13. Bohlen to Sec. State, Jan. 16, 17, 20, 1964, CIA Vol. 1, Agency File, NSFJ.

14. McGarvey, *Myth and the Madness*, pp. 15, 17, 25, 26; Marchetti and Marks, *CIA and the Cult of Intelligence*, p. 286–88; Kahin, *Intervention*, p. 220.

15. Memo, "Trends in the World Situation," by Willard Matthias of the CIA's Board of National Estimates, p. 43, covered by Sherman Kent's circulation note, June 9, 1964, in which Kent remarked that the Matthias memo had "general Board approval," folder "CIA Vol. 1," Agency File, NSFJ.

16. Memo, "A New Look at the Prospects for the African Nationalist Movements in

Angola and Mozambique," Nov. 17, 1965, by Sherman Kent, p. 13, folder "CIA Vol. 2," Agency File, NSFJ.

17. "Covert Action," *Hearings Before the Select Committee to Study Governmental Operations with Respect to Intelligence Activities of the United States Senate*, 94 Cong., 1 sess., pursuant to S. Res. 21, 7 vols., Vol. 7, Dec. 4 and 5, 1975, pp. 151, 161–63, 204.

18. December 4, 1964, document quoted in Horowitz, ed., *Rise and Fall*, pp. 4–5.

19. Horowitz in Horowitz, *Rise and Fall*, p. 4.

20. Marshall Sahlins, "The Established Order: Do Not Fold, Spindle or Mutilate," an address delivered to the November 1965 meeting of the American Anthropological Association and published in Horowitz, *Rise and Fall*: see p. 72.

21. *New York Times* quoted in Sahlins, "Established Order," p. 73.

22. Andres Aylwin quoted in Johan Galtung, *Papers on Methodology: Essays in Methodology*, 2:165.

23. Horowitz in Horowitz, *Rise and Fall*, pp. 11–12.

24. Sahlins, "Established Order," p. 71.

25. J. William Fulbright, "America in an Age of Revolutions," article reprinted in Horowitz, *Rise and Fall*: see p. 197.

26. Transcript, Richard Helms oral history interview, April 4, 1969, by Paige Mulhollan, p. 9, LBJ.

27. List of meetings and telephone conversations with McCone, supplied to President Johnson April 25, 1965, folder "Central Intelligence Agency," Gen FG 11–2, WHCF, LBJ.

28. McCone, Frantz, interview, pp. 17–18, 29.

29. Powers, *Man Who Kept the Secrets*, p. 206; Charles Bohlen to Sec. State, Jan. 13, 1964, folder "CIA. Vol. 1," Agency File, NSFJ.

30. The *Pueblo* affair—an intelligence incident, as opposed to problem—did feature prominently on the agenda in 1968, though that was after McCone's day: David C. Humphrey, "Tuesday Lunch at the Johnson White House: A Preliminary Assessment," *Diplomatic History* 8(Winter 1984):91–92, 98.

31. "Summary of Remarks made by John H. McCone, former Director of Central Intelligence (1961–1965)—October 9, 1975: United States Foreign Intelligence System and the Public Interest," p. 1, folder "Intelligence 11/1/75–12/31/75," ND6, Subj. WHCF, GRF.

32. Chester L. Cooper, "The CIA and Decision-Making," *Foreign Affairs* 50(Jan. 1972):227.

33. Freedman, *U.S. Intelligence and the Soviet Strategic Threat*, p. 111.

34. Thompson, *Rolling Thunder*, p. 40.

35. Special National Intelligence Estimate 10–3/1–65: "Communist Reactions to Possible U.S. Courses of Action against North Vietnam," Feb. 18, 1965, in Gareth Porter, ed., *Vietnam: The Definitive Documentation of Human Decisions*, 2 vols. (London: Heyden, 1979), 2:359–63.

36. Memo from McCone to Dean Rusk, Robert S. McNamara, McGeorge Bundy, and Maxwell D. Taylor, April 2, 1965, in *The Pentagon Papers as Published by the New York Times* (New York: Quadrangle, 1971), pp. 450–51.

37. Miss Mamie Raborn to the president, April 19, 1965, folder "Central Intelligence Agency," Gen FG 11–2, WHCF, LBJ.

38. Helms, Mulhollan, interview, p. 22.

39. McCone, Frantz, interview, pp. 22–23; Phillips, *The Night Watch*, p. 148; McGarvey, *Myth*, p. 207; anon. (but clearly Raborn), "Statement for the record," n.d. (but covered by a White House note dated Feb. 23, 1966), folder "CIA. Vol. 2," Agency File, NSFJ.

40. Walter LaFeber, "Latin American Policy," in Divine, *Exploring*, p. 76.

41. Memo, Jack Valenti to the president, April 30, 1965, folder "Central Intelligence Agency," Gen FG 11–2, WHCF, LBJ. Emphases in the original.

42. Raborn quoted in Cline, *CIA*, p. 236.

43. McGarvey, *Myth*, p. 207.

44. Raborn to the president, July 19, 1965, folder "Central Intelligence Agency," Gen FG 11–2, WHCF, LBJ.

45. Johnson to Raborn, July 27, 1967, folder "Central Intelligence Agency," Gen FG 11–2, WHCF, LBJ (not sent).

46. Johnson's aide Horace Busby deleted the passage in the original draft on the ground that it contained "unnecessary criticism of past performances of CIA," substituting a sentence that was "much more constructive and useful for Admiral Raborn's purposes." The new sentence was: "You know it is my hope that we can continue to build and strengthen the effectiveness of the Agency." Busby to the president and Johnson to Raborn, both July 29, 1967, in folder "Central Intelligence Agency," Gen FG 11–2, WHCF, LBJ.

47. C. M. Turnbull, *A History of Singapore 1819–1975* (Kuala Lumpur: Oxford University Press, 1977), pp. 293–99.

48. *New York Times*, Sept. 2, 1965.

49. "The Soviet and Communist Bloc Defamation Campaign," Sept. 1965, folder "Central Intelligence Agency," Gen FG 11–2, WHCF, LBJ.

50. Memo, Bromley Smith to Bill Moyers, Sept. 28, 1965, attached to above.

51. Memo, Office of Deputy Director CIA to McGeorge Bundy, Oct. 26, 1965, folder "Central Intelligence Agency," Gen FG 11–2, WHCF, LBJ.

52. Oleg Penkovsky, *The Penkovsky Papers*, pp. 66, 72–73, 92, 192.

53. London *Times*, Nov. 13, 1965.

54. Ranelagh, *Agency*, p. 424; *Washington Post*, Nov. 1, 1965; Bundy to the president (quoting Clifford), Jan. 26, 1966, in folder "Central Intelligence Agency," Gen FG 11–2,WHCF, LBJ.

55. In this connection, McGeorge Bundy remarked on Cline's "obsessive" personality: author's interview with Bundy, May 16, 1984; "These Men Run the CIA," *Esquire* 65(May 1966):167.

56. Cline, *CIA*, p. 223; Cline to the president, March 2, 1966, folder "Central Intelligence Agency," Gen FG 11–2, WHCF, LBJ.

57. Cline to the president, above.

58. Ranelagh, *Agency*, pp. 223–24.

59. Raborn to Moyers, March 3, and Moyers to White, March 7, 1966, in folder "Central Intelligence Agency," Gen FG 11–2, WHCF, LBJ.

60. Ransom, *The Intelligence Establishment*, p. 173; Eugene J. McCarthy, "The Expansion of the White House," *Center Magazine* 6(March 1973):53, 54; J. William Fulbright, "We Must Not Fight Fire with Fire" (originally published in *New York Times Magazine*, April 23, 1967), in Kim, ed., *The Central Intelligence Agency*, pp. 105–6.

61. The Soviet press took note of these events, which *Pravda* summarized on May 3, 1966.

62. Quotation and summaries in "Foreign Press Reaction to *Times* Series on CIA," May 3, 1966, enclosed with memo, Leonard H. Marks to the president, May 5, 1966, C. F. FG 1–1, WHCF, LBJ.

63. L. Natarajan, *American Shadow over India* (Bombay: People's Publishing House, 1952), p. (xvii).

64. See "Foreign Press Reaction" and Marks memo, above.

65. Memo, Helms to Bill D. Moyers and S. Douglass Cater, Jr., May 19, 1966, folder "CIA Vol. 2," Agency File, NSFJ.

66. Mansfield to Fulbright, May 25, 1966, folder "CIA Vol. 2," Agency File, NSFJ.

67. Clifford comment scrawled on memo, Rostow to the president, June 1, 1966, folder "CIA Vol. 2," Agency File, NSFJ.

68. On the "Patman Eight," see "Foreign and Military Intelligence" (Final Report of the Select Committee to Study Governmental Operations with Respect to Intelligence Activities, 5 Books, Book 1), *Senate Report*, 94 Cong., 2 sess., no 94–755 (April 26, 1976), p. 185.

69. On Fulbright's curiosity concerning Fulbright awards, see Ransom, *Intelligence Establishment*, p. 175. On 1950s resistance to the politicization of educational exchange programs, see Merrian Trytten, chairman, Conference Board of Associated Research Councils, Committee on International Exchange of Persons (CIEP), to Walter Johnson, chairman, Board of Foreign Scholarships, March 27, 1952, and "Comments on the Proposal to Establish Chairs of American Studies in Italian Universities," memo, Francis A. Young, executive secretary, CIEP, to J. Manuel Espinosa, chief, Professional Activities Division, International Educational Exchange Service, Department of State, May 22, 1956, both in ACLS, together with Walter Johnson and Francis J. Colligan, *The Fulbright Program: A History* (Chicago: University of Chicago Press, 1965), pp. 68, 82, 84, 127.

70. Memo, Mansfield to the president, June 6, 1966, folder "Central Intelligence Agency," Gen FG 11–2, WHCF, LBJ.

71. Raborn to the president, June 8, 1966, folder "Central Intelligence Agency," GEN FG 11–2, WHCF, LBJ.

Chapter 9
HELMS, JOHNSON, AND COSMETIC INTELLIGENCE

1. Powers, *The Man Who Kept the Secrets*, p. 23.

2. Helms as paraphrased in "Why LBJ Chose Helms to Run the CIA," *U.S. News and World Report*, 61(July 4, 1966):14.

3. Transcript, Richard Helms oral history interview, April 4, 1969, by Paige Mulhollan, pp. 7, 23–26, LBJ.

4. Memos, Harry C. McPherson to the president, 9 and 13 June 1966, folder "CIA," Box 5, OFHM.

5. Ransom, *The Intelligence Establishment*, p. 177.

6. NSA's Samuel W. Brown quoted in *Washington Post*, Feb. 18, 1967. By the time that Sol Stern's article "NSA and the CIA" appeared in *Ramparts* 5(March 1967), all its details had leaked into the press.

7. Transcript, Lewis B. Hershey oral history interview, May 7, 1975, by Robert Elder and James Hattersley, p. 26, LBH; W. Bedell Smith to Hershey, Sept. 15, 1950, Box 14, WBS; Groves to Cater, March 23, 1967, Gen FG 11–1, WHCF, LBJ.

8. *Washington Post*, Feb. 18, 22, and 23, 1967. The American Political Science Association president was Robert A. Dahl.

9. UPI printout, Feb. 15, 1967, and George E. Brown, Jr., and seven others to Lyndon B. Johnson, Feb. 14, 1967, both in folder "Ramparts—NSA—CIA," Subj NSFJ; Mansfield quoted in *Washington Post*, Feb. 17, 1967; Goldwater quoted in *New York Times*, Feb. 27, 1967.

10. Bates, Fulbright, and Russell quoted in *Washington Post*, Feb. 17, 18, and 22, 1967; Symington quoted in UPI printout, Feb. 21, 1967, in folder "Ramparts—NSA—CIA," Subj NSFJ.

11. Memo, Jack Rosenthal to George Christian, Feb. 15, 1967, in folder "Ramparts—NSA—CIA," Subj NSFJ.

12. Staff reporter Richard Harwood, on the anonymous authority of "one of the highest officials in both the Kennedy and Johnson Administrations," *Washington Post*, Feb. 17, 1967.

13. Helms, Mulhollen, interview, p. 41.

14. Reston in *New York Times*, Feb. 17, 1967; *Washington Post*, Feb. 16, 17.

15. Merrill Cody to Howland H. Sargeant, Feb. 28, 1967, covered by memo, Helms to Rostow, March 14, 1967, folder "Ramparts—NSA—CIA," Subj NSEJ.

16. To cap the story, Henri Perron is finally offered money from a wealthy Jewish banker: Simone de Beauvoir, *The Mandarins*, transl. Leonard M. Friedman (London: Collins, 1957 [1954]), p. 660.

17. E. Howard Hunt (under pseudonym David St. John), *Return from Vorkuta*, p. 22.

18. Malcolm Muggeridge, "Books," *Esquire* 68(Sept. 1967):12.

19. For an example of British indignation, see Andrew Kopkind, "CIA: the Great Corrupter," *New Statesman* (Feb. 24, 1967):249.

20. Morgan, *The Anti-Americans*, pp. 9–10; Claude Julien, *L'Empire américain*, pp. 307, 347–48.

21. Mader, *Who's Who in CIA*, pp. 284, 318; Mader, *Yellow List: Where is the CIA? A Documentary of Organizations and Institutions Set Up as Camouflage . . .* (Berlin: Julius Mader, 1968). Mader was the author of a best-selling work on Richard Sorge, the German who spied for the Soviet Union in the Far East. In 1984, he published a sequel under commission to the East German government, which was reviewed by Frederick Rubin in *Foreign Intelligence Literary Scene* 4(Feb. 1985):6.

22. Morris, *CIA and American Labor*, p. 100 and chapter 7, passim.

23. Bowles, *Promises to Keep*, pp. 392, 544, 545; *Seminar* issue devoted to "Academic Colonialism," 112(Dec. 1968); William McCormack, "Problems of American Scholars in India," *Asia Survey* 16:2(1976):1070.

24. "Another Scandal Laid to the CIA," undated editorial clipped from the *San Francisco Chronicle*, and attached to a letter from Sid Cowgill of the Redding, California, Chamber of Commerce to President Johnson, Aug. 20, 1968, Gen FG 11–2, WHCF, LBJ.

25. Gregorio Selser, *La CIA en Bolivia* (Buenos Aires: Hernandez Editor, 1970), pp. 5, 16–17, 22.

26. Dan Schechter, Michael Ansara, and David Kolodney, "The CIA as an Equal Opportunity Employer," *Ramparts* 7(June 1969):26, 32.

27. See McCormack, "Problems," p. 1071, and John Horton (CIA operations officer 1948–75, national intelligence officer for Latin America on National Intelligence Council 1983–84), "The Real Intelligence Failure," *Foreign Intelligence Journal* (Feb. 1985):25.

28. David Wise, the noted critic of intelligence policy and of the CIA, appears to have coined, or at least popularized, the phrase "credibility gap" in a May 23, 1965, article under that heading for the *New York Herald Tribune*. The article dealt with LBJ's extravagant promises on the issue of Vietnam.

29. *Washington Post*, Feb. 19, 1967; Katzenbach draft of a Feb. 22, 1967, statement by the president to the press, folder "CIA," Box 5, OFHM; Mansfield to the president, Feb. 22, the president to Mansfield, Feb. 23, 1967, Gen FG 11–2, WHCF, LBJ.

30. The paraphrase of Gardner's position is Katzenbach's: Katzenbach to the president, March 17, 1967, folder "Ramparts—NSA—CIA," Subj NSFJ.

31. Katzenbach statement in press conference no. 788-A, n.d., folder "CIA," Box 5, OFHM.

32. Ransom, *Intelligence Establishment*, p. 244; Julien, *L'Empire américain*, p. 307.

33. Larry D. Collins, "The Free Europe Committee: An American Weapon of the Cold War" (Ph.D., diss., Carleton Univ., 1973), p. 112.

34. "Foreign and Military Intelligence" (Final Report of the Select Committee to Study Governmental Operations with Respect to Intelligence Activities, 5 Books, Book 1), *Senate Report*, 94 Cong., 2 sess., no. 94–755 (April 26, 1976), pp. 188–89; Eugene Patterson testimony in "The CIA and the Media," *Hearings before the Subcommittee on Oversight of the Permanent Select Committee in Intelligence*, House, 95 Cong., 1 & 2 sess., Dec. 1977, and Jan. and April 1978, p. 242. Patterson was the editor of the *St. Petersburg Times*, Florida. He won the Pulitzer prize for editorial writing in 1966, and was in 1978 president of the American Society of Newspaper Editors.

35. See Green, *Taking Sides*, pp. 197, 201.

36. Quandt, *Decade of Decisions*, p. 50; Laqueur, *A World of Secrets*, pp. 219, 249; Helms, Mulhollan, interview, p. 36.

37. Ranelagh, *Agency*, p. 474.

38. All quotations from Helms, Mulhollan, interview, pp. 8, 9, 22.

39. McPherson quoted in Green, *Taking Sides*, p. 201.

40. Walt H. Rostow, *The Diffusion of Power: An Essay in Recent History* (New York: Macmillan, 1972), p. 358. Rostow's memory may have misled him on Helms's "regular" attendances in 1966, but a detailed investigation by the archivist at the LBJ Library in Austin, Texas, confirms that Helms's inclusion was probably earlier than, and certainly independent of, the June War prophecy: David C. Humphrey, "Tuesday Lunch at the Johnson White House: A Preliminary Assessment," *Diplomatic History* 8(Winter 1984):90.

41. Blaufarb, *Counterinsurgency Era*, p. 245.

42. Blaufarb, *Counterinsurgency Era*, p. 246.

43. Lewy, *America in Vietnam*, p. 280.

44. Colby, *Honorable Men*, p. 270.

45. Blaufarb, *Counterinsurgency Era*, p. 246.

46. "Intelligence Activities and the Rights of Americans" (Final Report of the Select Committee to Study Governmental Operations with Respect to Intelligence Activities, 5 Books, Book 2), *Senate Report*, 94 Cong., 2 sess., no. 94–755 (April 26, 1976), p. 97.

47. Memo, "A Right Cross to Left Temple," Peter Jessup to "S" (Walt Rostow and Bromley Smith were the originally designated recipients, but their names were crossed out), April 4, 1967, folder "Ramparts—NSA—CIA," Subj NSFJ.

48. *Report to the President by the Commission on CIA Activities Within the United States* (New York: Manor Books, 1975 [hereinafter *Rockefeller Report* after its chairman, Vice President Nelson A. Rockefeller]); pp. 130, 132; "Intelligence Activities and the Rights of Americans," p. 100.

49. *Rockefeller Report*, p. 132.

50. Quotations from dust jacket of record called *Joy to UC*, released on November 24, 1964: NLC.

51. "67,000 Soldiers Put Out of Action (Including 27,834 American and Satellite Troops) [in the first quarter of 1966])," *Vietnam Courier*, April 21, 1966.

52. Lansdale quoted in Lewy, *America in Vietnam*, p. 438.

53. Quotations from "Intelligence Activities and the Rights of Americans," p. 100. See, also, *Rockefeller Report*, p. 130.

54. Memo, Helms to the president, Nov. 15, 1967, enclosing CIA "International Connections of U.S. Peace Groups" (Nov. 15, 1967), in folder "U.S. Peace Groups—International Connections," Intelligence File, NSFJ.

55. Above memo, Helms to the president, Nov. 15, 1967.

56. Thompson, *Rolling Thunder*, p. 42.

57. *The Pentagon Papers as Published by the New York Times* (London: Routledge & Keegan Paul, 1971), p. 562; Laqueur, *World of Secrets*, pp. 179–80.

58. Sam Adams, "Vietnam Cover-up: Playing War with Numbers," *Harper's* (May 1975): 62, 64.

59. Lewy, *America in Vietnam*, p. 385.

60. Oberdorfer, *Tet*, pp. 20, 117–21, 159.

61. Herring, *America's Longest War*, p. 188.

62. *Denver Post*, Feb. 25, 1968.

63. Helms to the president, Feb. 28, E. Palmer Hoyt to Johnson, March 8, 1968, in folder "Central Intelligence Agency," Gen FG 11–2, WHCF, LBJ.

64. Clifford quoted in Schandler, *The Unmaking of a President*, p. 264.

65. Schandler, *Unmaking*, p. 222.

66. McCloskey to Ford, April 21, 1975, folder "Intelligence 6/24/75," ND6, Subj WHCF, GRF; Helms, Mulhollan, interview, p. 30; *Pentagon Papers*, p. 605; Adams, "Vietnam Cover-up," p. 66.

67. Laqueur, *World of Secrets*, p. 181.

68. Huizenga quoted in Ranelagh, *Agency*, p. 455.

69. McGarvey, *The Myth and the Madness*, pp. 10, 14; Marchetti and Marks, *The CIA and the Cult of Intelligence*, p. 55; Agee, *Inside the Company*, pp. 561–62, 597; Adams, "Vietnam Cover-up," 41; Snepp, *Decent Interval*, pp. 9, 263; McGehee, *Deadly Deceits*, pp. (ix)–(x).

70. For a discussion of Soviet Chief of General Staff Marshall V. D. Sokolovskiy's *Soviet Military Strategy*, see Laqueur, *World of Secrets*, p. 193.

71. Sargent, "The Soviet-American Strategic Competition," 1:10; Laqueur, *World of Secrets*, p. 188.

72. McGarvey, *Myth*, p. 7.

73. Freedman, *U.S. Intelligence and the Soviet Strategic Threat*, p. 140.

74. Epstein, "Disinformation: Or, Why the CIA Cannot Verify an Arms-Control Agreement," *Commentary* 74(July 1982); Martin, *Wilderness of Mirrors*, p. 210.

75. Freedman, *U.S. Intelligence*, p. 81.

76. Prados, *The Soviet Estimate*, p. 292; Freedman, *U.S. Intelligence*, pp. 110–11; Laqueur, *World of Secrets*, pp. 191–92.

77. See Alsop, *The Center*, pp. 228–29, and Sumner Benson, "The Historian as Foreign Policy Analyst: The Challenge of the CIA," *The Public Historian* 3(1981):18.

78. Les Aspin, "Misreading Intelligence," *Foreign Policy* (Summer 1981), reprinted in Department of Defense, *Current News* (June 11, 1981), 11–F.

79. Phillip A. Petersen, "American Perceptions of Soviet Military Power," *Parameters* 7(1977):72.

80. McGarvey, *Myth*, pp. 7, 14.

81. Blackstock, *The CIA and the Intelligence Community*, p. 10.

82. See Moulton, *From Superiority to Parity*, pp. (ix)–(xii), and Freedman, *U.S. Intelligence*, chapter 9: "Protecting Minuteman Through SALT." In explaining 1972's "asymmetrical parity," Moulton (p. [x]) pointed to the Vietnamese conflict rather than to the role of Soviet estimates: "The controversy surrounding the war and its high costs resulted in the curtailment of new strategic weapons programs in favor of substantial increases in conventional weapons systems and munitions. The Vietnamese conflict in effect allowed the United States to acquiesce in strategic nuclear parity with the Soviet Union without the nation's leaders ever having to justify its wisdom to the American people." Moulton's neglect of estimates only confirms, of course, their unimportance to the Johnson administration.

Chapter 10
NIXON, KISSINGER, AND THE FRUITS OF MANIPULATION

1. "Remarks to Top Personnel at the Central Intelligence Agency. March 7, 1969," *Public Papers of the Presidents of the United States. Richard Nixon* (Washington, D.C.: GPO, n.d.), p. 302.

2. Kissinger, *White House Years*, p. 36.

3. Nixon, *Memoirs*, 1:553, 638.

4. Nixon remarks at Cushman swearing-in, May 7, 1969, *Public Papers. Nixon*, p. 358.

5. Parmet, *JFK*, pp. 22–23; Halberstam, *The Best and the Brightest*, p. 31.

6. Lehman, *The Executive, Congress and Foreign Policy*, pp. 115–28.

7. Transcript, Richard Helms oral history interview, Sept. 16, 1981, by Ted Gittinger, pp. 6, 19–20, LBJ.

8. Kissinger, *White House Years*, p. 453.

9. The staff members were Walter Pincus and Roland Paul: see Hersh, *The Price of Power*, p. 197n.

10. Lehman, *Executive*, pp. 123, 129.

11. Ranelagh, *The Agency*, pp. 494–95.

12. Herring, *America's Longest War*, pp. 226–27.

13. Edward G. Lansdale, "A Comparison: Viet Nam & the Philippines" (written for the Institute for Defense Analyses, n.d. but after September, 1968), Box 8, EGL.

14. *The Nixon Presidential Press Conferences* (London: Heyden, 1978), Sept. 26, 1969, p. 61. Nixon hinted at his approval of CIA "paramilitary operations" in a passage criticizing President Kennedy in Richard Nixon, *No More Vietnams* (London: W. H. Allen, 1986), p. 56.

15. Kissinger, *White House Years*, pp. 660–61.

16. "Foreign and Military Intelligence" (Final Report of the Select Committee to Study Governmental Operations with Respect to Intelligence Activities, 5 Books, Book 1), *Senate Report*, 94 Cong., 2 sess., no. 94–755 (April 26, 1976), p. 54.

17. "Unauthorized Storage of Toxic Agents," *Hearings before the Select Committee to Study Governmental Operations with Respect to Intelligence Activities of the United States Senate*, 94 Cong., 1 sess., pursuant to S. res. 21, 7 Vols., Vol. 1, Sept. 16, 17, and 18, 1975, p. 202.

18. Helms quoted in *San Francisco Chronicle*, Sept. 18, 1975.

19. *San Francisco Chronicle*, Sept. 18, 1975; "Unauthorized Storage," p. 126.

20. Sihanouk, *My War with the CIA*, pp. 20, 270.

21. Hersh, *Price of Power*, p. 187n.

22. Kissinger, *White House Years*, pp. 660–61.

23. Marchetti and Marks, *The CIA and the Cult of Intelligence*, p. 13. The passage quoted was one of those deleted from the 1975 edition at the CIA's insistence, but restored in the 1980 edition.

24. Photographically reproduced fascimile of Helms memorandum on meeting with the president, Sept. 15, 1970, being exhibit 2 in "Covert Action," *Hearings before the Select Committee to Study Governmental Operations with Respect to Intelligence Activities of the United States Senate*, 94 Cong., 1 sess., pursuant to S. res. 21, 7 Vols., Vol. 7, Dec. 4 and 5, 1975, p. 96.

25. "Covert Action in Chile 1963–1973," staff report reproduced in "Covert Action," p. 196.

26. Inspector General memorandum of Sept. 11, 1972, quoted in "Intelligence Activities and the Rights of Americans" (Final Report of the Select Committee to Study

Governmental Operations with Respect to Intelligence Activites, 5 Books, Book 2), *Senate Report*, 94 Cong., 2 sess., no. 94–755 (April 26, 1976), p. 102.

27. "Intelligence Activities and the Rights of Americans," p. 113.

28. Excerpt from Helms's Sept. 17, 1971, speech enclosed with William E. Colby to the president, Dec. 24, 1974, "Oversize Attachment 4594," WHCF, GRF.

29. See Nixon, *Memoirs*, 1:630.

30. McGarvey, *The Myth and the Madness*, pp. 10, 14; Nixon, *Memoirs*, 1:631.

31. Nixon, *Memoirs*, 1:630.

32. The quotations are from, respectively, Szulc, *Compulsive Spy*, p. 91, and Hunt, *Undercover*, p. 146.

33. Powers, *The Man Who Kept the Secrets*, p. 326; Hersh, *Price of Power*, p. 478; Carl Bernstein and Bob Woodward, *All the President's Men* (London: Quartet, 1974), p. 306; H. R. Haldeman, *The Ends of Power* (New York: Times Books, 1978), pp. 161–62.

34. Transcript dated July 22, 1971, Appendix in "Inquiry into the Alleged Involvement of the Central Intelligence Agency into the Watergate and Ellsberg Matters," *Hearings before the Special Subcommittee on Intelligence of the Committee on Armed Services*, 94 Cong., 1 sess., May-June 1974, p. 1125.

35. "Inquiry into CIA in Watergate," p. 336.

36. Marchetti and Marks, *CIA*, p. 323; John Costa, *Legislation Introduced Relative to the Activities of the Intelligence Agencies, 1947–1972* (Washington, D.C.: Congressional Research Service of the Library of Congress, 1975), pp. 33, 36.

37. Costa, *Legislation Introduced*, p. 35.

38. Mickelson, *America's Other Voice*, pp. 130–31, 136.

39. State Department statement quoted in Collins, "The Free Europe Committee," p. 113.

40. Mickelson, *America's Other Voice*, p. 138.

41. Nixon, *Memoirs*, 2:128.

42. Powers, *Man Who Kept the Secrets*, p. 313.

43. Powers, *Man Who Kept the Secrets*, p. 314; Ranelagh, *Agency*, p. 538.

44. Agee, *Inside the Company*, pp. 599–630.

45. Marchetti and Marks, *CIA*, chap. 1.

46. Cover of the 1980 Dell paperback edition.

47. See the restorations in the 1980 Dell edition, pp. 70, 151. Successive editions of the book restored passages originally deleted as the information became public through congressional hearings and Freedom of Information Act applications. As of 1983, six thousand words were still missing: Ranelagh, *Agency*, pp. 537–38.

48. Kissinger, *Nuclear Weapons and Foreign Policy*, pp. 431, 434.

49. Kissinger, *White House Years*, p. 535.

50. Jackson's July 1972 statement quoted in Freedman, *U.S. Intelligence*, p. 168. See also Kissinger, *Nuclear Weapons*, pp. 211–14, and Smith, *Doubletalk*, pp. 111, 114–15, 173, and Prados, *The Soviet Estimate*, p. 230.

51. *CIA: The Pike Report* (London: Spokesman Books, 1977), pp. 249–53.

52. Paul N. McCloskey, Edwin B. Forsythe, and John N. Erlenborn to President Gerald R. Ford, April 17, 1975, folder "Intelligence June 24, 1975," Subj. ND6, WHCF, GRF; *Pike Report*, pp. 249–53; Cline, *CIA*, p. 318.

53. For a sample of the extensive speculation on this subject, see Bernstein and Woodward, *All the President's Men*, pp. 318, 334, Haldeman, *Ends of Power*, pp. 149–93, and Jim Hougan, *Secret Agenda: Watergate, Deep Throat and CIA* (New York: Random, 1984), pp. 269, 279.

54. See Nixon, *Memoirs*, 2:128–29.

55. Colby, *Honorable Men*, pp. 338–39.

56. See Price, *DCI's Role*, pp. 67–68, and Mark M. Lowenthal, *U.S. Intelligence*, pp. 35–36.

57. Stern quoted in Paul W. Blackstock, "The Intelligence Community under the Nixon Administration," *Armed Forces and Society* 1(Feb. 1975):240.

58. Freedman, *U.S. Intelligence*, p. 54.

59. In contrast to Soviet bloc propagandists, the authors of some of these attacks distinguished between the culpability of different branches of the U.S. government. For example, the anonymous author of *La CIA: ¿ Qué es? ¿ Qué hace en América Latina?* (Buenos Aires: Voz Latinoamericana, for Movimiento Argentino Antiimperialista de Solidaridad Latinoamericana, 1974) claimed that the CIA "acts with absolute disregard for the guidelines fixed by Congress" (p. 9).

60. Ambassador Daniel P. Moynihan remarked of Mrs. Gandhi's reaction to Allende's deposition: "She is not sure but that we would be content to see others like her overthrown": cable quoted in *Buffalo Evening News*, Sept. 18, 1974.

61. Willbur C. Eveland, *Ropes of Sand: America's Failure in the Middle East* (New York: Norton, 1980), p. 327.

62. "Inquiry into the Alleged Involvement of the Central Intelligence Agency in the Watergate and Ellsberg Matters," *Report of the Special Subcommittee on Armed Services*, House, 93 Cong., 1 sess., Oct. 23, 1973, as reproduced in Grover S. Williams, ed., *Legislative History of the Central Intelligence Agency as Documented in Published Congressional Sources* (Washington, D.C.: Congressional Research Service of the Library of Congress, 1975), p. 305.

Chapter 11
DEMOCRACY'S INTELLIGENCE FLAP

1. Cline, *CIA*, p. 248.

2. Colby, *Honorable Men*, pp. 411–12.

3. Gerald R. Ford and four other members of the Subcommittee on the CIA of the House Committee on Appropriations to President Kennedy, defending Dulles, May 15, 1961, Box 95, AWD; Ford, *A Time to Heal*, pp. 76, 90, 265; Seymour M. Hersh, "The Pardon," *Atlantic Monthly* (Aug. 1983):55, 56.

4. Buchen quoted in *Michigan Alumnus* (June 1975):11.

5. Ford, *Time to Heal*, pp. 24, 1973; Buchen in *Detroit Free Press*, July 14, 1974: "Jerry [is] going to be too old to try again after 1976. . . . I'm fearful of the futility of Jerry trying to run if the incumbent stays in through 1976."

6. "The CIA's New Bay of Bucks," *Newsweek* (Sept. 23, 1974):51.

7. Mondale quoted in D. Don Welch, "Secrecy, Democracy and Responsibility: The Central Intelligence Agency and the Congress" (Ph.D., diss., Vanderbilt University, 1976), p. 170.

8. Transcript, Martin Agronsky TV interview with Michael J. Harrington and Ray S. Cline, Sept. 11, 1974, folder "9.13 CIA(3)," Box 33, CHM; Harrington to Ford, Sept. 17, 1974, folder "Central Intelligence Agency; 8/9/74–12/13/74," FG 6–2, Subj. WHCF, GRF.

9. Michael J. Harrington, "The Problem and the Potential," in Howard Frazier, ed., *Uncloaking the CIA* (New York: Free Press, 1978), p. 5; Buncher, ed., *The CIA and the Security Debate*, p. 11; Abourezk circular letter, Sept. 20, 1974, folder "Central Intelligence Agency; 8/9/74–12/13/74," FG 6-2, Subj. WHCF, GRF.

10. Winks, *Cloak and Gown*, pp. 432–35; Wright, *Spycatcher*, pp. 273, 364. See also Martin, *Wilderness of Mirrors*, pp. 213–14, and Powers, *The Man Who Kept the Secrets*, p. 370.

11. *New York Times* editorial, Dec. 24, 1974; statement, with supporting documents, issued by the CIA director's office on July 8, 1975, in response to the *New York Times* (Hersh) story of Dec. 22, 1974, in "Oversize Attachment 4595," WHCF, GRF.

12. Hughes quoted in Stephen Goode, *CIA* (New York: Franklin Watts, 1982), p. 140; other quotations from "Foreign and Military Intelligence" (Final Report of the Select Committee to Study Governmental Relations with Respect to Intelligence Activities, 5 Books, Book 1), *Senate Report*, 94 Cong., 2 sess., no. 94–755 (April 26, 1976), pp. 151, 577.

13. Buncher, *1971–1975*, p. 11.

14. Collation of information from *Editorials on File*, 1970, 1975 (New York: Facts on File). In 1970, there were seven editorials on the use of the Agency for International Development as a cover for CIA funds flowing into Laos, but the Agency itself was not their prime focus.

15. Colby, *Honorable Men*, pp. 14–15.

16. Colby to Ford, Dec. 24, 1974, in "Oversize Attachment 4595," WHCF, GRF; Ford, *Time to Heal*, pp. 324–25.

17. The eight members were John T. Connor (businessman, former Secretary of Commerce 1965–67, Harvard Law School J.D.), Dillon (Harvard B.A.), Erwin N. Griswold (U.S. Solicitor General 1967–72, Harvard Law School J.D., later Dean), Ronald Reagan (actor, Governor of California 1966–74, no higher education), Lyman L. Lemnitzer (JCS chairman, 1960–63, graduate U.S. Military Academy), Edgar F. Shannon (Harvard faculty member, 1950–56, President of the University of Virginia, 1959–74), Joseph Lane Kirkland (Secretary-Treasurer AFL-CIO since 1969, Georgetown University B.S.), and Rockefeller (Dartmouth B.A.).

18. *New York Times*, Feb. 6, 1975.

19. Colby, *Honorable Men*, p. 16; Price to the president, Jan. 30, Buchen to Price, Feb. 10, 1975, both in folder "Central Intelligence Agency 1/1/75–6/30/75," FG 6–2, Subj. WHCF, GRF.

20. *Washington Star-News*, Jan. 18, 1975.

21. "Foreign and Military Intelligence," p. 3.

22. Ford, *Time to Heal*, p. 265.

23. Johnson's observation of Church's ambition recorded in transcript, Frank Church oral history interview, May 1, 1969, by Paige E. Mulhollen, pp. 2, 14, LBJ.

24. On Church's 1961 suspicions, see *Executive Sessions of the Senate Foreign Relations Committee*, Vol. 13, Pt. 1, 87 Cong., 1 sess., 1961 (Washington, D.C.: GPO, 1984), p. 323.

25. Johnson, *A Season of Inquiry*, pp. 30–31.

26. Conversation as recorded in Schorr, *Clearing the Air*, pp. 143–45.

27. Schorr, *Clearing the Air*, p. 153.

28. *New York Times*, May 10, 1975.

29. Buchen to Belin, March 31, 1975, folder "Intelligence 8/9/74–8/23/75," ND 6, Subj. WHCF, GRF.

30. "The Kennedy Connection," *Time* (June 2, 1975):10; Schorr, *Clearing the Air*, p. 155.

31. *New York Times*, May 8, 1975.

32. *New York Times*, June 15, 1975.

33. See Richard J. Barnet and Robert J. Borosage, "Does Rocky's Report Invite U.S. Gestapo?" *Los Angeles Times*, July 6, 1975.

34. *Report to the President by the Commission on CIA Activities Within the United States* (New York: Manor Books, 1975 [hereinafter *Rockefeller Report*]), p. 269.

35. Rockefeller quoted in a network-reaction summary entitled "Rockefeller CIA

Report Will Not Include Assassination Findings," folder "9.131 CIA Investigations (1)," Box 34, CHM.

36. Memo, Roland L. Elliott to the president, June 20, 1975, folder "4/1/75–1/20/75," FG 393, Subj. WHCF, GRF.

37. Memo, Gerald R. Ford to the attorney general, the assistant to the president for national security affairs, the director of the office of management and budget, and the director of central intelligence, August 16, 1975, folder "7/1/75–9/30/75," FG 6–2, Subj. WHCF, GRF.

38. *Rockefeller Report*, p. 17.

39. Interview reported in *San Francisco Examiner*, Sept. 16, 1975.

40. According to D. C. Watt, Stevenson Professor of International History at London University and chairman of Britain's Study Group on Intelligence: "Between 1972 and 1980, the American intelligence effort was severely crippled. The damage was done by a combination of political misjudgement in the White House and partisan ambition and purblindness in Congress." Watt, "Can the Secret Service become the Silent Service?" *Daily Telegraph*, Aug. 18, 1984.

41. London *Guardian*, Feb. 4, 1985; Shevchenko, *Breaking with Moscow*, p. 325. Edward Jay Epstein accused CIA of cosmetically enhancing Shevchenko's account of his own utility, making him "the most successful media-acknowledged spy since Oleg Penkowsky in *The Penkowsky Papers*": Epstein, "The Spy Who Came in to be Sold," *New Republic* (July 15 and 22, 1985), 41.

42. Cline, *CIA*, p. 262.

43. Richelson, *The U.S. Intelligence Community*, pp. 298–99, 330.

44. Kissinger quoting, with approval, President Carter's Defense Secretary Harold Brown: Kissinger, *Years of Upheaval*, p. 1,008.

45. "The National Intelligence Estimates A-B Team Episode Concerning Soviet Strategic Capability and Objectives," *Report of the Senate Select Committee on Intelligence Subcommittee on Collation, Production and Quality, Together with Separate Views*, 95 Cong., 2 sess. (Feb. 16, 1978), p. 2.

46. *The Pike Report*, pp. 196–98; Prados, *Presidents' Secret Wars*, pp. 313–15.

47. John Stockwell, "A CIA Trip—from Belief, to Doubt, to Despair," *Center Magazine* 12(Sept./Oct., 1979):20; Stephen Weissman, "The CIA and U.S. Policy in Zaire and Angola," in Ellen Ray, William Schaap, Karl van Meter, and Louis Wolf, eds., *Dirty Work 2: The CIA in Africa* (London: Zed, 1980), pp. 199, 202. Weissman's essay first appeared in the *Political Science Quarterly* 94:2(1972):263–86.

48. Robert Lindsey, *The Falcon and the Snowman* (Harmondsworth: Penguin, 1980), pp. 82–83.

49. Text of Angleton interview on the ABC program "Correspondents Report," June 12, 1977, in Freney, *Australian Connection*, pp. 75–80, at p. 76.

50. Freney, *Australian Connection*, pp. 27–28, 31; Lindsey, *Falcon and Snowman*, pp. 82–83; Buncher, *1971–1975*, p. 104.

51. James A. Nathan, "Dateline Australia: America's Foreign Watergate?" *Foreign Policy* 49(Winter 1982–83):184. Nathan was a professor of political science at the University of Delaware who had recently returned from an academic exchange in Australia.

52. Oriana Fallacci, "Otis Pike and the CIA," *New Republic* (April 3, 1976):9; *Pike Report*, pp. 249–53.

53. Taylor Branch, "The Trial of the CIA," *New York Times Magazine* (Sept. 12, 1976):116, 188.

54. Fallacci, "Pike," 9.

55. According to Church, "We're endeavoring in this investigation to avoid any

possible partisan bias." Statement in "Transcript Press Briefing with Senator Church Following Executive Session with Richard Helms June 13, 1975," cyclostyled copy interleaved with a second-hand set of the Church hearings and reports acquired by the author in the Strand Bookstore, New York City, Sept. 2, 1983.

56. Schorr, *Clearing the Air*, p. 156.

57. On the subject of Kennedy era assassination plots, Church had earlier assured newsmen there would be "a full disclosure of the facts to the American people": statement in "Transcript Press Briefing June 13."

58. Casey to Ford, Sept. 13, 1975, in folder "Church, Frank (Sen.) 1975," Name File, WHCF, GRF, enclosing Jack W. Germond, "Politics Today: Probe Aiding Church, but Could be Hazard," *Washington Star*, Sept. 10, 1975.

59. "THE PRESIDENT HAS SEEN . . . " was typed in capitals at the head of Casey's letter, above.

60. Memo, Ford to Secretary of State and others, Sept. 19, 1985, folder "Central Intelligence Agency 7/1/75–9/30/75," FG 6–2, Subj. WHCF, GRF.

61. Memo, Vice President and others to President, Sept. 18, and memo, Kissinger to Jack Marsh, Sept. 23, 1975, both in folder "Intelligence 10/6/75," ND 6, Subj. WHCF, GRF.

62. Mitchell Rogovin's account of events, reported in Branch, "Trial," p. 115. Rogovin was the CIA's special counsel during the investigation.

63. Buchen to Herbert J. Miller, June 25, folder "Central Intelligence Agency 7/1/75–9/30/75," FG 6–2, Subj. WHCF, GRF. A member of the Washington, D.C., legal firm Miller, Cassidy, Larroca & Lewin, Herbert Miller had advised Ford on the handling of the Nixon tapes during the trauma of Watergate, Nixon's resignation, and the pardon. See Hersh, "The Pardon," pp. 72, 75, 76.

64. Opening statement by Senator Church, in "Unauthorized Storage of Toxic Agents," *Hearings before the Select Committee to Study Governmental Operations with Respect to Intelligence Activities of the United States Senate*, 94 Cong., 1 sess., pursuant to S. res. 21, 7 Vols., Vol. 1, Sept. 16, 17, and 18, 1975, p. 1.

65. President Ford determinedly backed Buchen's blocking efforts up to the last minute: Buchen to Church and Senator John G. Tower (Republican, Texas, vice chairman of the Church committee), Oct. 9, 1975, folder "Intelligence 10/6/75," ND 6, Subj. WHCF, GRF; Ford to Church, Oct. 31, and Ford to James O. Eastland (President pro tempore of the U.S. Senate), Nov. 20, 1975, both in folder "Church, Frank (Sen.) 1975," Name File, WHCF, GRF. Ford's Nov. 20 letter failed to prevent publication on that day: "Alleged Assassination Plots Involving Foreign Leaders" (An Interim Report of the Select Committee to Study Governmental Operations with Respect to Intelligence Activities), *Senate Report*, 94 Cong., 1 sess., no. 94–465 (Nov. 20, 1975).

66. Norman Kempster, "CIA Professionals Hail Church Attack on Bush," *Washington Star*, n.d., clipping in folder "9.13 CIA(6)," Box 33, CHM.

67. Buchen to Pike, Dec. 6, 1975, in folder "Otis G. Pike," Name File, WHCF, GRF.

68. *Pike Report*, p. 66.

69. *Chicago Tribune*, Dec. 12, 1975.

70. Ford to Church, Oct. 31, 1975, in folder "Church, Frank (Sen.) 1975," Name File, WHCF, GRF.

71. Freney, *Australian Connection*, p. 30.

72. Joseph Heller, *Good as Gold* (London: Corgi, 1980 [1976]), p. 204.

73. Ronald W. Walters, "The Clark Amendment: An Analysis of U.S. Policy Choices in Angola," *The Black Scholar* 12(July–Aug. 1981):3–6; Meyer, *Facing Reality*, pp. 257–58.

74. For some speculation, see the *Christian Science Monitor*, April 20, 1976.

75. Smith, *Portrait of a Cold Warrior*, pp. 11–12. In spite of Welch's Latin American service, his name did not appear in the controversial Latin American biographical appendix to Agee's *Inside the Company*, pp. 599–624.

76. Mader, *Who's Who in CIA*, p. 411. Mader named Welch just as a secret agent, not as a CIA officer. Also, it is unclear how seriously his book was taken, as, with disinformation probably in mind, Mader omitted some obvious names and included some doubtful candidates.

77. Stockwell, "CIA Trip," 20; Schorr, *Clearing the Air*, p. 191; Tyrus G. Fain, ed., *The Intelligence Community: History, Organization, and Issues* (New York: Bowker, 1977), p. 133; Phillips, *The Night Watch*, pp. 193–95, 187–89; Colby, *Honorable Men*, p. 450; "An Attractive Fellowship," *Foreign Intelligence Literary Scene* 3(Feb. 1984):11.

78. Phillips interview, *New York Times*, May 10, 1975.

79. Generalizations based on tables in Ernest W. Lefever, "The Performance of TV Evening News," in Ernest W. Lefever and Roy Godson, eds., *The CIA and the American Ethic: An Unfinished Debate* (Washington, D.C.: Ethics and Public Policy Center, Georgetown University, 1979), pp. 104, 106, 110, 112, 113.

80. Robert F. Ellsworth, "Foolish Intelligence," *Foreign Policy* 36(1979):148, 154–55; Richard Pipes, "Team B: The Reality behind the Myth," *Commentary* 82(Oct. 1986):30.

81. Pipes, "Team B," p. 27.

82. Ellsworth, "Foolish Intelligence," p. 149.

83. Philip Hanson, "The CIA, the TsSU and the Real Growth of the Soviet Investment," *Soviet Studies* 36(Oct. 1984):571–81.

84. "Ford's Plan to Rein in the CIA—Its Impact," *U.S. News and World Report* (March 1, 1976):21; Cline, *CIA*, p. 263.

85. "Ford's Plan," pp. 18, 21.

86. "Foreign and Military Intelligence," pp. 441, 448, 470, 641.

Chapter 12
RESTRAINED INTELLIGENCE AND THE HALF-WON PEACE

1. Jimmy Carter, *Keeping Faith: Memoirs of a President* (New York: Bantam, 1982), p. 143.

2. Walter F. Mondale, "Reorganizing the CIA," *Foreign Policy* 23(Summer 1976):58.

3. "He made it his business to ensure that the CIA and FBI did not slip back into old lawless habits": Finlay Lewis, *Mondale: Portrait of an American Politician*, rev. ed. (New York: Perennial/Harper, 1984), p. 217.

4. Cline, *CIA*, p. 269.

5. Carter's remark in question-and-answer session with State Department employees, Feb. 24, 1977, in *Public Papers of the Presidents of the United States. James E. Carter. 1977* (Washington, D.C.: GPO, n.d.), p. 242.

6. Mondale "Reorganizing CIA," p. 61.

7. Aaron testimony, "Congressional Oversight of Covert Activities," *Hearings before the Permanent Select Committee on Intelligence*, House of Representatives, 98 Cong., 1 sess. (Sept. 20, 21, 22, 1983), p. 100.

8. Zbigniew Brzezinski, *Power and Principle: Memoirs of the National Security Advisor, 1977–1982* (New York: Farrar, Straus & Giroux, 1983), pp. 34–35.

9. Theodore C. Sorensen, *Kennedy* (London: Pan, 1966), pp. 343–44.

10. Harry Howe Ransom, "Secret Intelligence in the United States, 1947–1982: The CIA's Search for Legitimacy," in Andrew and Dilks, eds., *The Missing Dimension*, p. 219.

11. Woodward, *VEIL*, p. 27; Brzezinski, *Power and Principle*, pp. 64, 72–73; Turner, *Secrecy and Democracy*, pp. 88, 119; Richelson, *The U.S. Intelligence Community*, pp. 341–42.

12. Stansfield Turner interview with David Martin, *Newsweek* 91 (Feb. 6, 1978):19; Turner, *Secrecy*, pp. 196–97, 203.

13. Author's conversation with Theodore G. Shackley, Royal United Services Institute, London, Sept. 7, 1984; Shackley, *The Third Option*, pp. 158–59, 162.

14. *Newsweek* 91(Feb. 6, 1978):19, 21, 22.

15. Turner paraphrased in London *Guardian*, Sept. 29, 1984.

16. *Newsweek* 91(Feb. 6, 1978):22.

17. *Time* 111(Feb. 6, 1978):28.

18. Anne Karalekas, "Intelligence Oversight: Has Anything Changed?" *Washington Quarterly* 6(Summer 1983):25; Lowenthal, *U.S. Intelligence*, p. 53.

19. Johnson, "The U.S. Congress and the CIA: Monitoring the Dark Side of Government," *Legislative Studies Quarterly* 5(Nov. 1980):482.

20. Smith, *Portrait of a Cold Warrior*, pp. 44, 48.

21. Roy Godson, "Congress and Foreign Intelligence," in Ernest W. Lefever and Roy Godson, eds., *The CIA and the American Ethic: An Unfinished Debate* (Washington, D.C.: Ethics and Public Policy Center, Georgetown University, 1979), p. 28.

22. Johnson, "Congress and CIA," p. 496.

23. Lowenthal, *U.S. Intelligence*, p. 58.

24. CIA studies "Iran in the 1980s" (Aug. 1977) and "Iran after the Shah" (Aug. 1978) quoted in Sick, *All Fall Down*, p. 92.

25. Sick, *All Fall Down*, p. 91.

26. Lowenthal, *U.S. Intelligence*, p. 55.

27. For an outline of the "golden past" trend and for some qualifications to it, see Rhodri Jeffreys-Jones, "The Historiography of the CIA," *Historical Journal* 23(June 1980):489–96.

28. Meyer, *Facing Reality*, pp. 326–27; Oseth, *Regulating United States Intelligence Operations*, pp. 133–34.

29. Meyer, *Facing Reality*, pp. 326–27.

30. Meyer, *Facing Reality*, pp. 283–84; Brzezinski, *Power*, p. 427; "Afghanistan: Six Years of Soviet Occupation," Department of State, Bureau of Public Affairs, Special Report No. 135 (Dec. 1985), p. 1.

31. Krepon, *Strategic Stalemate*, p. 134; Philip J. Farley, "Verification: On the Plus Side of the SALT II Balance Sheet," in Potter, ed., *Verification and SALT*, p. 225.

32. Wilbur C. Eveland, *Ropes of Sand: America's Failure in the Middle East* (New York: Norton, 1980), p. 327; Mark M. Lowenthal, "U.S. Organization for Verification," in Potter, ed., *Verification*, pp. 79, 82.

33. Lowenthal, "Organization," pp. 79, 82.

34. Catherine P. Ailes, James E. Cole, and Charles E. Movit, "Soviet Economic Problems and Technological Opportunities," *Comparative Strategy*, 1:4(1979):268, 291, which includes discussion of the CIA National Foreign Assessment Center, *The Soviet Economy in 1976–77 and Outlook for 1978*, August, 1978 (No. ER 78–10512).

35. See Les Aspin, "Misreading Intelligence," *Foreign Policy* 43(1981):167, 168, and Robert F. Ellsworth and Kenneth L. Adelman, "Foolish Intelligence," *Foreign Policy* 36(1979):147, 151.

36. "The National Intelligence Estimates A-B Team Episode Concerning Soviet Strategic Capability and Objectives," *Report of the Senate Select Committee on Intelligence Subcommittee in Collection, Production, and Quality, Together with Separate Views*, 95 Cong., 2 sess. (Feb. 16, 1978), p. 4. Richard Pipes was dismayed that "some legislators" portrayed his B-Team as politically biased and out to "sabotage SALT II." Turner, he thought, used the Senate report as an excuse to rid himself of the troublesome President's Foreign Intelligence Advisory Board. See Pipes, "Team B: The Reality Behind the Myth," *Commentary* 82(Oct. 1986):35, 39.

37. Richard K. Betts, "Strategic Estimates: Let's Make Them Useful" (based on Betts's Feb. 20, 1980, statement before the House Intelligence Committee), *Parameters: Journal of the U.S. Army War College* 31(Dec. 1980):20–26.

38. See Pipes, "Team B," p. 33.

39. Pipes, 1970 testimony before the Senate Subcommittee on Strategic Arms Limitation Talks of the Committee on Armed Services, quoted in Krepon, *Strategic Stalemate*, p. 89.

40. See President Carter's admission during an April 30, 1979, news conference: "I don't know what comments Admiral Turner has made. I happen to know that he's basically in favor of the SALT treaty": *Public Papers. Carter*, p. 753.

41. Cyrus Vance, *Hard Choices: Critical Years in American Foreign Policy* (New York: Simon & Schuster, 1983), pp. 136–37.

42. "Principal Findings by Senate Select Committee on Intelligence on the Capabilities of the United States to Monitor the SALT II Treaty" (Oct. 5, 1979), Appendix in Potter, ed., *Verification*, pp. 237–41.

43. "An old rule of thumb was that to estimate events correctly 50 percent of the time was an unexpected achievement": testimony of Bruce C. Clarke, in "The Role of Intelligence in the Foreign Policy Process," *Hearings before the Subcommittee on International Security and Scientific Affairs of the Committee on Foreign Affairs*, House of Representatives, 66 Cong., 2 sess. (Jan. 28, Feb. 8, 11, 20, 1980), p. 76. A graduate of Syracuse, the Sorbonne, American University, and the National War College, Clarke had served in the CIA's intelligence directorate and National Foreign Assessment Center since 1953.

44. Cline, *CIA*, p. 275.

45. Turner's Feb. 21, 1980, testimony in *Congressional Digest*, 59(May 1980):152; Daniel P. Moynihan quoted in Ransom, "Secret Intelligence," p. 220.

46. Angelo Codevilla, "Reforms and Proposals for Reform," in Godson, ed., *Elements of Intelligence*, p. 95; Byrd quoted in Johnson, "Congress and CIA," p. 496; Karalekas, "Intelligence Oversight," p. 26.

47. Thomas M. Franck and James J. Eisen, "Balancing National Security and Free Speech," *Journal of International Law and Politics* 14(Winter 1982):340–41. See Snepp, *Decent Interval*.

48. Secretary of State Cyrus R. Vance nevertheless resigned over the raid, his replacement being Edmund S. Muskie.

49. Charles A. Beckwith and Donald Knox drew attention to the CIA's weakness on the ground in their book *Delta Force: The U.S. Counter-Terrorist Unit and the Iranian Hostage Rescue Mission* (London: Arms and Armour Press, 1984), pp. 199–221. Their attribution of this weakness to the Turner personnel cuts overlooks the relatively small scale of those cuts and the fact that the revolutionary Iranians, reacting to past CIA actions in their country, were determined to purge their nation of all traces of American espionage.

50. In the words of Allan J. Mayer and others, in "Bush Breaks Out of the Pack," *Newsweek* (Feb. 4, 1980):35.

51. Morton H. Halperin, "The CIA's Distemper," *New Republic* (Feb. 9, 1980):21, 22.

52. Quoted in Cline, *CIA*, p. 310.

Chapter 13
IGNORING THE CREDIBLE

1. Foreign opinion was, however, still volatile. In 1983, the CIA advertised for "senior insurgency/terrorism and political instability analysts" in the newsletter of the Latin American Studies Association: *LASA Forum* 14(Summer 1983):38. Some spokesmen for Latin American affiliates of the U.S.-sponsored association were furious and threatened withdrawal. LASA executive director Richard N. Sinkin (University of Texas) explained that the advertisement had been placed through an agency, without editorial approval. Author's interview with Sinkin, Austin, Texas, August 11, 1983.

2. Edwin Warner, "New Day for the CIA?" *Time* (Jan. 19, 1981):27; John P. Littlejohn (the CIA's recruitment officer) cited in David Wise, "Campus Recruiting and the CIA," *New York Times Magazine* (June 8, 1986):28.

3. On intelligence- and intelligence-related-courses, see Marjorie W. Cline, ed., *Teaching Intelligence in the mid-1980s: A Survey of College and University Courses on the Subject of Intelligence* (Washington, D.C.: National Intelligence Study Center, 1985). Several people from the CIA—openly designated as such on the program and wearing badges giving the "CIA" as their institutional affiliation—read papers at the 1986 conference of the American Association for Slavic Studies. In a session called "Changing Boundaries of Public Discussion in the USSR under Gorbachev," for example, Marc Zlotnik contributed a paper on "Greater Frankness within the Party: The 27th Party Congress and the 1985/86 Party Elections." According to Matjaz Klemencic, a conference participant from the University of Maribor, Yugoslavia, non-U.S. delegates' reaction to the open designations was favorable. Author's conversation with Klemencic, West Berlin, July 1986.

4. Cline, *CIA*, p. 309. Abshire went on to become U.S. ambassador to NATO and, in January 1987, a cabinet-level White House congressional liaison officer over the Iran-Contra affair.

5. Private information; quotations from Ranelagh, *Agency*, pp. 659–61, 664.

6. Quotations from transition team's November report in Ranelagh, *Agency*, pp. 660, 665.

7. Casey to Donald Rumsfeld, Oct. 17, 1975, folder "Wm. J. Casey," Name File, WHCF, GRF.

8. Haig, *Caveat*, pp. 141–42; John A. Bross, "William J. Casey," *Foreign Intelligence Literary Scene* 6(March-April 1987):2.

9. Lou Cannon, *Reagan*(New York: Putnam's, 1982), p. 275.

10. Stephen M. Meyer of MIT quoted in the *New York Times*, July 16, 1986. See also Bross, "Casey," p. 2; *New York Times*, Feb. 3, 1987; and *Wall Street Journal*, Feb. 3, 1987.

11. "Individual Views of Senator Barry Goldwater," in "Foreign and Military Intelligence" (Final Report of the Select Committee to Study Government Operations with Respect to Intelligence Activities, 5 Books, Book 1), *Senate Report*, 94 Cong., 2 sess., no. 94–755 (April 26, 1976), p. 586; Goldwater quoted in Warner, "New Day," p. 27.

12. "Individual Views of Senator Barry Goldwater," p. 592; Cline, *CIA*, pp. 312; Stephen Goode, *CIA* (New York: Franklin Watts, 1982), p. 143.

13. Chairman's opening statement, "National Historical Intelligence Museum," *Hearings before the Select Committee on Intelligence of the United States Senate*, 98 Cong., 1 sess., no. 98–519 (Nov. 3, 1983), p. 1.

14. Ira Glasser, "The Coming Assault on Civil Liberties," in Alan Gartner, Colin Greer, and Frank Riessman, eds., *What Reagan is Doing to Us* (New York: Harper & Row/Perennial, 1982), p. 235; Moynihan quoted in "Spooks on Ice: Unleashing the CIA," *Time* (Nov. 9, 1981):21. See also, "Freeing the CIA: Spooks want to Spy at Home," *Time* (March 23, 1981), and Cline and Alexander, *Terrorism*.

15. List of Soviet accusations against the CIA and response by Jeremiah Denton, chairman of the Senate Subcommittee on Security and Terrorism of the Committee of Judiciary, in Cline and Alexander, *Terrorism*, pp. 25–30.

16. *Economist* (April 11, 1981):34; *Scotsman*, Dec. 5, 1981; section 1.8(c), Executive Order 12333 of December 4, 1981, governing United States Intelligence Activities, in Leary, ed., *The Central Intelligence Agency*, pp. 169–79 at 174–75.

17. Massey quoted in Warner, "New Day?" p. 27.

18. Angelo Codevilla, "Reforms and Proposals for Reform," in Godson, ed., *Elements of Intelligence*, p. 95. Codevilla had been one of the Senate Committee on Intelligence staff members who served on Reagan's CIA transition team.

19. Barry Goldwater, "Congress and Intelligence Oversight," *Washington Quarterly* 6(Summer 1983):19.

20. "They're No Angels" (editorial), *Nation* 233(Dec. 19, 1981):660.

21. Glasser, "Coming Assault," p. 236; Inman paraphrased in Edward J. Epstein, "Disinformation: Or, Why the CIA Cannot Verify an Arms-Control Agreement," *Commentary* 74(July 1982):21–22.

22. Ray Cline had reminded the press that the "first amendment is an amendment," a statement that so infuriated American Society of Newspaper Editors president Eugene Patterson that he emotionally misquoted the CIA veteran as saying the "first amendment is only an amendment": "The CIA and the Media," *Hearings before the Subcommittee on Oversight of the Permanent Select Committee on Intelligence*, House, 95 Cong., 1 & 2 sess., Dec. 1977 and Jan. and April 1978, pp. 61, 243.

23. *Congressional Record*, April 26, 1983, p. 55240, quoted in computer-selected digest and printout of Congressional intelligence business (file CR98), supplied through the kind courtesy of Senator Barry Goldwater.

24. Quoted headline from London *Observer*, June 9, 1985; London *Daily Telegraph*, Nov. 29, 1984; *International Herald Tribune*, July 21, 1986; London *Guardian*, Oct. 10, 1986.

25. Woodward, *VEIL*, p. 180; David M. Alpern and others, "America's Secret Warriors," *Newsweek* (Oct. 10, 1983):30–32.

26. The White Paper is reproduced in Warner Poelchau, ed., *White Paper Whitewash* (New York: Deep Cover Books, 1981), pp. A–1 to A–87.

27. Jeane Kirkpatrick, "The Threat America Cannot Ignore," London *Guardian*, April 25, 1983; *The Soviet-Cuban Connection in Central America and the Caribbean* (Washington, D.C.: Departments of State and Defense, 1985), pp. 5, 28.

28. McGehee, *Deadly Deceits*, pp. 174, 198. See, also, Joanne Omang (national staff reporter for the *Washington Post*), "A Historical Background to the CIA's Nicaragua Manual," in *Psychological Operations in Guerrilla Warfare* (New York: Vintage, 1985), p. 19, and LaFeber, *Inevitable Revolutions*, p. 296.

29. Francisco d'Escoto quoted in *Scotsman*, May 11, 1985.

30. Quotations in Alpern, "Secret Warriors," 30.

31. Text of the Boland amendment quoted in Schulzinger, *American Diplomacy in the Twentieth Century*, p. 324.

32. These details emerged at the start of the "Irangate" scandal, when the *Jerusalem Post* revealed the scheme and alleged U.S. officials had pressed Israel to help. U.S. attorney general Edwin Meese claimed, however, that Israeli officials took the initia-

tive, a claim that elicited an official denial from the Israeli government. See London *Guardian*, Dec. 5, 31, 1986.

33. Shultz statement to Senate Foreign Relations Committee, Feb. 23, 1983: United States Information Service official text, p. 5.

34. Quotations from, respectively, Michael White, "A Barrage of Rhetoric to Hot Up the Covert War," London *Guardian*, Feb. 26, 1985, and Donald Cameron Watt, "Can the Secret Service become the Silent Service?" London *Daily Telegraph*, Aug. 18, 1984. Watt is chairman of the British Study Group on Intelligence.

35. "House Intelligence Committee Report on Covert Operations in Nicaragua," reprinted in *First Principles*, 8 (July/Aug. 1983), 7.

36. Boland, early August statement quoted in Turner, *Secrecy and Democracy*, p. 168, and Boland in "Congressional Oversight of Covert Activities," *Hearings before the Permanent Select Committee on Intelligence House of Representatives*, 98 Cong., 1 sess. (Sept. 20, 21, 22, 1983), p. 1.

37. London *Guardian*, Apr. 15, 1984.

38. Senator Daniel P. Moynihan's complaint recorded in London *Times*, April 17, 1984; *Facts on File* 44 (1984): 273.

39. Edgar Chamorro and Jefferson Murphy, "Confessions of a 'Contra'," *New Republic* (Aug. 5, 1985):21.

40. Goldwater quoted in *Time* (April 23, 1984):6; London *Guardian*, April 28, 1984. Commenting, in 1980, on his change of heart concerning oversight, Senator Goldwater said the "honest exchange of information and views has probably done more for the agencies than anything in the last five years": "The Role of Intelligence in the Foreign Policy Process," *Hearings before the Subcommittee on International Security and Scientific Affairs of the Committee on Foreign Affairs*, House, 66 Cong., 2 sess. (Jan. 28, Feb. 8, 11, and 20, 1980), p. 171.

41. See Hersh, *The Target is Destroyed*, pp. 244–46, 249–50. R. W. Johnson, a scholar at Magdalen College, Oxford, England, argues that the Korean airliner, though not a spyplane itself, was on a surveillance mission. The purpose of the mission was to make the Russians switch on their new, massive radar installations at Krasnoyarsk. U.S. ground and orbital listening posts would then be able to monitor the radar emissions, perhaps showing that their source-size was in excess of SALT I provisions, a convenient circumstance for Reaganite hawks who wanted an excuse to withdraw from arms-reduction talks with the Soviet Union. According to Johnson's interpretation, CIA director Casey would have been instrumental in setting up the civilian probe, because he had close personal links with the Korean CIA, which in turn was powerful enough to get things done within Korea, "the KCIA state." If Johnson is correct, then the Reagan administration's disregard of the NSA's sound intelligence finding was more calculated than casual. See Johnson, *Shootdown: The Verdict on KAL 007* (London: Chatto & Windus, 1986), pp. 255, 257, 260, 261.

42. McGehee, "The CIA and the White Paper on El Salvador," *The Nation* (April 11, 1981):425; McGehee, *Deadly Deceits*, p. 193; *Facts on File* 44(1984):470.

43. John Horton, "The Real Intelligence Failure," *Foreign Service Journal* (Feb. 1985):25; Philip Taubman, "Intra-Agency Rifts Laid to Nicaraguan Operation," *New York Times*, Aug. 5, 1983; *Facts on File* 44(1984):486.

44. Chamorro, "Confessions," p. 23. See also: Christopher Dickey, *With the Contras: A Reporter in the Wilds of Nicaragua* (New York: Simon & Schuster, 1985), p. 254.

45. Reagan in United States Information Service transcript of second Reagan-Mondale debate, Oct. 21, 1984, p. 3; Dickey, *With the Contras*, reviewed in Aryeh Neier, "The U.S. and the Contras," *New York Review of Books* 33(April 10, 1986):3–6; Ferraro quoted in *Facts on File* 44(1984):809.

46. London *Guardian*, Sept. 28, Nov. 2, 1985; London *Weekly Guardian*, April 13, 1986; London *Times*, Dec. 4, 1986.

47. London *Observer*, Nov. 16, 1986; London *Guardian*, Nov. 28, 1986, Jan. 14, 1987; *The Tower Commission Report* (New York: Bantam, 1987), pp. 18, 22, 27–28, 38, 112.

48. Durenberger quoted in Omang, "Historical Background," p. 25; London *Guardian*, Oct. 10, 18, 1986; London *Observer*, Oct. 12, 1986.

49. Figure compiled from *Editorials on File, 1985* (New York: Facts on File).

50. According to a local Gallup Poll affiliate, 92 percent of Costa Ricans, 89 percent of Hondurans, and 63 percent of El Salvadorans regarded Nicaragua as militarily threatening to their respective countries: *Scotsman*, March 18, 1986.

51. London *Guardian*, March 21, June 28, 1986.

52. London *Weekly Guardian*, April 13, 1986.

53. Alpern, "Secret Warriors," p. 34.

54. Bob Woodward and Patrick R. Taylor paraphrasing intelligence sources in the *Washington Post*, April 10, 1986.

55. Jeffrey T. Richelson, "Old Surveillance, New Interpretations," *Bulletin of the Atomic Scientists* 3(Feb. 1986):18; *Washington Post*, April 10, 1986.

56. *Facts on File* 44(1984):66; Richelson, "Old Surveillance," p. 18; *New York Times*, July 16, 1986.

57. *Facts on File* 44(1984):75.

58. Don Oberdorfer, "U.S. Arms Spending Has Outpaced that of Soviets, CIA Says," *Washington Post*, Feb. 22, 1985.

59. Ibid.

60. Shevchenko, *Breaking With Moscow*, pp. 39, 325; Edward Jay Epstein, "The Spy Who Came in to be Sold," *New Republic* (July 15 and 22, 1985):39–41; Ashbel Green (Knopf editor-in-chief), *New Republic* (Aug. 26, 1985):23; Adler, *Reckless Disregard*, pp. 5, 224.

61. Gates quoted in the London *Sunday Times*, March 31, 1985.

62. Richelson, "Old Surveillance," pp. 18–19.

63. London *Guardian*, Aug. 12, 1985.

64. Durenberger quoted in *Washington Post*, Nov. 14, 1985. Other critics faulted the CIA for its weak analyses of terrorism: London *Weekly Guardian*, April 13, 1986. Durenberger had, by the end of 1985, come to the conclusion that one "could not fault the intelligence community" in relation to the crisis that led to Marcos's downfall: Durenberger quoted in Christopher Madison, "Committee Leaders Prod Intelligence Chiefs to Develop National Strategy," *National Journal* (Jan. 11, 1986):79.

65. *Washington Post*, April 10, 16, 1986.

66. London *Guardian*, Oct. 10, 1986. For a retrospective account by one of the journalists involved, see Woodward, *VEIL*, p. 476.

67. North called his secret Contra backup network "Project Democracy." The quotations are from Woodward, *VEIL*, p. 467.

68. London *Guardian*, Jan. 3, 1987; President Reagan's disclaimer quoted in the London *Daily Telegraph*, Nov. 26, 1986; "Iran-Contra Affair," *Report of the Congressional Committees*, 100 Cong., 1 sess. (Nov. 17, 1987), p. 375.

69. London *Observer*, April 26, 1987.

70. Senator Tower quoted in London *Guardian*, Feb. 27, 1987. The political scientist James Bill challenges the view that the episode was an aberration, portraying it instead as part of a National Security Council policy-and-intelligence muddle over Iran that characterized the Carter administration and continued under Reagan. See Bill, *The Eagle and the Lion*, chapter 10: "The United States in Iran: Diplomats, Intelligence Agents, and Policy-Making," especially p. 410.

71. *Tower Report*, pp. 79–80, 92–93, 96–97.
72. "Iran-Contra Affair," pp. 375, 382–84.
73. "Iran-Contra Affair," pp. 381–82.

CONCLUSION

1. Goldwater statement in "The Role of Intelligence in the Foreign Policy Process," *Hearings before the Subcommittee on International Security and Scientific Affairs of the Committee on Foreign Affairs*, House, 66 Cong., 2 sess. (Jan. 28, Feb. 8, 11, and 20, 1980), p. 171.

2. Those steeped in comparative intelligence history usually isolate the CIA's advanced technology as the element which gives the Agency its ascendancy. See, for example, Andrew, *Secret Service*, p. 497, and Laqueur, *A World of Secrets*, pp. 227, 230.

3. Professor Higgins's complaint in "My Fair Lady," the U.S. stage and film adaptation of George Bernard Shaw's *Pygmalion*.

4. Boland and Goldwater statements in "Role of Intelligence," pp. 170–71, 177.

5. The intelligence debate of the mid-1970s helped to educate people, and the ensuing pressures and expectations no doubt encouraged Presidents Ford and Carter to adopt fresh approaches to the CIA. The spread of intelligence courses on U.S. campuses in the 1980s was a further educative factor. But the field was relatively immature and dominated by intelligence veterans who had firsthand experience but subjective viewpoints.

BIBLIOGRAPHY

I. MANUSCRIPT SOURCES

Dwight D. Eisenhower Library, Abilene, Kansas.
C. D. Jackson Papers; Walter Bedell Smith Papers.
Gerald R. Ford Library, Ann Arbor, Michigan.
Gerald R. Ford, Papers as President—White House Central Files; White House Staff Files.
Harry S. Truman Library, Independence, Missouri.
Eben A. Ayers Papers; Clark M. Clifford Papers; George M. Elsey Papers; National Security Council Papers; John C. O'Gara Papers; Post Presidential Files; Records of the Psychological Strategy Board; Samuel I. Rosenman Papers; Sidney W. Souers Papers; Ralph H. Stohl Papers; Papers of Harry S. Truman, White House Central Files—Official File, President's Secretary's File.
Hoover Institution Archives, Stanford, California.
Edward G. Lansdale Papers.
John F. Kennedy Library, Boston, Massachusetts.
National Security Files.
Library of Congress, Washington, D.C.
Records of the American Council of Learned Societies; Records of the National Urban League.
Lyndon Baines Johnson Library, Austin, Texas.
National Security Files; Office Files of the White House Aides; Papers of Lyndon Baines Johnson as President, White House Central Files.
National Archives, Washington, D.C.
Modern Military Headquarters Branch: Record Group 218, William D. Leahy files as Chairman, Joint Chiefs of Staff, 1942–48; unlabeled boxes containing materials

on the Central Intelligence Group, the Doolittle Report, and the Taylor Board of Inquiry.

Modern State Section: Record Group 59, General Records of the Department of State, Decimal File, 811.20/1–6.

Navy Section: Record Group 80, Secretary of the Navy and Chief of Naval Operations Top Secret Files, 1945.

Public Record Office, London, England.
CAB 122/1021.

Seeley G. Mudd Manuscript Library, Princeton University, Princeton, New Jersey.
Allen W. Dulles Papers; Ferdinand Eberstadt Papers; James V. Forrestal Papers.

U.S. Army Military History Institute, Carlisle Barracks, Pennsylvania.
George H. Decker papers; Lewis B. Hershey Papers.

Yale University Library, New Haven, Connecticut.
Hanson W. Baldwin Papers.

2. UNPUBLISHED ITEMS

Bissell, Richard M., Jr. Oral history interview, Sept. 7, 1966.

Boatner, Helene L. "CIA's Intelligence Analysis: How Good Is It?" Paper at Conference on World Affairs, Boulder, Colo., April 1985.

Bruce-Lockhart, John. "What Is Intelligence?" Paper at Royal United Services Institute, London, Sept. 7, 1984.

Bundy, McGeorge. Interview with author, May 16, 1984.

Bunnell, Fred. "The American Response to the 1965 Radicalization of Guided Democracy: From Accommodation to Low Posture." Paper at International Studies Association Convention, Los Angeles, May 1980.

"C. D. Jackson." *Time* in-house biography, n.d.

Church, Frank. Transcript of press briefing, June 13, 1975.

———. Oral history interview, May 1, 1969.

Colby, William E. Transcript of statement to House Select Committee on Intelligence, Aug. 6, 1975.

Collins, Larry D. "The Free Europe Committee: An American Weapon of the Cold War," Ph.D. diss., Carleton University, 1973.

Computer-selected printout of congressional intelligence business, Oct. 11, 1978–Jan. 31, 1983. File CR 98.

Computer-selected printout of CIA entries in *Who's Who in America*, Chicago: Marquis, 1982–84. DIALOG File 234.

Cooper, Chester. Oral history interview, May 6, June 9, 1966.

Decker, George. Oral history interview, Dec. 18, 1972.

Dulles, Allen W. Oral history interview, May 17–June 3, 1965.

Elsey, George M. Oral history interview, Feb. 10, 1964.

Fletcher, Catherine B. "The CIA Apostates," postgraduate paper, University of Edinburgh, 1984.

———. "The Secret Agent Portrayed in American Spy Fiction—with Particular Reference to the History of the Central Intelligence Agency," M.Sc. diss., University of Edinburgh, 1985.

Foot, Peter. "The American Origins of NATO: A Study in Domestic Inhibitions and West European Constraints," Ph.D. diss., University of Edinburgh, 1984.

Handel, Michael I. "The Politics of Intelligence." Paper at Royal United Services Institute, London, Sept. 8, 1984.

Helms, Richard M. Oral history interviews, April 4, 1969, Sept. 16, 1981.

Hershey, Lewis. Oral history interview, May 7, 1975.

Hilsman, Roger. Oral history interviews, May 15, 1969, Aug. 14, 1970.

McCone, John A. Oral history interviews, Aug. 19, 1970, July 26, 1976.

Raat, William D. "U.S. Intelligence Operations and Covert Action in Mexico during the Twentieth Century." Paper at Society for Historians of American Foreign Relations conference, Stanford University, June 28, 1985.

Rabe, Stephen G. "Eisenhower and the Overthrow of Rafael Trujillo." Paper at Society for Historians of American Foreign Relations conference, Stanford University, June 28, 1985.

"Report on the Covert Activities of the Central Intelligence Agency" (Doolittle Report), Sept. 30, 1954.

Rifkind, Bernard D. "OSS and Franco-American Relations, 1942–1945," Ph.D. diss., George Washington University, 1983.

Ross, Andrew C. Interview with author, May 31, 1983.

Sargent, Richard E. "The Soviet-American Strategic Competition: The Action-Reaction Process Reconsidered," 2 vols., Ph.D. diss., University of Edinburgh, 1976.

Shackley, Theodore G. Conversation with author, Sept. 7, 1984.

Smith, Bradley F. "Admiral Godfrey and Co-operation with U.S. Intelligence." Paper at Royal United Services Institute, London, Sept. 8, 1984.

Trohan, Walter. Oral history interview, Oct. 7, 1970.

Troy, Thomas F. "CIA's British Parentage—and the Significance Thereof." Paper at Society for Historians of American Foreign Relations meeting, Washington, D.C., Aug. 3, 1984.

Unattributable Source A. Author's conversation with a senior White House official with responsibility for intelligence, Sept. 6, 1984.

Unattributable Source B. Letters to author, dated July 10 and August 7, 1985, from a senior CIA official.

Unattributable Source C. Letter to author, dated July 16, 1985, from a former CIA official historian.

United States Congress, Senate, Committee on Armed Services. "Nomination of Lieutenant General Walter Bedell Smith to be Director of the Central Intelligence Agency," Hearing, Executive Session, Aug. 24, 1950.

United States Information Service. Texts of recent statements by American officials and politicians.

Wall, Jim. Conversations with the author in the academic year 1983–84, notably on March 15, 1984.

Welch, D. Don. "Secrecy, Democracy and Responsibility: The Central Intelligence Agency and Congress," Ph.D. diss., Vanderbilt University, 1976.

3. PUBLISHED OFFICIAL DOCUMENTS

"Alleged Assassination Plots Involving Foreign Leaders" (An Interim Report of the Select Committee to Study Governmental Operations with Respect to Intelligence Activities), *Senate Report*, 94 Cong., 1 sess., no. 94–465 (Nov. 20, 1975).

"The CIA and the Media," *Hearings before the Subcommittee on Oversight of the Permanent Select Committee on Intelligence*, House of Representatives, 95 Cong., 1 & 2 sess. (Dec. 1977 and Jan. & April 1978).

CIA: The Pike Report. London: Spokesman Books, 1977.

Commission on the Organization of the Executive Branch of the Government (Hoover Commission), *Task Force Report on National Security Organization*. Washington, D.C., 1949.

Commission on the Organization of Government for the Conduct of Foreign Policy (Murphy Commission). *Report*. Vol. 7: *Appendix U: Intelligence Functions Analyses*. Washington, D.C., 1975.

"Congressional Oversight of Covert Activities," *Hearings before the House Permanent Select Committee on Intelligence*, 98 Cong., 1 sess. (1984).

Congressional Record

Etzold, Thomas H., and John L. Gaddis, eds. *Containment: Documents on American Policy and Strategy, 1945–1950*. New York: Columbia University Press, 1978.

"Electronic Surveillance Within the United States for Foreign Intelligence Purposes," *Hearings before the Subcommittee on Intelligence and the Rights of Americans of the Select Committee on Intelligence of the United States Senate*, 94 Cong., 1 sess. (June 29, July 1, Aug. 6, 10, and 24, 1976).

Executive Sessions of the Senate Foreign Relations Committee (Historical Series), Vol. 13, Pt. 1, 87 Cong., 1 sess. (1961: made public 1984).

Final Report of the Select Committee to Study Governmental Operations with Respect to Intelligence Activities (Church Report), *Senate Report*, 94 Cong., 2 sess., no. 94–755 (1976): Book 1: "Foreign and Military Intelligence"; Book 2: "Intelligence and the Rights of Americans"; Book 3: "Supplementary Detailed Staff Reports on Intelligence Activities and the Rights of Americans"; Book 4: "Supplementary Detailed Staff Reports on Foreign and Military Intelligence"; Book 5: "The Investigation of the Assassination of President John F. Kennedy: Performance of the Intelligence Agencies."

Gantenbein, James W., comp. and ed. *The Evolution of Our Latin-American Policy: A Documentary Record*. New York: Columbia University Press, 1950.

Hearings before the Select Committee to Study Governmental Operations with Respect to Intelligence Activities of the United States Senate, 94 Cong., 1 sess. (1975): Vol 1: "Unauthorized Storage of Toxic Agents" (Sept. 16, 17, and 18); Vol. 2: "Huston Plan" (Sept. 23, 24, and 25); Vol. 3: "Internal Revenue Service" (Oct. 2); Vol. 4: "Mail Opening" (Oct. 21, 22, and 24): Vol. 5: "The National Security Agency and Fourth Amendment Rights" (Oct. 29 and Nov. 6); Vol. 6: "Federal Bureau of Investigation" (Nov. 18 and 19, and Dec. 2, 3, 9, 10, and 11).

"Inquiry into the Alleged Involvement of the Central Intelligence Agency in the Watergate and Ellsberg Matters," *Hearings before the Special Subcommittee on Intelligence of the Committee on Armed Services*, 94 Cong., 1 sess. (May–June 1974).

"Iran-Contra Affair," *Report of the Congressional Committees*, 100 Cong., 1 sess. (Nov. 17, 1987).

Jackson, Henry M., ed. *The National Security Council: Jackson Subcommittee Papers on Policy-Making at the Presidential Level*. New York: Praeger, 1965.

"National Historical Intelligence Museum," *Hearing before the Select Committee on Intelligence of the United States Senate*, 98 Cong., 1 sess., no. 98–519 (Nov. 3, 1983).

"The National Intelligence Estimates A-B Team Episode Concerning Soviet Strategic Capability and Estimates," *Report of the Senate Select Committee on Intelligence Subcommittee on Collection, Production and Quality, Together with Separate Views*, 95 Cong., 2 sess. (Feb. 16, 1978).

"National Security Act of 1947," *Hearing before the Committee on Expenditures in the Executive Departments*, 80 Cong., 1 sess. (June 27, 1947).

Operation Zapata: The "Ultrasensitive" Report and Testimony of the Board of Inquiry on the Bay of Pigs (Taylor Report). Frederick, Md.: University Publications of America, 1984.

The Pentagon Papers as Published by the New York Times. London: Routledge & Kegan Paul, 1971.

Porter, Gareth, ed. *Vietnam: The Definitive Documentation of Human Decisions*, 2 vols. London: Heyden, 1979.

Public Papers of the Presidents of the United States: Richard Nixon, 1969; *Jimmy Carter,* 1977, 1979; *Ronald Reagan,* 1981.

Report to the President by the Commission on CIA Activities Within the United States (Rockefeller Report). New York: Manor Books, 1975.

Resolution to Create a Select Committee to Inquire into the Activities of the CIA in Quasi-foreign and Domestic Activities, S. Res. 85, 90 Cong., 1 sess. (Feb. 23, 1967).

"The Role of Intelligence in the Foreign Policy Process," *Hearings before the Subcommittee on International Security and Scientific Affairs of the Committee on Foreign Affairs,* House, 66 Cong., 2 sess. (Jan. 28, Feb. 8, 11, 20, 1980).

Ryan, Jr., Allan A. *Klaus Barbie and the United States Government: The Report, with Documentary Appendix, to the Attorney General of the United States.* Frederick, Md.: University Publications of America, 1984.

The Tower Commission Report. New York: Bantam, 1987.

Turner, Stansfield. "Should Congress Relax Present Limitations on the Conduct of Covert U.S. Intelligence Operations (pro)," *Congressional Digest* 59(May 1980):152, 154, 156, 158.

United States Congress, House. *Hearings before the Select Committee on Assassinations,* 95 Cong., 2 sess. 13 vols. (1979).

Williams, Grover S. *Legislative History of the Central Intelligence Agency as Documented in Published Congressional Sources.* Washington, D.C.: Congressional Research Service, 1975.

4. NONACADEMIC PERIODICALS AND NEWSPAPERS

Atlantic Monthly
Baltimore Sun
Buffalo Evening News
Center Magazine
Chicago Sun-Times
Chicago Tribune
Christian Science Monitor
Collier's
Commentary
Congressional Digest
Davenport (Iowa) *Democrat*
Detroit Free Press
(Edinburgh) *Scotsman*
Evansville Courier
Esquire
Facts on File
Foreign Affairs
Foreign Intelligence Literary Scene
Foreign Policy
Foreign Service Journal
Fortune
(Geneva) *La Suisse*
Harper's
(Havana) *Tricontinental*
Houston Chronicle
(London) *Daily Herald*
(London) *Daily Telegraph*

(London) *Economist*
(London) *Guardian*
(London) *New Statesman*
(London) *Observer*
(London) *Reynolds News*
(London) *Sunday Times*
(London) *Times*
Los Angeles Times
Lugano Review
(Madrid) *Pueblo*
Miami Herald
Michigan Alumnus
(Moscow) *Pravda*
Nation
New Republic
Newsweek
New York Herald Tribune
New York Review of Books
New York Times
(Paris) *La Liberation*
Ramparts
Richmond (Va.) *News Leader*
San Francisco Chronicle
San Francisco Examiner
Saturday Evening Post
St. Louis Post-Dispatch
Time
(Toronto) *MacLean's*
U.S. News and World Report
Washington News
Washington Quarterly
Washington Star
Washington Times-Herald

5. MEMOIRS, PUBLISHED PAPERS, AND ADDRESSES

Acheson, Dean. *Present at the Creation: My Years in the State Department.* New York: Norton, 1969.
Adams, Sam. "Vietnam Cover-up: Playing War with Numbers," *Harper's* (May 1975):41–44, 62–73.
———. *Who the Hell Are We Fighting Out There? A Story of American Intelligence on the Viet Cong.* New York: Norton, 1984.
Bohlen, Charles E. *Witness to History 1929–1969.* London: Weidenfeld & Nicolson, 1973.
Bowles, Chester. *Promises to Keep: My Years in Public Life 1941–1969.* New York: Harper & Row, 1971.
Braden, Spruille. *Diplomats and Demagogues: The Memoirs of Spruille Braden.* New Rochelle, N.Y.: Arlington House, 1971.
Brzezinski, Zbigniew. *Power and Principle: Memoirs of the National Security Advisor, 1977–1981.* New York: Farrar, Straus & Giroux, 1983.
Byrnes, James F. *Speaking Frankly.* New York: Harper, 1947.
Carter, Jimmy. *Keeping Faith: Memoirs of a President.* New York: Bantam, 1982.

Castro, Fidel. *Playa Girón, a Victory of the People*. Havana: Editoriel en Marcha, 1961.

Colby, William, and Peter Forbath. *Honorable Men: My Life in the CIA*. London: Hutchinson, 1978.

Cooper, Chester L. *The Lion's Last Roar: Suez, 1956*. New York: Harper & Row, 1978.

Dickey, Christopher. *With the Contras: A Reporter in the Wilds of Nicaragua*. New York: Simon & Schuster, 1985.

Eisenhower, Dwight D. *The Eisenhower Diaries*, ed. Robert H. Ferrell. New York: Norton, 1981.

Eveland, Wilbur C. *Ropes of Sand: America's Failure in the Middle East*. New York: Norton, 1980.

Ford, Gerald R. *A Time to Heal: The Autobiography of Gerald R. Ford*. New York: Harper, 1979.

Galbraith, John K. *Ambassador's Journal: A Personal Account of the Kennedy Years*. Boston: Houghton Mifflin, 1969.

Gehlen, Reinhard. *The Gehlen Memoirs*. London: Collins, 1972.

Haig, Alexander. *Caveat: Realism, Reagan and Foreign Power*. London: Weidenfeld & Nicolson, 1984.

Haldeman, H. R., with Joseph DiMona. *The Ends of Power*. New York: New York Times Book Co., 1978.

Hunt, E. Howard. *Undercover: Memoirs of an American Secret Agent*. New York: Holt, Rinehart & Winston, 1971.

Johnson, Lyndon B. *The Vantage Point: Perspectives of the Presidency 1963–1969*. New York: Holt, Rinehart & Winston, 1971.

Kennan, George F. *Memoirs 1950–1963*. London: Hutchinson, 1972.

Kennedy, John F. *The Kennedy Presidential Press Conferences*. London: Heyden, 1978.

Killian, James R., Jr. *Sputniks, Scientists and Eisenhower: A Memoir of the First Special Assistant to the President for Science and Technology*. Cambridge, Mass.: MIT Press, 1982.

Kissinger, Henry. *White House Years*. Boston: Little, Brown, 1979.

———. *Years of Upheaval*. London: Weidenfeld & Nicolson, 1982.

Krock, Arthur. *Memoirs. Sixty Years on the Firing Line*. New York: Funk & Wagnalls, 1968.

Langer, William L. *In and Out of the Ivory Tower: The Autobiography of William L. Langer*. New York: Watson Academic Publications, 1977.

Lansdale, Edward G. *In the Midst of Wars: An American's Mission to Southeast Asia*. New York: Harper, 1972.

McGehee, Ralph. *Deadly Deceits: My 25 Years in the CIA*. New York: Sheridan Square Publications, 1983.

Meyer, Cord. *Facing Reality: From World Federalism to the CIA*. London: University Press of America, 1983.

Nixon, Richard M. *The Memoirs of Richard Nixon*, 2 vols. New York: Warner, 1979.

———. *Six Crises*. London: W. H. Allen, 1962.

Philby, Kim. *My Silent War*. New York: Ballantine, 1983 (1968).

Phillips, David A. *The Night Watch*. New York: Atheneum, 1977.

Roosevelt, Kermit. *Countercoup: The Struggle for the Control of Iran*. New York: McGraw-Hill, 1979.

Schorr, Daniel. *Clearing the Air*. Boston: Houghton Mifflin, 1977.

Shevchenko, Arkady N. *Breaking with Moscow*. New York: Alfred A. Knopf, 1985.

Sihanouk, Norodom. *My War with the CIA: The Memoirs of Prince Norodom Sihanouk*, as related to Wilfred Burchett. Harmondsworth: Penguin, 1974.

Smith, Joseph B. *Portrait of a Cold Warrior*. New York: Putnam's, 1976.

Smith, Walter B. *My Three Years in Moscow*. New York: Lippincott, 1950.

Wright, Peter. *Spycatcher: The Candid Autobiography of a Senior Intelligence Officer*. New York: Viking, 1987.

Stockwell, John. "A CIA Trip—from Belief, to Doubt, to Despair," *Center Magazine* 12(1979):18–29.

———. *In Search of Enemies: A CIA Story*. New York: Norton, 1978.

Truman, Harry S. *Memoirs*, 2 vols. Garden City, N.Y.: Doubleday, Vol. 1: *Year of Decisions*, 1955. Vol. 2: *Years of Trial and Hope*. 1956.

Turner, Stansfield. *Secrecy and Democracy: The CIA in Transition*. Boston: Houghton Mifflin, 1985.

Vance, Cyrus. *Hard Choices: Critical Years in American Foreign Policy*. New York: Simon & Schuster, 1983.

Walters, Vernon A. *Silent Missions*. New York: Doubleday, 1978.

Wofford, Harris. *Of Kennedys and Kings: Making Sense of the Sixties*. New York: Farrar, Straus, & Giroux, 1980.

Woodhouse, Christopher M. *Something Ventured*. London: Granada, 1982.

6. WORKS OF REFERENCE

Costa, John. *Legislation Introduced Relative to the Activities of the Intelligence Agencies, 1947–1972*. Washington, D.C.: Congressional Research Service, 1972.

Great Soviet Encyclopedia, 37 vols. New York: Macmillan, 1973–82. Trans. from 3d Russian-language ed., 1970–79.

Grimmett, Richard F. *Reported Foreign and Domestic Covert Activities of the United States Central Intelligence Agency*. Washington, D.C.: Congressional Research Service, 1975.

Lowenthal, Mark M. *The Central Intelligence Agency: Organizational History*. Washington, D.C.: Congressional Research Service, 1978.

Mader, Julius. *Who's Who in CIA: A Biographical Reference Work on 3,000 Officers of the Civil and Military Branches of the Secret Services of the USA in 120 Countries*. East Berlin: Julius Mader, 1968.

———. *Yellow List. Where is the CIA? A Documentary of Organizations and Institutions Set Up as Camouflages*. East Berlin: Julius Mader, 1970.

Whitnah, Donald R., ed. *Government Agencies*. Greenwood Encyclopedia of American Institutions, vol. 7. Westport, Conn.: Greenwood, 1983.

Who's Who in America. Chicago: Marquis, 1980–.

7. BIBLIOGRAPHIC AIDS

Blackstock, Paul W., and Frank L. Schaf, Jr., eds. *Intelligence, Espionage, Counterespionage, and Covert Operations: A Guide to Information Sources*. Detroit: Gale Research, 1978.

Burns, Richard D., ed. *Guide to American Foreign Relations since 1700*. Santa Barbara, Cal.: ABC-Clio, 1983.

Cline, Marjorie W., Carla E. Christiansen, and Judith M. Fontaine, eds. *Scholar's Guide to Intelligence Literature: Bibliography of the Russell J. Bowen Collection*. Frederick, Md.: University Publications of America, 1983.

Constantinides, George C. *Intelligence and Espionage: An Analytical Bibliography.* Boulder, Colo.: Westview Press, 1983.

DIALOG Computer Search Facility. Files 7, 35, 38, 47, and 93.

Goehlert, Robert, and Elizabeth R. Hoffmeister, eds. *The CIA: A Bibliography.* Monticello, Ill.: Vance Bibliographies, 1980.

Haight, David. "The Papers of C. D. Jackson: A Glimpse at President Eisenhower's Psychological Warfare Expert," *Manuscripts* (Winter 1976):27–37.

Hanke, Lewis, ed. *Guide to the Study of United States History Outside the U.S., 1945–1980,* 5 vols. Kraus International Publications for American Historical Association, 1985.

Smith, Myron J., Jr., ed. *The Secret Wars: A Guide to Sources in English,* 3 vols. Santa Barbara: ABC-Clio. Vol. 1: *Intelligence, Propaganda and Psychological Warfare, Resistance Movements and Secret Operations, 1939–1945,* 1980. Vol. 2: *Intelligence, Propaganda and Psychological Warfare, Covert Operations, 1945–1980,* 1981. Vol. 3: *International Terrorism 1968–1980,* 1980.

8. SELECT LIST OF OTHER BOOKS AND OF ARTICLES

Adler, Emanuel. "Executive Command and Control in Foreign Affairs: The CIA's Covert Activities," *Orbis* 23(Fall 1979):671–95.

Adler, Renata. *Reckless Disregard: Westmoreland v. CBS et al.; Sharon v. Time.* New York: Vintage, 1988 (1986).

Agee, Philip. *Inside the Company: CIA Diary.* Harmondsworth: Penguin, 1975.

Agee, Philip, and Louis Wolf, eds. *Dirty Work: The CIA in Western Europe.* Seacaucus, N.J.: Lyle Stuart, 1978.

Ailes, Catherine P., James E. Cole, and Charles H. Movit. "Soviet Economic Problems and Technological Opportunities," *Comparative Strategy* 1(1979):267–305.

Allison, Graham. *Essence of Decision: Explaining the Cuban Missile Crisis.* Boston: Little, Brown, 1971.

Alsop, Stewart. *The Center: The Anatomy of Power in Washington.* London: Hodder & Stoughton, 1968.

Ambrose, Stephen E. "The American Response to Soviet Imperialism since World War II," in Rhodri Jeffreys-Jones, ed., *Eagle against Empire,* below.

———. *Eisenhower,* 2 vols. New York: Simon & Schuster. Vol. 2: *President and Elder Statesman, 1952–1969,* 1984.

———. *Ike's Spies: Eisenhower and the Espionage Establishment.* Garden City, N.Y.: Doubleday, 1981.

Andrew, Christopher M., and David Dilks, eds. *The Missing Dimension: Governments and Intelligence Communities in the Twentieth Century.* London: Macmillan, 1984.

Andrew, Christopher M. "Whitehall, Washington and the Intelligence Services," *International Affairs* 53(July 1977):390–404.

———. *Secret Service: The Making of the British Intelligence Community.* London: Heinemann, 1985.

Aron, Raymond. *The Imperial Republic: The United States and the World, 1945–1973,* trans. from French by Frank Jellinek. Englewood Cliffs, N.J.: Prentice-Hall, 1974.

Aspin, Les. "Misreading Intelligence," *Foreign Policy* (Summer 1981): 166–72.

Astre, Georges-Albert, and Pierre Lépinasse. *La Démocratie contrariée: Lobbies et jeux du pouvoir aux Etats-Unis.* Paris: Armillaire/La Découverte, 1985.

Ayers, Bradley E. *The War that Never War: An Insider's Account of CIA Covert Operations against Cuba.* Indianapolis: Bobbs-Merrill, 1976.

Baldwin, Hanson W. "Intelligence I . . . V," *New York Times*, July 20, 22, 23, 24, and 25, 1948.

———. *The Price of Power*. New York: Harper, 1947.

Bamford, James. *The Puzzle Palace: A Report on America's Most Secret Agency*. Boston: Houghton Mifflin, 1982.

Barnes, Trevor. "The Secret Cold War: The CIA and the American Foreign Policy in Europe, 1946–1956," *Historical Journal*, 2 parts: 24(1981):399–415, and 25 (1982):649–70.

Barron, John. *KGB: The Secret Work of Soviet Secret Agents*. London: Hodder & Stoughton, 1974.

Beck, Kent M. "Necessary Lies, Hidden Truths: Cuba in the 1960 Campaign," *Diplomatic History* 8(Winter 1984):37–59.

Beichman, Arnold, and Mikhail S. Bernstam. *Andropov: New Challenge to the West*. New York: Stein & Day, 1983.

Benson, Sumner. "The Historian as Foreign Policy Analyst: The Challenge of the CIA," *The Public Historian*, 3(1981):15–25.

Bernstein, Barton J., ed. *Towards a New Past: Dissenting Essays in American History*. London: Chatto & Windus, 1970.

Betts, Richard K. "Strategic Intelligence Estimates: Let's Make them Useful," *Parameters* 31(Dec. 1980):20–26.

Bill, James A. *The Eagle and the Lion: The Tragedy of American-Iranian Relations*. New Haven: Yale University Press, 1988.

Bissell, Richard M., Jr. "Response to Lucien S. Vandenbroucke, 'The "Confessions" of Allen Dulles: New Evidence on the Bay of Pigs'," *Diplomatic History* 8(Fall 1984):377–80.

Bitzer, Lloyd, and Theodore Rueter. *Carter vs. Ford: "The Counterfeit Debates of 1976*. Madison: University of Wisconsin Press, 1980.

Blackstock, Paul W. *The CIA and the Intelligence Community*. St. Charles, Mo.: Forum Press, 1974.

———. "The Intelligence Community under the Nixon Administration," *Armed Forces and Society* 1(Winter 1975):231–62.

———. *The Strategy of Subversion: Manipulating the Politics of Other Nations*. Chicago: Quadrangle, 1964.

Blaufarb, Douglas S. *The Counterinsurgency Era: U.S. Doctrine and Performance, 1950 to the Present*. New York: Free Press, 1977.

Blum, William. *The CIA: A Forgotten History. U.S. Global Interventions since World War 2*. London: Zed, 1986.

Bonner, Raymond. *Weakness and Deceit: U.S. Policy and El Salvador*. New York: Times Books, 1984.

Braden, Tom. "The Birth of the CIA," *American Heritage* 28(Feb. 1977):4–13.

———. "I'm Glad the CIA is 'Immoral'," *Saturday Evening Post*, May 20, 1967.

Branch, Taylor. "The Trial of the CIA," *New York Times Magazine*, Sept. 12, 1976.

Brown, Anthony C. *The Last Hero: Wild Bill Donovan*. London: Michael Joseph, 1982.

Buncher, Judith F., ed. *The CIA and the Security Debate, 1971–1975*. New York: Facts on File, 1976.

———. *The CIA and the Security Debate, 1975–1976*. New York: Facts on File, 1977.

Bundy, McGeorge. "The National Security Council in the 1960s", in Henry M. Jackson, ed., *The National Security Council*, section 3, above.

Bunnell, Frederick P. "The Central Intelligence Agency—Deputy Directorate for Plans 1961 Secret Memorandum on Indonesia: A Study in the Politics of Policy Formulation in the Kennedy Administration," *Indonesia* 22(Oct. 1976):131–69.

Burnham, Walter D. "Democracy at Home and Imperial Policy Abroad," *Commonweal* 80(Sept. 1964):639–42.

Bushkoff, Leonard. "The CIA Rides Again. . . , " *Times Higher Education Supplement*, Jan. 18, 1985.

Cannon, Lou. *Reagan*. New York: Putnam's, 1982.

Casey, William J. "The Real Soviet Threat in El Salvador—And Beyond," *U.S. News and World Report*, March 8, 1982.

Chace, James. *Endless War: How We Got Involved in Central America—And What Can Be Done About It*. New York: Vintage, 1984.

Chamorro, Edgar, and Jefferson Murphy. "Confessions of a 'Contra'," *New Republic* (Aug. 5, 1985):18–23.

Cline, Ray S. *The CIA under Reagan, Bush and Casey: The Evolution of the Agency from Roosevelt to Reagan*. Washington, D.C.: Acropolis, 1981.

Cline, Ray S. and Yonah Alexander. *Terrorism: The Soviet Connection*. New York: Crane Russak, 1983.

Codevilla, Angelo. "The Substance and the Rules," *Washington Quarterly* 6(1983): 32–39.

Cohen, Warren I. *Dean Rusk*. Totowa, N.J.: Cooper Square Publishers, 1980.

Colby, William E. "A New Charter for the CIA," *America* 142(March, 1980):243–44.

———. "Reorganizing the CIA: Who and How," *Foreign Policy* 23(Summer 1976): 53–63.

Copeland, Miles. *Without Cloak or Dagger: The Truth about the New Espionage*. New York: Simon & Schuster, 1974.

Corson, William R. *The Armies of Ignorance: The Rise of the American Intelligence Empire*. New York: Dial, 1977.

Cumings, Bruce, ed. *Child of Conflict: The Korean-American Relationship, 1943–1953*. Seattle: University of Washington Press, 1983.

Cummings, Robert. "African and Afro-American Studies Centers: Towards a Cooperative Relationship," *Journal of Black Studies* 9(March 1979):291–310.

Davis, Earle D. "Howard Hunt and the Peter Ward-CIA Spy Novels," *Kansas Quarterly* 10(1979):85–98.

Divine, Robert A., ed. *Exploring the Johnson Years*. Austin: University of Texas Press, 1981.

Divine, Robert A., *Foreign Policy and U.S. Presidential Elections, 1952, 1960*. New York: New Viewpoints, 1974.

Donner, Frank J. *The Age of Surveillance: The Aims and Methods of America's Political Intelligence System*. New York: Vintage, 1981.

Donovan, Robert J. *Conflict and Crisis: The Presidency of Harry S. Truman, 1945–1948*. New York: Norton, 1977.

Donovan, Thomas A. "The CIA Investigation: Asking the Unthinkable?" *Foreign Service Journal* 52(1975):19–20.

Dorwart, Jeffery M. *Conflict of Duty: The U.S. Navy's Intelligence Dilemma, 1919–1945*. Annapolis, Md.: Naval Institute Press, 1983.

Duggan, Ronnie. *The Politician: The Life and Times of Lyndon Johnson: The Drive for Power, from the Frontier to the Master of the Senate*. New York: Norton, 1982.

Dulles, Allen W. *The Craft of Intelligence*. London: Weidenfeld & Nicolson, 1963.

———. *Germany's Underground*. New York: Macmillan, 1947.

Eaton, Cyrus. "Nixon the FBI and the CIA." *New Humanist* 89(July 1973):86–88.

Editorials on File. New York: Facts on File, 1970, 1975, 1985.

Edwards, Robert, and Kenneth Dunne. *A Study of a Master Spy (Allen Dulles)*. London: Housemans/Chemical Workers' Union, 1961.

Elder, Robert E. *The Policy Machine: The Department of State and American Foreign Policy.* Westport, Conn.: Greenwood, 1974.

Ellsworth, Robert F., and Kenneth L. Adelman. "Foolish Intelligence," *Foreign Policy* 36(1979):147–59.

Elwell-Sutton, Lawrence P. *Persian Oil: A Study in Power Politics.* London: Lawrence & Wishart, 1955.

Epstein, Edward J. "Disinformation: Or, Why the CIA Cannot Verify an Arms-Control Agreement," *Commentary* 74(July 1982):21–28.

———. *Legend: The Secret World of Lee Harvey Oswald.* London: Hutchinson, 1978.

———. "The War Within the CIA," *Commentary* 66(Aug. 1978):35–39.

Erickson, John. *Stalin's War With Germany,* 2 vols. Vol. 2: *The Road to Berlin.* London: Weidenfeld & Nicolson, 1983.

———. "The Soviet Weapons Build-Up, 1965–1970/71: Roles and Capabilities," *Waverley Papers,* Ser. 3, No. 6 (1972):1–23.

Faenza, Roberto, and Marco Fini. *Gli Americani in Italia.* Milan: Fetrinelli, 1976.

Fallacci, Oriana. "Otis Pike and the CIA," *New Republic* (April 3, 1976):8–12.

Felstead, S. Theodore. *Intelligence: An Indictment of a Colossal Failure.* London: Hutchinson, 1941.

FitzGibbon, Constantine. *Secret Intelligence in the Twentieth Century.* London: Hart-Davis, MacGibbon, 1976.

Fletcher, Catherine B. "Evolution of the Modern American Spy Novel," *Journal of Contemporary History* 22(April 1987):319–30.

Franck, Thomas M., and James J. Eisen. "Balancing National Security and Free Speech," *Journal of International Law and Politics* 14(Winter 1982):339–69.

Frazier, Howard, ed. *Uncloaking the CIA.* New York: Free Press, 1978.

Freedman, Lawrence. *U.S. Intelligence and the Soviet Strategic Threat.* London: Macmillan, 1977.

Freeland, Richard M. *The Truman Doctrine and the Origins of McCarthyism: Foreign Policy, Domestic Politics, and Internal Security 1946–1948.* New York: Schocken, 1974.

Freney, Denis. *The CIA's Australian Connection.* Sydney: Denis Freney, 1977.

Fulbright, J. William. "We Must not Fight Fire with Fire," in Young Hum Kim, ed., *The Central Intelligence Agency,* below.

Gaddis, John Lewis. *Strategies of Containment: A Critical Appraisal of Postwar American National Security Policy.* New York: Oxford University Press, 1982.

Galambos, Louis. *The New American State: Bureaucracies and Policies since World War II.* Baltimore: Johns Hopkins University Press, 1987.

Galich, Manuel. "Playa Girón desde Buenos Aires, hace dos decadas," *Casa de las Américas* 21(March-April 1981):54–65.

Gallucci, Robert L. *Neither Peace Nor Honor: The Politics of American military Involvement in Vietnam.* Baltimore: Johns Hopkins University Press, 1975.

Galtung, Johan. "After Camelot," in Galtung, *Papers on Methodology: Essays in Methodology,* vol. 2. Copenhagen: Christian Ejlers, 1979.

Gardner, Lloyd C. *Covenant with Power: American and World Order from Wilson to Reagan.* London: Macmillan, 1984.

Gartner, Alan, Colin Greer, and Frank Riessman, eds. *What Reagan Is Doing to Us.* New York: Harper, 1982.

Geismar, Peter. *Fanon.* New York: Dial, 1971.

Gelb, Leslie H., with Richard K. Betts. *The Irony of Vietnam: The System Worked.* Washington, D.C.: Brookings Institution, 1979.

Glasser, Ira. "The Coming Assault on Civil Liberties," in Alan Gartner and others, eds., *What Reagan is Doing to Us,* above.

Godfrey, E. Drexel, Jr. "Ethics and Intelligence," *Foreign Affairs* (April 1978):624–34.

Godson, Roy, ed. *Elements of Intelligence*. Rev. ed. Washington, D.C.: Consortium for the Study of Intelligence/National Strategy Information Center/Transaction Books, 1983.

———. *Intelligence Requirements for the 1980s: Covert Action*. Washington, D.C.: Consortium for the Study of Intelligence/National Strategy Information Center/ Transaction Books, 1981.

Godson, Roy, and Richard Shultz. "Intelligence—The Evaluation of a New Teaching Subject," *International Studies Notes of the International Studies Association* 9(Fall-Winter 1981–82):3–4.

Golitsyn, Anatoliy. *New Lies for Old: The Communist Strategy of Deception and Disinformation*. London: Bodley Head, 1984.

Goode, Stephen. *CIA*. New York: Watts, 1982.

Goodman, Allan E. "Dateline Langley: Fixing the Intelligence Mess," *Foreign Policy* 17(Winter 1984–85):160–79.

Gosnell, Harold F. *Truman's Crises: A Political Biography of Harry S. Truman*. Westport, Conn.: Greenwood, 1980.

Graebner, Norman A. *America as a World Power: A Realist Appraisal from Wilson to Reagan*. Wilmington, Del.: Scholarly Resources, 1984.

Green, Stephen. *Taking Sides: America's Secret Relations with a Militant Israel 1948–1967*. London: Faber & Faber, 1984.

Greene, Graham. *The Quiet American*. Harmondsworth: Penguin, 1983 (1955).

———. *Ways of Escape*. London: Bodley Head, 1980.

Greenstein, Fred I. *The Hidden-Hand Presidency: Eisenhower as Leader*. New York: Basic, 1982.

Halberstam, David. *The Best and the Brightest*. New York: Fawcett Crest, 1973.

Halperin, Morton H. "The CIA's Distemper," *New Republic* (Feb. 9, 1980):21–23.

Hauser, Thomas. *Missing*. Harmondsworth: Penguin, 1982.

Herken, Gregg. *The Winning Weapon: The Atomic Bomb in the Cold War, 1945–1950*. New York: Alfred A. Knopf, 1980.

Herring, George C. *America's Longest War: The United States and Vietnam, 1950–1975*. New York: Wiley, 1979.

Hersh, Seymour. *The Price of Power: Kissinger in the Nixon White House*. London: Faber & Faber, 1983.

———. "The Pardon: Nixon, Ford, Haig, and the Transfer of Power," *The Atlantic Monthly* (Aug. 1983):55–62, 64, 67–78.

———. *The Target Is Destroyed: What Really Happened to Flight 007 and What America Knew About It*. London: Faber & Faber, 1986.

Higgins, Trumbull. *The Perfect Failure: Kennedy, Eisenhower, and the CIA at the Bay of Pigs*. New York: Norton, 1987.

Hilsman, Roger. "On Intelligence," *Armed Forces and Society* 8(Fall 1981):129–43.

———. *Strategic Intelligence and National Decisions*. Westport, Conn.: Greenwood, 1981 (1956).

———. *To Move a Nation: The Politics of Foreign Policy in the Administration of John F. Kennedy*. Garden City, N.Y.: Doubleday, 1967.

Hinckle, Warren, and William W. Turner. *The Fish is Red: The Story of the Secret War against Castro*. New York: Harper, 1981.

Hinsley, Francis H. *British Intelligence in the Second World War: Its Influence on Strategy and Operations*, 2 vols. London: Her Majesty's Stationery Office, 1979, 1981.

Hoeksema, Renze L. "The President's Role in Insuring Efficient, Economical, and Responsible Intelligence Services," *Presidential Studies Quarterly* 8(1978):187–98.

Höhne, Heinz, and Hermann Zolling. *Network: The Truth about General Gehlen and American Foreign Policy*. Chicago: University of Chicago Press, 1960.

Holt, Robert T., and Robert Van de Velde. *Strategic Psychological Operations and American Foreign Policy*. Chicago: University of Chicago Press, 1960.

Holzman, Franklyn D. "Are the Soviets Really Outspending the U.S. on Defense?" *International Security* 4(Spring 1980):86–104.

———. "Is There a Soviet-U.S. Military Spending Gap?" *Challenge* 23(Sept.-Oct. 1980):3–9.

Hood, William J. *Mole: The True Story of the First Russian Intelligence Officer Recruited by the CIA*. London: Weidenfeld & Nicolson, 1982.

Hoopes, Townsend. *The Devil and John Foster Dulles*. Boston: Little, Brown, 1973.

Horowitz, Irving L., ed. *The Rise and Fall of Project Camelot: Studies in the Relationship between Social Science and Political Parties*. Cambridge, Mass.: MIT Press, 1967.

Horrie, Chris. "The War against 'Communism'," *New Statesman* (Nov. 2, 1984):19–21.

Horton, John. "The Real Intelligence Failure," *Foreign Service Journal* (Feb. 1985): 22–25.

Humphrey, David C. "Tuesday Lunch at the Johnson White House: A Preliminary Assessment," *Diplomatic History* 8(Winter 1984):81–101.

Hunt, E. Howard. *Bimini Run*. New York: Macfadden-Bartell, 1971 (1949).

———. *Return from Vorkuta*. New York: Signet, ca. 1973 (1965 under pseudonym David St. John).

Immerman, Richard H. *The CIA in Guatemala: The Foreign Policy of Intervention*. Austin: University of Texas Press, 1982.

Isaacs, Arnold R. *Without Honor: Defeat in Vietnam and Cambodia*. Baltimore: Johns Hopkins University Press, 1983.

Jaworski, Leon. *The Right and the Power, The Prosecution of Watergate*. New York: Reader's Digest, 1976.

Jeffreys-Jones, Rhodri. *American Espionage: From Secret Service to CIA*. New York: Free Press, 1977.

———. "The CIA and the Demise of Anti-Anti-Americanism," in Kroes and Rossem, eds., *Anti-Americanism in Europe*, below.

———. "The Socio-Educational Composition of the CIA Elite: A Statistical Note," *Journal of American Studies* 19(Dec. 1985):421–24.

Jeffreys-Jones, Rhodri, ed. *Eagle against Empire: American Opposition to European Imperialism, 1914–1982*. Aix: Publications Université de Provence for European Association for American Studies, 1983.

Jeffreys-Jones, Rhodri, and Bruce Collins, eds. *The Growth of Federal Power in American History*. Dekalb: Northern Illinois University Press, 1983.

Johnson, Loch K. "Controlling the Quiet Option," *Foreign Policy* 39(1980):143–53.

———. "Legislative Reform of Intelligence Policy," *Polity* (Spring 1985):549–72.

———. *A Season of Inquiry: The Senate Intelligence Investigation*. Lexington, Ky.: University Press of Kentucky, 1985.

———. "The U.S. Congress and the CIA: Monitoring the Dark Side of Government," *Legislative Studies Quarterly* 5(Nov. 1980):477–99.

Johnson, R. W. *Shootdown: The Verdict on KAL 007*. London: Chatto & Windus, 1986.

Jordan, Kent A. "The Extent of Independent Presidential Authority to Conduct Foreign Intelligence Activities," *Georgetown Law Journal* 72(1984):1855–63.

Julien, Claude. *L'Empire américain*. Paris: B. Grasset, 1968.

Kahin, George McT. *Intervention: How America Became Involved in Vietnam*. New York: Alfred A. Knopf, 1986.

Kahn, David. *The Codebreakers: The Story of Secret Writing*. London: Weidenfeld & Nicolson, 1966.

Kalb, Madelaine G. *The Congo Cables: The Cold War in Africa from Eisenhower to Kennedy*. New York: Macmillan, 1981.

Karalekas, Anne. *History of the Central Intelligence Agency*. Laguna Hills, Cal.: Aegean Park Press, 1977.

———. "Intelligence Oversight: Has Anything Changed?" *Washington Quarterly* 6(Summer 1983):22–30.

Katz, Barry. *Herbert Marcuse and the Art of Liberation: An Intellectual Biography*. London: Verso, 1982.

Kendall, Wilmoore. "The Function of Intelligence," *World Politics* 1(1948–49):542–52.

Kennan, George F. *The Nuclear Delusion: Soviet-American Relations in the Atomic Age*. New York: Pantheon, 1982.

Kent, Sherman. *Strategic Intelligence for American World Policy*. Princeton, N.J.: Princeton University Press, 1949.

Kim, Young Hum, ed. *The Central Intelligence Agency: Problems of Secrecy in a Democracy*. Lexington, Mass.: D.C. Heath, 1968.

Kirkpatrick, Lyman B. *The U.S. Intelligence Community: Foreign Policy and Domestic Activities*. New York: Hill & Wang, 1975.

Kissinger, Henry A. *Nuclear Weapons and Foreign Policy*. New York: Harper, 1957.

Krepon, Michael. *Strategic Stalemate: Nuclear Weapons and Arms Control in American Politics*. London: Macmillan, 1984.

Kroes, Rob, and Maarten van Rossem, eds. *Anti-Americanism in Europe*. Amsterdam: Free University Press, 1986.

Kroes, Rob, ed. *Neo-Conservatism: Its Emergence in the USA and Europe*. Amsterdam: Free University Press, 1984.

Kumar, Satish. *CIA and the Third World: A Study in Crypto-Diplomacy*. London: Zed, 1981.

LaFeber, Walter. *America, Russia, and the Cold War 1945–1971*. 2d ed. New York: John Wiley, 1972.

———. *Inevitable Revolutions: The United States and Central America*. New York: Norton, 1984.

Laqueur, Walter. *A World of Secrets: The Uses and Limits of Intelligence*. New York: Basic, 1985.

Lasch, Christopher. "The Cultural Cold War: A Short History of the Congress for Cultural Freedom," in Barton J. Bernstein, ed., *Towards a New Past*, above.

Leary, William M. *Perilous Mission: Civil Air Transport and CIA Covert Operations in Asia*. University, Ala.: University of Alabama Press, 1984.

Leary, William M., ed. *The Central Intelligence Agency: History and Documents*. University, Ala.: University of Alabama Press, 1984.

Leary, William M., and William Stueck. "The Chennault Plan to Save China: U.S. Containment in Asia and the Origin of the CIA's Aerial Empire, 1949–1950," *Diplomatic History* 8(Fall 1984):349–64.

Lederer, William J., and Eugene Burdick. *The Ugly American: A Novel; with a factual epilogue*. London: Victor Gollancz, 1959.

Lefever, Ernest W., and Roy Godson, eds. *The CIA and the American Ethic: An Unfinished Debate*. Washington, D.C.: Ethics and Public Policy Center, Georgetown University, 1979.

Lehman, John. *The Executive, Congress and Foreign Policy: Studies of the Nixon Administration*. New York: Praeger, 1976.

Leuchtenburg, William E. *In the Shadow of FDR: From Harry Truman to Ronald Reagan*. Ithaca: Cornell University Press, 1983.

Lewis, Findlay. *Mondale: Portrait of an American Politician*. Rev. ed. London: Harper, 1984.

Lewy, Guenter. *America in Vietnam*. New York: Oxford University Press, 1978.

Lilly, Edward P. "The Psychological Strategy Board and its Predecessors: Foreign Policy Coordination 1938–1953," in Gaetano L. Vincitorio, ed., *Studies in Modern History*, below.

Lindsey, Robert. *The Falcon and the Snowman*. Harmondsworth: Penguin, 1980.

Lowenthal, Mark M. *U.S. Intelligence: Evolution and Anatomy*. New York: Praeger, 1984.

Lowther, William. "Academic Cloaks and Daggers," *MacLean's*, 93(Nov. 1980):34.

Lundestad, Geir. "Empire by Invitation: The United States and Western Europe," *Society for Historians of American Foreign Relations Newsletter* 15 (Sept. 1984):1–21.

Madison, Christopher. "Committee Leaders Prod Intelligence Chiefs to Develop National Strategy," *National Journal* (Jan. 11, 1986):79–81.

Mahoney, Richard D. *JFK: Ordeal in Africa*. New York: Oxford University Press, 1983.

Marchetti, Victor, and John D. Marks. *The CIA and the Cult of Intelligence*. New York: Dell, 1975.

Martin, David C. *Wilderness of Mirrors*. New York: Harper, 1980.

May, Ernest R., ed. *Knowing One's Enemies: Intelligence Assessment before the Two World Wars*. Princeton, N.J.: Princeton University Press, 1985.

McCarthy, Eugene J. "The Expansion of the White House," *Center Magazine* 6 (March-April 1973):53–55.

McCormack, William. "Problems of American Scholars in India," *Asian Survey* 16(1976):1064–80.

McGarvey, Patrick J. *CIA: The Myth and the Madness*. New York: Saturday Review Press, 1972.

McGehee, Ralph. "The CIA and the White Paper on El Salvador" *Nation* (April 11, 1981):423–25.

Melosi, Martin V. *The Shadow of Pearl Harbor: Political Controversy over the Attack, 1941–1946*. College Station: Texas A & M University Press, 1977.

Merry, Bruce. *Anatomy of the Spy Thriller*. Dublin: Gill & Macmillan, 1977.

Mickelson, Sig. *America's Other Voice: The Story of Radio Free Europe and Radio Liberty*. New York: Praeger, 1983.

Miller, James E. "Taking Off the Gloves: The United States and the Italian Elections of 1948," *Diplomatic History* 7(Winter 1983):35–55.

Mondale, Walter F. "Reorganizing the CIA: Who and How," *Foreign Policy* 23(Summer 1976):53–63.

Mooney, Peter J. *The Soviet Superpower: The Soviet Union 1945–1980*. London: Heinemann, 1982.

Morgan, Thomas B. *The Anti-Americans*. London: Michael Joseph, 1967.

Morris, George. *CIA and American Labor: The Subversion of the AFL-CIO's Foreign Policy*. New York: International Publishers, 1967.

Mosley, Leonard. *Dulles: A Biography of Eleanor, Allen and John Foster Dulles and their Family Network*. London: Hodder & Stoughton, 1978.

Moulton, Harland B. *From Superiority to Parity: The United States and the Strategic Arms Race, 1961–1971*. Westport, Conn.: Greenwood, 1973.

Movimiento Argentino Antiimperialista de Solidaridad Latino-americana. *La CIA: ¿qué es? ¿qué hace en América Latina?* Buenos Aires: Ediciones Voz Latinoamericana, 1974.

Muggeridge, Malcolm. "Books," *Esquire* 68(Sept. 1967):12–16.

Mumford, Lewis. *The Myth of the Machine: The Pentagon of Power.* New York: Harcourt Brace Jovanovich, 1970.

Natarajan, L. *American Shadow over India.* Bombay: People's Publishing House, 1952.

Nathan, James A. "Dateline Australia: America's Foreign Watergate?" *Foreign Policy* 49(Winter 1982–83):168–85.

Neff, Donald. *Warriors at Suez: Eisenhower Takes America into the Middle East.* New York: Simon & Schuster, 1982.

Neu, Charles. "The Rise of the National Security Bureaucracy," in Louis Galambos, ed., *The New American State,* above.

Newfield, Jack. *Robert Kennedy: A Memoir.* New York: Dutton, 1969.

Ninkovich, Frank A. *The Diplomacy of Ideas: U.S. Foreign Policy and Cultural Relations 1938–1950.* Cambridge: Cambridge University Press, 1981.

Nixon, Richard M. *No More Vietnams.* London: W. H. Allen, 1986.

Noer, Thomas J. "The New Frontier and African Neutralism: Kennedy, Nkrumah, and the Volta River Project," *Diplomatic History* 8(Winter 1984):61–79.

Oberdorfer, Don. *Tet! The Turning Point in the Vietnam War.* New York: Da Capo, 1984 (1971).

Oseth, John M. *Regulating United States Intelligence Operations: A Study in Definition of the National Interest.* Lexington, Ky.: University of Kentucky Press, 1985.

Oshinsky, David M. *A Conspiracy So Immense: The World of Joe McCarthy.* New York: Free Press, 1983.

Parker, Phyllis R. *Brazil and the Quiet Intervention, 1964.* Austin: University of Texas Press, 1979.

Parmet, Herbert S. *JFK: The Presidency of John F. Kennedy.* New York: Dial, 1983.

Patti, Archimedes L. A. *Why Viet Nam? Prelude to America's Albatross.* Berkeley: University of California Press, 1980.

Pearson, John. *The Life of Ian Fleming.* London: Jonathan Cape, 1966.

Penkowsky, Oleg. *The Penkowsky Papers.* London: Collins, 1965.

Peter, F. W. "Stimmen die Angaben der CIA doch?" *Politische Studien* 32(1981):405–13.

Petersen, Phillip A. "American Perceptions of Soviet Military Power," *Parameters* 7(1977):71–82.

Petrusenko, Vitalii V. *A Dangerous Game: CIA and the Mass Media,* trans. from Russian by Nicolai Kozelsky and Vladimir Leonov. Prague: Interpress, 1979.

Pettee, George S. *The Future of American Secret Intelligence.* Washington, D.C.: Infantry Journal Press, 1946.

Pipes, Richard. "Team B: The Reality behind the Myth," *Commentary* 82(Oct. 1986):25–40.

Podhoretz, Norman P. "Making the World Safe for Communism," *Commentary* 61(April 1976):31–41.

Poelchau, Warner, ed. *White Paper Whitewash: Interviews with Philip Agee on the CIA and El Salvador.* New York: Deep Cover Books, 1981.

Potter, William C., ed. *Verification and SALT: The Challenge of Strategic Deception.* Boulder, Colo.: Westview Press, 1980.

Powers, Thomas. *The Man Who Kept the Secrets: Richard Helms and the CIA.* New York: Washington Square Press, 1981.

Prados, John. *Presidents' Secret Wars: CIA and Pentagon Covert Operations since World War II.* New York: William Morrow, 1986.

———. *The Soviet Estimate: U.S. Intelligence Analysis and Russian Military Strength.* New York: Dial, 1982.

Price, Victoria. *The DCI's Role in Producing Strategic Intelligence Estimates.* Newport, R.I.: Naval War College, 1980.

Propas, Frederic L. "Creating a Hard Line Toward Russia: The Training of State Department Soviet Experts, 1927–1937," *Diplomatic History* 8(Summer 1984): 209–26.

Prouty, L. Fletcher. *The Secret Team: The CIA and its Allies in Control of the United States and the World.* Englewood Cliffs, N.J.: Prentice-Hall, 1973.

Psychological Operations in Guerrilla Warfare. New York: Vintage, 1985.

Quandt, William B. *Decade of Decisions: American Policy Toward the Arab-Israeli Conflict, 1967–1976.* Berkeley: University of California Press, 1977.

Radosh, Ronald. *American Labor and United States Foreign Policy: The Cold War in the Unions from Gompers to Lovestone.* New York: Vintage Books, 1970.

Ranelagh, John. *The Agency: The Rise and Decline of the CIA: From Wild Bill Donovan to William Casey.* New York: Simon & Schuster, 1986.

Ransom, Harry H. "How Central is our Intelligence?" *Saturday Review* (June 27, 1964): 25–26.

———. *The Intelligence Establishment.* Cambridge Mass.: Harvard University Press, 1970.

———. "Secret Intelligence in the United States, 1947–1982: The CIA's Search for Legitimacy," in Christopher M. Andrew and David Dilks, eds., *The Missing Dimension,* above.

Ray, Ellen, and others, eds. *Dirty Work II: The CIA in Africa.* London: Zed, 1980.

Reeves, Thomas C. *The Life and Times of Joe McCarthy: A Biography.* New York: Stein & Day, 1982.

Rice, Gerard T. "The American Government's Harnessing of the Overseas Voluntary Spirit—The Peace Corps," in Rhodri Jeffreys-Jones and Bruce Collins, eds., *Growth of Federal Power,* above.

———. *The Bold Experiment: JFK's Peace Corps.* Notre Dame: University of Notre Dame Press, 1985.

Richelson, Jeffrey T. "Old Surveillance, New Interpretations," *Bulletin of the Atomic Scientists* 3(Feb. 1986):18–23.

———. *The U.S. Intelligence Community.* Cambridge, Mass.: Ballinger, 1985.

Robbins, Christopher. *The Invisible Air Force: The Story of the CIA's Secret Airlines.* London: Macmillan, 1979.

Robertson, Ken G., ed. *British and American Approaches to Intelligence.* London: Macmillan, 1987.

Rogger, Hans. "America in the Russian Mind—or Russian Discoveries of America," *Pacific Historical Review* 47(1978):27–51.

Rogow, Arnold A. *James Forrestal: A Study of Personality, Politics and Policy.* New York: Macmillan, 1963.

Rositzke, Harry. *The CIA's Secret Operations: Espionage, Counterespionage, and Covert Action.* New York: Reader's Digest Press, 1977.

Rossem, Maarten van. "The Intellectual Roots of Neo-Conservatism," in Rob Kroes, ed., *Neo-Conservatism,* above.

Rubin, Barry. *Paved with Good Intentions: The American Experience and Iran.* New York: Oxford University Press, 1980.

Rystad, Göran. *Prisoners of the Past? The Munich Syndrome and Makers of American*

Foreign Policy in the Cold War Era. Scripta Minora Regiae Societatis Humaniorum Litterarum Ludensis, 2. Lund: CWK Gleerup, 1982.

Schandler, Herbert Y. *The Unmaking of a President: Lyndon Johnson and Vietnam*. Princeton, N.J.: Princeton University Press, 1977.

Schechter, Dan, Michael Ansara, and David Kolodney. "The CIA as an Equal Opportunity Employer," *Ramparts* 7(June 1969):25–33.

Schlesinger, Arthur M., Jr. *The Imperial Presidency*. New York: Popular Library, 1974.

———. *Robert Kennedy and His Times*. Boston: Houghton Mifflin, 1978.

———. *A Thousand Days: John F. Kennedy in the White House*. London: André Deutsch, 1965.

———. "Who was in Charge? A Debate about the CIA and Presidential Authority," *Commonweal* (Feb. 29, 1980):108–11.

Schlesinger, Stephen, and Stephen Kinzer. *Bitter Fruit: The Untold Story of the American Coup in Guatemala*. New York: Doubleday, 1982.

Schram, Martin. *Running for President: A Journal of the Carter Campaign*. New York: Pocket Books, 1978.

Schulzinger, Robert D. *The Making of the Diplomatic Mind: The Training, Outlook, and Style of United States Foreign Service Officers, 1908–1931*. Middletown, Conn.: Wesleyan University Press, 1975.

———. *American Diplomacy in the Twentieth Century*. New York: Oxford University Press, 1984.

Selser, Gregorio. *La CIA en Bolivia*. Buenos Aires: Hernández Editor, 1970.

Shackley, Theodore G. *The Third Option: An American View of Counterinsurgency Operations*. New York: Readers' Digest, 1980.

Shannon, William V. *The Heir Apparent: Robert Kennedy and the Struggle for Power*. New York: Macmillan, 1967.

Sick, Gary. *All Fall Down: America's Tragic Encounter with Iran*. New York: Random House, 1985.

Sivachev, Nikolai, and Nikolai Yakovlev. *Russia and the United States: US-Soviet Relations from the Soviet Point of View*, trans. from Russian by Olga Adler Titelbaum. Chicago: University of Chicago Press, 1979.

Smith, Bradley F. *The Shadow Warriors: OSS and the Origins of CIA*. London: André Deutsch, 1983.

Smith, E. Timothy. "The Fear of Subversion: The United States and the Inclusion of Italy in the North Atlantic Treaty," *Diplomatic History* 7(Spring 1983):139–55.

Smith, Gerard. *Doubletalk: The Story of the First Strategic Arms Limitations Talks*. New York: Doubleday, 1980.

Smith, Joseph B. "Life Without Badges: The Cost of Cover in the CIA," *The Washington Monthly* 10(May 1978):44–48.

Smith, R. Harris. *OSS: The Secret History of America's First Central Intelligence Agency*. New York: Delta, 1973.

Snepp, Frank. *Decent Interval: The American Debacle in Vietnam and the Fall of Saigon*. London: Allen Lane, 1980.

Snow, Edgar. *Red Star over China*. London: Victor Gollancz, 1937.

Solberg, Carl E. *Oil Power: The Rise and Imminent Fall of an American Empire*. New York: Mentor, 1976.

Sorensen, Theodore C. *Kennedy*. London: Pan, 1966.

The Soviet-Cuban Connection in Central America and the Caribbean. Washington, D.C.: Departments of State and Defense, 1985.

Spanier, John W. *The Truman-MacArthur Controversy and the Korean War*. New York: Norton, 1965.

Stavros, Nikolas. *Allied Policy and Military Intervention: The Political Role of the Greek Military*. Athens: Papazissis, 1976.

Stein, Jean. *American Journey: The Times of Robert Kennedy*, ed. George Plimpton. New York: Harcourt Brace Jovanovich, 1970.

Steinfels, Peter. *The Neoconservatives: The Men Who Are Changing America's Politics*. New York: Simon & Schuster, 1979.

Stephens, Ian. *Pakistan: Old Country/New Nation*. Harmondsworth: Penguin, 1964.

Stern, Sol. "NSA and the CIA," *Ramparts* 5(March 1967):29–39.

Stevenson, William. *A Man Called Intrepid: The Secret War 1939–1945*. London: Macmillan, 1976.

Stueck, William W. *The Road to Confrontation: American Policy toward China and Korea, 1947–1950*. Chapel Hill: University of North Carolina Press, 1981.

Supperstone, Michael. "The Law Relating to Security in Great Britain," in Ken. G. Robertson, ed., *British and American Approaches to Intelligence*, above.

Szulc, Tad. *Compulsive Spy: The Strange Career of E. Howard Hunt*. New York: Viking, 1974.

Taylor, Maxwell D. *The Uncertain Trumpet*. London: Atlantic Books, 1960.

Temple, Harry. "Deaf Captains: Intelligence, Policy, and the Origins of the Korean War," *International Studies, Notes of the International Studies Association* 8(Fall-Winter 1981–82):19–23.

Theoharris, Athan G. *Spying on Americans: Political Surveillance from Hoover to the Huston Plan*. Philadelphia: Temple University Press, 1978.

Theoharris, Athan G., ed. *The Truman Presidency: The Origins of the Imperial Presidency and the National Security State*. London: Heyden, 1979.

Thompson, James C. *Rolling Thunder: Understanding Policy and Program Failure*. Chapel Hill: University of North Carolina Press, 1980.

Tovar, B. Hugh. "Strengths and Weaknesses in Past Covert Action," in Roy Godson, ed., *Covert Action*, above.

Trask, Roger R. "The Impact of the Cold War on United States-Latin American Relations, 1945–1949," *Diplomatic History* 1(Summer 1977):271–84.

Treverton, Gregory F. *Covert Action: The Limits of Intervention in the Post-war World*. New York: William Morrow, 1987.

Troy, Thomas F. *Donovan and the CIA: A History of the Establishment of the Central Intelligence Agency*. Frederick, Md.: University Publications of America, 1981.

———. "Knifing of the OSS," *International Journal of Intelligence and Counterintelligence* 1, no. 3 (1986):95–106.

Tully, Andrew. *Central Intelligence Agency: The Inside Story*. London: Arthur Barker, 1962.

Ungar, Sanford J. *The Papers and "The Papers": An Account of the Legal and Political Battle over the Pentagon Papers*. New York: Dutton, 1972.

Vandenbroucke, Lucien S. "The 'Confessions' of Allen Dulles: New Evidence on the Bay of Pigs," *Diplomatic History* 8(Fall 1984):365–75.

Verrier, Anthony. *Through the Looking Glass: British Foreign Policy in an Age of Illusions*. London: Jonathan Cape, 1983.

Vincitorio, Gaetano L., ed. *Studies in Modern History*. New York: St. John's University Press, 1968.

Walker, David. "OSS and Operation Torch," *Journal of Contemporary History* 22 (Oct. 1987):667–79.

Walters, Ronald W. "The Clark Amendment: An Analysis of U.S. Policy Choices in Angola," *The Black Scholar: Journal of Black Studies and Research* 12(July-August 1981):2–11.

Watt, D. Cameron. "Can the Secret Service Become the Silent Service?" *Daily Telegraph*, Aug. 18, 1984.

———. *Succeeding John Bull: America in Britain's Place 1900–1975*. Cambridge: Cambridge University Press, 1984.

Weissman, Stephen R. "CIA Covert Action in Zaire and Angola: Patterns and Consequences," *Political Science Quarterly* 94(Summer 1979):263–86.

———. "The CIA and U.S. Policy in Zaire and Angola," in Ellen Ray, ed., *Dirty Work*, above.

Wells, Samuel F. "The Lessons of the War," *Wilson Quarterly* 2(1978):119–26.

Wills, Garry. *The Kennedys: A Shattered Illusion*. London: Orbis, 1983.

Winks, Robin W. *Cloak and Gown: Scholars in the Secret War, 1939–1961*. New York: Morrow, 1987.

Wise, David. *The American Police State: The Government against the People*. New York: Random House, 1976.

Wise, David, and Thomas B. Ross. *The Invisible Government*. London: Jonathan Cape, 1964.

———. *The U-2 Affair*. New York: Random House, 1962.

Wohlstetter, Roberta. *Pearl Harbor: Warning and Decision*. Stanford, Cal.: Stanford University Press, 1962.

Wolff, Robert L. "William Leonard Langer," *Massachusetts Historical Society Proceedings* 89(1977):187–95.

Wood, Bryce. "The End of the Good Neighbor Policy: Changing Patterns of U.S. Influence," *Caribbean Review* 11(Spring 1982):25–27, 54.

Woodward, Bob. *VEIL: The Secret Wars of the CIA 1981–1987*. New York: Simon & Schuster, 1987.

Wriston, Henry M. *Executive Agents in American Foreign Relations*. Baltimore: Johns Hopkins University Press, 1929.

Wyden, Peter. *Bay of Pigs: The Untold Story*. London: Jonathan Cape, 1979.

Yakovlev, Nikolai. *CIA Target: The USSR*, trans. from Russian by Victor Schneierson and Dmitry Belyavsky. Moscow: Progess Publishers, 1982.

Yergin, Daniel. *Shattered Peace: The Origins of the Cold War and the National Security State*. Boston: Houghton Mifflin, 1977.

9. SUPPLEMENTARY BIBLIOGRAPHY ON THE CONTEMPORARY CIA

Boren, David L. "The Intelligence Community: How Crucial?" *Foreign Affairs* (Summer 1992): 52–62.

Casey, William J. *Scouting the Future: The Public Speeches of William J. Casey*, comp. Herbert E. Meyer. Washington, D.C.: Regnery Gateway, 1989.

Commission on the Roles and Capabilities of the United States Intelligence Community. *Preparing for the 21st Century: An Appraisal of U.S. Intelligence* [Aspin/Brown Commission Report]. 1996.

Dorn, A. Walter. "The Cloak and the Blue Beret: Limitations on Intelligence in UN Peacekeeping." *International Journal of Intelligence and Counterintelligence* 12 (Winter 1999–2000).

Draper, Theodore. "Is the CIA Necessary?" *New York Review of Books*, Aug. 14, 1997; Oct. 23, 1997: 76–78.

FitzGerald, Frances. *Way Out There in the Blue: Reagan, Star Wars and the End of the Cold War*. New York: Simon and Schuster, 2000.

Gates, Robert M. *From the Shadows: The Ultimate Insider's Story of Five Presidents and How They Won the Cold War*. New York: Simon and Schuster, 1996.

Gooding, John. *Rulers and Subjects: Government and People in Russia, 1801–1991.* London: Arnold, 1996.

Goodman, Allan E. "The Future of U.S. Intelligence." *Intelligence and National Security* 11 (Oct. 1996): 645–56.

Goodman, Allan E., and Bruce D. Berkowitz. "Intelligence without the Cold War." *Intelligence and National Security* 9 (April 1994): 301–19.

Hersh, Seymour M. "Missed Messages." *New Yorker,* June 3, 2002: 40–48.

Hodgson, Godfrey. *The Gentleman from New York: Daniel Patrick Moynihan, A Biography.* Boston: Houghton Mifflin, 2000.

In from the Cold: The Report of the Twentieth Century Fund Task Force on the Future of U.S. Intelligence. New York: Twentieth Century Fund Press, 1996.

Jeffreys-Jones, Rhodri. *Cloak and Dollar: A History of American Secret Intelligence.* New Haven: Yale University Press, 2002.

Johnson, Loch K. *Secret Agencies: U.S. Intelligence in a Hostile World.* New Haven: Yale University Press, 1996.

Kessler, Ronald. *The Bureau: The Secret History of the FBI.* New York: St. Martin's, 2002.

Moynihan, Daniel Patrick. "Do We Still Need the CIA: The State Dept. Can Do the Job." *New York Times,* May 19, 1992.

———. "Our Stupid but Permanent CIA: What Are We Going to Do about Reforming the Agency? Nothing." *Washington Post,* July 24, 1994.

———. *Secrecy: The American Experience.* New Haven: Yale University Press, 1998.

Schweizer, Peter. *Victory: The Reagan Administration's Secret Strategy That Hastened the Collapse of the Soviet Union.* New York: Atlantic Monthly, 1994.

Shukman, Harold, ed. *Agents for Change: Intelligence Services in the 21st Century.* London: St Ermin's/Little, Brown, 2000.

Villadsen, Ole R. "Prospects for a European Common Intelligence Policy." *Studies in Intelligence* 9 (Summer 2000): 81–96.

INDEX